Withdrawn

Original Questionnaire (Questionnaire construction)
attitude scales
historical - critical analysis
interviews as a data-collection technique
interaction analytic study P30

Research in Speech Communication

RAYMOND K. TUCKER
Bowling Green State University

RICHARD L. WEAVER, II
Bowling Green State University

CYNTHIA BERRYMAN-FINK
University of Cincinnati

Prentice-Hall, Inc., Englewood Cliffs, New Jersey 07632

Library of Congress Cataloging in Publication Data

TUCKER, RAYMOND K
   Research in speech communication.

   Bibliography.
   Includes index.
   1. Oral communication—Research. 2. Oral communi-
cation—Methodology. I. Weaver, Richard L.,
(Date), joint author. II. Berryman, Cynthia L.,
(Date) joint author. III. Title.
P95.3.T8   302.2'2   80-26537
ISBN 0-13-774273-8

*P
95.3
.T8
1981*

Printed in the United States of America

10 9 8 7 6 5 4 3 2 1

Editorial/production supervision: Jeanne Hoeting
Interior Design: Edith Riker
Cover Design: Mariam Recio
Manufacturing Buyer: Edmund W. Leone

Prentice-Hall International, Inc., *London*
Prentice-Hall of Australia Pty. Limited, *Sydney*
Prentice-Hall of Canada, Ltd., *Toronto*
Prentice-Hall of India Private Limited, *New Delhi*
Prentice-Hall of Japan, Inc., *Tokyo*
Prentice-Hall of Southeast Asia Pte. Ltd., *Singapore*
Whitehall Books Limited, *Wellington, New Zealand*

We dedicate this book to

Donald T. Campbell, Karl R. Wallace, and Chuck Fink

Contents

4   HISTORICAL-CRITICAL RESEARCH   66

5   DESCRIPTIVE RESEARCH   89

6 THE EXPERIMENTAL METHOD 123

SPECIFIC CONCERNS
PART THREE

Preface

In a rapidly changing, complex world fraught with a multitude of social, economic, political, environmental, educational, and technological problems, there is a persistent need to ask questions, to provide answers, to change, to grow, and to advance—in short, to *discover.* Research is the process by which we do just that. Research frequently has the connotation of being stodgy, laborious, and dull. With this book we hope to change that image. For us, research is contemporary, challenging, and *fun.*

However, we are not denying the rules and guidelines that must be followed. We are not denying that good research is rigorous. It means carefully planning, systematically following certain procedures, and insightfully deliberating over reams of information. But there is no mystery about the whole process. We have tried to make that fact plain throughout the book. Research can be easily understood, and procedures can be easily followed if one is willing to learn the fundamental precepts.

This book is an introduction to research in speech communication. It is designed for those just entering serious study in the area: juniors and seniors in college, beginning graduate students, those interested in research or those planning to write a thesis or dissertation.

We feel the book has several strengths. First, it is readable. We have tried to convey information in down-to-earth, easy-to-read language—a style that the student should find comfortable and enjoyable. We assume no background in speech on the part of the reader. Nor do we expect the student to be familiar with any research methodology.

Second, this book is a straightforward, no-nonsense guide to research. We have written another "how-to" book in the spirit of offering practical, specific guidelines to getting immersed in research. Wherever we could, we offer shortcuts and suggestions for streamlining research activity. All of us thoroughly understand and appreciate the time and effort that research demands.

The third strength of the book is that it encourages the reader to go on. Wherever we could, we offer other journal references and books that can be explored. If the reader gets the "research bug," the reading of this book will be just a beginning. Our goal is to get the readers out into the literature of the profession and doing research of their own.

Another strength is that this book is written by people who *do* what they talk about. Each author has extensive background in research—a combined professional experience of close to thirty-five years. Further each also teaches research methods courses. Thus, the material in this book benefits from actual in-class use and testing and is presented in such a way as to make it easily taught. In addition, one of the authors recently finished graduate school. This perspective has helped us all by keeping our approach and suggestions close to the immediate needs of students; we feel we are directly in touch with those needs.

Perhaps this book's greatest strength is that it is the first comprehensive research book written in the field of speech communication in twenty years. We saw a glaring gap and sought to fill it. This volumne is traditional in its overview of the research process (Chapters 1 and 2) and its explanation of the various types of research methods (Chapters 3-6), but it is contemporary and unique in its detailed coverage of quantitative data (Chapter 7), statistical models (Chapter 8), writing and publishing (Chapter 10), practical suggestions (Chapter 11), and evaluation procedures (Chapter 9). In addition, Chapter 12 provides a comprehensive view of the speech communication field. We hope this serves as an introspective self-evaluation for researchers already in the field as well as an orientation for novice speech communication researchers.

What may be considered a weakness in the book is an occasional lapse into redundancy. However, we have chosen to retain a level of redundancy to stress the importance of certain points and because a restatement of material from a different author's perspective and may offer new insight. We are fully aware, too, that instructors tend to assign some chapters and not others. With the goal of making the chapters relatively self-contained, then, a certain amount of redundancy was necessary.

In this book, we have tried to convey both the importance and excitement of being researchers. We hope that you will sense this enthusiasm and perhaps feel it also.

ACKNOWLEDGEMENTS

To the thirty-five distinctly human beings whose doctoral dissertations I directed or co-directed, and to the remaining ten who will soon join them: I owe you everything.

E. Scott Baudhuin, Kenneth R. Albone, Christine E. Bergen, Arthur P. Bochner, Lawrence J. Chase, James C. Clymer, Roger N. Conaway, Michael F. Curran, Fran Dickson-Markman, Kathi Dierks-Stewart, Dennis P. Dunne, Robert L. Duran, Donald L. Grigsby, Karen J. Gritzmacher, Richard B. Haynes, Phyllis Hershman, Clifford W. Kelly, Charles W. Kneupper, Desmonde F. Laux, James L. Laux, Robert W. Loesch, Ronald L. Lomas, Edward A. Mabry, Eleanor A. W. McCreery, Gilbert J. Maffeo, Jr., David L. Mathison, Bonnie L. McEndree, Gary W. Melton, Keith A. Miller, Mark J. Nolan, Susan C. Parrish, Sandra D. Perky, Joseph C. Philport, Eileen M. Redden, Timothy E. Rook, Gary N. Rubin, Carol L. Sloman, Jessie Swihart, Paul D. Ware, Roger D. Wimmer, Leanne O. Wolff, Sandra E. Wright, Janet L. Yerby, Leslie J. Young, and Walter Zakahi.

R.K.T.

Books are products of our whole background—all our experience. This author (Weaver) is indebted to many students and colleagues, more than can be mentioned by name. For the part he played in introducing me to research in the field of speech communication, I wish to thank Kenneth E. Andersen. For continuing to provoke an interest in research, I also want to acknowledge Raymond G. Smith and Robert G. Gunderson. For their help in furnishing materials, offering suggestions, and providing support, I also wish to thank my colleagues at Bowling Green State University, Donald K. Enholm, James R. Wilcox, John T. Rickey, and Delmer M. Hilyard. I want to express genuine appreciation as well to my co-authors on this project, Ray and Cindy. It has been a pleasure working with both of them. The interchange of ideas, suggestions, and materials has been rewarding. For her excellent work in typing the manuscript, I would like to thank Judy Harris. I also wish to express appreciation to Gloria Gregor and Mary Lou Willmarth for their continuing help in duplicating materials. For their unceasing support, I also wish to thank my wife and family: Andrea, Scott, Jacquie, Anthony, and Joanna. Without all of you, there would be little reason for what I do.

R.L.W., II

The first spark of interest for this book came while I was being interviewed by my then future but now present colleagues at the University of Cincinnati. I thank them for igniting that spark which originated this volume. Specifically within this group, I offer my appreciation to Kathleen and Rudolph Verderber and Gail Fairhurst for their editorial assistance, theoretical suggestions, and endless empathy. For helping me understand the difference between architects and carpenters of research, I am indebted to James R. Wilcox. For innumerable reasons and for just "being there" when I needed them, my thanks go to Gertie and Chuck.

C.B-F.

PART ONE

FOUNDATIONS

The Need for Research in Speech Communication

Change is a certainty in contemporary society. Technological advancements are occurring so rapidly that most scientists have become technically obsolete within ten years after graduation from college. So much new knowledge is being generated that even a professional operating in a narrow field may find it impossible to keep current on information in that one speciality. To illustrate the rapid rate of progress, think of the technological and social advances that have been made within your own lifetime. Such a list can be difficult to generate because we take for granted and assimilate into our lives changes that have occurred within our lifetime. But for the brief time period from 1940 through 1980 history has recorded the development of television, oral contraceptives, the computer, solar energy, space travel, a cure for polio, and artificial creation of DNA. The rapid rate of change is further evidenced by the following statistics:[1]

1. The gross national product of goods and services in advanced nations of the world is doubling every one-and-a-half decades.
2. Between 85 and 90 percent of all scientists who ever lived were alive in 1970.
3. The speed of transportation never exceeded twenty miles per hour until the mid-nineteenth century. Rockets now travel at over twenty thousand miles per hour and commuter speeds for many exceed the speed of sound.
4. In four and one-half centuries, the publication of new books has increased from one thousand a year to one thousand a day.
5. The number of scientific journals and articles appears to be doubling every fifteen years, with a current output of some 20 million pages per year.

6. Approximately half of the energy consumed in the last two thousand years was consumed in the last hundred years.
7. Aproximately 36 million people move from one place to another each year in the United States.

Alvin Toffler, in his book *Future Shock,*[2] suggests that we are utterly unprepared to cope with this accelerated rate of change. Our images of reality are useless when we come to realize that the world we were educated to believe in does not exist.

RESEARCH IS THE NEW FRONTIER

What do these changes have to do with research? Research is responsible for these accelerating technological and social advances. And research will ultimately find the remedy for the social and psychological problems caused by the burgeoning change. Our increasingly mobile population, bombarded with a changing environment, faces "future shock." Research in the social sciences may be the means by which we cope with it.

Today greater emphasis than ever before is being placed on research. Among advanced nations, scientific, technological, and social knowledge is equated with international influence. Government policies of various nations give high priority to applied research and technology. Institutions of higher education in the United States are increasingly emphasizing research. Teachers are being replaced by teacher-researchers. Academic institutions, small and large alike, are requiring their faculty to demonstrate proficiency in both teaching and research. As the job market for graduates in the social sciences shrinks employability requires more than demonstrated ability in teaching.

Our world is rapidly changing, and research is both the harbinger and consequence of that change. This chapter discusses the meaning of research, the mode of thought and norms followed by the researcher, the relationship between research and the development of an academic community, the stages through which research evolves, the revolutionary process of discovery, the functions of research, and the research obligations of an academic community.

WHAT IS RESEARCH?

Recognizing that research is so prevalent in today's society and most of us will be expected to engage in research, we are justified in asking "What is research?" As a noun, *research* usually is defined as systematic inquiry into a subject in order to discover or revise facts or theories. As a verb, it means to study, to inquire, to examine, to scrutinize. Given these definitions, it would seem that all human endeavor involves research. As a student of some sixteen or more years, you have had ample practice in study, inquiry, examination, and scrutiny. Certainly on occasion we have all done "research"—that is, we have conducted a systematic inquiry to discover or revise facts or theories. The difference between research in the general sense and research in a more academic sense lies in the word *systematic*. How does a systematic inquiry differ from a nonsystematic inquiry? The remaining chapters in this book are devoted to explicating the procedures and methods of systematic inquiry, or scholarly research. For now let it suffice to say that systematic research is guided by reflective thought and inquiry.

All research, whether it is conducted according to a historical, descriptive, or experimental methodology, follows a systematic form of reflective thinking, often called the scientific method. Dewey's *How We Think* presents the general procedures in reflective thinking.[3] The steps he presents correspond to the procedures involved in systematic research.

HOW DOES THE RESEARCHER THINK?
THE SCIENTIFIC METHOD

Research begins with the researcher experiencing an obstacle to understanding, a curiosity about some phenomena. This curiosity, uncertainty, or unrest must then be expressed in the form of a problem. Only when it is verbalized or formulated as a problem does the curiosity take on a researchable form. The researcher thinks about the problem, ponders it, and imagines possible causes. A hypothesis, or tentative statement, about the variables relating to the problem is then proposed. The hypothesis essentially predicts that if X or Y occurs, then Z should result. At this stage, the researcher studies the hypothesis and tries to deduce the implications or consequences of the hypothesis. This deductive reasoning may change the problem as the researcher comes to realize the initial problem is really just part of a broader, more important problem. The original hypothesis may change as the researcher works out the testable implications of the initial hypothesis. The researcher then puts the hypothesis to the test by making observations or collecting information, data, or evidence. On the basis of the information collected, the hypothesis is either accepted or rejected. When the predicted *then* does not follow from the *if*, the hypothesis is rejected. Essentially, systematic research follows the sequence of question, problem, possible causes, hypothesis, implications, revised hypothesis, observation, and acceptance or rejection of hypothesis.

A simple example will illustrate the scientific method as the mode of thinking in systematic research. Suppose, as a speech-communication instructor, you notice that certain course assignments bring vociferous complaints from your students. You observe that students more often complain about public-speaking assignments than about other communication performance assignments such as interviews, dyadic encounters, group discussions, or debates. As an effective and sensitive teacher, you begin to wonder why public-speaking assignments elicit such student criticism. Following the scientific method, you ponder the problem and think of possible causes. Perhaps the students dislike being graded, you surmise. Yet other performance assignments are graded, and they do not lead to such negative reactions. Perhaps students dislike public-speaking assignments because they must complete the assignment individually, as opposed to working with others. But what is it about individual performance that generates negative reactions? After much thinking, questioning, and observing, you formulate the hypothesis: If students are fearful of public speaking, then they will negatively evaluate the assignment.

This hypothesis implies that students will negatively evaluate any classroom assignment that engenders fear. It indicates that the initial problem (student complaints about public speaking) is really part of a broader problem (the relationship between fear and negative reactions to course assignments). You revise your hypothesis to test this more general implication: The greater the fear of a class assignment, then the more negative the attitude toward the assignment. Note that your hypothesis is stated so as to predict a relationship between the two variables of fear and negative attitudes. You are now ready to make observations, to collect information, data, or evidence. There are many ways of collecting information to test your hypothesis. In this instance you might administer questionnaires to determine how fearful each student is about each course assignment and how negative or positive that same student's attitude is regarding each assignment. A simple comparison will show whether the assignments that are most feared are most negatively evaluated. If increased fear correlates positively with increased negative attitudes, then your hypothesis is accepted.

Note how employing the scientific method allows you to refine and systematically investigate what was initially a vague curiosity.

1. Curiosity: Why are students complaining?
2. Problem: Students dislike public-speaking assignments.
3. Possible causes: Grades, individual performance, fear.
4. Hypothesis: If students fear public speaking, then they will negatively evaluate the assignment.
5. Implication: There will be a positive relationship between fear of a classroom assignment and negative attitude toward that assignment.
6. Revised hypothesis: The greater the fear of a class assignment, then the more negative the attitude toward the assignment.
7. Observation: Administration of questionnaire.
8. Evaluation: Acceptance or rejection of hypothesis.

RESEARCH NORMS: HOW DOES THE RESEARCHER BEHAVE?

Besides following the scientific method or mode of reflective thinking, researchers are expected to observe certain norms. A few of the generally accepted norms of the research community, regardless of the speciality in which the research is conducted, include:[4]

Universalism: Scientific laws are the same everywhere. A scientific law states a relation between phenomena that is invariable under the same conditions.

Organized skepticism: Researchers are responsible for verifying the results on which they base their work.

Communality: Researchers are willing to share knowledge freely and contribute to public knowledge.

Disinterestedness: Researchers must ban ulterior motives and be relatively free from bias. Any known or possible biases must be admitted.

Researchers seek to draw conclusions about the relationship between phenomena. Once a definitely established relationship between phenomena (a law) exists, researchers accept that the relationship is invariant. They agree that the established relationship exists in all circumstances, under all conditions, and for all time. There can be no exception to the law. Because laws are virtually nonexistent in the social sciences, the norm of universalism may be a moot point for social science researchers; however, the norm is nevertheless endorsed. Agreement on this basic assumption encourages researchers to pursue questions and problems until they can know such invariant answers as a law provides.

Researchers continually question their own and their colleagues' work. They accept a research finding only after it has been repeatedly verified. By endorsing the norm of organized skepticism, researchers detect errors, force themselves to verify tentative answers, and allow only definite results to be labeled *knowledge*.

By agreeing to make their results public, researchers can scrutinize, revise, and build on the work of others. Without the norm of communality, the value of research would be lost, and a piece of knowledge would be nothing more than the private fantasy of an individual. Knowledge becomes knowledge through sharing and consensual validation. The researcher in private possession of information is akin to the one-eyed person in the land of the blind: His or her reality is nonexistent since reality inherently consists of shared perceptions.

Competent researchers seek knowledge through careful and controlled inquiry. Those who allow biases and prejudices to confound their investigations come up with nothing more than distorted, slanted, or incorrect findings. Only by agreeing to the norm of disinterestedness can researchers control, as much as possible, their private desires, influences, and expectations from affecting their investigations.

HOW DOES RESEARCH RELATE TO THE DEVELOPMENT OF AN ACADEMIC COMMUNITY?

We have briefly examined how researchers conduct their inquiry and what norms govern such inquiry; now we will look at how research evolves and shapes an academic community. Research is guided by and contributes to theory. To test specific hypotheses without attempting to relate these hypotheses to the larger whole is to deal in triviality. Hypotheses are to theories as the short-range answer is to the long-range solution. Imagine that as a researcher, you test and accept several hypotheses relating to a given problem. As you continue to test varied hypotheses relating to this problem, common sense would tell you to consult the research of others, to avail yourself of past answers or past experiences with the problem. To ignore relevant past experience is to work in a vacuum and to deny yourself the wisdom and benefit of history. What an utter quandary we would find ourselves in throughout our day-to-day functioning if memories of past experiences were not imprinted in our minds! Each endeavor would be totally new and foreign for us, and we would be quite unable to cope with daily existence were it not for our capacity to use our accumulated knowledge of similar endeavors. The researcher can use existing theory to guide each new test of an hypothesis and then feed back the results of that hypothesis-test into the existing theory to revise or expand the knowledge base.

While we have been using the term *theory* in a rather general sense, *theory* is more accurately defined as a set of interrelated concepts that present a systematic view of phenomena by specifying relations for the purpose of explaining and predicting the phenomena.[5] The level or amount of theory that exists to guide investigations depends on how much or how little a problem has been investigated. The researcher who inquires about a never-before-investigated problem area is akin to the child experiencing an event for the very first time. Just as the child is baffled by a new experience and repeatedly asks its parent "why," the researcher without the guide of theory operates with a childlike puzzlement and speculation. We can expect then, that the more mature the discipline, the more it is characterized by theoretical development.

Research in a particular discipline evolves through stages, just as the child proceeds through stages in its explanation of the world. Ziman outlines the stages characteristic of scientific developments, which we will expand to include the steps in the evolution of theory in an academic field.[6]

Research Stages

1. Conjecture: At this stage, researchers simply ask why; they question a phenomenon with little or no past experience to apply in projecting an answer. Here, researchers can rely only on the conventional wisdom of other related disciplines.

2. Discovery: As research progresses, a body of existing knowledge develops to guide present investigations. But at this stage, researchers propose many speculative and contradictory theories that generate much debate. Resistance and conflict emerges as various theoretical positions are advanced, argued, and debated. The research literature of the field is fraught with inconsistencies, statements, and counterstatements.

3. Breakthrough: At this stage a general explanatory pattern begins to be adopted. Inconsistencies are resolved, resistance lessens, and opposing theories give way to a unified explanatory system.

4. Acceptance: The theoretical system successfully explains and predicts phenomena; consequently, it is accepted by the majority who do research in the discipline. The puzzle is assembled and researchers clearly see how the pieces fit together.

These stages in the evolution of theory as an academic discipline develops correspond to the course of scientific development charted by Thomas Kuhn in his classic volume, *The Structure of Scientific Revolutions.*[7] Although Kuhn describes the progress of scientific developments, it must be noted that the term *scientific* is used in its broadest sense. The accumulation of knowledge in any subject area follows the evolutionary and revolutionary course described by Kuhn.

THE EVOLUTION (REVOLUTION?) OF KNOWLEDGE

The development of a body of knowledge proceeds through an incremental process of accumulation. Early fact gathering is nearly a random activity, and each investigation adds just one small detail to what is already known. In the early developmental stages of a discipline, researchers have varied ways of seeing the field and of practicing research in it. Each researcher adopts a paradigm or a view of the field, which specifies assumptions of how research ought to be conducted in that field. This view determines what are considered relevant phenomena for investigation and acceptable methods for discovering relationships among those phenomena. Since each researcher is looking at the field differently, each is likely to interpret the same phenomena in a different way. In the absence of a universally accepted paradigm, model, or viewpoint, all the various and frequently inconsistent interpretations are equally valid—for who is to say which view of the field is the correct one? At this stage we see continual competition among a number of distinct views of the field. Researchers join different "camps" or "schools of thought" that are often at cross purposes.

As one paradigm comes to better explain and predict phenomena, it gains additional supporters. Professional allegiances gradually shift until one paradigm gains the lead. More and more researchers explore, improve, and refine this paradigm. Investigations and articles based on it multiply as competing paradigms receive less and less attention. More people adopt the guiding paradigm, and resisters become the minority.

The paradigm is accepted as long as it continues to allow us to successfully attack our problems and explain the phenomena we investigate. When puzzles or problems evolve that cannot be attacked within the realm of our "world view" or existing interpretations, we at first dismiss the problems. Rather than question the basic and guiding assumptions, researchers dismiss the unexplainable phenomenon. But as the unexplainable event keeps rearing its ugly head, researchers begin to study it, to focus attention on it, to magnify it, and to speculate why the event is occurring. If the unexplainable phenomenon cannot be assimilated into the existing paradigm, the paradigm comes into question and a scientific revolution begins. We try to adjust the paradigm to explain the violating phenomenon. The discipline experiences professional insecurity as proponents of the paradigm resist its demise and advocates of a changed or new paradigm seek to renounce the old. Competition, conflict, and debate reemerge as a new world view replaces the old. The novel interpretation emerges with great difficulty, and the guiding paradigm is declared invalid only when the new one is sufficiently developed and refined to take the place of the old. Led by a new paradigm, researchers look in new places to solve new puzzles. In effect, they view the discipline differently. Kuhn likens this process to one of government revolution, whereby the status quo or existing system cannot be overthrown until a new system is available to take its place.

What does this have to do with speech communication? Kuhn's chronicle is cited to demonstrate the cycle through which knowledge in a particular discipline progresses and to provide a basis for commentary on the speech-communication field. Although study, analysis, and commentary concerning the area of speech began over two thousand years ago with the insights and observations of Plato and Aristotle, the academic discipline of speech communication as we know it today is still at a nascent state. Systematic research in speech communication is in many areas still in the realm of conjecture, with speech-communication scholars borrowing heavily from other academic disciplines. Competition among paradigms is evidenced by distinct schools of thought. Some speech-communication scholars posit that we are moving from an aparadigmatic to a preparadigmatic stage[8] while others resist the move to a single paradigm, stating that it will restrict our research options.[9] Different perspectives that are currently endorsed by various groups of speech-communication scholars include the covering-laws perspective, the rules perspective, the systems perspective, the mechanistic perspective, the psychological perspective, the interactionist perspective, and the pragmatic perspective, among others.

Now that we have a basic awareness of the prevalence and importance of research in contemporary society, a definition and description of the research process, the norms for its conduct, and the evolution of research knowledge in an academic community, we can turn to the question, "So what?" Specifically, why is research conducted? What are its purposes or functions? What can research do for us?

WHAT ARE THE FUNCTIONS OF RESEARCH?

Basic Versus Applied Research: Advancing Knowledge or Solving Problems?

We frequently hear stated two broad objectives of research, objectives that correspond to the two generic types of research. The first type, *basic* or *pure research*, seeks to advance knowledge. The urge to explain the world around us emerges from our basic human curiosity. As we find answers to satisfy our curiosity, our storehouse of knowledge grows. We elevate ourselves from animals and gain our very humanness in our capacity to think, to ask questions, to reason, to remember, and to advance knowledge. Surely, we all can recall situations where we sought an answer to a question not so much because we needed the answer to solve a pressing problem but merely because we wanted to know. We were curious. The basic researcher seeks knowledge for its own sake; he or she has no immediate need for that knowledge other than to settle a plaguing curiosity.

The second generic type of research, *applied research,* seeks knowledge to solve a problem. Just as basic research is guided by the question of why, applied research deals with questions of how, how should . . . , or how could . . . . In this sense, research is applied to problems; the researcher is seeking to better the conditions of mankind. By doing research, we not only contribute to knowledge but learn from this knowledge and profit by making enlightened choices based on understanding.

This classic distinction between basic and applied research is really rather arbitrary and is designed more so to classify researchers rather than to distinguish research activity per se. One may argue that since all good research draws on existing knowledge and theory, no research can be "pure." Any knowledge generated by basic research will be used to guide further research, thereby changing the initial research from pure to applied. And of course, as an individual's knowledge increases, that person's prestige, power, and capacity for making enlightened choices or decisions increase. Thus, all knowledge is applied and "knowledge for its own sake" becomes a meaningless phrase.

The dichotomy between basic and applied research more often reflects the motives and conditions under which researchers pursue their investigations. Basic researchers are often conceptualized as academicians in the university community; they are seen as exercising considerable freedom in choosing their research topics, as pursuing their investigations relatively unhampered by outside constraints and directions, and as seeking their own sources of funding for research, if they seek any at all.

In contrast, the applied researcher is viewed as one who conducts investigations aimed at solving problems that are often posed by sponsoring agencies or companies. Since this researcher is usually hired by the sponsoring agency to solve a specific problem, the sponsor usually provides more direction, perhaps even specifying the research topic, more consultation, and more assistance in the day-to-day conduct of the investigation. This researcher usually receives some funding or monetary reimbursement for the project. Examples of applied researchers include, among others, the communication consultant to government, business, or service organizations; marketing researchers; and those on the research and development staff of an organization.

As with any category system that seeks to classify or separate, the distinctions it sets up frequently obscure similarities and emphasize differences, and the classifications begin to take on a hierarchical order. Basic or pure research has frequently been placed at the top of the hierarchy and labeled a more legitimate or more scholarly type of research. We see evidence of this elitism in the very term *pure research,* which by comparison implies that applied research is impure or less pure. In our opinion such evaluative assumptions concerning pure and applied research are unnecessarily restrictive. A piece of research should be judged in terms of the norms and methods for conducting research set forth by the research community. The quality of a research project does not necessarily depend on whether the investigation is commissioned, funded, or directed by a specific agency to solve a problem or by an individual researcher who seeks to advance knowledge and receives no funding or direction by others for doing so. True, the myth exists that pure research is nobler, but who would deny that both Einstein and Edison were great researchers?

As researchers increasingly engage in both basic and applied research, the distinctions and implicit evaluations between the two are probably lessening. No longer is one either a basic or an applied researcher. University faculty, traditionally associated with basic research, are increasingly being commissioned and funded by government and private agencies to conduct research projects. Increasingly, faculty members are offering their research skills to the public, investigating specific problems, and applying research findings to the solution of those problems.

In the overall sense, then, research serves two general functions—advancing knowledge and solving problems—and the two are not mutually exclusive. To be more specific, however, we can enumerate many functions of research within these two general purposes. Research also enables us to organize existing knowledge, relate new information to existing information, understand, explain, and predict events, generate instructional curricula, refine and improve research methodologies, and generate new research questions.

Organizing Existing Knowledge: What Do We Already Know?

As human beings we feel a need to organize and synthesize the world in some meaningful way. As research findings accumulate bit by bit into a body of knowledge, we need a way to compile, systematize, and synthesize that knowledge. To generate facts without organizing those facts into unified generalized statements precludes the value of those facts. Thus, as research in an area progresses, statements that synthesize, criticize, organize, or reorganize knowledge in that area frequently appear. Only by periodically examining where we are to date or by describing the status quo can we move forward and make progress. Examples of speech-communication investigations that seek to organize and provide a commentary on existing knowledge include, among others: Robert L. Nwankwo, "Communication as Symbolic Interaction: A Synthesis"; David R. Seibold, "Communication Research and the Attitude-Verbal Report-Overt Behavior Relationship: A Critique and Theoretic Reformulation"; C. David Mortensen, "The Status of Small Group Research"; Sidney Kraus, "Mass Communication and Political Socialization: A Reassessment of Two Decades of Research"; and Arthur Bochner, "Conceptual Frontiers in the Study of Communication in Families: An Introduction to the Literature."[10]

As research studies in many areas of speech communication proliferate, such summary articles serve the important need of organizing existing knowledge. Because they provide a quick and often thorough overview of research already conducted in a specific area, they are invaluable to the beginning researcher. Rather than having to start anew with each investigation, the researcher can draw on the organized knowledge of previous generations of scholars. As a beginning researcher, you would be wise to consult the summary articles to gain a general perspective on a topical area. Research that organizes existing knowledge can help us avoid engaging in a process of reinventing the wheel.

Resolving Inconsistent Findings: Who Do We Believe?

As we have mentioned, immature disciplines frequently are fraught with inconsistencies. Since a single study does not prove or disprove anything, many researchers engage in testing the same hypotheses. Each research finding becomes one small additional piece of evidence in the quest for an answer. Only when a phenomenon has been repeatedly investigated do we begin to gain a semblance of "truth." As researchers pursue the same questions and test the same hypotheses, the waters often become more muddied. Given a number of researchers investigating phenomenon X, half are likely to report one finding and the other half a different and often opposite finding. For every example, there is a counterexample, for every statement a counterstatement, and for every research finding a counterfinding. As you embark upon your course of research in speech communication, you will no doubt find these inconsistencies at least mildly if not highly frustrating. This prophecy may not be very consoling, but rest assured that inconsistencies will be resolved in time. In an attempt to detect research errors, researchers scrutinize their own and their colleagues' work. No one research result is blindly accepted or believed by the members of the research community. Scholars seek to explain or resolve inconsistent research findings by studying them; examining the paradigm, theories, and methodologies upon which they are based; and debating, discussing, and reinterpreting the inconsistencies. Examples of speech-communication studies that seek to resolve inconsistent findings include, among others: Michael O. Watson, "Conflicts and Directions in Proxemics Research;" Ernest G. Bormann, "The Paradox and Promise of Small Group Research;" Thomas S. Frentz, "Toward a Resolution of the Generative Semantics/Classical Theory Controversy: A Psycholinguistic Analysis of Metaphor"; Howard S. Erlich, "Populist Rhetoric Reassessed: A Paradox"; and Carl I. Hovland, "Reconciling Conflicting Results Derived from Experimental and Survey Studies of Attitude Change."[11]

With the proliferation of inconsistent findings in many speech-communication areas, such articles serve an important need. Without such attempts to resolve inconsistencies, progress would give way to endless factional debates. By providing commentary and reinterpretations of seemingly incompatible research results, inconsistencies may give way to consistent explanations and increased understanding of human communication.

Relating New Information to Existing Information:
Is There Really Anything New Under The Sun?

Much of our understanding of the world derives from our capacity to remember, relate, and compare. In fact, the abstract terms and concepts in our vocabularies have meaning for us only in a relative sense.[12] Can we truly appreciate happiness, for example, if we have never known sadness? There can be no such thing as love for a person who does not know hate. Similarly, wealth and poverty, work and play, good and bad, pleasure and pain gain meaning only in the relative sense.

Besides achieving meaning through paired comparisons, we often draw upon the comparative function of analogy, simile, and metaphor to conceptualize the unknown in terms of the known. A classic example is the various metaphorical explanations of a supreme deity—God is light, wisdom, love, and so forth.

In the progress of research, there also exists a tendency to compare, relate, or conceptualize the new or unknown with the old or known. The capacity to juxtapose a new idea with an old idea is often labeled the essence of creativity. The creative individual is one who sees a unique application of standard information. By relating new knowledge to existing knowledge the researcher furthers understanding and expands the creative frontiers of his or her discipline. Examples of speech-communication investigations that seek to relate new information to existing information include, among others: Kathleen J. Turner, "Comic Strips: A Rhetorical Perspective"; Carol Weiher, "American History on Stage in the 1960's: Something Old, Something New"; L. L. Lane, "Communication Behavior and Biological Rhythms"; Gerald M. Phillips, "Rhetoric and Its Alternatives as Bases for Examination of Intimate Communication"; and Richard L. Weaver, "Role Playing and the Five Rhetorical Canons."[13]

Such investigations enable us to draw on the past to broaden our perspective of the present so that we can better understand the complex phenomenon of human communication. By applying new perspectives to familiar information or familiar perspectives to new information, such articles expand the scope of speech-communication research.

Understanding, Explaining, and Predicting Events:
What Will Happen Next?

We have already stated that research is guided by theory and contributes to theory. Thus, we can say that one function of research is to advance theory. But this theory-building function remains incomprehensible and esoteric without an understanding of how human communication theory relates to the communication process.

Theoretical statements, by specifying relationships among phenomena, allow us to infer causes. A theory not only describes what relationship the phenomena have to each other, but it also explains why the relationship among the phenomena exists. When we know why something exists, we know its cause. When we know the cause of an event, we can predict the future occurrence of the event. The capacity to predict events allows us to control those events. Thus, theory enables us to understand, explain, predict, and control.

Although the idea of predicting and controlling human behavior frequently evokes the image of an Orwellian society, it must be emphasized that the aim of scientific research is to control. The ability to control is not inherently good nor bad. Rather, the ethical, moral, or evaluative question arises with respect to how we employ the ability to control. An example of the functional use of control in human behavior will illustrate what we mean.

Imagine a relationship that you have had with a close friend. You see yourself as devoting time and energy to develop the relationship into a strong and mutually satisfactory one. You perceive that your friend does the same. Over the course of the relationship, in words and actions you disclose your identity, thoughts, and feelings to this person. You communicate a great deal of affection for your friend, and your friend communicates a similar caring for you. He or she performs valuable favors for you, is the first to help you in financial crisis, and brings you thoughtful gifts. But despite the mutual demonstration of affection, you find yourself becoming dissatisfied with the relationship. You feel guilty about your negative feelings. Your changed attitudes hurt your friend, yet you are at a loss to explain why the relationship is disintegrating. You simply feel that something is missing in the relationship.

This frequent and ironic problem in relationships can be understood, explained, predicted, and controlled (if you so desired) by applying Homan's theory of social exchange[14] as it relates to Villard and Whipple's concept of relational currencies.[15] The theoretical knowledge generated by these researchers can explain your disintegrating relationship. Social exchange theory states that all interaction involves the exchange of costs and rewards. You will be satisfied with a relationship and want it to continue if the rewards of the relationship exceed the costs. The rewards for the other party must also exceed their costs if he or she is to find the relationship satisfying. Villard and Whipple explain that parties in a relationship can exchange two different types of relational currencies—intimate and economic. In terms of your hypothetical relationship, you were offering affection through intimate currencies (self-disclosure and affect displays), while your friend was returning affection through economic currencies (favors, money, and gifts). If you were seeking intimate currencies and not receiving them, your costs in the relationship (need-frustration) may have exceeded your benefits (need-fulfillment), thus causing your dissatisfaction. If you understood the theory of social exchange as it applied to relational currencies, you could have explained to yourself and to your friend the cause of your dissatisfaction. You could have predicted the disintegration of the relationship and controlled or eliminated the relational problems through discussion, compromise, and change by either you or your friend.

This example is somewhat oversimplified and does not do justice to the more complex theory of social exchange, but it does illustrate that the ability to predict and control human behavior does not necessarily restrict our freedom. Rather, with the increased understanding, prediction, and control that we gain through theory, we can expand our options and widen our choices in human interaction.

Theory construction as a goal of research allows us to determine the what and why of events, giving us the freedom to consciously change those events and so exercise greater control in our lives. As research in human communication progresses, researchers engage in theory building and propose theoretical statements. Examples of speech-communication studies that increase our ability to understand, explain, predict, and control human communication include, among others: Judee K. Burgoon, "Unwillingness to Communicate as a Predictor of Small-Group Discussion Behaviors and Evaluations"; Charles R. Berger and Richard J. Calabrese, "Some Explorations in Initial Interaction and Beyond: Toward a Developmental Theory of Interpersonal Communication"; Randall Harrison and Mark Knapp, "Toward an Understanding of Nonverbal Communication Systems"; Donald Enholm, "Rhetoric as an Instrument for Understanding and Improving Human Relations"; and Peter R. Monge, "The Systems Perspective as a Theoretical Basis for the Study of Human Communication."[16]

Such investigations serve the important need of interrelating concepts to present a systematic view of phenomena so that we can understand, explain, predict, and control those phenomena.

Generating Instructional Curricula:
To be a Teacher or Researcher

It cannot be denied that research in communication education has provided scientific facts and principles to guide curriculum building. Kuhn describes the typical relationship between research results and educational curricula: When research results, theories, and paradigms are still at a tentative stage, they are discussed in professional articles, which are disseminated only in a limited portion of the academic community. As researchers come to have more faith in their research results, theories, and paradigms, their ideas are incorporated into textbooks, which are intended for the larger and more general audience. This dissemination of research findings to the lay community often represents the legitimization and acceptance of that subject area by the academic discipline. By the time we incorporate the researcher's results in our teaching, we assume those results are correct and the knowledge generated from them sound. True, an instructor may introduce students to tentative and speculative ideas, but these tentative results will seldom be included in textbooks and seldom receive widespread treatment in the educational curriculum.

This common view of the relationship between research and teaching includes an implicit hierarchical dimension. Research findings filter down through the research community, eventually reaching the educators and the general public. We can depict the assumed relationship as a pyramid, with a few researchers at the top of the pyramid who dedicate their time and energy to discovering facts, which eventually are shared with the masses at the bottom of the pyramid.

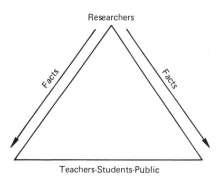

Figure 1-1   Research Pyramid

Source: Fred P. Barnes, "We Are All Researchers," *The Instructor,* 69:10 (1960), 7.

Perhaps this pyramidlike relationship has evolved because many teachers and students have held research in awesome fear and viewed the research process as a mysterious, incomprehensible, and difficult endeavor. We feel this view makes an unnecessary, unrealistic, and incorrect distinction between teachers and researchers. The time-honored formula of researchers as specialists who discover new and exciting ideas and teachers as users of those ideas is not an accurate depiction.

Increasingly, those who teach or plan to teach are expected to be aware of research that is being done, to pass judgment on it, to apply it, and to engage in it. Even if we accept the dichotomy of researchers as producers and teachers as consumers of research, we can raise these objections: (1) Can teachers who have never conducted research critically examine research results or do they accept research findings as gospel truths? and (2) Can teachers who have never conducted research understand the ideas developed by researchers and effectively incorporate them into the curriculum?

The very assumption that teachers are not researchers violates the tenets of effective teaching. Does not the teacher hypothesize a relationship between classroom actions and student learning and then collect information to accept or reject the hypothesis? Does not planning a course involve making the prediction that if I do X in terms of methods, materials, content, or activities, then students will do, learn, believe, or feel Y? The difference between teaching and doing research lies not in the method of conducting the investigation but in the level of formality in planning, observing, and reporting the investigation.

Barnes, writing on educational research, points out the similarities in the reflective thinking, teaching, and research process.[17]

As defined by the academic community, the teacher and the researcher are one in the same. The question, then, is not "Will I be a teacher or researcher?" but "How will I integrate my research into my teaching and conduct research investigations to answer classroom questions?"

Unless teachers conduct research and researchers engage in teaching, both teachers and researchers become stagnated. Educators do a disservice to their

Table 1-1 Common Elements In Reflective Thinking, The Teaching Process, And The Research Process

5 Steps in Reflective Thought				
Awareness of perplexing situation	Defining the difficulty	Proposing a hypothesis for problem solution	Reasoning out implications of the hypothesis	Testing the hypothesis against experience

7 Steps in the Teaching Process						
Awareness of general goal-directed teaching-learning object	Assessing state of affairs & diagnosing needs within the group	Selection of activities to meet these needs	Carrying through the activities planned	Evaluating the success (or failure) of the activities	Reassessing the activities	Replanning

7 Steps in the Research Process						
Sensing the problem area	Defining the specific problem	Formulating a hypothesis	Designing the test of the hypothesis	Obtaining evidence	Challenging and generalizing data	If necessary, retest

students, and researchers isolate themselves in their "ivory towers." Only with the notion of the combined teacher-researcher in speech-communication does knowledge become meaningful and relevant to improved human communication. Speech-communication investigations that seek to guide curriculum design and improve teaching methods, materials, and evaluation include, among others: Michael D. Scott and Lawrence R. Wheeless, "The Relationship of Three Types of Communication Apprehension to Classroom Achievement"; Michael McGuire, "Rethinking the Public Address Curriculum"; Daniel T. Hayes, "Toward Validation of a Measure of Speech Experience for Prediction in the Basic College-Level Speech Communication Course"; James L. Golden and Goodwin F. Berquist, "The Rhetoric of Western Thought: A Case Study in the Evolution of an Undergraduate Lecture Course;" and Stafford H. Thomas, "Teaching Stagecraft Through Models."[18]

Such studies investigate pedagogical issues and show how research ideas apply to the communication classroom. They integrate the teacher's and the researcher's knowledge for improved instruction.

Refining Research Methodologies:
Are We Using Sound Tools?

As we develop and employ methods and tools for answering questions and solving problems. we must examine those methods and tools. Just as the philosopher examines methods of reasoning and logic in resolving abstract issues and the artisan determines whether his or her tools satisfactorily perform the tasks for which they were designed, researchers too must scrutinize, question, and revise their methods and tools. This is especially important in research because the intangibility of the researcher's tools frequently leads to their misapplication. Imagine that you are collecting information about a concrete, tangible object, such as a table. Your perception and description of a particular table—its color, size, shape, and weight— will probably be fairly consistent with the perceptions and descriptions of most other individuals. This is because there are well-accepted tools to measure such things as size and weight of the table, for example. Next imagine a group of individuals collecting information about an abstract, intangible concept, such as intelligence, credibility, power, or conformity. Since we cannot see or touch credibility, for example, each individual will probably perceive and describe it differently. Although researchers frequently investigate such concepts, there are no obvious, widely used tools for measuring them.

If research tools were tangible objects like the artisan's hammer, wrench, and chisel, and if they were applied to concrete objects like tables, then we could immediately tell when the tools were being employed for the wrong purpose. But because many researchers, especially in the social sciences, do not work with tangible tools, opinions differ as to what tools perform what functions. Different methods of collecting and analyzing information generate much debate in the research community. Therefore, there is a need to hypothesize, theorize, and test the relationship between research methods and research outcomes. Some researchers specialize in methodology, systematically investigating the structure, practices, and procedures employed by the research community. In an attempt to detect research errors, they investigate whether we are answering research questions as validly, objectively, accurately, and economically as possible.

The task of improving research methodologies reflects the self-correcting nature of research. As researchers, we should critically examine our own methods and tools, but should we neglect our own duties as researchers, our research colleagues will make sure this obligation is fulfilled. Our colleagues will question our research results, and should our investigations not conform to generally adopted research practices, they will discredit our findings.

Many investigations attempt to resolve the professional debate concerning appropriate methods of collecting and analyzing information. Methodological research studies in speech-communication include, among others: Ronald L. Applbaum and Steve Phillips, "Subject Selection in Speech Communication Research"; Raymond K. Tucker and Herschel L. Mack, "Speech as Process: Effects of Experimental Design"; Dennis Alexander, "A Construct of the Image and a Method of Measurement"; Dan F. Hahn and Ruth M. Gonchan, "Studying Social Movements: A Rhetorical Methodology"; and James E. Fletcher, "Semantic Differential Type Scales in Communication Research."[19]

Such investigations fulfill the important need of examining current research methodologies. Because such researchers study the effects of existing methods and posit improved and refined methods and tools, we can gain increased confidence in the results of speech-communication research.

Generating Additional Questions:
Will We Ever Know all the Answers?

Besides giving tentative answers to questions, research investigations generate additional research questions. In fact, research multiplies questions far faster than it answers them. As each new bit of information expands our understanding and awareness of the world, we come to perceive this larger picture of the world in a slightly different way. We become curious about new phenomena. If we know nothing of a particular event, we cannot ask questions about it. It is only as we perceive and begin to understand an event that we can formulate the questions that will help us validate our perceptions and increase our understanding. The more we know, the more we realize there is to know. Think, for example, of a time when you were first introduced to a new subject. Before studying it, you probably had few if any questions, for it takes knowledge to ask questions in the first place. As you learned more about the subject, most likely your questions multiplied and your curiosity expanded. Perhaps you even became frustrated with the massive amount of information that could be known in the subject area. No one can master and know all there is to know, even in a narrow speciality, for increased knowledge leads to the capacity to ask more questions, and the question-answer cycle proceeds to infinity.

You can readily see that research investigations generate more questions than they answer when examining any research report. Read any thesis, dissertation, or published journal article and near the end of the report you should find suggestions or implications for further research. Here the researcher lists all the additional questions raised by the very answers provided by the study. The researcher is expected to indicate the questions or issues raised by his or her research results, thus allowing future research to be ongoing, cumulative, and a natural outgrowth of previous research.

RESEARCH AS AN OBLIGATION
OF THE ACADEMIC COMMUNITY

Whether you intend to pursue a career in academe or to use the knowledge and skills you gain as a temporary member of the academic community in a nonacademic occupational sphere, you will be expected to engage in some kind of research during your academic tenure. Whether it be a seminar project, a publishable paper, a thesis, or a dissertation, the academic community requires some degree of research experience from its members. The day of passively accepting the wisdom of the sage is over, if indeed it ever existed. In a world where change is constant, accelerating, and ubiquitous, our educational system must instill a capacity to cope with change. As Postman and Weingartner[20] explain, a relevant education is one that teaches survival strategies for coping with future shock. Education must do more than disseminate old facts, which will be outdated and useless even before they are learned. Education must teach the process of asking and answering questions—the systematic methods of pursuing and discovering knowledge. For once we learn how to ask questions, collect information, and draw conclusions from our observations, we have learned how to acquire and advance knowledge. Then no one can keep us from learning whatever we want or need to know. The world may change and our storehouse of information may become outdated, but we can keep pace and survive when we know the method of answering questions—the research method. For this reason a relevant education includes instruction and practice in conducting research.

For those who choose an academic career, especially in higher education, the capacity to do research becomes a right of passage into the academic community. The ongoing execution of research investigations and the sharing of research results become an obligation of the academician. Research is the lifeblood of academe: Sound administrative and policy decisions are based on research, the updating and revising of curricula require research, and devising and evaluating teaching practices depend on research.

Not only is the teacher in higher education expected to conduct research, but his or her professional standing among colleagues is dependent upon it. Typically, the criteria for evaluation of faculty at academic institutions include demonstrated contributions in teaching, research, and university and community service. A jack-of-all-trades and a wearer of many hats, the contemporary educator who wishes to remain in good favor (and in continued employment) must perform satisfactorily in all these categories. In some universities, one's research contributions may be the most heavily weighted criterion in determining salary, promotion, and tenure issues. The bottom line in higher education today is research. The adage "publish or perish" is increasingly being applied in the academic environment. The teacher who does not publish research studies perishes in terms of a career; the discipline that does not produce a body of scholarly research perishes as an academic field. As we have indicated, the teacher-researcher dichotomy has been replaced by a combination teaching-research proficiency. All members of the academic community must do their share in advancing knowledge, solving problems, and expanding frontiers of their profession.

Pressures Toward Excess and Abuse

Dedicated and sincere interest in answering questions, solving problems, generating knowledge, and advancing one's profession are—ideally—the catalysts to research endeavors. But unfortunately there are pressures in the research community that undermine the ideal functions and purposes of research inquiry. The glutted job market for educators has had a detrimental effect on the motives and quality of research. What was once research for the sake of knowledge can become research for the sake of one's resume. That is, as research becomes necessary for professional prestige and advancement in academe, and as competition limits the chance of advancement, the merit and quality of research projects may give way to an emphasis on quantity. A large number of published research articles may be seen as the path to a faculty position, promotion, tenure, job mobility, and visibility. With an emphasis on research quantity, quality is likely to take a back seat. In order to gain a number of resume items in a short time, individuals may spend less time on any one research project, leading to errors resulting from haste. As researchers face increasing demands to publish, the norms of careful and deliberate study, thorough planning, and careful execution—long inextricably a part of the research process—may deteriorate. With an emphasis on quantity, researchers are likely to avoid complicated, in-depth, long-term projects that could take years to complete adequately. Thus, the scholarly and thorough could give way to the quick and shoddy.

Even students feel the pressure of competition for grades, visibility within a department, admittance into graduate programs, and acquisition of jobs, which can obscure the ideal purpose of study: acquiring knowledge. When means become confused with ends, problems necessarily arise.

Our purpose is not to paint a bleak, dismal future for academe, but we do feel these pressures toward excess and abuse in the research realm need to be raised. If research is to fulfill its ideal functions and be conducted according to high standards, each practicing or would-be researcher must question his or her motives, methods, and procedures. The research community as a whole must address these issues to make sure the adage "publish or perish" does not become "publish *and* perish." Since research leads to progress, we must decide if we are progressing in a desirable and beneficial way. As we see burgeoning scientific, technological, and social change in our world, the research process and the motives and means by which it is conducted can enable us to cope with future shock. But only when research is sound and scholarly can we put any faith in its findings and truly advance understanding, knowledge, and freedom of choice in a rapidly changing world.

SUMMARY

Contemporary society places an ever-increasing emphasis on research. The ability to acquire and advance knowledge through systematic research is a necessary skill in a rapidly changing world. Systematic research is guided by reflective thought, or the scientific method, which follows a sequence of question, problem, possible causes, hypothesis, implications, revised hypothesis, observation, and hypothesis acceptance or rejection. Researchers observe the norms of universalism, organized skepticism, communality, and disinterestedness. Research is guided by and contributes to theory, which evolves through the stages of conjecture, discovery, breakthrough, and acceptance. The extent of theory that exists to guide investigations in a given field depends on the maturity of the discipline. Young disciplines frequently are characterized by less theoretical development, competing paradigms, inconsistent interpretations of phenomena, and factional debates among different schools of thought. As a discipline matures, its research is usually guided by a generally accepted paradigm, which can be replaced only through a process of scientific revolution. The speech-communication field frequently is labeled at the preparadigmatic stage, and speech-communication scholars disagree as to the necessity of a guiding paradigm.

Research is often characterized as basic or pure when its goal is to advance knowledge. Applied research attempts to solve specific problems. This dichotomy is a questionable one, however, and may simply serve to distinguish research projects that are funded and directed by sponsoring agencies from those that receive no funding or outside direction. Besides advancing knowledge and solving problems, research functions include: organizing existing knowledge, resolving inconsistencies in knowledge, relating new information to existing information, explaining, understanding, and predicting events, generating instructional curricula, improving research methodologies, and generating new research questions.

The ability to engage in research is a necessary condition of a relevant education and an expectation the academic community has for its members. Researchers must be aware of the pressures toward excess and abuse that could potentially undermine the value of research.

An Overview
of Research Procedures

"How do I go about conducting research?" This is likely to be the most important question you face as a beginning researcher. At this point, you are probably asking yourself some very practical questions: "Where do I find a research topic?" "Where do I find the necessary background information?" "How do I collect information?" "What should be included in the written research report?" "How long will it take me to complete the research?" "What problems will I encounter?"

This chapter discusses the procedures that apply to research and attempts to answer these and other questions that you will face as you begin a research project. The procedures for conducting research are fairly standard across various types of research and various subject areas. All researchers must choose their research area, formulate the research problem, select research questions or hypotheses, review relevant literature, design the research investigation, collect, analyze, and interpret information, draw conclusions, and write the research report. In this chapter we will elaborate on each of these stages, which are inevitably involved in the actual conduct of research, and provide suggestions and guidelines to ease you through each stage of your investigation.

PLANNING: THE KEY TO QUALITY RESEARCH

Ask any experienced researchers what their secrets are for avoiding problems and pitfalls and insuring a smooth, trouble-free research project, and they are likely to reply "planning." Where research is concerned, it pays to plan. As you will see throughout the pages of this chapter, there is a sequence of steps that you must proceed through when conducting research. Unlike in other sequential tasks, in the research process you cannot simply plod through step one, enter step two, begin step three, and so on. Rather, the entire research process must be carefully planned in advance. Before you even begin to collect information, you must give thought to why you are going to collect that information, what results you expect from the information, how you tentatively intend to analyze the information, and in what form and for what purpose you will report the information. It is imperative that the vital parts of the research project be outlined in detail at the beginning. As an experienced student you have probably heard this advice countless times and chuckled as you wrote a project's outline as an afterthought upon completion of the project. In research, however, the planning and outlining of subsequent procedures is the only way to insure quality results.

The initial plans can be revised as you move through the project. It is better to plan carefully and revise later than to do little planning and face unexpected problems along the way. Without thorough initial planning, unexpected problems will abound and sour even the most enthusiastic researcher. Among researchers, Murphy's Law is a commonly espoused adage: If anything can go wrong, it will. The only way to control most potentially devastating problems during a research project is to plan ahead. By thorough initial planning, possible errors can be foreseen and forestalled. As an example of the problems that befall the researcher who fails to plan in advance, consider the hypothetical case of Professor X. Professor X intended to conduct an experimental study using three hundred students from his introductory speech course to complete a series of questionnaires. Unfortunately, it took Professor X longer than he expected to devise, type, and duplicate the questionnaires, and he soon faced time pressures in the execution of the experiment (he was scheduled to present his findings at an upcoming speech-communication conference). Hastily, he arranged for the three hundred students to assemble in a large lecture hall on the sixth Tuesday evening of the term. Bewildered and disappointed when only fifty of the total three hundred students turned up for the experiment, he inquired as to the cause, only to learn that the largest rock concert of the year was being held on campus that evening. His last-minute planning coupled with his failure to attend to a minor detail—checking his schedule for possible conflicts—proved to be a major disaster for the researcher.

Considering all possible details and anticipating all possible problems at the start is the key to successful research. Setting up a research timetable and adhering to it will help to eliminate the time pressures that can frequently turn a thorough, well-organized project into a quick, shoddy, and sloppy one. The researcher would be well advised to chart the various stages of the research against the dates when they should be completed. Even so simple a formula as setting aside one-third of the time for planning, one-third for collecting and analyzing information, and one-third for writing will help the researcher avoid the last-minute time crunch. We cannot overemphasize the point that planning is perhaps the most important aspect of research.

CHOOSING THE RESEARCH AREA

The discipline of speech-communication is broad and encompasses many subareas. Within those subareas are still more narrow speciality areas. Thus, choosing a research area may seem like a most formidable problem. You may already have aligned yourself with a certain area of the discipline; that is, your speciality may be public address, mass communication, communication education, theatre, rhetorical theory, speech and language sciences, forensics, interpretation, or interpersonal, small-group, or public communication. But within each of those specialities lies a vast realm of research possibilities. Take, for example, the area of interpersonal communication: within its realm are such topics as nonverbal communication, self-disclosure, feedback, listening, perception, conflict, assertiveness, interviewing, self-concept, and intercultural communication, to name but a few. Choose one of those topics—nonverbal communication, for example—and you see a myriad of additional subtopics: proxemics, kinesics, chronemics, paralanguage, territoriality, olfactory communication, and many more.

If one tries to pick a research area out of mid-air, applying no prior criteria to the choice, then this stage of the research process necessarily will be frustrating. Research areas are not chosen randomly—or so we would hope. Instead, the scholar, through his or her coursework, independent reading, and genuine interest gradually becomes aligned with a speciality area. When the time approaches to begin a thesis or dissertation, there should be little doubt about the research area. The dedicated scholar will have been reading and developing an acute interest in a particular topic area, with an eye toward a specific research problem. You establish a solid basis for selecting a research area by becoming interested in a topic area, finding out as much as possible about it, discussing it with colleagues, and reading about it with a critical, questioning attitude. By immersing yourself in your discipline, you will not be faced with the task of selecting a research area. Rather, the research area and problem will slowly evolve as a natural outgrowth of your interest and proficiency. Recall from Chapter 1 that the researcher experiences a curiosity, an obstacle to understanding, an unrest that stems from genuine interest and theoretical understanding of an area. The research problem represents a felt need, not a question plucked from mid-air.

As the researcher becomes increasingly familiar with a topic area, reading and thinking about the topic suggests numerous researchable problems. It cannot be denied that the more we know about a topic, the more likely we are to ask intelligent questions, and the more we realize there is to know. You will have noticed that the final sections of published articles, theses, and dissertations usually provide a multitude of additional questions for research. These can inspire the beginning researcher. Most research studies need to be repeated before the findings can be accepted by the research community; replication provides another valid and necessary source of research projects. Researchers can investigate the same problem, using the same procedures and data analysis, and compare their findings to those of the original study. Still another source of research ideas comes from the work situation. Life in the classroom, on the job, or in the graduate program inevitably suggests issues and questions to be investigated. Many applied research problems can be discovered by looking at our daily surroundings.

Beginning or experienced researchers should have little difficulty selecting research areas if they immerse themselves in their discipline, become knowledgeable in a subject area, read with healthy skepticism, engage in shop talk with colleagues, consult the most recent professional articles, consider replication, and pay attention to practical problems in the working environment.

As you tentatively settle on a research problem, you must devote some time to scrutinizing the problem to determine the feasibility or workability of researching the problem. Careful thinking about the subsequent stages may convince you that the problem is unresearchable. Here is where the planning we emphasized earlier begins. Several criteria can be applied to the research problem to decide if it is workable, given one's limitations and situational constraints. Carter V. Good provided ten criteria for selecting a research problem, and these guidelines are just as important and applicable today as they were when he ennumerated them in 1942.[1] By evaluating a potential research problem in light of these criteria, the researcher can make a sound judgment concerning the value or feasibility of his or her study.

Novelty and Avoidance of Unnecessary Duplication

Is your research idea new and worthwhile, or are you merely reinventing the wheel? Many questions that intrigue researchers have already been answered. Unless you are thoroughly familiar with a subject area, you may fail to realize that definitive answers already exist for the research problem you are contemplating. Discussion with colleagues or faculty advisers and a thorough investigation of the literature in all related fields may show that a particular problem has been sufficiently researched. Unless you can investigate a slightly different aspect of the problem or provide new insights, you should most likely abandon the problem. This is not to say that duplication is forbidden. Planned duplication, as in a replication study, is a necessary and valuable research endeavor. Accidental duplication, however, results from poor planning and could be the downfall of one seeking a graduate degree. In thesis and dissertation research, an original contribution to knowledge is required. Research investigations can and should build upon previous investigations, adding to the accumulation of information. Many studies, though merely slight variations on previous studies, add new and useful pieces of information and contribute, in some small way, to knowledge. Unnecessary duplication of research, however, should be avoided, for it offers no contribution to one's discipline and the quest for knowledge.

Importance for the Field

All researchers should ask of their research proposals, "So what?" Before embarking on a research investigation, we should question whether the knowledge our research problem will generate is significant or trivial. What will the information do for the field? Is the question significant enough to deserve investigation? Will anyone else be interested in our results?

There are ample important questions to be answered in the field of speech communication. To investigate trivial, insignificant questions and to accumulate information that no one wants or needs is a waste of time. Researchers must justify to themselves and to their professional colleagues their choice of research topics. While it may seem difficult to distinguish a significant research topic from an insignificant one, consensual validation among the research community will prevail. Faculty committees, journal editors, and convention critics inevitably will suppress the trivial and applaud the significant research project.

Interest and Intellectual Curiosity

Do you have a genuine interest in the research topic? Or have you merely settled on a topic so you can begin your research and be done with it? Only with a genuine interest in the research area can most researchers discipline themselves to complete the investigation. A research project can take months or even years to complete. If your curiosity about the subject area is only superficial you are less inclined to find the will power to stick to the task at hand. Little benefit comes to those who jump from one research project to another without ever completing any. Investigating changing whims and fancies does little to advance the professional community. It is imperative that you select a research area that interests you, excites you, and makes you eager to pursue the project.

Although this fervor may sound idealistic, genuine enthusiasm for research projects is a very real phenomenon among dedicated researchers. They are eager to search for sources, to examine the data, to compare findings with projected outcomes, to discover the original document, or to discuss their progress with colleagues. Yet, despite this excitement that can accrue when one becomes immersed in one's research, most scholars will admit that at some point in the investigation, they usually become bored or frustrated and wish that they could abandon the entire project. This is hardly surprising; research is time-consuming. Ask someone who has recently completed a seminar paper, thesis, or dissertation about their research, and they are likely to say they never want to think about it again. After months or years of researching a problem, this temporary desire to escape the subject is quite natural. Because of the extensive time you will be devoting to a particular piece of research, you must have genuine interest and curiosity from the onset to insure continued enthusiasm through the project's completion.

Training and Personal Qualifications

Are you qualified to carry out the research investigation? Or will personal limitations hinder your completion of the project? Beginning researchers frequently take on more than they can handle, quite convinced that they will be capable of carrying out the research as proposed. It is important that the investigator examine his or her qualifications to conduct the proposed research. The researcher who plans to construct an original questionnaire or attitude scale, for example, must be well schooled in the intricacies of questionnaire construction or must at least be assured the assistance of qualified colleagues. Those planning a historical-critical analysis of public discourse should be knowledgeable in historiography or methods of rhetorical criticism. A sophisticated statistical analysis of data may require knowledge and skills in statistics. Some research may require the ability to translate documents written in a foreign language.

The researcher must question whether he or she possesses or can receive assistance with the necessary methodological knowledge, tools, or skills to investigate the research problem. While it may be noble to set one's sights high, having to abandon a project because you lack the necessary capacities and qualifications is not a desirable position to put yourself in. Besides determining what methodological skills are needed, you must consider your knowledge of content. If you plan an investigation in the area of contemporary rhetoric, for example, consider whether your past and future course work, independent reading, and availability of assistance enables you to gain sufficient proficiency in the subject matter. Ask if you can rely on the help of others with the necessary expertise. To attempt to become an expert in a subject area without the aid of others in the working environment to assist in your training is a difficult and lonely endeavor. Beginning researchers especially should choose research areas in which they have some knowledge, and they should realistically evaluate their research proposals in light of methodological expertise and limitations.

Availability of Data

Having determined that you are qualified to investigate the research problem, you must next ask yourself if the necessary information will be readily available to you. Will your investigation be halted at the data-collection stage because you are unable to locate or get access to the necessary information? Researchers who plan to administer questionnaires to specific populations may find that those populations do not exist. One researcher, for example, attempted to survey the communication problems of one hundred upper-level managerial women in nontraditional business careers. Despite the assistance of countless directories, government publications, and organizational contacts, this researcher found that one hundred such women simply do not exist.

Research that depends on the interview as a data-collection technique may be hampered because interviewees are unwilling, unable, or reluctant to provide the desired information. Such a problem may plague the researcher, for example, who attempts to interview couples concerning family communication problems. The researcher choosing a documentary or historical investigation must be certain that the desired documents exist. Have the historical documents been destroyed or lost? Is the necessary primary information thousands of miles away and not accessible through interlibrary loan services? These are questions the researcher must ask during the preliminary, planning stages of a project. That information is frequently unavailable is an unfortunate fact that can render even the most worthwhile and significant problems unresearchable.

Special Equipment and Working Conditions

Even if the information is available, the means for acquiring that information may not be. If you need special equipment or certain working conditions during the course of the research, you should plan in advance your means for acquiring the materials or setting up the conditions. An interaction analytic study, for example, may require video and audio tape equipment. An audiological study may require expensive and sophisticated audiological equipment. If the necessary equipment is not available, you may have to abandon the research project. Sometimes the researcher is unable to use various psychological tests and scales because the administration of such instruments is restricted to licensed psychologists. Many statistical analyses of data require access to computers. It is also extremely risky to depend on certain conditions occurring in the natural environment. The crisis communication researcher, for example, who waits for a natural disaster to occur to investigate victims' communication may be hampered by an unexpected benevolence of the elements. And research can be halted by an uncontrollable change in the conditions under investigation. A colleague who attempted to investigate attitude-behavior discrepancy regarding the national program of swine flu vaccination surveyed people regarding their intentions to be vaccinated, then found her research terminated when the government abandoned the vaccination program. For the laboratory researcher, suitable conditions may necessitate soundproof rooms, two-way mirrors, and qualified assistants. Without prior consideration of necessary equipment and working conditions, the researcher may face unexpected pitfalls when attempting to investigate the research problem.

Sponsorship and Administrative Cooperation

This criterion in selecting a research problem involves some very practical issues: Will there be someone to advise you on this project? Will the committee or department support the project? Will you be able to establish a good working relationship with the adviser and committee? Your choice of a research area must be guided by consideration of available assistance and advice. Although it is not necessary nor even recommended that you choose a research area that corresponds to the research speciality of a faculty member, it is advantageous to have someone with an interest in your research project. You should find some individual or individuals that you can rely on as resource persons during your investigation. If you have chosen a novel, significant problem that fits your capabilities, then administrative support and cooperation should be forthcoming.

Cost and Returns

Some research projects are costly—in time and money. As you settle on a research problem, you must evaluate the cost of the project against projected returns. Will you have to travel long distances to obtain necessary materials, documents, or information? Will you incur the costs of purchasing or renting equipment, paying subjects, fieldworkers, or assistants, or mailing questionnaires? For some fortunate or aggressive researchers, such costs may be covered by the department or through research grants. If these costs will be your responsibility, however, we recommend that you make an initial assessment of feasibility. Perhaps returns such as salary increases, promotion, job acquisition, enhancement of professional reputation, or personal satisfaction may serve to balance your expenses. In any event, you should evaluate the cost-benefit ratio at the time you plan your research problem.

Hazards and Penalties

All researchers should attempt to determine whether the benefits of the research to themselves and to their academic spheres justify the research. Some types of research may be negatively sanctioned by colleagues, and the researcher ostracized for working on that project. Some research methods may be regarded as unethical or unprofessional. Pursuit of a certain line of research may create an undesirable reputation for the researcher. Perhaps a new area within a discipline is regarded as faddish, superfluous, trivial, dangerous, or radical. Certainly, researchers from Galileo to Darwin to those currently investigating nuclear physics or parapsychology have faced such charges. However, you will want to examine the potential consequences of being associated with a particular type of research and determine whether hazards or penalties warrant conducting the research.

Time

As stated earlier, beginning researchers frequently attempt massive projects. You must examine the scope of a research project according to a time criterion. Longitudinal studies, for example, may best be postponed by the graduating senior or one-year master's student, and executed at some later time in one's professional career. A rhetorical analysis of all the speeches of a political candidate might best be reduced to the criticism of selected discourse. Sometimes you can conduct the initial or pilot research for a comprehensive project as a seminar project or a master's thesis, reserving the follow-up research for your doctoral dissertation. We are not suggesting that researchers avoid time-consuming, in-depth studies in favor of quick, miniscule investigations. As indicated in Chapter 1, avoidance of comprehensive, time-consuming research may result in the "publish and perish" syndrome for researchers and academic disciplines. Rather, we suggest that researchers examine the feasibility of projects in advance of embarking upon the project. A frequently stated maxim in the research community is that the only good study is a completed study. The time factor, an important though not the only criterion, deserves consideration.

DEFINING THE PROBLEM

Once the research area has been selected, the specific research problem must be defined. Simply choosing an area of research does not give you enough specificity or direction to proceed with your investigation. The exact problem must be formulated before you can begin to plan the details of executing the research. Although deciding on the broad research area may be easy, defining the specific problem is likely to be more difficult. The initial formulation of the research problem must be examined with an eye toward simplicity. The early, broad—and often vague—research idea may have to be reduced to a manageable size, a step that will also help bring the central issue into focus. It would be wise to sketch out several drafts of the research problem, continually refining the idea into a researchable project. The statement of the research problem should be clearly and concisely worded, it should raise a question about the relationship between variables, and it should suggest a method of researching the problem. The following example illustrates the refining process involved in the statement of a research problem.

Imagine you are interested in research in the area of self-disclosure. You are curious about why some people disclose more than other people do. What leads Person A to be a high self-discloser whereas Person B rarely discloses? At this stage you have a vague curiosity about the phenomenon. You have selected a research area and initially narrowed the problem to the variables that affect amount of self-disclosure. As you examine the material written on the topic, you find that such factors as the age, sex, race, geographical background, socioeconomic background, and personality of the discloser, as well as the topic and its relevance to the listener, seem to influence the amount of self-disclosure. You recognize that any attempt to investigate all these variables would be cumbersome, if not impossible, and therefore decide to narrow the problem to personality factors that affect self-disclosure.

But still the problem is unwieldy; numerous personality variables such as sociability, self-esteem, need for approval, dogmatism, extroversion, and competitiveness may affect self-disclosure. You must narrow the research problem still further. Suppose you become interested in the dogmatic or closed-minded personality as it relates to amount of self-disclosure. Here, the relationship between specific variables emerges, allowing you to formulate a more precise problem. Yet, your problem is still ambiguous, for the questions of determining dogmatism as a personality characteristic and measuring amount of self-disclosure remain unresolved. Next, you discover that Rokeach's Dogmatism Scale and Jourard's Self-Disclosure Questionnaire are valid measures of dogmatism and self-disclosure, respectively. Now, after several phases of refining and reworking, you formulate the specific problem of dogmatism (as measured by the Rokeach scale) as it relates to amount of self-disclosure (as measured by the Jourard questionnaire). The research problem has changed significantly from the initial formulation. It is worded clearly and concisely, it raises a question about the relationship between variables, and it suggests a method of researching the problem.

Through several stages of systematic delineation, you have narrowed the problem into a researchable one:

Step 1: What factors influence amount of self-disclosure?

Step 2: What personality factors influence amount of self-disclosure?

Step 3: How does the personality factor of dogmatism influence amount of self-disclosure?

Step 4: How will dogmatism, as measured by the Rokeach Dogmatism Scale, relate to amount of self-disclosure, as measured by the Jourard Self-Disclosure Questionnaire?

SELECTING RESEARCH QUESTIONS OR HYPOTHESES

By following the steps in the above hypothetical example you can begin to see not only how a research problem is formulated, but also how the researcher words it as a question that can be answered by the investigation. Perhaps the researcher is in a position to specify even further the relationship between variables through the use of a hypothesis. Recall that the hypothesis is a tentative if-then statement predicting the direction of the relationship between the variables. It is a conditional or provisional solution to the problem or answer to the question. Suppose that some information on this topic suggests that dogmatic individuals tend to disclose less than nondogmatic ones do. If there is any previous basis for doing so, the researcher will specify a tentative directional relationship between the variables: If dogmatism increases, then amount of self-disclosure will decrease. A directional hypothesis is not a prerequisite to every investigation. There are some questions where the exact nature of the answer cannot be anticipated. In an exploratory study where a topic has not previously been investigated, the research question substitutes for the research hypothesis. When a hypothesis is used, it should be worded in a declarative form, it should describe a relationship between the variables, it should be testable, and it should reflect a guess at the solution or outcome.

Some people link hypotheses only to experimental studies, perhaps because of the obvious nature of hypotheses in experimental research. But a hypothesis can be investigated by any method of research. Even the historian examines data, formulates hypotheses, and tests these conjectures by seeking fresh evidence or reexamining the old. Researchers who specify hypotheses must beware of projecting desires and biases into their perceptions during data collection, analysis, and interpretation. The tentative prediction of results must not guide the researcher into necessarily discovering those results. An unconfirmed hypothesis sheds light on the research problem and contributes to the cumulation of knowledge.

REVIEWING THE LITERATURE

Before, during, and after formulating the research problem, investigators face the task of reviewing the literature that relates to the research area. By familiarizing yourself with the body of existing knowledge and theory on the topic, you are better able to integrate your projects into existing theory and build on the work of predecessors. Your purpose in reviewing the literature is to define the boundaries of knowledge. The felt need or problem stems directly from the review of literature. All the previous relevant studies form the foundation on which your present investigation will be built. Since we are not lone pioneers operating in a vacuum but cooperators in the research community, we must thoroughly acquaint ourselves with what is known in a given area.

Those initial trips to the library, the archives, or the private collections of documents may prove to be overwhelming as sources unfold and everything or nothing seems relevant. As you try to select a research area, delineate a specific problem, and formulate questions or hypotheses, the sheer volume of information you encounter may prove discouraging. Each article you read includes a long list of new references to consult. The number of sources in your working bibliography expands exponentially. It may seem impossible to plod through the literature review. Or you may find yourself facing the opposite problem: Locating even one relevant source may prove a painstaking and fruitless process. The early stages of a literature review are frequently discouraging. But gradually the discovery of some helpful leads, the location of summary articles, or previous authors' clues to additional material makes the detective work easier and even enjoyable. The elusive information is found or additional references begin to look familiar.

For historical and library researchers, this phase of the investigation represents the major work of the project. They often must search at great length to discover primary sources, to identify authorship, and to verify the authenticity of documents. They must be concerned with the accuracy and thoroughness of documents, unraveling the possible biases, hindsights, and selective perceptions of those who have recorded the information.

For all researchers, however, the review of the literature involves thorough and critical searching and reading. All possible information that relates to the research problem must be examined. The researcher must locate, read, analyze, evaluate, organize, and report all the relevant sources to provide a solid justification for his or her research. The literature review provides a purpose for one's research questions or hypotheses and demonstrates the relationship between past work and the present investigation.

Several cautions are presented at this point to forewarn you of some common pitfalls in reviewing literature.

1. *Beware a skimpy literature review.* Some researchers, in their eagerness to get to the investigation, provide a skimpy literature review. They find that reading existing information seems boring when compared to the thought of collecting original information, making personal observations, or drawing

independent conclusions. But for most research, a thorough and careful review of the literature is the only way to insure a solid justification for the research project.

2. *Beware of getting bogged down in the literature.* Frequently in a search for relevant information, we discover the most fascinating tangential or irrelevant information. We are lured into reading other material that very well may make us more knowledgeable in our discipline, but does little to advance the progress of our present research. When you discover interesting but irrelevant sources, make note of them and return to read them at a more appropriate time. We do not aim to discourage perusal of the literature, but we do suggest making judgments that correspond to your timetable for a particular project. Frequently the fascination with reading an entire journal issue when only one article in it is relevant to the research project represents a desire to postpone or escape the work at hand.

3. *Beware of spending too much time in an effort to exhaust the review of all related literature.* An obsession with finding, reading, rereading, copying, or reporting every detail of relevant information may also upset your timetable. Furthermore, such a search is impossible and unnecessary. A review of literature need not include every detail of every source. Such a practice is unnecessarily time-consuming, leads to an accumulation of useless paper, and may be the path to plagiarism for many an unsuspecting student. Summarize information in your own words, make critical or evaluative comments, take down the full bibliographic citation, and copy only that which will serve to illustrate writing style or will be used as direct quotations. Lengthy details of previous studies need not be included in the written literature review of one's research report. Page upon page of reviewed literature does little to increase readers' understanding of the relationship between the past and present investigations. Instead, concise statements that summarize existing knowledge and reference to summary articles create a smooth-flowing, easily comprehended literature review.

DESIGNING THE RESEARCH INVESTIGATION

Designing a research investigation involves planning the method for collecting information to answer the research question or test the research hypothesis. Investigators determine which method of data collection best suits the research problem and then detail the procedures for collecting that information. A thorough delineation of the research problem should suggest an appropriate method of data collection. A researcher investigating the campaign persuasion of a local politician might choose face-to-face interviews, personal correspondence, or direct observation as the most appropriate data-collection methods. The researcher would then plan the schedule of interviews and devise relevant interview questions. He or she might have to locate or train observers and schedule the events to be observed. An investigator studying the nature of speech education programs at United States colleges and universities might rely on mail surveys as the method of collecting information. If so, the researcher must decide what questions the survey will ask, what format the survey will take, who the survey will be mailed to, and how the respondents' answers will be tabulated and analyzed. A scholar researching the effect of propaganda appeals on listeners' attitude change might choose an experimental method of research. This could entail planning a stimulus message that included various propaganda appeals, testing that message for validity and reliability, selecting a group of listeners, planning the procedures for administering the message to the subjects, and devising measures of attitude change.

Whatever the research problem, careful consideration must be given to the methods of data collection and procedures for carrying them out. The specifics of designing the research investigation will become clearer as you gain a better understanding of the various research methods detailed in subsequent chapters of this book. At this point, let it suffice to say that careful and thorough planning of the research design will help insure a well-executed study that generates the most appropriate information for answering the research questions.

COLLECTING INFORMATION

If the researcher plans all the details of the research design, then he or she should encounter few major problems at the data-collection stage. In the initial evaluation of the research problem, the investigator determines whether necessary information sources are available and whether he or she is capable of acquiring the appropriate information.

We are all experienced in acquiring information, but the researcher's task of collecting information differs from that of the ordinary layperson. Researchers collect information in a deliberate, planned, and controlled fashion that differs from one's casual perceptions of everyday life. Researchers must attempt to suppress biases in their collection of information. Little justice is done to a research problem when evidence is selected to prove a hypothesis or neglected when it points to a different conclusion. As researchers, we must question our motives and try to overcome our biases when collecting information. The historian's healthy skepticism of information is a trait that all researchers should cultivate. Doubt, examination, and critical testing of information helps eliminate prejudices and naiveté. It is crucial to remember that any research is only as good as the information collected. We can subject the information to sophisticated statistical manipulations, or we can report it in eloquent terms, but that does not improve the basic information. The information-collection stage is a most important aspect of the research process, deserving careful planning and an honest, unbiased accumulation.

ANALYZING, INTERPRETING, AND DRAWING CONCLUSIONS

We must organize our raw data, the information we accumulated in the data-collection phase, into a form that can be analyzed. This may mean studying, coding, transferring, or tabulating the information. The historical researcher in possession of reams of primary-source accounts of phenomena must organize it in some coherent manner before he or she can make much sense of it. The experimenter with hundreds of completed measurements in hand can do little to decipher the information until it is organized and tabulated. Other researchers may have to transcribe tape-recorded discourse, code and summarize respondents' written replies, or sort information into chronological time periods. Only when the information is organized can the process of analysis begin.

Analyzing information, for most researchers, means long hours of studying the information, "eyeballing the data," categorizing it, and determining patterns. It may mean analyzing documents, determining authorship and dates, and detecting forgeries, plagiarism, or erroneous identification of sources. For researchers employing statistical analyses, this stage may involve calculating mathematical formulas, writing computer programs, studying computer printouts, or constructing data tables.

Analyzing the information extracts the "meat" from the material and allows the research findings to emerge. Then, the findings must be explained or interpreted. Interpreting research results requires hard conceptual and theoretical thinking. The researcher studies the findings in light of projected outcomes, previous findings on the subject, and existing theoretical explanations. If the results are consistent with hypothesized predictions, then these results must be integrated with previous knowledge. They must be shown to be consistent with expectations and explained according to existing theory. If no errors have occurred during the investigation, then the researcher's findings generate a bit of new knowledge and provide additional evidence in support of existing theory.

If the research hypothesis is unconfirmed—that is, if results differ from the earlier prediction of outcomes—then the researcher must explain the inconsistency. The researcher evaluates his or her study, asking why the unexpected findings occurred. Perhaps he or she made mistakes somewhere in the research process which led to distorted, unreliable, invalid information. Maybe forged documents were accepted as authentic, unreliable sources were believed, or untrained observers or interviewers were used. When unexpected results surface, researchers must critically examine and evaluate their projects. They must retrace every step in the research process with an eye toward possible errors. If the study was soundly planned and executed, then perhaps this unexpected finding cannot be discredited. Instead, it may represent a significant, new finding that sheds doubt on the work of predecessors. If so, other scholars in the research community most likely will direct their attention to this anomaly as it becomes the focus of further investigation.

Whatever the outcome, research results must be interpreted or explained. It is not sufficient to merely state results. They must be related to previous research. This may mean tying the findings into the previous review of the literature or returning to the library for further literature review. No research finding stands on its own. Rather, the interpretation phase explains, refutes, discusses, or accounts for the present research finding.

Finally, we offer two cautions to the researcher regarding possible pitfalls in the interpretation stage of an investigation:

1. *Beware of overinterpreting your findings.* It is wise to be conservative in interpreting findings. You should be able to support or provide evidence for any statements you make. Let the principle of parsimony guide your interpretations. Oftentimes, the simplest interpretation or explanation is best. This is not to say that you should suppress any complex explanations of discovered phenonema. Rather, we stress the importance of making sure you can justify your interpretations. Tempting as it is to stretch our findings, honesty, a lack of bias, and unselfish motives should prevail when we interpret our research results.

2. *Beware of leaving findings uninterpreted.* Many beginning researchers think that merely stating, describing, or reiterating research results constitutes interpretation. To interpret is to explain, to create an understanding for the reader, to translate the findings into theoretical terms. Here, the researcher uses his or her own judgment backed by evidence. At this point, the researcher makes original statements, uses personal expertise, and offers insights. It is your responsibility as a researcher to explain the information for your readers.

As a final stage in the research process, the investigator must summarize and draw conclusions. The conclusions should stem directly from the information and must not generalize beyond the data. By offering generalizations, we project that what we have found will be found again and always under the same conditions. As in interpreting, the researcher must be cautious in drawing conclusions that cannot be supported by the data. Our ego-involvement in the research must not tempt us to color our interpretations or overextend our conclusions. In the conclusion phase of a research project, we may offer implications that we see as stemming from our research and suggest to future scholars research ideas that grow out of our work. We provide suggestions that will advance research on this topic, allowing the research community to share, build, and cooperatively seek the advance of knowledge.

REPORTING OR WRITING

Since an entire chapter in this volume is devoted to the writing of research reports, the writing phase is discussed only briefly here and only as it relates to the overall research process. This process is not complete until the research report is written. Whether it be for a class project, a master's or doctoral degree, a convention presentation, or a journal publication, the researcher must write a report to be shared with some audience of interested scholars. The writing style and sections to be included differ according to target audience. Before writing, the researcher should consider the target audience, medium, writing style, and organization of content. Consulting the format of similar research reports will provide examples of writing style, organizational scheme, and bibliography or footnote format. Department, graduate school, or journal editors' guidelines usually provide writing suggestions for the researcher.

For some researchers, writing each section as the investigation proceeds makes the task of writing a polished final draft easy and enjoyable. For the researcher who has planned and outlined the entire investigation in advance, the writing phase represents an enjoyable culmination of the research project.

SUMMARY

Planning is the key to quality research. The researcher who initially outlines in detail the vital parts of a research project is likely to conduct a smooth-flowing research investigation, unhampered by unexpected problems. Topics for research come from immersing oneself in a discipline, becoming knowledgeable in a subject area, reading extensively, developing a critical attitude, engaging in conversation with colleagues concerning research ideas, and examining practical issues in the working environment. The researcher should evaluate research problems to determine feasibility of investigating the issue. Questions of novelty, significance, interest, personal qualifications, availability of data, equipment, and working conditions, sponsorship, cooperation, costs and returns, consequences, and time should be considered in the choice of a research problem.

After selecting a problem to research, the investigator must define, delineate, or further specify the problem in an attempt to formulate it into a researchable one. Research problems should be worded as questions and, where possible, stated as hypotheses with directional predictions of outcomes. The research hypothesis states a relationship between variables, is testable, and provides a tentative outcome of the investigation.

An important early step in the research process involves reviewing relevant literature. By familiarizing themselves with existing theory and the results of previous investigations, researchers can provide direction, purpose, and justification for their projects. Researchers should avoid too skimpy a review of the literature, should avoid becoming distracted by tangential or irrelevant literature, and should not attempt to completely exhaust or report all related information.

The research design specifies the method and procedures for collecting data. A carefully planned design will assist the researcher in generating the appropriate information for answering research questions or testing research hypotheses. The information-collection stage represents the deliberate, planned, and controlled acquisition of information. Here, the researcher must possess a critical, unbiased attitude to insure sound and valid information. The raw data must be organized and analyzed in order to extract the research results. The researcher must then interpret the findings in the light of existing knowledge and theory. The results must be explained, completed research procedures must be evaluated, and original insights must be offered and supported. Conclusions should include summary statements, generalizations that are supported by the data, and implications or suggestions for further research. Finally, the researcher writes the research report according to a specified writing style and organizational format.

All researchers, regardless of subject area or research method, proceed through the stages of choosing a research area, formulating a research problem, selecting research questions or hypotheses, reviewing relevant literature, designing the research investigation, collecting, analyzing, and interpreting information, drawing conclusions, and writing the research report. Thorough advanced planning and careful thought at each stage of the process can make research an enjoyable, exciting, and rewarding endeavor.

PART TWO

METHODS

3

Documentary
or Library Research

The hardest part of any job is getting started. We sit, look at a blank page, and wonder how will we ever do it. But we must begin if we are to accomplish anything. Doing research is no exception. In the last chapter, we presented an overview of research procedures; now we examine specific research tools and sources.

In this chapter we will discuss the methods of doing documentary or library research. We will clarify and specify procedures so that little time will be wasted. When time is used efficiently *and* profitably, research is more fun. Time is precious, especially in graduate school when all the conflicting demands on your time seem to converge. It will be our goal, throughout this chapter, to help you utilize your research time to the best advantage. We will make suggestions for streamlining procedures; we will offer precautions which, if taken, will prevent repetitious and unnecessary duplication of effort. *We* are interested in saving time too.

We intend to focus on several specific areas. After a definition of documentary or library research, we will clarify the definition by describing several different types of effort. We will be even more specific as we present procedures most commonly used in library research. Toward the end of the chapter we will make suggestions for the library researcher and briefly outline and explain some of the pitfalls and problems. Finally, we will discuss some of the values and limitations of the whole process.

One more overall comment is necessary before we begin. Think of the process of documentary and library research as detective work—not the kind of detective work we often see on television, where a complicated case can be solved in a half-hour or hour, but real-life detective work. It takes hours, days, weeks, and sometimes years to solve a case. It requires much effort—prolonged effort. To lay the foundation for the final resolution of the case, many different lines of investigation must be pursued. Facts must be piled on facts. Each must be scrutinized and related to other facts. An intricate and complex web of relationships is established, each with its own body of knowledge, each with its own base in evidence, each with its own peculiarities and uniquenesses. The detective plods along slowly, always aware of what is behind and on either side and cautious, too, of what lies in front. This is the methodology of the true researcher. Cases are seldom spectacular and they cannot be quickly resolved. The qualities of the successful detective and the successful researcher are almost identical: care and accuracy. Neither wants to come up with the wrong facts, the wrong inferences, or the wrong solution. If the researcher is careful, he or she is likely to be accurate. As your specialized quest for knowledge begins, decide to be a first-rate detective.

DEFINITION

Beginning graduate students may find themselves floundering in large and apparently confusing libraries, unable to isolate material that will help them quickly and efficiently. We emphasize those words, *quickly* and *efficiently.* We hear graduate students make comments like, "I could have gotten so much more out of graduate school if I just knew then what I know now." If they had learned procedures for efficient use of time, they could have accomplished so much more. And yet the resources—the opportunities to learn—are so much more available today than before. We know, however, that unless students actually apply the procedures to investigate a problem, they are unlikely to acquire the necessary skills. A tour of a library facility is not the same as using its resources. This chapter provides a tour. To get the most from documentary and library research, students must use the procedures. Also, students whose professors use the library will learn to use it themselves.[1]

The researcher should realize at the outset that library methods and techniques in the United States are the most advanced in the world. Concepts such as the free circulation of books, open shelves, bibliographical tools, and reference and research services originated in America.[2] Thus, we have at our disposal one of the most advanced systems in the world.

Not long ago libraries were thought of as dark, dingy mausoleums of culture. Filled with antiquated, backbreaking furniture and gloomy, silent tiers of bookshelves, they were remote from the lives and interests of anyone but those with nothing better to do. They served scholars who poured over dusty, dog-eared, out-of-date books in pursuit of ideas of little relevance or significance. Libraries have undergone a revolution. With their modern architecture, good lighting, efficient ventilation, comfortable and attractive furniture, and pleasing color schemes, they invite inquiry. On many campuses they are bright, cheerful, informal, and lively meeting places. In towns and cities they have become community centers. To the benefit of all, they portray an atmosphere of service and an eagerness to please.[3]

To define our goal specifically, we intend to answer one essential question: How can the researcher make the best use of the resources and services that libraries have to offer? We understand research to be exact, patient, and prolonged study. We are using the term loosely to mean investigating a subject—not necessarily the process of searching for individual items of information. It will often be the researcher's intent to find out all there is to know about a subject. There is a distinction between research designed to cross the frontiers of knowledge through the development of new inventions and discoveries and research that aims at drawing fresh conclusions from facts already known. Both, however, require knowledge of what facts are already known. It is how to tap that reservoir of knowledge that concerns us in this chapter.[4]

We will be using the terms *documentary research* and *library research* to mean the same thing. We are discussing careful collection of records relating to the investigator's topic, the thorough analysis of those records, and a synthesis of the conclusions derived from them. Thus, location, evaluation, and interpretation are the important processes in this type of research. We will be dealing, primarily, with "location" in this chapter, leaving evaluation and interpretation for our next chapter, entitled "Historical-Critical Research." The location of documents is often the most time-consuming part of the task.[5]

TYPES OF LIBRARY RESEARCH

When the researcher begins the task of investigation, the overall purpose should be clear. Notice that the paragraphs above make a distinction between two goals: One is to discover new knowledge; the other is to draw new conclusions from established knowledge. These distinctions can delineate certain lines of inquiry. For example, is it the researcher's intent simply to discover how present knowledge is organized? Many survey or "state of the art" papers do just this. What is the state of the art with respect to research done on ethos, conflict, small-group leadership, self-disclosure, ethics, Marxist rhetoric, or some other topic? A similar purpose— with similar methodologies—would be to devise a scheme, or construct, whereby present knowledge can be organized. A construct is simply an image or idea that results from a synthesis; it might be a framework that indicates how the various parts are put together. To build such a construct, the researcher must discover the nature and extent of present knowledge. Even if the researcher simply wished to make recommendations based on present knowledge, he or she would still have to discover what is known.

Would the work of the researcher be different if he or she was interested in designing curricula for presenting knowledge? Basically, no; however, the end product or goal would be different. For the purposes of discussion, we will separate the three different approaches: (1) the researcher who wants to organize existing knowledge, (2) the researcher who wants to make recommendations based on existing knowledge, and (3) the researcher interested in designing curricula for presenting this knowledge.

Organizing Existing Knowledge

Before you even grab for a volume from the shelves you should, through questioning of the reference librarian, prior knowledge, or other recommendation, know
something about the source. Do not waste time consulting sources that, for your
topic and investigation, do not meet the following criteria: (1) relevance to your
topic; (2) up-to-dateness; (3) coverage of subjects of current interest and importance; and (4) reputation for accuracy, reliability, and thoroughness.

The number of reference books *is* overwhelming. There is considerable duplication, overlapping, and repetition among them. Frequently, answers to a research
question can be found in a number of sources. As a rule, however, no two sources
are alike; thus, knowing their special qualities will speed your investigation.

The best way to see how knowledge is organized is to try to get a picture of the
whole. To do this we must strive to find the most general source: not just a bibliography, but a bibliography of bibliographies. Because it is up-to-date and because
of its wide coverage, the best such source is *Bibliographic Index: A Cumulative
Bibliography of Bibliographies.*[6] If you were attempting to do research on world-
famous orations, this source would lead you to indexes where such speeches would
be listed. It would also lead you to annotated bibliographies that have been compiled in a variety of areas. For example, you might start by looking at a topic such
as sex differences in language, speech, and nonverbal communication; or sources
of additional information if you wanted to investigate the use of humor in communication; or the dynamics of communication in organizations. No matter what
the topic, if it relates to speech communication and contains sources of information
that have been written, it is likely to appear in the *Bibliographic Index.* The researcher should look under both "Speech" and "Communication"—as a starting
point—because sources are listed in *both* areas as well as in many other related
areas. It is wise to look for information under as many different descriptors as you
can think of; speech and communication are just two.

The *Bibliographic Index* is also a source for finding ideas on a broad, undefined
scale. That is, if you do not know where to begin, what interests you, or what
topics might even be relevant, the *Index* might serve as a launching pad to fire
your imagination. One of the bibliographies to which the *Index* refers, is Ronald
and Irene Matlon's *Index to Journals In Communication Studies Through 1974.*[7]
This bibliography indexes articles that appear in thirteen journals that relate to
speech-communication studies. They are indexed according to the chronology of
when they appeared in each journal, according to the subject, and according to the
author of the article. This is the key bibliography in the field of speech communication and should become part of the library of anyone who plans to go into the field
or pursue serious research in the field. Also, the student of speech-communication
should use *Communication Abstracts.*[8] This is a "comprehensive source of information about communication-related publications worldwide." It abstracts "major
communication-related articles, reports, and books from a variety of publishers,
research institutions, and information sources." It is one source to consult to find
recent literature in almost all areas of speech communication: communication

theory, intrapersonal and interpersonal communication, small-group communication, organizational communication, broadcasting, radio, and television, as well as advertising, marketing, public relations, and journalism. Material is catalogued by subject at the beginning of each quarterly volume and by author at the end of each volume.

Like the *Bibliographic Index* these sources are a useful beginning point for finding ideas if one has no idea where to begin. But they also provide a way to get an overview of a particular subject-matter area. If one goes to a subject listing, one can often see:

1. How much has been written on a subject
2. How recent—or how old—the material is
3. Who has done much of the writing in the area
4. What specialized topics, or subtopics, have attracted the most attention
5. What topics have not been written on
6. What other topics relate to this one

The researcher should remember that *all* indices are "dated" immediately upon publication; that is, before they are even published, they are out-of-date. To make certain that one has full knowledge of what has been written since the publication of a bibliography or index, one must go to the journals themselves. Most journals contain an index to subjects and authors at the end of the final issue for a year. For an incompleted year, one must scan the contents pages of each issue. In most quarterly academic journals, this would only involve looking at three issues.

Bibliographies provide a way of systematizing and classifying knowledge. To go to them first in an investigation provides an overview. But because communication is an interdisciplinary process, researchers should not limit themselves to speech-communication bibliographies.

The *Current Index to Journals in Education* (CIJE)[9] covers more than seven hundred publications that represent the core of periodical literature in the field of education. It is compatible with the ERIC information retrieval system that will be referred to shortly. The main entry section of the CIJE includes the actual title and author of a selection with an annotation and the availability of a piece to the researcher. Other sections include a subject index, author index, and journal-contents index, which lists the contents of the various journals and the number of each article so that a researcher can get a copy of it.

Because it is closely related, we also recommend *Resources in Education* (RIE), the source that indexes and abstracts ERIC documents. ERIC is an acronym for Educational Resources Information Center.[10] Established by the U.S. Office of Education in 1964, it provides bibliographic control over a wide variety of educational documents. ERIC consists of sixteen clearinghouses, each affiliated with universities or professional associations across the country, that collect and process documents and journal articles in their particular area of education. The Speech Communication Association supports one of these. Most of the material in RIE is uncopyrighted and unpublished. It includes such items as innovative curriculum designs, conference proceedings, research reports, bibliographies, directories, speeches, and other types of information useful to educators. These documents are available on microfiche—single plastic sheets that include miniature photocopies of each page of the manuscript from left to right. They must be read in a microfiche reader.

Because using RIE tends to be a bit more complex than using other indexes, we will briefly explain the procedure. The following five-step methodology is, perhaps, the clearest statement on how to do it, but it will be confusing unless one goes to the source itself and tries it out.

1. Use the *Thesaurus of ERIC Descriptors* to find appropriate indexing terms.
2. Look in the subject index of the monthly RIE or in the cumulative RIE index under the appropriate descriptors. Author or institution indexes can be used if searching for a specific person or an institution.
3. Note the titles that seem relevant to the topic and the ED number located beneath and to the right of the title.
4. After listing all the ED numbers, turn to the documents' resumes section, where the documents are arranged numerically by ED number.
5. After reading the abstract, the microfiche can be obtained to read the entire document. Microfiche are arranged numerically by ED number.[11]

We also recommend the *Education Index*[12] as a guide to educational material. It is a cumulative author-subject index that will lead the user primarily to periodicals but also to proceedings, yearbooks, bulletins, monographs, and material printed by the United States Government. The committee responsible indexes more than two hundred periodicals in this source.

Four other sources will help make the organization of existing knowledge easier. The first source is *Dissertation Abstracts,* published by University Microfilms, Ann Arbor, Michigan. This source lists the author, title, and a brief abstract of doctoral dissertations written at a number of cooperating universities. They are listed alphabetically by subject and university. To find an abstract by author or subject, the researcher must go to the *Index to American Doctoral Dissertations,* published separately.

The second is *Psychological Abstracts* (PA)[13] which provides the reader with "Nonevaluative summaries of the world's literature in psychology and related disciplines." According to information found in each monthly volume, PA gets its material from over 950 journals, technical reports, monographs, and other scientific documents. Of the sixteen major classification categories used, "Communication Systems" is one, and "Language and Speech" is a subcategory. But one should not limit examination to these categories alone. Material on auditory and speech perception appears under the heading "Experimental Psychology (Human)," as does material on "Attention." Material on marriage and the family, as well as sex roles, appears under the heading, "Social Processes and Social Issues." Material on group and interpersonal processes appears under "Experimental Social Psychology."

Anything on encounter groups, sensitivity training, or speech therapy falls under "Treatment and Prevention." Organizational behavior can be found in the section labeled "Applied Psychology." Each issue contains an author index and a brief subject index.

Of equal importance is *Sociological Abstracts*.[14] Just as in the previous index, monthly subject and author indexes as well as cumulative indexes are available. The number of sections and areas covered varies with the information for that month. One should, however, use the table of contents in the same manner as for *Psychological Abstracts*. Anything on small groups and small-group interaction, personality and culture, or leadership comes under "Social Psychology." Inter-action between large groups such as races, however, can be found in the "Group Interactions" category. Communication, social movements, collective behavior, public opinion, and mass culture can be found under "Mass Phenomena." The better one can define and refine one's area of research, the more specific one can be in using these abstracts. The point, again, however, is to cover all the bases. Each of these sources is simply an aid to getting all the information available—the quest of the good detective.

The final source includes those guides to periodicals, newspapers, and popular journals. There are three major sources. The first is the *New York Times Index*,[15] which has provided the "master-key to the News since 1851." This serves as a guide to the complete *New York Times* on microfilm.

The second guide is *The Times Index*,[16] which is compiled from the final edi-tions of *The Times, The Sunday Times, The Times Literary Supplement, The Times Educational Supplement, The Times Educational Supplement Scotland,* and *The Times Higher Education Supplement*. This is a British source originating in London.

The third source is the *Reader's Guide to Periodical Literature*.[17] This is a cumulative author-subject index to periodicals of general interest published in the United States. Most graduate students who have done any research previous to graduate school will be familiar with it. It is, perhaps, the source most often used when students are assigned speeches on subjects of social or political importance.

By examining the above sources and any others that might relate to a specific area or discipline, one can usually find out whether or not anyone else has dealt with the subject in print. For a list of books in print, the student is referred to *Books in Print*.[18] This source will help to fill gaps that card catalogs inevitably reveal. *Books in Print,* published since 1948, is an index to the *Publishers' Trade List Annual* (PTLA), compiled annually since 1873. Arranged alphabetically by the publishing firm, the *PTLA* is a collection of the catalogs of the major American publishing firms. Since a one-year edition of *PTLA* may require as many as six or more volumes, an index was required. *Books in Print* provides one-line entries under author or title that state publisher and price. To get further information, one must then go to the *PTLA. Books in Print* is often consulted to secure the exact author, title, or publisher so that the book can be found in a bookstore or ordered. There is also (since 1957) a *Subject Guide to Books in Print*. It should be remembered that books may appear under several different subjects. It should also be noted that *PTLA* does not include books published outside the United States or those published by smaller publishers.

Also published by the same company are *Forthcoming Books* and its companion, *Subject Guide to Forthcoming Books,* published bimonthly. *Publishers Weekly* provides up-to-date information on newly published books. In addition, a number of foreign countries also have their own editions of books in print that are distributed in the United States.[19] Books listed that are not held by the researcher's own library may be ordered through interlibrary loan. The only warning is to allow plenty of time—several weeks or even a month—for this process.

A complete listing of all material published in the United States is contained in the *National Union Catalog,* sometimes referred to as *United States Catalog.*[20] This is a dictionary catalog that lists each book by author, title, and subject. Some are also listed under joint author, editor, and additional subjects. Many of the entries give enough detail so that a book could be ordered. With a fairly complete list of descriptors, even the use of the *United States Catalog* can be enhanced. The researcher is encouraged to begin accumulating a list of descriptors at the outset of the research endeavor.

Making Recommendations Based on Existing Knowledge

If the researcher has pursued the various lines of inquiry suggested above and has taken thorough notes, he or she should have a way of knowing the contours of existing knowledge. These do not often spring out from titles and subjects without the analysis and synthesis of the researcher. But as one works and accumulates information, one begins to see trends, similarities, and relationships. The researcher begins to perceive the answers to such questions as:

1. In what areas has research been most intensive?
2. In what areas has research been weakest?
3. What areas of investigation have been avoided?
   a. replication?
   b. further clarification?
   c. further documentation or support?
   d. further research and development?

Often, initial research efforts are made simply to discover answers to questions like these. One has not really begun the intense leg work and perspiration; one has simply defined perimeters that will help in making recommendations based on existing knowledge.

To know how to answer the above questions, one must have performed a serious, systematic, and complete examination of what exists. To overlook one of the areas for available information might cause one to begin an investigation that has already been done and might result in a waste of time and energy. It could, as well, lead other researchers on similar investigations for which there is no need—the proverbial "wild goose chase."

Designing Curricula for Presenting Existing Knowledge

The graduate student may have an opportunity to either teach a course or design a syllabus for a course he or she would like to teach. To design a current, contemporary curriculum that reflects all the literature (all that has been published in an area), the student must first amass that information. From an overview of what has been done, he or she can begin to see natural breaks or divisions in the material. From such an overview one can also determine the best way to present the material. Some possible approaches would include:

1. *Topical:* using general subject-headings for each unit.
2. *Chronological:* using a time sequence (usually beginning to end) that covers the developments in the evolution of a subject. This is often the approach used when considering an historical subject.
3. *Cause-effect:* using a sequence that would begin with the first stimulation and end with the final results (a problem-solution order would be similar: beginning with the cause of the problem and moving to the solution or solutions recommended)
4. *Inductive or deductive:* using an approach that would either present the specifics and build to the general (inductive) or present the general (perhaps, an hypothesis) and then move to specific examples.

These various curricula-organizational possibilities are presented simply to suggest that the scheme selected should depend on the nature of the existing knowledge. We often pursue knowledge so that we can present it to others. To present it in a logical and understandable manner one must first have a clear picture of the whole. The parts of the whole can best be understood if the umbrella unifying them is clear and distinct. When we think of developing a syllabus or curriculum, we often think of chronology because a syllabus lends itself to the gradual unfolding of knowledge over time—chronology. Our suggestion is to let the organization of knowledge dictate the scheme. The blinders we wear are often determined by what we have experienced or how we think things should be: To remove the blinders, we must let the information we find speak to us.

PROCEDURES IN LIBRARY RESEARCH

In this section, the bulk of this chapter, we will try to get the researcher to ask questions: questions about selecting the problem-question, questions about stating the problem-question, questions about reviewing previous research, and questions about organizing material. Question, challenge, and ask others. We will try to raise the important points, but how you approach those points, and how you use our information, will depend on you and your investigation.

Selecting the Problem-Question

No part of the research process is more important than the selection of the problem-question. A well-selected problem-question is half the battle. It clearly delineates that which is to be included in the investigation, but more important, it spells out, by lack of inclusion, that which is to be excluded. Since, inevitably, more is excluded than included, a well-phrased problem-question tells the researcher what he or she does *not* have to do. To phrase it well, then, narrows the focus and channels the energies toward productive ends.

The problem-question serves as a motivator. A well-phrased problem-question can excite us. It can get us interested in pursuing the investigation and keep us going until the investigation is complete.

The problem-question also serves as a unifier. It is the theme that relates the disparate elements, thus, drawing them together in a meaningful way. As you move through the research process, ask yourself from time to time, "But how does this relate to my problem-question?" If you cannot answer that question, we can assure you that your readers will have difficulty answering it.

Finally, the problem-question provides a goal. It allows us to move efficiently from a starting point to an end point that can be clearly, if not exactly, perceived. We do not go out and do research just to be doing research. As dedicated to research as some people are, *that* is a waste of time. The well-phrased, specific question helps prevent us from moving thoughtlessly in unprofitable directions.

But, you might ask, from where does the problem-question come? How does one "get it"? This is like asking, "What is creativity?" or "How does one acquire ideas?" Actually, however, the answer is not that elusive. We know where we get research ideas. To name just a few sources, we get ideas from:

1. *Personal observation and thought.* As astute, alert, and responsive observers of life, we pick out problems and concerns that, if answered or confronted, might help improve the quality of life on this planet. Being an active sponge for knowledge in our own personal sphere of activity can lead to meaningful and significant research questions.

2. *Reading.* One must consider *all* the reading one does as having one invaluable purpose: to serve as a spark for new ideas.

3. *Courses.* Although reading is often an inherent part of courses, so is discussion and dialogue with the teacher and other students. From such discussions can often come questions, problems, or challenges that might lead to research. Assignments and papers can lead to theses and dissertations or research projects and publications.

4. *Other people.* Rebounding ideas off others, whether casually or formally, can serve as an invaluable resource. As authors we can remember published articles that resulted from informal, unplanned, casual conversation with colleagues.

5. *Brainstorming.* The methods mentioned above tend to be ones where ideas may occur accidentally—just by being alert, reading, being in a course, or talking to friends. Brainstorming is getting together with others (or by oneself) for the expressed purpose of suggesting ideas in a rapid-fire succession, with *no* evaluation.

One person should write the ideas down. We suggest brainstorming with others because of the value of hitchhiking: that is, attaching ideas to those of others or reworking their ideas.

6. *Professional meetings.* The more active you are in attending conferences, meetings, and annual conventions, the more likely you will be exposed to ideas. Published papers often result from participation in round-table discussions and panel-forums that occur at such meetings.

Once you get an idea, you should begin testing it for strength and durability. Often, without testing you do not know just how good the topic is. Because the ideas must withstand thorough investigation, and because you will be intimately involved with it for awhile, it is wise to begin finding the answers to the questions raised in Chapter 2 regarding novelty, importance, interest, training, availability of data, special equipment, sponsorship, costs, hazards, and time. Do not be like the graduate student who could guarantee to the instructor that his topic and approach were *completely* original: He said that he knew they were completely original because he had consulted no other sources and had done no other reading. In today's society, it is unlikely that a graduate student—or any researcher—will come up with a problem area or topic that has received *no* previous attention.

One need not begin the search for answers in the library; however, if other people cannot answer the questions to your satisfaction, then the library is likely to be a good starting point. It might save a trip, however, if you first ask colleagues and teachers. If you begin by asking your peers, your teachers, and other teachers at your institution, you begin to learn whether the topic appears to be significant and interesting. If all these sources tell you the idea is not new, worthwhile, interesting, or feasible, a trip to the library may be avoided until another topic is decided upon. But do not *just* listen to others; *you* have resources available to answer those questions quickly and efficiently for yourself. Use the views of others as guides.

If a library trip can be justified and is taken, the overview we recommended in the section entitled, "Organizing Existing Knowledge" is likely to provide rather definitive answers to these questions. Also, pursue any specific sources that others have recommended. Do not rely on your own knowledge alone! You may have to read some of the key articles or books on the subject to determine whether your topic has strength and, especially, durability. One point in the quest for a *durable* subject is the answer to the question, "Am I likely to maintain interest in this topic?" Again, you will be breathing, sleeping, and eating this idea for some time— can you stand it?

Stating the Problem-Question

We all have good minds, but almost all of us are subject to forgetfulness. As we are reading—amassing facts, opinions, and other evidence—that which we first read becomes dimmer, replaced with new facts, opinion, and other evidence, only to be replaced with . . . This is a fact of life. We *all* forget things. Can you imagine what our minds would be like if we did not?

A key reason for stating the problem-question in writing is to protect it against the frailty of our minds. To write it is *not* to etch it in stone, never to be altered. The whole process of investigation is likely to bring to light new data, new ramifications of the problem, and new insights. Possibly, in light of these discoveries, the problem-question can be refined or narrowed. This polishing can occur only if it has first been clearly stated. You must have a concrete, specific base from which to begin work. That base then becomes more and more exact—more and more reflective of *exactly* what you want to do.

The problem-question is the most important part of the researcher's outline or prospectus. It is not to be left until the end or even pushed aside. The investigation one does can contribute to its precision. It should be phrased in such precise terms and presented so fully that no doubt is left in anyone's mind about the goal of the investigation. It is also helpful to state those areas that will not be studied.

As part of the exact phrasing of the problem-question, the researcher must define concepts or words that will either be unfamiliar to the reader or be used in specific ways. Definitions should not only be simple, concrete, and avoid connotative terms, but they should also be suited to the particular reading audience. For example, you would define a word differently for a professional in that field than you would for a layperson unfamiliar with that field.

The exact nature of the problem-question depends in part on the type of methodology that will be used to pursue the answer. There are differences, for example, between historical problem-questions and experimental problem-questions. These will be clarified in the appropriate chapters that follow. Let us, at present, clarify some of the broad expectations for final phrasing:

1. Problem-questions should be phrased as questions. This does not rule out statements, but questions tend to be more provocative and challenging. Some examples: What rhetorical processes characterize the emergence of leaders in task groups? What characteristics determine upward mobility in an organization? What effect did Indian rhetoric from 1850-1879 have on government policy toward the Indian?
2. They should be full sentences.
3. They should be unambiguous. Clarity is important.
4. They should not be biased. They should not beg the question but should allow the research to prove or disprove the question.
5. They should be simple sentences rather than compound or complex ones. If a compound or complex sentence is needed, it is better to go to a second question or include subparts that help delimit the main question.
6. They should be broad enough to allow for worthwhile and productive scholarship, but narrow enough to confine the research to definite and workable limits.

We tend to err on the side of breadth as we formulate our problem-question because our sights and expectations in the beginning are larger, more encompassing, and more optimistic than our behavior can possible satisfy. Being realistic and considering the natural proclivities of humans, it is better to err on the side of narrowness. We can always expand our sights, perimeters, and research when we have first exhausted the narrow base from which we began.

Some students may not realize that the agreement on a problem-question may be taken as an informal contract between himself or herself and another person: the teacher, an advisor, or a committee. It is especially important, then, that it be as narrow as is reasonable. It would be to the student's advantage, in such a situation, to be able to go back and expand or extend the problem-question if necessary.

For example, a possible problem-question would be how the contemporary labor movement—after the union of the AFL-CIO (American Federation of Labor-Congress of Industrial Organizations)—has influenced worker attitudes through the views manifest in labor-related speeches. Significant? Yes! Interesting? Yes! Too broad? Yes! Can you imagine trying to research this topic? It would be better to examine the rhetoric of George Meany, the primary spokesman for the AFL-CIO after its merger in 1955, to see how that rhetoric affected worker values and attitudes. But how can worker attitudes and values be measured? It might be better still to assume the effect on worker attitudes and values, or disregard it and simply try to understand what values and attitudes are manifest in the rhetoric of George Meany from 1955 to the present. You begin to see how the narrowing process can occur. It could even be limited to an examination of his speeches from 1955 to 1965—depending on the number of speeches and their availability.

Reviewing Previous Research

Having arrived at a narrow, precisely defined problem-question, we are now ready to review the literature. Our goal is to find out what is known about the problem. At the end of this process the library researcher should be familiar with all pertinent previous studies and with all the main sources of data. The review of the literature provides others with evidence that the researcher has this background.

The first place to start is with the bibliographies. These sources do not get listed in the review; they simply lead the library researcher to sources that provide the content.

If, for example, you wanted to investigate the problem of improving student performance in the classroom—a broad topic—you would want to know what others have done. But notice that classroom performance relates to every field; thus, relevant material could be found in every field. The review of literature becomes an impossible task before you have even begun.

How about narrowing the topic to the use of written critiques on student performance as motivational tools? This narrows the search to those courses where student performances occur—primarily, perhaps, speech, English, and education courses—but not necessarily. One would not have to talk to many people to discover that much information on this topic has been published in the speech and education literature. One would want to find books on the topic: Books on education would be an obvious choice, but books on motivation, self-concept, and personality should not be overlooked. Academic journals that might include articles would be *Communication Education, Human Communication Research,* and the other speech-communication journals. The *Journal of Educational Psychology, Journal of Experimental Education,* and *Journal of Personality and Social Psychology* would help, as would *Improving College and University Teaching. Dissertation Abstracts* would undoubtedly yield positive results too. This brief mention of sources indicates the breadth of investigative work that needs to be done. What we have outlined above is a start—a mere beginning. Every article found leads to other articles and each additional source needs to be pursued as if it alone contains the key! The search can seem unending, and because of the ongoing nature of investigation and discovery, it often is. The closure one finds is that happy feeling when one has done all that can be done within the confines of time and effort available.

As you gather sources, maintain a working bibliography. What you want, at all times, is a complete listing of all the sources you have found to date. This, of course, is one reason note cards are highly recommended: They can be arranged alphabetically and new cards can easily be added. When the same book or article is found in several bibliographies, it can be checked against the working bibliography to avoid duplication. Having such an updated, progressing, or developing bibliography always available is a time saver. When a source is referred to over and over, the researcher might want to add an asterisk in the margin by that source to indicate this fact. Frequently mentioned sources may be landmark studies, those involving key issues, those completed by important researchers, or those that provide comprehensive reviews of the literature. They should be noted because you may also want to include them in your own final product.

As a working bibliography becomes extensive, its usefulness may decrease proportionately. When too many sources are listed, the list begins to get unwieldy. At this point, it might be useful to divide it into three categories:

1. Sources most likely to be cited in the footnotes. This would cover all sources most pertinent to the subject.
2. Sources read or examined that relate directly to the subject, contributed background information to the subject, and would prove useful to other researchers investigating the subject. These sources would not be specifically cited in the footnotes.
3. Sources that seemed to be likely sources of information, but on closer examination, proved to be irrelevant or erroneous.

In a bibliography to a paper, all items in the first category would be included. If asked to include in the bibliography all items that have contributed substantially to the paper, the second category would also be included. In research, an annotated list of items in the third category is often helpful. The annotation would indicate their inadequacy and also where they might prove useful.[21]

Note Taking

One other item is important with respect to reviewing previous research, and this suggestion may save time as well as improve your research: As you compile your review of the literature, keep complete bibliographic information. By complete, we mean that which not only satisfies either the *MLA Style Sheet* (from the Modern Language Association) or the *APA* guidelines (from the American Psychological Association)[22] but also includes notes for yourself about location and worth. If an article was found only after a great deal of searching or only in a remote source, make note of that information so that you can find it again. If an article is consulted and read at any point in the investigation, make notes on the article's major findings or essential worth. Too often we go back and reread whole articles that were discovered to be of little value the first time around. We rely on our memories —"Oh, I'll remember that!"—and we should not. Several points on note taking are important:

1. Be certain notes are readable.
2. Check them for accuracy.
3. Avoid excessive abbreviations.
4. Put material quoted in quotation marks.
5. Be consistent in the form used. (Do not switch styles, size of cards, or from cards to paper.)
6. Recheck notes before leaving a source.

Notes well taken and systematically filed are reliable. Too many notes are far better than too few. Above all, do not plan to bring all your books, articles, documents, and records to a single location when you begin the assimilation process. This is an exercise in futility! Shuffling note cards is far more efficient.

Inefficient note taking is one of the biggest causes for wasted time and sheer frustration in the investigative process. We cannot overemphasize the six steps above. The *MLA* or *APA* guidelines should be checked first since one of these two will likely be used in the final writing (and publishing) of the manuscript. To know what they demand with respect to form is essential so that all the necessary information is recorded first and recorded in proper sequence. To do it right the first time saves time later. You might not think, for example, that proper sequencing is important in the early stages. But think how much time you will save if you can copy your footnotes or bibliography directly from your notes, knowing they are correct, without having to make adjustments in form.

The methods used to take notes are important, for it is easiest to organize material if it can conveniently be put into categories or units. Obviously, however, note taking involves more than recording sources. You must capture a summary of the content of the material and, equally important, carefully record the context. If we have no context, or incomplete context, we may interpret the material incorrectly. We may distort or misinterpret it inadvertently. Using something out of context can inadvertently occur when no context has been noted and we depend on our memories to supply it correctly.

Different authors prefer different systems for taking notes. Some use three-by-five, four-by-six, or five-by-eight cards. These can be stored upright for quick reference and can be easily handled. Some writers prefer 8½ by 11 sheets of paper.

Notes should capture the essence. Overly detailed note taking can waste precious time and energy. It is, however, better to have too much information than not enough.

In most libraries permission can be secured to use a portable typewriter. The researcher using a typewriter can take far more notes than someone writing in longhand. When typing, however, because of the speed of note taking, you must be careful to avoid typographical errors and misspellings. In some of the historical libraries, researchers are allowed only pencils or typewriters—no ink pens. Librarians feel this is necessary to protect manuscripts.

Whether writing or typing, the note taker must copy direct quotations exactly, even if the direct quotation contains errors. If the quotation has an error in spelling, punctuation, or syntax, the note taker should insert *sic* in brackets following the error to indicate that the error appears in the original.

It is wise to establish a system for identifying directly quoted material in your notes. Placing quotes before and after the material works fairly well, but one must remember to use single quotation marks for internal quotes to identify instances when the source is quoting someone else. Because quotation marks are inconspicuous and easily overlooked, it is wise to note direct quotations in the margin or devise some other system of marking them.

Also, when you leave out material, use three dots (. . .) to symbolize the omission. This is known as an *ellipsis* and is very common in scholarly writing. Why, for example, cite a big hunk of material in the middle of a paragraph when that which is most relevant and pertinent to your idea is contained in the first and last part? You not only save your reader time, but you also tighten up your argument and make your writing briefer and more cogent. Use of ellipsis requires good judgment, but what aspect of researching and writing does not?

If an ellipsis is used at the end of a sentence in a direct quotation, the quotation should include the original punctuation. If the original ends with a period, the notes would include four periods: the ellipsis plus the period of the original. If it occurs before a semicolon, the semicolon should be added. The main point is that the notes of the researcher should contain an exact record of the original, including the punctuation.

If you want to insert your own comments in your notes, place them in brackets [like this] to avoid later confusion. It is better to avoid parentheses unless they are included in the original source. If a source quotes another source, make certain this is indicated. It is the other source who originated the idea, not the one you are quoting.

Since few researchers know when taking notes exactly how material will be used, it is wise to have copy that is as complete as possible to retain the greatest flexibility. You can decide later how to use material and how to arrange it in the text of the research report. To try to make such decisions when taking notes is limiting and frustrating. Generally, it cannot be done, simply because the researcher has not yet acquired a broad enough perspective. But discrimination and restraint are advised, otherwise the note-taking process alone can expand indefinitely.

One reason for choosing to use 8½-by-11-inch sheets of paper for notetaking is for the convenience of including large amounts of additional material. Material like diary pages, letters, and original transcripts can be photocopied and added to the notes.

Another consideration in note taking is the distance you must travel to find information. If you must visit numerous, small libraries over considerable distance and will not be able to make second trips, you will want to make the best, most complete set of notes possible in a single visit. Because of one oversight or error you may have to write a librarian for the missing information. Getting the exact response may take several weeks.

Photoduplication processes insure completeness and accuracy; they are generally inexpensive and quite widely available. But before photoduplicating material consider its probable value to your research. Why waste money photoduplicating a worthless document when it could be recorded in the bibliography and its worth and strengths and weaknesses noted?

Because of the ease, availability, and lack of expense of photoduplication, we tend to pay now and read later. "I'll just get the material home, and I can judge its relative worth once I have time to read it." If you have plenty of money and do not mind spending it this way, there is nothing wrong with this method. With an article in hand, you can highlight the important parts and go on. This will increase the amount of paper shuffling later on—especially on a project with numerous (hundreds) of sources. Notes are brief, condensed, and much more efficient.

To help eliminate the problem of gathering too many articles, we suggest perusing each before duplicating it. To find out if it is worth the cost of copying, read the opening for both the purpose and the review of literature. Read only as far as your interests and needs require. With background in your field, you can tell whether this one is relevant. Skim the central part and read the final paragraphs or conclusion. Are there findings or conclusions that appear, at first glance, relevant and useful? Only then would it matter how the author came to those conclusions; then you may want the meat of the article.

When a large number of articles are copied, efficient organization becomes important. One useful system is to staple the pages of each article together at the top left corner, write a quick index code—a subject, title, author, or other category—in the upper-left corner over the staple. In this way you can quickly find the piece you need by looking in the upper-left corners alone. Labeling in the upper right-hand corners does not work as well because the pages are not secured together in that corner, thus, it may take a great deal of thumbing to reach the labeled pages.

A method suggested by one writer for keeping track of items of no value is to maintain a reject file. This researcher uses three-by-five-inch cards. He copies the full bibliographic citation at the top of each and briefly notes why the source is weak or cannot be used. The cards are filed by author's name. This record of sources that have already been examined and found wanting can be a time saver.

Abstracting

A method often taught in graduate school for handling large amounts of material is called abstracting. When you must review great masses of literature and want to preserve the essential ingredients from each article or experiment for future reference, this is a method that works. Our feeling, however, is that it has largely been supplanted by photoduplication and consequent highlighting. Most people would agree that their time is more valuable than the money paid out for photoduplicating. Abstracting takes time.

When abstracting, the researcher briefly responds to each of the major categories of the reading or article. One writer suggests that three essential procedures are involved: (1) to retain the order and sequence of the original ideas; (2) to include all the major divisions in the original structure; and (3) to maintain approximately the same proportion and emphasis as the original.[23] Summarizing the major points of the article lets the researcher know if returning to a source will be useful and productive. The essential abstract categories for most experimental studies would follow an order similar to this:

1. Full bibliographic citation (MLA or APA style)
2. Brief synopsis of problem (define concepts where necessary and relate problem to theoretical framework or previous research, if possible)
3. Hypothesis of article
4. Design of study (controls, subjects, environment, tests used, sampling, methods of gathering data)
5. Results (describe)
6. Conclusion (provide a thumbnail summary)
7. Evaluation (strengths, weaknesses, further research needed or suggested)
8. Other sources (other important sources should be noted)

One graduate student who saw this outline remarked, "Why not just copy the whole article?" It is true that these categories represent the central features of most experimental studies; however, the researcher will quickly find shortcuts for recording the information. The name of a journal like *Quarterly Journal of Speech* becomes *QJS,* the word *subjects* becomes Ss, and other quick notational devices are used. An abstract file can be conveniently maintained on four-by-six or five-by-eight-inch cards. Beyond immediate research needs, they become a useful research file for both teaching and future writing and publishing.

Goals

The documentary or library researcher does not do research or pursue an investigation for its sake alone. The effort is directed toward specific goals. Most involve a class assignment, a thesis, a dissertation, or a paper to be presented at a convention and submitted for publication. If it is to be a presentable or publishable paper,

Chapter 10, "Writing and Publishing," provides practical advice for reaching those goals. If it is to be a thesis or dissertation, we suggest designing a prospectus as a guide for that effort. An outline for a prospectus is also presented in Chapter 10.

Whatever the final goal, it is wise to make certain that the research investigation fulfills some basic categories. No matter the outcome or goal, it is wise to outline your material first. This serves several important purposes: First, it organizes your thinking. Second, it allows you to make certain that the fundamental requirements of the research effort are being satisfied. Third, it gives you a check to make certain you are not missing anything—or have not overlooked any major factors or in- gredients. And finally, it gets you started.

The following outline, as general as it is, can be considered a goal. It is developed in some detail in the chapter on writing and publishing as we examine the develop- ment of the prospectus. Since that is still several chapters away, we provide a general overview here to give direction (and to get you started). The major headings are:

1. Problem Statement (Be precise, clear, and thorough.)
2. Purpose Statement (Give reasons for doing the study—new knowledge, bene- fits, importance, etc.)
3. Review of Literature (What is known about the topic?)
4. Tentative Hypothesis
   What are the probable conclusions?
   What is the likely hypothesis and the likely alternative hypotheses? (Al- ternatives simply prepare the investigator to accept results different from those expected.)
   Describe the nature and scope of the facts you hope to uncover.
5. Methods and Procedures (In detail, describe the exact steps to be taken in gathering data and testing the hypothesis.)[24]

This broad outline for organizing your ideas should be considered a tentative beginning. One must get specific requirements from the instructor, adviser, depart- ment, college, or university, depending on what one is going to do. An outline of some kind is important as one begins to amass the facts. We will add, too, that a specific content outline will be dictated by the methodology one chooses to follow (historical, descriptive, or experimental), and these will be treated in forthcoming chapters.

SUGGESTIONS FOR THE LIBRARY RESEARCHER

Our suggestions for the person with little if any experience in library research fall into two major categories: (1) characteristics of the researcher, and (2) the pitfalls of library research and how to avoid them. These grow out of the comments al- ready made and can be viewed as a summary of what has preceded.

Characteristics of the Library Researcher

These five general characteristics will alert you to what you can expect, so that you can gear up, brace yourself, and be prepared. The library researcher:

1. *Considers the process important and necessary.* What this requires is a proper frame of mind. Some people, frankly, have no use for the past and generally do not make good library researchers.

2. *Enjoys discovery.* The person who actually finds pleasure in searching through books, journals, and reports is likely to be the person who gets more out of it, who benefits from the search. To enjoy discovery, you must enjoy the search, and if you enjoy it you are likely to get more out of it.

3. *Is willing to commit the requisite time.* To do a thorough, accurate, and careful job takes time. We cannot expect immediate results. We may not even be able to expect "fair" compensation for the time and effort expended.

As teachers, we often hear from the student who says, "But I put so much work into this course. Surely I deserve better than a C." The fallacy, of course, is that time expended does not equal the grade given. It is the same in documentary and library research. Time expended does not guarantee results, which is why points one and two are important. If you, first, consider the process necessary and, second, enjoy doing it, you will not consider the time invested a total waste if results are not immediately forthcoming or are not consistent with your expectations.

4. *Is willing to ask questions.* Library research is often a process of probing and searching—the life of a detective. Solutions, answers, and connections between ideas do not all of a sudden pop out at you. They occur as a result of questioning, analysis, and synthesis. If an idea does suddenly pop out, it is probably because you have been toying with it or rolling it around in your mind. We develop this concept further in Chapter 11, "General Suggestions for the Researcher," when we discuss the creative process.

Just because you ask questions does not mean that answers can immediately be found, or even that answers exist. Volumes could be filled with unanswered questions. But, rest assured, good results are most likely to occur because of good questions. You just have to make certain that you are asking enough of them. Err on the side of quantity.

5. *Is accurate and complete.* The frustration, pain, and personal agony that is likely to result from inaccuracy and incompleteness is likely to be so intense that it alone will drive you right out of the library! Enough said.

Avoiding the Pitfalls

Some of the pitfalls are the negative corollaries of the characteristics just mentioned. For example, we would list not considering the process important to be a pitfall, just as we might list moving too quickly or jumping to conclusions, viewing material found as sacred rather than maintaining a questioning or skeptical posture, or failure to be thorough, accurate, and complete. But there are several other important pitfalls.

1. *Not going far enough.* We may stop too early and fail to locate all the available sources of information. One never really knows what "far enough" is until he or she has exhausted all leads.

2. *Not getting enough advice.* When we listen to just one or two other people regarding what sources are important or what lines of pursuit would be most advantageous, we may be misled. We need input—all we can get. We must seek information and opinions widely, and after all is said and done, we must rely on our own best judgment as it reflects, draws together, or denies the information and opinions we get.

3. *Not letting the materials at hand become the end of our search.* We should not allow the limitations of the library in which we worked to dictate the limitation in our background knowledge. We must be willing to take advantage of inter-library-loan programs, to write for books and articles, to travel, and to pursue sources that are not within immediate reach.

4. *Not assuming something does not exist because it did not appear in the sources we investigated.* We should realize that it is, after all, almost impossible for us to find everything. This is especially true when we consider the volume of unpublished works, convention-program papers, and other reports and documents. We can strive to find everything and keep that as a goal. But when we think we have met that goal, we should also be realistic, knowing that the chances of missing something are fairly great. Scholarly restraint is essential. Have we discovered everything? The answer must be, "Based on the material found . . . ," or "Considering available information . . . ," or "With respect to the information noted in this paper . . ."

5. *Not following every lead.* Sometimes we get too sure of ourselves. We arbitrarily decide—before seeing it—that a source is not important or not relevant based on the date, journal, author, title, or some other factor. We become omniscient, and such omniscience can result in overlooked sources and missed information.

VALUES OF LIBRARY RESEARCH

The values of library research should be clear. We must view the library as one arm of the researcher. The other arm is his or her own ingenuity, creativity, and insight—including his or her ability to synthesize and draw together the essential elements of that discovered. We function best with both arms. Not only that, but we use each to help the other. They can work separately at times, but reinforcement and synchronization are obvious in final products. The value of the library lies in what the researcher can and will do with it. What is found there is enhanced, unified, and brought alive by the active, involved, and alert library researcher.

That which is found in the library does not stand by itself. Library information and data are just that: information and data. They have no unique or unusual properties that make them stand out from other information and data. It is the researcher who, using all his or her unique characteristics, breathes that special life or outstanding quality into lifeless information and data. The value in library research is limited by the value that the library researcher can demonstrate. It is he or she that makes what is found esteemed, desirable, or useful. Its worth, merit, or importance is directly dependent on the researcher.

LIMITATIONS OF LIBRARY RESEARCH

Libraries do not contain all the answers. And just because an answer can be found there does not make that answer right. There is nothing sacrosanct about material found in the library or in published form. We should not stand in awe of this information. We must keep an objective, open, and responsive mind—questioning the process, questioning the materials, and questioning the information. Not only should we be open and flexible enough to let our materials speak to us, to let their essential worth and significance sink in, and to compare their information with what we find in other materials, but we must continue the process of interrogation. We must strive not to allow our approach to be clouded by our own biases or by the biases of what we discover. Despite the wealth of materials we discover, we must continue to ask, "But what if . . . ?" or "What about . . . ?" or "What else?" And when we have asked that final question, we need to ask it again, "But, what else?"

Documentary and library research can be mind-boggling. How small we sometimes feel when we look at the mass of literature and the mass of available knowledge and when we think of how many others have come before us. How small our contribution can seem when we consider the contributions of so many others. A humbling experience, to say the least. But we should not let this perspective limit our objectives and goals. We should not let it limit our abilities and potentials, our insights and creativity. It is precisely such individual efforts, often miniscule, often seemingly insignificant, that add up to knowledge breakthroughs. Individual efforts, over and over again, provide us the knowledge base by which we advance.

Although there are limitations in documentary and library research, some limitations are self-imposed and unnecessary. We are often limited by our own perspective, and that perspective can be changed. We can make a contribution, and that contribution can be significant. We must keep our sights realistic, however. In the advance of knowledge, no contribution is insignificant. But we are entering an area where giant leaps are rare, startling discoveries are the exception. We must strive to be content with making *a* contribution, not *the* contribution.

SUMMARY

We have discussed the most important part of the investigative process: documentary or library research. These skills are not only basic to everything else in this book, they are also essential. That person who develops and polishes these skills will find the research process enjoyable and rewarding. In this chapter we have focused on locating materials rather than evaluating or interpretating them. We attempted to make the process practical and specific—to remove any mystery or doubt about it.

When the researcher has no topic or is first investigating a topic, he or she should try to secure a vantage point: a way of looking at the whole before the parts are analyzed in detail or even separated. Bibliographies, as perhaps the most general of the reference sources, offer a way of examining the contours of existing knowledge.

Once a topic is selected and some initial bibliographic groundwork is laid, the researcher should begin selecting the phrasing the problem-question. The problem-question serves as a delineator, motivator, unifier, and goal, and the library researcher should not view this selection and phrasing phase of the process as trivial or unessential. Once a problem-question is determined, it must be tested for its strength and durability. Several test questions were suggested along with criteria that can be used to phrase it in the most concise, unambiguous, unbiased, and narrow manner possible.

The next phases of the library-researcher's procedure should be intensively reviewing the literature, organizing the material, and taking careful notes. We stressed the importance of a working bibliography. We also noted that any organizational scheme should be based upon the ease and comfort of its use. However one chooses to organize material, the end product, or goal, of the whole process should be kept in mind. Details for any scheme will be supplied by the researcher, instructor, adviser, department, college, or university. We provided basic essentials.

Our final suggestions for the library researcher fell into the categories of characteristics and pitfalls. Although we want to be encouraging and positive, we must also be realistic. We have sought to provide information that will present the research context as we see it but that will save time and energy as well. To be well informed is not only to be prepared, but to be understanding and accepting of the demands and expectations.

Researchers must be active users of library resources. The pleasure derived from library investigations results from knowledge of what materials are there and where they can be found. Not knowing is both frustrating and time-consuming. With experience we can get the information we want, when we want it. We feel successful. We feel like detectives who have just heard the final court decision in their favor. Documentary and library research is a skill, and like any skill, it can be learned.

Historical-Critical Research

Why study history? It seems so out of place in our fast-moving scientific world. Isn't the future far more important than our past? There are several important reasons for studying history. For one, it is a major literary form. We are all historians since we are all interested in what occurred in the past, but much of what passes as "history" today—in the form of the historical novel, documentary, film, or movie—is designed to entertain. It could not meet the demands of scholarship that historical research requires. Second, we study history as a vicarious experience. When we think, we use recollections of the past as the meat or thought. We incorporate our personal experience with that of others, now and in the past, to better understand the present and, thus, prepare ourselves to face the problems of the future. It is true that no two events are the same, but because patterns recur we can act with the confidence that comes when we are dealing with the familiar. To be known as a practical person, one must be able to select the path of safety and progress. Such choices require cognizance of the past. With the past as a base, we can help shape the future.

A final reason for studying the past is as professional training. Few if any subjects are taught devoid of any historical base. Thus, professional training need not mean training to teach history alone, as a pure subject. Many fields and professions realize that historical study is indispensable to their own proficiency. Thus, a familiarity with historical methodology broadens our professional base.[1] And as we acquire this professional training, we are also likely to acquire the values that result from a study of the past: perspective, understanding, tolerance, and appreciation.

Too often we think of historical research as that which is intended to discover and describe past events. That is a narrow view. A more contemporary view is that historical research provides a perspective for the interpretation of the present, understanding present facts, customs, traditions, trends, and movements. Characteristics of present society can be traced to the past. We can ask, for example, in what ways the conditions that drove Reverend James Jones and his followers to Jonesville, Guyana, were similar to those that caused the Puritans to leave England in their fervor for experiential religion and devout living in 1629. In addition, we can examine other cults and movements and, using these same characteristics or predictors, forecast the possible occurrence of other splintering or fractionalization from mainstream society. History, then, would be used in formulating predictions for the future.[2]

In this chapter, we will begin with a definition of historical-critical research. We will briefly examine several types of historical-critical research, then discuss the important procedures in pursuing this kind of research. Within this development of procedures we will briefly distinguish the critical methodology. We will also try to answer the question, "What distinguishes historical-critical research from the other methodologies we will be discussing in other chapters?" Summarizing much of what we said in the chapter, we discuss the pitfalls of historical-critical research. We then end the chapter with a brief consideration of the limitations of this type of research.

DEFINITION

The historical-critical method is not an academic subject; it is a way of thinking. It is one of the three basic methods that educators use to solve problems—the historical, descriptive, and experimental. The historical-critical method enlarges our world experience. It provides a deeper appreciation of and more thorough insight into the essential nature and uniqueness of people. It makes us aware of what it means to be human. Historical research can give us better understanding of ourselves and of how the contemporary scene (no matter the topic area) was set. Because history includes all that has ever been thought, felt, or said by human beings, a synthesis of the knowledge of the past may help us make decisions about current problems with greater intelligence and greater economy of effort. True, it may not provide exact predictive powers, but it can tell us what has been tried before and what actions have been successful or unsuccessful; it can even give criteria to better appraise alternative courses of action.[3]

Using the past to aid in interpreting the future is nothing new. It was indeed, the very goal of Thucydides, a writer of historical accounts in the fifth century B.C. He based his writings on his own observations and on the reports of eyewitnesses that he subjected to "rigorous" tests of reliability. Certainly the "rigor" Thucydides used was different from that of current scholarship, but he had exacting methods and lofty aims as he engaged in a critical search for truth—the goal of modern historical research. Indeed, the Greek word from which we derive "history" meant an inquiry, *any inquiry*, intended to elicit truth.

Historical-critical research involves reconstruction of the past in a systematic and objective manner by collecting evidence, evaluating it, verifying it, and synthesizing it to establish facts and to reach defensible conclusions. This is usually done in relation to particular hypotheses.[4] To engage in this methodology is to follow a systematic body of rules and procedures for collecting all possible evidence of an era or event, evaluating it, and ordering the proven facts to indicate causal connection, verifying it and, finally, presenting this ordered knowledge of events in a way that will stand the test of critical examination.[5]

Why use the historical-critical method? It can serve many functions. In the following list, we have tried to be as broad as possible to provide the general perimeters of possible investigations. The historical-critical method might be used to:

1. Ascertain the meaning and reliability of past facts. A researcher might want to know how an audience interpreted a particular message, or if the local media misinterpreted the audience's impressions.

2. Appraise past facts. A researcher might want to evaluate the effect of a lobby on legislators or on how they voted over a period of time on a particular issue about which the lobby had concern.

3. Study trends and the mechanics by which they have occurred. A researcher might investigate a movement or genre as well as the speakers, messages, and situations that gave rise to, sustained, or caused their downfall.

4. Make comparisons of likenesses and differences. A researcher might compare and contrast the positions of political candidates on prominant issues. Such comparison and contrast might occur on rhetorical strategies used to approach various situations or crises as well.

5. Study changes in social structure. A researcher might examine the religious rhetoric of a prominent minister, rabbi, priest, or evangelist to determine its impact on a society's social structure. Another study might examine Mormon religious rhetoric to determine the effect that the ERA (Equal Rights Amendment) or Women's Liberation has had on that religion.

6. Study the transition from one status to another. Researchers might study the change in values reflected in the rhetoric of a politician as he or she moves from state legislator to governor to national legislator and then, perhaps, to president.[6]

7. Provide an indepth examination of a past event and to draw conclusions from it. A researcher might investigate a local demonstration, a state issue, a national cause, or a world-wide phenomena to draw meaningful insights from it. Why did workers picket the local factory? Why did a ballot issue pass or fail? What contributed to a change in patriotism? How have world events changed the nature of UN rhetoric?

8. Better predict the future. Researchers want to know how to control factors to better predict outcomes. What ingredients best serve to move audiences to action? Political speeches that cause people to vote for one candidate over another? Evangelical speeches that bring people forward? Television addresses that keep people from turning the dial?

The demands for objectivity in historical-critical research are high. The demands, however, are hard to meet because of the nature of the data. As a result, historical research (as opposed to descriptive or experimental research) is perhaps the most difficult research to do well. It is important, though, because it gives us insight into some problems that could be gained by no other technique. For example, a careful examination of the speeches, speakers, and audiences in a given campaign may give us broad insights into the nature of human motivation or the factors that cause people to vote. These could be critical factors contributing to the success or failure of future politicians or could offer clues for obtaining voter support. Applied to other campaigns, such a study might provide a general understanding of variables that operate in campaigns. Historical research not only provides a backdrop for experimentation but can also guide and direct it.

Whereas historical-critical research attempts to reconstruct the past to establish facts and reach conclusions with respect to specific hypotheses, descriptive research attempts to describe factually, accurately, and systematically the facts and characteristics of a given population or area of interest. Both contrast sharply with experimental research, where cause-and-effect relationships are investigated by exposing experimental groups to treatment conditions and comparing the results with control groups not given the treatment. Experimental research is generally done in the laboratory.[7] Just as not all experimental research uses control groups, not all experimental research occurs in the laboratory. More on this in Chapter 6.

TYPES OF HISTORICAL-CRITICAL RESEARCH

Every problem, as we have already noted, has its roots in the past. Even studies not primarily historical must consider background. Whether history is the central focus or simply incidental to a study, every speech-communication scholar should know how to study the past. Historical-critical methods do not stop with a description of what has been. They must also suggest interpretation of the past to serve three important purposes: (1) to show why things developed as they did; (2) to show how they compared with other similar developments; and (3) to indicate a judgment of worth—how effective or ineffective, good or bad, or right or wrong.[8]

Many different kinds of problems in speech communication require the historical-critical approach; however, most fall under three categories: biographical studies; movement or idea studies; and rhetorical criticism.

Biographical Studies

There have been numerous studies of orators. A student may examine a prominent politician, religious leader, or teacher. To see what a carefully prepared, well-documented biographical study looks like, we suggest that you examine *A History and Criticism of American Public Address.*[9] Movement leaders are also possible subjects. For example, a leader of the women's movement, the civil-rights movement, or the Jesus-movement could be examined. George Meany, as a labor leader, could be a focus for study, as could a leader of any prominent business or industry.

For other examples, see works such as *Agnew: Profile in Conflict* by Jim G. Lucas, *Eldridge Cleaver: Post-Prison Writings and Speeches,* edited by Robert Scheer, or *The Rhetoric of Black Americans* by James Golden and Richard Reike. Also, almost any issue of the *Quarterly Journal of Speech* includes articles on prominent orators.

Movement or Idea Studies

In movement or idea studies the history of ideas or great religious-political-social-economic movements are examined. Such studies cover a wide variety of topics: factors that give rise to movements; conditions under which leaders emerge and followers are welded together; roles played by authorities; stages through which movements develop; comparative merits of alternative modes of influence for achieving different goals; varied consequences of movement activity; and varied fates of movements.[10] Such a study might examine religious cults or the great awakening. Studies in the past have focused on the great debates, the road to the whitehouse, or the Progressive movement. Women's liberation, civil rights, and the Indians' struggle for freedom are other examples. For some examples of movement or idea studies, see:

> *Antislavery and Disunion,* 1858-1861: *Studies in the Rhetoric of Compromise and Conflict,* edited by **J. Jeffery Auer** (New York: Harper & Row, Publishers, 1963).
>
> **Waldo W. Braden,** editor. *Oratory in the Old South,* 1828-1860 (Baton Rouge: Louisiana State University Press, 1970).
>
> **Wayne Brockriede** and **Robert L. Scott.** *Moments in the Rhetoric of the Cold War* (New York: Random House, 1970).
>
> **DeWitte Holland,** editor. *Preaching in American History* (Nashville, Tenn.: Abingdon Press, 1969).
>
> **Arthur L. Smith.** *The Rhetoric of Black Revolution* (Boston: Allyn & Bacon, 1969).

Rhetorical Criticism

In rhetorical criticism the researcher focuses on any artifact that is subject to analysis. For example, a researcher could focus on the rhetoric of a prominent personality, a cartoon character, a piece of music, or a television program. Utilizing all of one's knowledge of the social milieu that provided the essential backdrop, the researcher attempts to draw conclusions about the effort. Since this is a specialized form of historical analysis, we refer the reader to the sources of information listed under "Critical Methodology" on p. 305.

PROCEDURES IN HISTORICAL-CRITICAL RESEARCH

The steps involved in historical-critical research are essentially the same as those in other research projects: You must find and define a problem-question, which should involve formulating a hypothesis as well. You must then choose the historical or critical approach to be used. Next, the data must be collected and verified. Finally, the data must be interpreted and synthesized and conclusions drawn. There are, however, some important differences in the way these steps are carried out for an historical-critical study.

Before we explain and develop each of these steps from the historical-critical frame of reference, the researcher who plans to use this methodology should ask himself or herself some important questions. This methodology involves some difficulties, but many of these can be overcome if the researcher can be honest in answering the following questions:

1. Do you like reading serious history books? If serious history books bore you, we suggest you try another kind of research.

2. Do you like working in the library? Your world will become the world of books and documents. Back files of periodicals, microfilm, and obscure sources will make up a good deal of your research base. Do you enjoy pursuing the hard-to-find source? The historical-critical researcher must be dedicated to the spirit of critical inquiry—a desire to find the whole truth. Historical-critical research requires an endless search for facts and statements. Knowing in advance that the historical record is incomplete and that all gaps are unlikely to be filled, the researcher attempts the impossible: to complete the record and to fill the gaps. Patience and persistence are essentials.

3. Are you accurate and organized? In collecting bibliographical, biographical, and other substantive information, an unsystematic classification scheme will cause frustration and endless amounts of additional work. The historical-critical researcher is careful. He or she is concerned about the need for numerous evaluations: weighing of standards and material. He or she is willing to allow the data to speak and avoids jumping to conclusions before the data is in. He or she also shows strict regard for scientific method—not scientific method interpreted in its narrow sense by its use in the physical sciences, but scientific method defined in terms of its reliance on critical methods of discovery and scholarship. Care means adhering to the same principles and practices and the same scholarship and accuracy that characterize (or should characterize) all scientific research. Cautiousness is essential. Also, although the data may be imprecise, the various weighings and evaluations indefinite, some of the content discovered inexact, and even some of the interpretations and conclusions incorrect, the researcher must still strive for precision, definiteness, exactness, and correctness.

4. Can you go to your sources? In pursuing serious research, often you must go to your primary sources. Are they available? Can you travel to where they are located? Although microfilm and interlibrary loan can bring some material within reach, manuscripts, letters, diaries, and early periodicals often cannot be secured or used unless you can travel to where they are housed. The historical-critical researcher must be willing to go where the facts lead or where the information lies. Finding the data may mean extensive correspondence, phone calls, or traveling. It may lie in dusty archives, antiquarian societies, or in the back room of a local historical society. Most of this material is seldom handled and cannot be mailed.

Often, its location is dubious. To view the process of locating the information as an adventure puts one in the appropriate frame of mind. The researcher must be ready to face such challenges.

5. Do you like to write? Most historical studies require more writing than studies using other methodologies. Are you prepared to sit at a desk hour after hour, day after day, carefully and painstakingly developing and polishing your manuscript?[11]

6. Are you a questioner—a doubter? The historical-critical researcher must also assume the posture of historical doubt and skepticism. He or she must be a questioner. Assumptions must be accounted for; conjectures must be challenged; guesses must be questioned so that hypotheses can be satisfied. It is an uncomfortable role because one is often unhappy with the status quo; there are too many unknowns, and often the responses to all the inquiries simply result in more unaccounted-for stirrings—stirrings that multiply geometrically rather than arithmatically. Diligence and industriousness are necessary.

Our intent is not to scare you, rather to prepare you. The above are some of the realities of historical-critical research. To choose this methodology is to choose to fulfill the above prerequisites.

Finding a Problem-Question

Historical-critical research begins when you question some idea, event, development, or experience of the past. "I wonder how people came to believe . . ." "Why did the audience respond that way?" "How could that have occurred?" "I don't understand the full meaning of what happened." Sometimes the historical-critical researcher will discover new source materials that, when interpreted, will shed new light on or provide new answers about past events. It is like the information scientists received back from the Venus probes: Some scientists were known to respond that on the basis of that new knowledge alone, they would have to go back and revise or redesign their theories about how our universe was conceived; new knowledge was applied to already established ideas. Sometimes, too, the historical-critical researcher will question an established interpretation of existing data and devise a new hypothesis that will provide a more satisfactory or parsimonious explanation of past events. Reasons for engaging in the research process were developed in Chapter One.

The historical-critical researcher may begin with a large, general, diffused, and even confused notion of the problem. By isolating the crucial points that gave rise to the doubt or concern—one by one—the researcher begins to formulate a simple, clear, complete description of the problem. Then, before proceeding, he or she checks to make certain that the problem will be answerable. Several questions could be posed before commiting oneself too fully:

1. Is the problem adaptable to historical-critical research methods? Can it be adequately treated using this approach?

2. Is the problem a significant one? Is it too trivial to consider? To what extent, for example, will the conclusions drawn be applicable to other problems and concerns?
3. To what extent is data available on this topic? Can you use this data without having to travel long distances?

Historical-critical research, like any scientific inquiry, stems from a well-phrased problem-question that starts the researcher on a quest for a solution. It requires the setting up of specific, testable hypotheses. Without such hypotheses, historical-critical research can become little more than aimless gathering of facts. A specific, testable hypothesis directs the researcher's attention to related information. In this way, he or she has a reasonable chance of extracting a meaningful body of data that can be synthesized to provide new knowledge or new understandings. But even when a specific and testable hypothesis has been framed, the researcher must exert strict self-control. In reading historical documents, it is easy to find oneself collecting large amounts of information that, though interesting, is not related to the topic. Delimited and specific hypotheses help prevent the researcher from becoming distracted and led astray by information that is not pertinent to the specific field of investigation.

Below are examples of specific hypotheses previous researchers have used.

In what ways can one explain the success of Barbara Jordan's keynote address to the 1976 Democratic Convention?[12]

What is the significance of Booker T. Washington's decision to speak on the Southern race question at the opening ceremonies of the International and Cotton States Exposition in Atlanta, 18 September 1895?[13]

What are the rhetorical results when a pressure group—"popular" atheists in the United States—fail to achieve their end?[14]

CHOOSING THE HISTORICAL APPROACH OR CRITICAL CRITERIA

In choosing the historical method you also choose critical criteria. You use critical criteria no matter the method: descriptive, experimental, or historical. But when the critical method serves the leading role it receives the major emphasis and as with any method, certain basic understandings are essential.

On what does the critic focus? What might prompt a person to use this method? We cannot suggest all the possible concerns—nor would we want to—but we can suggest some focal points. A speech, a series of speeches, or a speaker are observable objects and events. A kind of speaking, listening, or viewing might also be observed as might an event, campaign, or movement. Less traditional objects might include scrutinizing novels, plays, or editorials from a rhetorical stance. As a literary genre, one writer suggests that the critical method "focuses upon the artistry of the maker; it has as its end interpretation, appreciation, elucidation, appraisal, of a work of art."[15]

Why would a person want to engage in this kind of research? That is, what is its purpose? There are several. One purpose is to indicate, point out, or draw attention to phenomena of speech communication. By this we mean that a researcher will point out or set forth the outlines of a campaign, the career of a speaker, or the impact of a speech or series of speeches.[16] Researchers have examined a keynote address as adaptive rhetoric[17] or as a juxtaposition of contradictory values.[18] One investigator, too, examined the public discourse that surrounds political corruption.[19]

Another purpose is to evaluate phenomena of speech. By this we mean that the critic will interpret or judge the data as he or she perceives it. Is the effort well done? On what basis is this decision made? One researcher examined remarks made by Jimmy Carter in his *Playboy* interview and determined that the stylistic level was inappropriate to Carter.[20] Another researcher studied the public speaking of John Bright between 1850 and 1860 and found it to be clear, eloquent, and impressive.[21]

Some critics exclude any evaluation of the critical object from their work. They label their efforts "descriptive" and claim description was their sole goal. We feel that this is inappropriate, although we understand why some might wish to do so. Evaluation should not be entirely eliminated. The process of describing—of indicating, pointing out, and drawing attention to—seems to imply that the phenomenon is worth attending to. The interpretative and evaluative process are an inherent part of the critical method. Description and evaluation may merge into each other in the presentation, one preparing for the other or one reflecting back on the other, but both are necessary and essential.

A third purpose for engaging in critical research is to persuade. The critic should not overlook the persuasive function. Whether admitted or not, the critic through his or her work says, "Come to understand this as I do." Such critical acts can have consequences. Think about, for example, the impact that a critic of a presidential address might have. When we make judgments, especially about important occurrences, whether contemporary or historical, our judgments are likely to foster counterjudgments. People do not always agree. Just because the well-educated, erudite, critic says something is true, does not make it true—in any area where criticism occurs. One researcher sought to convince the reader that Frederick Jackson Turner functioned optimally as a persuader.[22] Another writer focused on a single rhetorical form—the rhetorical use of calamity—and argues that it has been a significant pattern in the rhetorical history of colonial North America and the United States.[23]

A fourth purpose for pursuing criticism is simply to learn. Important as this purpose is, we do not mention it first but rather in passing because it can be and often is a stimulus for pursuing research of any kind. Criticism can lead to new insights. These new insights could be phrased as principles or hypotheses that can be subjected to further testing.

Learning may not be confined to speech communication. That is, it need not be confined to what the researcher might learn about communication principles, concepts, and ideas. Communication is an artifact—whether it be a conversation, speech, editorial, or other media production; we may study it to learn about other matters. For example, we may want to reconstruct the lives and the ways of the people who produced the communication. Their presentation then becomes one window we have for looking into their culture or time.[24] In her book *A Distant Mirror,* Barbara Tuchman uses the life of one man as a vehicle for developing, explaining, and analyzing the life and times of the fourteenth century.

A fifth purpose for choosing the critical method is to test. Critical researchers contribute by testing conventional or accepted principles. If the principles we teach about communication are sound, they should be capable of being demonstrated in the communication of others. Thus, the critical researcher can confirm our theories and concepts through critical examination of the practice of effective communicators.[25] For example, in his work on "The Fall of Wellington," Michael C. McGee offered a case study of the relationships between theory, practice, and rhetoric in history.[26] In "Music and the Three Appeals of Classical Rhetoric," Gerard G. LeCoat applied the three classical rhetorical appeals of *logos, ethos,* and *pathos* to musical compositions.[27]

Jesse G. Delia presented one of the best defenses of the need for testing theories and methodologies in his article, "Constructivism and the Study of Human Communication." He summarizes his thesis in the final challenge he presents to the reader:

> Coherent theoretical frameworks, of course, are created only by the hard work of individual researchers elaborating, refining, and defending their entire programs—assumptions, concepts, methods, and all. Some frameworks doubtlessly will fail or be rejected; others will surely win admiration and adherents.[28]

What are the criteria by which the critical researcher judges? On what does his or her evaluation rest? This is not an easy question to answer because there are many different sets of criteria, kinds of phenomena to be studied, and purposes that the criticism can serve. These reasons suggest the importance of studying the critical method in more depth than what we can offer here. Many issues are implicit in the above comments. For example, who is to say that the traditional perspective —or set of criteria—is better or more appropriate than the dramatistic approach suggested in the writing of Kenneth Burke?[29] In another instance, who is to say which criteria would be most appropriate for the study of Lincoln's first inaugural as opposed to the speeches delivered by a political candidate in his or her bid for the presidency? Finally, who is to say which critical approach would be most appropriate for a critique designed to persuade the public that the president's latest approach (reflected in his speeches) to control inflation or energy usage is unworkable, as opposed to a critique designed to show why Adolph Hitler was one of the finest speakers in history? These are by no means all the difficulties, but they raise several of the important problems. Even the problem of focusing on immediate effects versus long-term effects can pose problems for the researcher. When this problem is resolved, then there is the question concerning which effects to focus upon.

As the critic employs his or her method, he or she is placed in the lead role of judge—judge not only of the material to be criticized, but also of all the criteria, kinds of phenomena, and purposes. The role of judge begins as the researcher decides that this or that is the best method to employ.

Following the critical method means following a rather specific approach. We will try, briefly, to clarify this approach—assuming that the person intent on using this approach will supplement our material with other books and materials of far greater depth.

A researcher must first discover and structure the research problem. This is a common procedure, no matter the method, and we developed this idea in Chapters 2 and 3. Second the researcher must establish the need for the study, a procedure that, like the first, is both common and developed elsewhere. It was treated briefly in Chapter 3 when we discussed the general goals of the research investigation, and it will be discussed in detail in Chapter 10 as we present the details of prospectus writing. At this point the researcher should know if the critical method is, indeed, best for this problem, how the problem relates to other pertinent research, and what contribution this investigation is likely to make. It is at this point that the peculiarities or unique features of the critical method become apparent.

The researcher begins by thoroughly mapping the territory of the problem. All the parts—the bits and pieces—should be related. With the territory defined, a plan of investigation can be created to fit the phenomena to be criticized. Not to match the plan of investigation with the territory is to cast doubt on the validity of the results. One would not, for example, use the same criteria to analyze a social move-ment as to analyze a speech. There is no limit to the amount of borrowing that can be done from other methodologies—this is how one tailors an investigative procedure to meet unique problems—but the approach must be specified at the outset. To piece a plan of attack together as one proceeds can create serious problems and result in loss of time and energy. A total perspective may be lost, important stages omitted, necessary preparations neglected or materials not acquired.

If researchers think of this mapping and planning process in terms of a precision-balance scale, they can begin to understand the nature of the process.[30] On one side of the balance rest the prescribed standards of judgment; on the other the phe-nomenon to be observed. The researchers' goal is to observe whether there is an imbalance and the nature of its direction. They must then weigh each side of the scale against the other and make the appropriate adjustments. This may not be easy; the necessary adjustments may not be clearly evident, predictable, or pre-cise; but again, the outcome of this effort may determine the significance, validity, relevance, or acceptance of the results. Care in determining requisite adjustments is mandatory.

From reading the above, you may get the impression that certain rules or norms are followed to pursue critical research. It is true that certain general norms exist; these can be found by studying the literature. But note that although these norms are associated with traditional categories, researchers can derive their specific criteria from any combination of norms. Moreover, the communication phenomena that may be examined by appropriate criteria are not restricted. Determining which phenomena are to be studied and which criteria are used to judge the phenomena are two highly creative functions of critical researchers; a third is controlling the synthesis, or the way these two are brought together. When one considers the possible combinations of critical criteria, the number of combinations grows toward infinity.

Several of the most often used critical approaches are described briefly below. This list is by no means exhaustive; it is intended to suggest sources where specific critical criteria can be located.

In the traditional critical approach, the classical canons of rhetoric (invention, arrangement, style, delivery, and memory) are applied and the discourse analyzed in terms of classical modes of proof.[31]

In psychological criticism, the critic focuses on the speaker and audience and on the means speakers use to activate and direct audience needs and motives. The critic attempts to determine whether the speaker's goals were achieved as well as how and why.

In dramatistic criticism, the critic analyzes language and thought as modes of action, not as means of conveying information. The crucial element of concern is the creation and identification of meaning as it determines changes in attitude and action. The critic examines the speaker's language as it affects the symbolic behavior of both speaker and audience.[32]

In a critical study, the researchers need to draw conclusions from their work. The criticism is the composite judgment and should be structured to fit the problem as it was outlined at the outset. The conclusions answer the questions asked in the beginning.

The conclusions should be limited to the available data. A typical question might be: To what degree is a researcher allowed freedom to go beyond the data? How far can a researcher go beyond the evidence? Every study should end with a brief and clear statement of the essential facts or points. But following the summary and conclusions, the researcher should experience the freedom earned by seriousness of purpose and rigor in implementation: That freedom involves the joy of giving advice and guiding future investigators. As long as the section is appropriately labeled and clearly distinguished from the summary and conclusions, the researchers should not feel restricted from simply recommending further research. Few writers, we feel, are willing to realize their potential in this creative area. They are boxed in to the point that many ideas are not expressed simply because they are unwilling to take the risk that this freedom involves.

Many researchers may not realize that at this point in their research they are in a unique position. They have a better command of the information, a better perspective of the problem, and a better idea of how various puzzle parts fit together than most other people. Not to use this position as a launching pad for creative insight and expression is to waste an opportunity for constructive contribution to the field.

It may help the critical researcher to view the critical method as more qualitative than quantitative. Quantitative methodology is explained in Chapter 6. The evaluations should be tied to the corresponding link between standards and phe-nomena being measured, but to suggest that this link is exact is to suggest that this methodology is more precise than it is. Whenever one interprets data, subjectivity is present. Even the most objective research is subjective—at least in its critical phases.

Goals of the Critical Researcher

What is the aim or objective of the critical researcher? He or she should aim, first, for dependability. Dependability is reflected in validity: Did the researcher measure what he or she claimed to measure? It is also reflected in reliability. In experimental work the key question is: If the study were repeated, would the same results occur? In critical work, the question is different. The statistical reliability of critics is not as crucial as the reliability of evidence; often excellent criticism distinguishes itself because other critics have *not* agreed. Even the critic may disagree with himself or herself at a later time; that is the nature of criticism.

Dependability also relies on clarity and accuracy of style. The way the material is presented becomes crucial to the critic's success. This confirms the "theory of the weakest link," which will be discussed in some detail in Chapter 10, "Writing and Publishing." (The theory of the weakest link contends that any part that lacks strength or effectiveness is likely to cast a shadow of doubt on other parts—whether weak or strong.) A creative effort that is slightly inaccurate, inadequately sup-ported, or poorly phrased does not look like a creative product. It needs revision to be recognized. It is more likely that results will get published, that visibility will come, and that success will be assured (through dependability) if the researcher presents results with clarity and accuracy.

Excellence in criticism also results from the authenticity of sources: checking to see that the material used conforms to an original (this will be discussed next in this chapter). Originality in design and execution are also important. The critical methodologist has, perhaps, greater freedom in imposing his or her personal stamp or mark on the study. As a result, the expectation is higher, and the criteria of originality is used in determining excellence.

Excellence is also determined by the criteria of application: Can the results be applied to life? The critical methodologist must strive to be relevant. Will his or her research serve to guide future researchers? This is also known as educational poten-cy. The critic is on a quest to help people perceive, interpret, and judge what they might otherwise ignore or misevaluate.

COLLECTING AND VERIFYING EVIDENCE

After finding a problem-question, and having decided on the historical approach or the critical methodology—a choice that, in the final analysis, will likely be com-bined—the researcher must collect and verify the evidence. This process involves the careful scrutiny of the material or phenomena to be evaluated and, as explained earlier, can determine the acceptability of the final outcome of the study. To phrase this a bit differently, unless care is taken and rigor pursued, the time and effort expended at this stage of the research (or at later stages) may be for naught. The backbone of historical-critical research is evidence. In this section, we will discuss primary and secondary sources, external criticism of documents and writers, and internal criticism of documents.

Primary and Secondary Sources

Once the historical researcher has defined the perimeters of the category of events to be reconstructed, he or she must establish sources from which inferences can be made about the nature of events. One common classification of sources is *primary* and *secondary*. A primary source is one with some direct physical relationship to the events being studied. A researcher investigating a particular speech might interview a member of the audience or examine a film, videotape, sound recording, or photograph of the event—all primary sources. In addition, the researcher might correspond with the speaker and use other speeches, articles, or books of the speaker. An actual transcript of the speech or a diary of the events would also be considered primary materials.

We might note, too, a growing dependence on tapes and transcripts—oral history—in historical-critical research. Numerous repositories for oral-history documents already exist and more are being developed. The *Directory of Archives and Manuscript Repositories in the United States* and the New York Times Oral History Program's master index to oral-history transcripts—all computer based—are available tools for the discovery of these primary sources.

Secondary sources, on the other hand, bear no direct physical relationship to the event. Their relationship to the event is secondary—through some intermediate process. The researcher investigating the speech mentioned above, might read newspaper or magazine accounts. Although the person writing the account may have been present at the speech, the researcher is dependent not on the person but on his or her account—a secondary source. To gain additional insight, the researcher might talk with the speaker's friends, might read an account written by a person who never knew the speaker but accumulated data by interviewing the speaker's associates—all secondary sources. In all secondary sources, distortions occur in the researcher's information; the further removed from the speaker, the greater the decrease in the adequacy of the information.

Some sources the researcher will discover combine both primary and secondary elements. Consider, for example, a biography written by a close personal friend of the speaker. The friend relies on both personal observations and other material. The researcher must try to sort out the differences; often, this cannot be done. But this distinction can be a vital issue when the researcher must determine the inferences that can be made based on the material. Here is where the concept of cross-validation enters in: Sources are checked against each other. Obviously, the more information the researcher has as a basis for inferences, the more likely he or she will uncover distortions, exaggerations, and errors. Also, the more he or she can rely on strictly primary materials, the more likely sound inferences can be made.

As a general rule, the researcher should not accept secondhand data or use sources that have derived their information from other sources. A newspaper story, for example, should not be relied on as a major source if more direct means of determining the facts are available. In historical research, the researcher must use the best available information—whatever records have survived. The point of the general rule is to lead the researcher away from encyclopedias, almanacs, digests, and textbooks. Whenever a quotation from another source appears in a book or article, the researcher should find the original quotation to check it against two criteria: (1) What is its context? Has the current author distorted its meaning by taking it out of context? (2) Is it accurately stated? Sometimes an inadvertant error can change the entire meaning of a passage.

When a researcher relies on secondary sources, he or she opens the way for error. They are less reliable than primary sources and sometimes represent nothing more than unverified rumor or hearsay. The best use the historical researcher can make of secondary sources is as hypotheses designed to bridge the gaps between pieces of primary evidence. If numerous or wide gaps occur in the primary material, the researcher should question whether to proceed with the study at all. The greater the reliance the researcher places on carefully evaluated primary sources, the more accurate his or her conclusions are likely to be.

External Criticism of Documents

After the data is collected, the researcher subjects it to careful scrutiny to establish both authenticity and accuracy. Establishing authenticity is called *external criticism*. This involves determining the genuineness of the material. If you were studying a historical figure and discovered letters she had written to a friend that revealed her feelings about speaking in public, you would need to establish the authenticity of the letters. Authenticity can be established in various ways; in this case, you might want to:

1. Determine from an analysis of the paper and ink if it could have existed at that time.
2. Compare the handwriting with other documents she might have written.
3. Check the language to be sure it is representative of the language at the time when the letters were written and that it is representative of the language she tended to use.

No record has value for the study unless it is genuine. Manuscripts, letters, artifacts, books, or biological remains can be forged. If personal recollections are required as data, they, too, should be verified by other supporting evidence.

In examining speeches and official correspondence, the researcher should be aware of the problem presented by ghostwriters. Most people in prominent positions—especially *public* positions—use ghostwriters. Since speeches and letters composed by ghostwriters are not genuine, one must take great care in the inferences based on such material.

In rhetorical criticism, textual authenticity is the primary problem. How accurately does the printed text represent what the speaker said in the immediate speaker-audience-message-situation interaction? What are the confounding—confusing, perplexing, or puzzling—variables? That is, what are the causes for confusion? We want to know if there was a difference between what the speaker actually said and what was printed. For example,

1. Could the reporter hear? Were there distractions?
2. Did the speaker deviate from his or her notes?
3. Could the reporter transcribe well?
4. Was the speech edited by someone other than the speaker?
5. Did the printer follow the text accurately?
6. Was the speech abridged?
7. Was the reporter biased?
8. Was the editor prejudiced?
9. Did the speaker change his or her own speech?
   a. Did he or she revise and polish it?
   b. Did he or she change it to make it contain what he or she wished had been said?
10. Was an exact, unedited, audio or video transcription made of the speech?

One must be skeptical of printed copies of speeches found in newspapers, articles, or books. Often, an editor or reporter can dictate what portions of a speech are printed. They can also, consciously or subconsciously, distort both the content and the tone of the synopses. Although such contamination of the original may be difficult to detect, it is highly important in external criticism.

External Criticism of Writers

As the researcher investigates documents, he or she will quickly learn that some authors can be excellent sources of information and others worthless sources. Evaluations of writers must be made; those characteristics most commonly considered are:

1. Is the writer a trained observer and reporter? We give more credence to experts. Also, with respect to training, was the writer an expert at recording the events?

A newspaper reporter is more likely to provide an accurate report than a casual bystander. Going one step further, might the writing habits of the writer interfere with his or her accurate reporting? Talented writers often embellish, seek the effective turn of phrase or apt analogy, or allow their imagination to interfere with fact. These questions are all important and should be added to the very basic, fundamental questions that refer to training, like:

a. When was the writer born?
b. How old was he or she at the time of the event?
c. What was his or her educational background?
d. Where did he or she live?
e. What kind of training did he or she receive?
f. What were his or her professional affiliations?
g. Was he or she intelligent?

The researcher must also find out if the person was in a position to know or observe the facts, aware of the significance of his or her comments, in a reliable position to observe, physically able to observe, intellectually competent to understand and report, and morally able to report only what he or she observed. Did the witness know what he or she ought to have known? Did the witness claim to know what he or she could not have known? Finally, do other witnesses support him or her?[33]

2. What is the writer's relationship to the event? Was he or she present? We give more credibility to those who are closer to the event.

3. What was the intent of the writer? Was the writer under any obligation to say nice things about the politician? Was an observer unlikely to criticize a person because of a close friendship? Was public face an important ingredient? Was the writer trying to inform or to persuade? Was he or she trying to change an impression? Was it cathartic release? The intent of the writer, if it can be determined, can have a significant effect on the evaluation of a document.

4. What is the likelihood of boldness in reporting? Some judgment might have to be made regarding the boldness or timidity of the writer. Some writers want to avoid all possibility of being sued for libel. Every writer wants to avoid this, but some will report more boldly and with less distortion. The researcher must try to see a pattern in the writer's method.[34]

The importance of external criticism underscores the need for a posture of historical doubt. Doubt is the circumstance that forces researchers to question. They must question the material until the evidence forces a conclusion. Every possible reason for disbelief must be explored. Finally, unable to question any longer, and after a comprehensive and careful search of all events and motives, and the study of all other contemporary accounts, the researcher can conclude that in all probability, given the available evidence, this appears to be an accurate picture of what happened.

Internal Criticism of Document

Internal criticism begins where external criticism ends. There is little sense in establishing the validity of the content—the accuracy of the statements in a document—until you are absolutely convinced of its genuineness. Forgeries should be discarded; internal criticism begins when it is certain that the documents are either originals or as close to originals as one can get. Just because a document has been established as authentic does not mean the researcher should jump to the conclusion that what it says is credible. Internal criticism evaluates the meaning, truth, and believability of the statements in the document. It may be closely tied to judgments you have made externally about the observer, for it is true that the more credible the source, the more likely one can trust and believe in his or her statements. But this should not lead the researcher into being too trusting.

Meaning. What does a statement mean? Several problems confront the researcher with respect to meaning. Passages must be studied in context. Terms must be understood, which may lead the researcher to ask some or all of the following questions:

1. What is the meaning of technical terms?
2. What is the meaning of obsolete terms?
3. What was the original or intended meaning of terms that have shifted meaning since the document was written?
4. What is the connotation of terms that have shifted meaning with the passage of time?
5. What is the meaning of terms used differently in various regions of the country? Various countries? Various continents?
6. What is the meaning of figurative language? Many gaps in meaning occur when a speaker or writer relies on allegory, allusion, hyperbole, irony, metaphore, or simile.
7. What is the meaning of phrases, asides, digressions, humor, or sarcasm? To distinguish real meaning from apparent meaning is difficult when the researcher cannot actually observe the position of the tongue in cheek.

These questions emphasize the importance of a general knowledge of the period. How else can a researcher discover the meaning of obscure allusions to contemporary people, issues, or events?

Truth. Once we know the meaning of what is written, out next concern is its truth: Is the statement true? The researcher asks this question with respect to individual statements, building the study piece by piece. Again, the credibility of the speaker or writer—established through external criticism—helps us in this inquiry. The author's possible biases are immediately suspect. The researcher should be led by the answer to this question: Is there any reason to doubt the accuracy of the statement? Examining the full context will help the researcher discover biases. When examining anonymous statements, partial statements, unsigned newspaper or journal articles, the researcher should attempt to understand the point of view of the periodical as a whole.

Internal consistency of the document also provides information about the truth. Are there contradictions within the document? Are these same contradictions found in other documents produced by the same author? When compared with documents produced by others at the same time, are there contradictions? When reports are contradictory, the researcher must decide in favor of one or the other or provide a rationale for resolving the contradiction. When reports agree, the researcher can be reasonably sure of having discovered the truth.

Believability. Belief is not dependent on any single criterion; it is an accumulated phenomenon: It depends on the aggregate effect of having proceeded through all the previous stages. To believe or not to believe is a final decision to either accept or reject based on:

1. Evaluation of the genuineness of the statement or document.
2. Estimation of the credibility of the source.
3. Discovery of other support independent of the source. Special attention must be given to the "reluctant witness" who provides information contrary to his or her personal position, political affiliation, or group interests.
4. Appraisal of statements in light of the period under study. The researcher must examine the people, events, and issues—the total milieu—and assess the critical event with reference to the whole.[35]

It is always possible for new information to upset preconceptions and to reverse judgments. The researcher must maintain an open and responsive mind. If the presentation of history were merely a process of digging out facts, it would be simple. But the study involves answering puzzling problems, and researcher judgment is always involved in determining the extent to which inferences have a high probability of being correct.

The researcher must not become too narrow in this pursuit; the question is not primarily, what is the *substance* of particular ideas. The researcher should also be looking for the function—the dynamics—of ideas.[36]

Interpreting Evidence and Drawing Conclusions

We have found a problem-question, we have chosen the approach, we have collected and verified the data, we are now ready to interpret the evidence and draw conclusions. This is the process of synthesizing the data: drawing everything together into a meaningful whole. No single procedure works for all data and for all researchers: Researchers proceed differently as they reason connections between facts and infer causes and relationships. This is, once again, a highly creative phase. It may involve attributing motives, deducing characteristics, or deriving causes, and two people studying the same events may not arrive at the same conclusions.

The possibility that two scholars may not reach the same conclusion should not deter the researcher. Indeed, it should inspire. History pursued as a set of objective facts is dull and lifeless. The researcher must attempt to add flesh to the facts. Historical reconstruction involves presenting real people with their very human values, hates, loves, fears, internal struggles, and external conflicts. People are more than empty frames, events are more than empty rooms, and history is more than the skeleton of a house. The interesting historical writer must make numerous assumptions about human nature—assumptions that future researchers may prove to be unsound.

To evaluate data and draw sound conclusions, the researcher needs more than mere knowledge of the specific event under investigation. He or she also needs:

1. A rich fund of historical knowledge
2. A wealth of general knowledge
3. An intelligent understanding of human nature
4. A keen mind
5. Good common sense
6. A strong grasp of the present
7. Historical perspective[37]

The historical researcher does not allow facts to speak for themselves; facts do not talk. It is this process of synthesis—putting all this together—that is the essential part of historiography. Anything less is the work of the antiquarian, who simply collects facts or relics for their own sake. "The University student must learn among his first lessons" wrote John W. Burgess, an early writer on historical methodology, "that truth, as man knows it, is no ready-made article of certain and objective character, that it is a human interpretation, and subject therefore to the fallibility of human insight and reasoning—one sided, colored, incomplete."[38] "The study of history," echoed Albert Hart, "means the attempt to form for one's self an independent judgment upon historical events, a judgment based upon the most trustworthy accounts within reach."[39] It is the historian who interprets for the purpose of determining the light history can shed on men, women, and events.

We close this section on historical-critical procedures with a plea. In general, historical research tends to take a too narrow interpretation of the data. The complex sociopolitical and socioemotional climate that creates the need for change is often ignored. History is approached segmentally whereas it should be a reflection of the people—their aspirations, values, and mores. Because communication touches all aspects of life, whether it be social, political, cultural, economic, religious, or technological, it cannot be studied completely or successfully without examining the various forces. Communication critically affects and is critically affected by every aspect of society. To date it has been narrow and segmented. Greater perspective into the broad interactions of historical phenomena is needed.

The process of organizing, writing, and publishing the historical report will be treated in Chapter 10, "Writing and Publishing." Clear, appropriate, impressive, and effective communication should be the goal of anyone engaged in historical research in speech communication.

PITFALLS OF HISTORICAL-CRITICAL RESEARCH

Many of the pitfalls of historical-critical research can be deduced from the material presented thus far. There are, of course, many—an infinite number. Rather than catalogue all the errors to which the human mind is susceptible, we will focus on the common pitfalls of the historical method. All are not necessarily unique to this method; many relate to the other methods described as well. Since they are important, they bear repeating.

Blinders. The concept of selective perception suggests that we see what we want to see, and we hear what we want to hear. In research, we must be wary of the tendency to find exactly what we are looking for. Without doubt, selecting one all-powerful purpose has benefits: It controls the focus and direction of a study from conception to writing. But it is too easy to prove what one sets out to prove. The effective researcher must be willing to suspend judgment—to remove the blinders that restrict a full, free, and open examination of the material.

Proportion. One goal of the researcher must be to examine the matrix—the social milieu—into which a person or an event is fitted. The relationship of the play and players to the backdrop provides depth, perspective, and relationship. In historical research, it is this association that offers significance and relevance: proportion. The greatness of a person or a movement is commensurate with the times in which the person lived or the era in which the movement flourished.

In selecting a particular person or movement to study, the researcher makes a choice about the worth of this individual or event. Sometimes this choice, along with the time and effort spent in investigating it, causes the researcher to lose perspective, to break the symmetry of the relationship between the person and the times or the movement and its era. The researcher becomes a partisan and can no longer be an objective, impartial, dispassionate, and unbiased reporter—the goals of quality historical reporting.

Doubt. The importance of cultivating doubt, touched on earlier, bears reemphasis, especially in this context. Too often the researcher sits in awe of the written word, assuming that because something has been written (and preserved), it is valid. For many beginning researchers, not having been published themselves increases the reverence. Our esteem, regard, and respect for those who have accomplished this feat is immeasurable.

In much the same way, some researchers find it hard to believe that writers would deliberately falsify evidence or change historical fact. Some historians of the past have examined history in its broadest spectrum, being casual in matters of detail. Jared Sparks is known to have improved the grammar of George Washington's letters[40] much as those who transcribed the Nixon tapes left many expletives deleted. Because newspapers had fewer competitors, factual errors or misrepresentations were less likely to be exposed. And by tradition, papers were often partisan; they engaged in yellow journalism, replete with alarming headlines in large type, lavish use of pictures, pseudoscientific articles, sensational features, and ostentatious crusading for popular causes. Their purpose was to sell newspapers, and it guided some newspapers' philosophies for five years prior to and shortly after the turn of the century. Some of the techniques of yellow journalism have taken root and are widespread even today.

Bias. We must recognize our own biases. Our prejudices, beliefs, affections, upbringing, social and economic experience, and even our humor will affect our selection and ordering of materials. We must not only admit them but own up to them. We must strive to overcome them as well. Our goal should be to try to understand a point of view, a philosophy, an approach that is foreign to our own.

Although few of us are able to achieve complete impartiality and objectivity, we must not let that fact cloud our minds or obscure our attempts to achieve a fair and equitable approach toward all varieties of people, movements, and ideas.

Interpretation. Although we stated earlier that a historical-critical researcher characteristically has a strong grasp of the present, we must be careful not to criticize the past based on our contemporary ideas and values. Using today's standards will pervert our judgment about the motives, character, and attitudes of the past. Think, for example, of the changes in public attitude toward words like democracy, slavery, and religious toleration over just the past hundred years. Imagine the infinite number of other such changes. To project today's values on yesterday's history is like suggesting, in reverse, that yesterday's laws fit today's circumstances. We must look at history in light of the time in which it occurs.

Cause. As a historical-critical researcher, you will be looking for the causes of events. Why did this happen? Finding causal links is not easy; usually there is no *one* cause, but rather a multiplicity of interlocking causes. Just as research has demonstrated that the immediate impact of a speech generally has little effect on basic value structures, it has shown that persuasion works more effectively as a result of a two-step flow, the second step being the effect of information once it has been discussed with friends and evaluated in terms of group memberships.[41] This two-step process makes the discovery of causal links more difficult. Causation should not be inferred, however, just because one event closely follows another; chronology or juxtaposition does not guarantee that one caused the other. We must not mistake casual relationships for causal ones.

Certainty. No matter how overwhelming the evidence, no matter how impressive the evaluations, no matter how convincing the conclusions, there is little certainty in history. New evidence, evaluations, and conclusions cast new light on old events and circumstances. As impressed as you are with your results and as carefully as you documented your material, you must still be cautious in drawing your conclusions. They are, indeed, a function of the time in which they are written and, thus, subject to change. As Mencken said, "The public . . . demands certainties . . . But there *are* no certainties."[42]

LIMITATIONS OF HISTORICAL-CRITICAL RESEARCH

Studying history or engaging in historical-critical research has great value, but it also has some limitations. History should be read and interpreted with guarded cautiousness. Taking into consideration the following limitations will help:

1. History cannot be wrong because it is, by definition, what occurred. But the way it is interpreted or presented can be wrong—or at least misleading. To depend too heavily on the written word—especially a single source—without constant cross-checking and questioning, can be a serious limitation. We must strive to read broadly and in depth.

2. Language distorts. The meanings we have for words are not the same meanings that writers had for the words they used. Those writers of history we enjoy reading made their writing interesting. Often their flair or enthusiasm for their subject becomes a limitation. We must be careful not to consider history dull because it was written about in a boring manner, just as we must be careful not to consider a period or person flamboyant because it was written about in an ostentatious manner.

3. We must strive to know as much as possible of the history writers on whom we depend. Just as personality characteristics help determine whether a person should pursue historical-critical research, personality characteristics surely influenced the success others had in writing their history. Were they dedicated pursuers of information who were careful, accurate doubters?

SUMMARY

This chapter is but an introduction to historical-critical methodology. If it has served as a guide to the challenges and problems of applying historical methodology to events and people, it has served its purpose. If you plan to pursue an historical topic, consult the professional historian.

Historical research enlarges our world experience by providing a deeper appreciation and more thorough insight into the essential nature and uniqueness of people and events. It involves the reconstruction of the past in a systematic and objective manner: collecting evidence, verifying it, synthesizing it, and formulating conclusions.

Interpreting data and drawing conclusions requires a broad base of knowledge and understanding. Here is where the historical-critical researcher exercises ingenuity, imagination, insight, and scholarliness, but in doing so he or she must also exhibit restraint and caution. He or she must not allow personal biases to affect the outcome. In approach, as well as in frame of mind, the researcher should keep the goals of scientific research in mind. Historical methodology applies scientific methods to the description and analysis of past events. To meet the goals of scientific research will help assure success.

Historical research is not two-dimensional, like following a route on a road map. It has many alternate routes that lead in many different directions. It is much like the tangle of scaffolding that can be found around and within a building under construction. The historical researcher is like the construction supervisor. He or she helped construct the maze, knows why it exists, can find the way through it, and with persistence will, in an orderly manner, be able to disassemble it to leave a new creation: the synthesis to which all the scaffolding lent support. All parts of the tanglement are important, but the new building is the final goal. To be effective, the final product stands alone; the mechanical aspects of its creation are no longer evident. The role of the historical researcher on this project is complete, and he or she may now strike out on a new endeavor—though in the true believer the nagging feeling that one more stone can be turned or one more gap can be filled will persist. Oh, the persistence of that feeling: If I just had more time . . . .

Descriptive Research

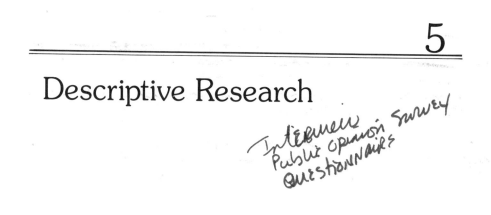

Imagine that you are walking across campus and an individual stops you to ask if you would provide some opinions concerning university services and facilities. Imagine that you open your mail and find a questionnaire from your state senator soliciting your views on various political issues. Imagine that an individual from the U.S. Census Bureau rings your doorbell and proceeds to ask you a series of questions concerning number, ages, and occupations of your household members. These hypothetical situations are not uncommon. At some time in your life, you have probably been asked to provide specific information on your lifestyle, interests, attitudes, opinions, beliefs, or behaviors. Such incidents provide examples of how the descriptive method of research is carried out. Unlike documentary, historical or library research, which examines written records of phenomena, descriptive research involves the collection of information directly from individuals who possess the information. It is a common and familiar method of research that is applicable to a wide variety of research questions.

This chapter explains descriptive research methodology, discusses its purposes or functions, and suggests various ways of conducting descriptive research, including surveys, interviews, and observations. It explains several types of structured and naturalistic observation techniques. Its aim is to provide the reader with an understanding of descriptive research methods and practical suggestions for conducting descriptive research.

OVERVIEW OF THE DESCRIPTIVE METHOD

Recall from Chapter 2 that after you have formulated a specific problem worthy of investigation, determined research hypotheses or questions, and reviewed rele-

[handwritten annotations: "Descriptive Researcher Paints a Picture of the status quo or present state of affairs. Systematically; Objectively describe what is happen..."]

vant literature, you are ready to design your investigation—that is, to plan the specific method for collecting information. The descriptive methodology represents one means of collecting the desired information. The descriptive researcher collects, through various specific techniques, information about conditions that exist, practices that prevail, beliefs or attitudes that are held, processes that are going on, effects that are being felt, or trends that are developing.[1] In short, descriptive research paints a picture of the status quo or the present state of affairs. It depicts or characterizes current conditions. Unlike experimental researchers, descriptive researchers do not manipulate conditions or arrange for events to happen. Rather, they systematically and objectively describe what is happening, how people feel about what is happening, or what people would like to have happen.

PURPOSES OF DESCRIPTIVE RESEARCH

In examining what descriptive research is, we already have alluded to its purpose or function. The overall purpose of the descriptive method is to describe—events, beliefs, attitudes, values, intentions, preferences, or behaviors. There are several more specific points, however, concerning what we describe and why we describe it. Let us present here some specific uses of the descriptive method that are relevant to the speech-communication researcher. This list of functions is not exhaustive nor mutually exclusive. The hypothetical research questions are not refined, nor is the descriptive method necessarily the only suitable method for investigating all of the following research examples. We provide these functions and examples merely to illustrate possible uses of the descriptive method.

1. To describe individuals, events, programs, or groups.
   Example: "What are the characteristics of graduate students in speech communication at U.S. colleges and universities?"
   A mail survey to speech-communication graduate students could determine such characteristics as age, sex, race, religion, area of concentration, and career goals.
2. To compare individuals, events, programs, or groups.
   Example: "How do U.S. and Canadian public schools compare in speech-communication curricula?"
   Telephone interviews with selected communication teachers in both countries could determine teaching philosophy, numbers and types of courses offered, and textbooks used.
3. To determine motivations.
   Example: "Do television advertisements motivate people to buy economy cars?"
   Interviews with selected economy car owners could determine their recall of television advertisements and their reported reasons for such purchases.
4. To determine needs, desires, or problems.
   Example: "What problems do managers encounter when communicating with their subordinates?"

Surveys, interviews, or direct observation could determine communication problems or communication training needs.

5. To determine preferences or make predictions or projections.

   Example: "Which candidate will individuals vote for in the next election?"

   Surveys or interviews could determine individuals' voting intentions.

6. To determine effects, results, or consequences.

   Example: "How does a couple's marital conflict affect their children's attitudes toward marriage?"

   Observations of marital interactions and interviews with the children could determine such effects.

7. To determine relationships or associations.

   Example: "How do individuals' religious values relate to their attitudes toward the Equal Rights Amendment?"

   Surveys or interviews with selected individuals concerning their religious values and attitudes toward the amendment could be compared to determine this relationship.

8. To link attitudes to behavior.

   Example: "How do employers' attitudes toward communication training influence their hiring of communication majors?"

   A survey of employers' attitudes toward communication training could be compared with their hiring behavior, as determined by personnel records or interviews with employers.

As you can see, the descriptive methodology serves many purposes for the speech-communication researcher and for researchers at large. The descriptive method is also widely used in public opinion polls, election predictions, consumer market studies, and population censuses.

With an understanding of the general goal of descriptive research and some of its specific purposes, let us now turn to the more pragmatic question of how descriptive research is conducted. The descriptive researcher follows the systematic, sequential process discussed in Chapters 1 and 2. He or she must be concerned with the theoretical basis of the investigation, should follow the norms of the research community, and must proceed through each step of the research process from discovering the problem to writing and disseminating the research report.

The descriptive researcher has available some specific techniques, however, for collecting data. Descriptive data-collection techniques fall into three general categories: surveys, interviews, and observations. Each category represents a certain tool, means, or method for gathering information. Some descriptive research studies combine elements of two or all three of these categories. Some investigators, for example, will conduct interviews prior to launching a survey. A researcher may observe a phenomenon and then interview participants in the phenomenon to gain additional, in-depth information. Techniques from each of these categories can be used as sequential steps in the collection of information. We use these three general categories as a classification device to aid in our explanation of these tools and to allow the reader to compare and contrast the different techniques.

SURVEYS

A survey is a technique for gathering information, in writing, directly from those individuals who possess the information. Sometimes the term *questionnaire* is used synonymously with the word *survey*. Most researchers, however, use *questionnaire* to refer to a written list of questions and reserve the term *survey* for the larger process of collecting information through the use of a questionnaire. The questionnaire is seen as the tool, whereas a survey refers to the development, administration, and analysis of the questionnaire.

In our discussion of the survey as a research technique, we will examine the conditions that are appropriate to conducting a survey, the criteria for choosing possible respondents, incentives for insuring an adequate response rate, guidelines for constructing questionnaires, cover letters and follow-up letters, and suggestions for arranging, printing, duplicating, and disseminating questionnaires.

When is it Appropriate to Conduct a Survey?

If you are unsure whether a survey would be the appropriate technique for gathering information concerning your research problem, ask yourself this question: "Can I obtain the necessary information through any other means?" If your answer is yes, then perhaps you should not be conducting a survey. Most surveys are time-consuming and costly. They represent an inconvenience to respondents. A respondent will resent providing information that is readily accessible through other means. Consider this hypothetical example: A researcher wishes to investigate speech-communication graduate programs in the United States. She mails questionnaires to the chairperson of every university that offers a graduate degree in speech communication. Assume she asks each respondent to indicate number of graduate faculty members: their names, ranks, and degree-granting institutions; and the titles and descriptions of graduate courses offered by that department. Should this researcher have been using the survey method? No. An easier, less costly, and quicker method for gaining this information would be to examine graduate college catalogs. A week or so spent reading catalogs at the university library would be preferable to conducting a national mail survey to collect this information. By failing to evaluate the appropriateness of the survey method to this research problem, our hypothetical investigator has needlessly spent a large sum of money, foolishly wasted valuable time, and inconsiderately alienated professional colleagues.

The point is that public records and documents often contain the information we need. Documents we may not be aware of may contain the data that we fallaciously assume should be collected through a survey. Before deciding on a survey check out all possible resources. Ask colleagues, librarians, and officials of target organizations whether such records exist. We should ask people to complete questionnaires only when those individuals are the sole keepers of the data, as is the case when we want to know their personal attitudes or intentions.

Time and money are other considerations in determining the appropriateness of the survey method. National or international surveys, in particular, take time and cost money. A local or regional mail survey, or one in which questionnaires are personally administered to an assembled group of individuals, may not be as costly or as time consuming. If you do not have or cannot acquire the time or money that your survey requires, you would be well advised to revise your research design and use an alternate method of data collection.

Choosing Survey Respondents

Once you have decided to collect data through a survey, you must determine who will be surveyed. Ideally, this would be every person to whom the research question applies. If we were able to question each and every relevant individual, then we would be in a position to make a very accurate description of the phenomenon under study. Suppose we want to determine which candidate the voters intend to elect in an upcoming election. If we assume that individuals' reported intentions accurately correspond to their subsequent behavior, then surveying every potential voter would allow us to make a precise and correct prediction of the election outcome. But obviously, the cost and effort of such a survey would be prohibitive. Our task, then, becomes one of choosing a more reasonable number of voters to represent the total population of voters. We choose a sample (a smaller number of cases) whose answers represent the responses of the larger population (the total number of cases). Choosing this subset of cases to represent the total group is called sampling.

Several considerations are involved in sampling. One concern is the number in the sample. In this case, we would ask, "What is the minimum number of people we could survey to arrive at a potentially accurate prediction of the election outcome?" Common sense would tell us that questioning ten people would not allow us to put much faith in our prediction. Would twenty, fifty, one hundred, five hundred, or one thousand people increase the accuracy of our prediction? Unfortunately, there are no absolute answers to this question, since we are dealing in the realm of probability. The topic of sampling is discussed in Chapter 7, but we mention it here to emphasize that it is a question that frequently faces the descriptive researcher.

A second issue facing the survey researcher is representativeness of the sample. We must decide who we will survey. If we question all the members of a church group concerning their voting intentions, we may get a different prediction than if we questioned the members of a business organization. Sampling eighteen-year-olds may provide different data than sampling sixty-year-olds. Questioning Republicans and Democrats probably would result in two very different outcomes. Males may report different intentions than females; lower socioeconomic groups may differ from upper socioeconomic groups.

The basic problem is to determine what characteristics the individuals in the sample must possess to be representative of the larger population. One solution would be to survey people at random, assuming that a random sample would insure fairly equal numbers of men and women, old and young, rich and poor, Republicans and Democrats. As indicated, these sampling concerns are discussed in greater detail in Chapter 7. Survey researchers should familiarize themselves with these issues. It is difficult to make valid descriptions of the status quo without thoroughly understanding the assumptions and techniques of sampling.

Sometimes the researcher can survey every member of the population under study. Suppose a minister wanted to determine the audience's attitudes toward the sermon he just delivered. Rather than questioning a portion of the audience and inferring the entire audience's attitudes from the sample, the minister could distribute a questionnaire to the entire audience. This survey would take little time, would cost little money, and would provide data from the entire target population. Assuming the individuals answered honestly, the minister could make an accurate statement of the audience's attitudes without having to deal with questions of sample size and representativeness.

Incentives for Insuring an Adequate Response Rate

Whether the researcher surveys a sample as representative of the population or questions every member of the particular population, he or she faces the task of generating cooperation from possible respondents. When using the survey method, responsibility is placed on the individuals surveyed. In the data-collection stage, the survey researcher is at the mercy of others. If no one responds, the researcher collects no data. If potential respondents who are sole possessors of the desired information are unwilling or unable to provide that information, the research project comes to a standstill. Unlike the documentary or library researcher, who has the responsibility of discovering the data, the survey researcher is dependent on others' willingness and cooperation in providing the data. Thus, the survey researcher must furnish incentives or inducements to potential respondents. These incentives vary somewhat depending on the purpose and the topic of the survey, the nature of potential respondents, and the procedures of organizing and disseminating the questionnaire.

Let us first examine how the purpose and topic of the survey relate to response incentives. If the purpose of the survey seems important, relevant, or salient to respondents, they will be more likely to supply the necessary information. If the purpose, in their perception, is insignificant or unimportant, they may feel that answering the survey is a waste of their time. A topic that is interesting and that relates to the lives of respondents will generate more response than a boring, irrelevant, or seemingly trivial one. The difficulty lies, however, in discrepant perceptions of researcher and respondent. Most researchers feel their studies are valuable, interesting, and significant. What researcher will admit that his or her study is trivial? A questionnaire topic that seems inherently interesting and valuable to the researcher may not generate such perceptions among those surveyed. The researcher must create these positive perceptions in respondents. He or she must persuade possible respondents that it is in their best interest, worthwhile to them or to society at large, and important that they respond.

The nature, characteristics, or identities of potential respondents also affect the survey response rate. Certain individuals have a greater understanding of and respect for the need for research. Anyone who previously has conducted research should have empathy for researchers. We would expect this commonality of experience to generate increased cooperation from potential respondents. Yet, some individuals are skeptical of anyone who seeks to ask them questions. They may regard a survey as threatening or as an invasion of their privacy.

It is not easy to determine what types of people typically do or do not respond to surveys, but it is felt that respondents and nonrespondents differ on a number of dimensions. A recent study of demographic characteristics of nonrespondents to speech-communication surveys showed that respondents differ from nonrespondents in terms of sex, academic rank, educational degree, teaching area, academic affiliation, and experience.[2]

People do differ in the strength of their needs. This need-fulfillment characteristic also affects whether they respond or fail to respond to surveys. Gorden states several response incentives that appeal to certain individual needs.[3]

1. Recognition. A respondent may be flattered to think that he or she is recognized for having some information that someone else needs.
2. Altruism. Since human beings often identify with causes, they may be motivated out of a sense of helping.
3. New experience. As a means of experiencing the novel, respondents may be motivated out of a sense of curiosity.
4. Catharsis. Respondents may be motivated to cooperate from a need to verbalize their feelings, disclose their attitudes, or "air their gripes."
5. Extrinsic rewards. A desire to get money, a free gift, a copy of the research results, or some other direct benefit from the study may motivate respondents.

The format of the questionnaire and the means of its dissemination also affect the response rate. The researcher can provide incentives in the way he or she designs and disseminates the questionnaire. Anything the researcher can do to minimize inconvenience to respondents acts as an inducement to respond. The shorter the questionnaire, the more likely the response. Neatness and professional appearance of the questionnaire increases the likelihood of response. Questions that are clearly and concisely worded, multiple-choice answers that are easily understood and require little or no elaboration, and directions that are explicit and helpful facilitate response.

If the survey is disseminated through the mail, it should be addressed to a specific individual whenever possible and should include a stamped, self-addressed envelope. The researcher should consider the time of the year when conducting surveys. Surveying college professors during the summer may significantly decrease the response rate. When questioning individuals associated with business organizations, income-tax time may be less than ideal. Surveying the general public on or near major holidays would not be recommended.

The researcher should also provide survey respondents with a deadline for submitting their completed questionnaires. Approximately two weeks is a reasonable amount of time, but this may vary depending on the length of the questionnaire and the types of answers desired. Most survey researchers use some type of follow-up contact (letter, postcard, telephone call) after the deadline to induce those who have not responded to reply.

As we discuss the specifics of designing, wording, arranging, and administering questionnaires, we will provide additional information relating to response incentives, including details of wording cover and follow-up letters. Virtually every decision in the process of surveying should be made with an eye toward response rate. A research study is only as good as the information that is collected. Even the most significant or sophisticated studies are rendered worthless if insufficient or inadequate data are collected.

You may be asking yourself, "What is an adequate response rate? How do I calculate response rate?" Response rate is the ratio between the number of usable questionnaires returned and the number of reachable respondents sampled. Some sampled respondents are never reached because they have died or have moved. In a mail survey, you frequently get unopened questionnaires returned with the notation "Insufficient Address," "Addressee Unknown," or "Addressee Deceased." These returns should be subtracted from the total number in the sample. Suppose you mail 1000 questionnaires, receive 50 undelivered returns, 20 incomplete questionnaires, and 465 returned, usable questionnaires. You would compute the response rate in the following manner:

$$
\begin{array}{r}
1000 \quad \text{TOTAL SAMPLE} \\
- \quad 50 \quad \text{UNDELIVERED} \\
- \quad 20 \quad \text{INCOMPLETE} \\
\hline
930
\end{array}
$$

$$465 \div 930 = 50\% \text{ RESPONSE RATE}$$

There is no absolute cut-off point for determining an adequate response rate. What is considered acceptable may depend on the purpose of the study, the type of survey, and the nature of the population being investigated. In an exploratory study, for example, enough data to indicate patterns or trends may suffice to meet the research purpose. At the other extreme, the descriptive researcher whose results may decide widespread and costly policy changes may want a very high response rate before making such decisions.

Some researchers have suggested general guidelines for determining the adequacy of response rate. We offer these guidelines, proposed by Lin, as a basis for your judgments.[4]

50 percent or higher is adequate
60 percent or higher is good
75 percent or higher is very good

Guidelines for Constructing Questionnaires

Constructing a questionnaire requires careful planning, for this is the means by which you translate research objectives into specific questions, the answers to which provide the data for testing research hypotheses. In this section, we will discuss types of questions, the wording and sequencing of questions, and instructions to respondents.

Types of Questions. There are two basic types of questions: open and closed. Open questions are broad and basically unstructured. They simply indicate the topic and let the respondent structure the answer as he or she sees fit. The respondent provides a written statement, paragraph, or essay in answer to the question. Examples of open questions include:

Please describe your reaction to the speech you just heard.
What communication skills does your job require?
Please state three major leadership problems facing this group.

Closed questions greatly narrow the respondent's range of possible answers. They not only state the specific topic but also include an exhaustive list of mutually exclusive alternatives from which the respondent chooses the appropriate answer. Alternatives may be of the yes-no or multiple-choice type. Examples of closed questions include:

Which of the following best describes your reaction to the speech you just heard?
_____ extremely favorable
_____ moderately favorable
_____ neutral
_____ moderately unfavorable
_____ extremely unfavorable

Please indicate which of the following communication skills are required in your job. (You may check as many answers as applicable.)
_____ interviewing   _____ public speaking
_____ leadership   _____ assertiveness
_____ group decision-making   _____ conflict management
_____ persuasion   _____ public relations

Have you ever taken a leadership training course?
_____ yes   _____ no

Open questions usually require more time for the respondent to answer, but they are likely to generate a more in-depth answer. Open questions take little time to create but are difficult to tabulate. Closed questions are more difficult to formulate, but they are easier and quicker for respondents to answer and require less time to tabulate. Closed questions may help to keep the respondent on the subject, but they assume a certain knowledge base on the part of respondents and may overly restrict the respondent's answer.

Each type of question has its advantages and disadvantages. In an effort to provide response incentives and to facilitate the tabulation process, researchers frequently opt for closed questions. Some questions, however, require an open-ended format simply because the researcher cannot imagine or cannot list all possible answers. Asking a respondent to list the textbooks used in a particular course, for example, would be more practical than generating an exhaustive list of all possible textbooks for a multiple-choice answer. Open questions can be used in an exploratory or pilot study to generate response alternatives for a subsequent closed-format questionnaire. Many researchers use a majority of closed questions and include a few open questions for those answers that cannot be determined any other way. Sometimes marketing researchers or psychologists prefer open-ended responses that can be analyzed for underlying motivations, needs, fears, or anxieties. They feel that open questions can subtly reveal things that the respondent may be unwilling or unable to indicate consciously. As a survey researcher, your choices of open or closed questions must be personal decisions, guided by considering the purpose of the question, the nature of the respondent, and projections of response rate.

Wording of Questions. Regardless of whether you use open or closed questions or a combination of the two, you must word each question carefully to avoid ambiguity, double-barreled items, negatives, leading language, and socially desirable responses. Clarity is of prime importance in questionnaires. What seems clear to you as researcher may not be clear to respondents. Consider this question: "How frequently is the student evaluated in this course?" Even if the response alternatives include such items as "Every class period," "Twice a week," "Once a week," and "Once every other week," this question is still ambiguous. The first alternative is meaningless unless we know how many times a week the class meets. Nor is this the only ambiguity. Do we want to know about written or oral evaluation, or both? Do we mean teacher or peer evaluation, or both? Perhaps this question would be clearer if it were divided into four separate questions. To insure clarity, use technical language or jargon only when you are certain that the respondent will understand it. Use a list of synonyms for potentially ambiguous words and define your terms as much as possible. We suggest that when wording questions you proceed through several drafts, refining the question until it is clear and measures exactly what you want it to measure. Get feedback from others regarding the clarity of the question. Administer the final draft of the questionnaire to a subset of your sample to get further suggestions regarding clarity. If respondents do not attach the same meaning to a question as you intended, then your data become meaningless.

A double-barreled question is two or more questions disguised as one. A clue to a possible double-barreled question is the word "and." Examine these double-barreled questions:

What is your attitude toward evaluation and grading in communication courses?
Do you believe in and participate in consciousness-raising groups?
How frequently do you self-disclose to your spouse and children?

These examples demonstrate the response difficulties involved in double-barreled questions.

As you probably recall from taking course examinations, questions that include negatives often are confusing. The respondent has to study or ponder the following sample questions and alternatives, for example, to determine the appropriate answer.

Please indicate which of the following channels of communication you do not use in your job·

———— memos   ———— face-to-face

———— telephone   ———— bulletin boards

(*Note:* Asking which channels they *do* use would provide identical information.)

Which of the following statements does not represent your teaching philosophy?

———— Students learn by doing   ———— Grading should be abolished

———— Punishment does not motivate   ———— A teacher should model com-

———— students   munication skills

(*Note:* Including negative items creates confusion; asking which statements *do* reflect one's philosophy would provide identical information.)

Leading questions bias the respondent toward a particular answer. They may contain grammatical structures, hyperbole, or emotionally loaded words that suggest to the respondent that one answer is more appropriate than another. Examine the following leading questions:

Don't you believe that television is affecting communication in the family?

(*Note:* The word *don't* obviously biases respondents to an affirmative answer.)

Do you favor wage and price controls as a means of reducing inflation? (*Note:* By linking wage and price controls to a desired outcome, the question leads respondents to an affirmative answer.)

What is your attitude toward radical women's liberationists? (*Note: Radical* is hyperbolic and *women's liberationist* is an emotionally charged term, leading respondents to a negative attitude.)

Social desirability is another biasing factor in the wording of questions. On some issues society conditions us to believe that certain reactions, feelings, beliefs, or behaviors are unacceptable. Socially desirable questions lead the respondent to feel that a particular answer is expected, morally sound, or ethically perferred. Examine the following socially desirable questions:

Which of your parents was more supportive of your career goals?

———— Mother   ———— Both

———— Father   ———— Neither

(*Note:* A respondent may be reluctant to choose one parent over another or may feel guilty in making the underlying assumption that the parents were deficient.)

Do you use manipulation when communicating with your spouse?

(*Note:* Because of the negative connotation of manipulation, respondents may be reluctant to perceive or admit such a practice.)

What television shows do you watch regularly?

(*Note:* Respondents may report more viewing of news and documentary shows and less viewing of cartoons and situation comedies because of an assumed societal negative evaluation of their actual viewing habits.)

Sequencing of Questions. In addition to considering the wording of questions, you must decide on proper sequencing of questions. A questionnaire that jumps from one subject to another burdens respondents. The organization and sequencing of a questionnaire also can influence a respondent's level of cooperation, thereby affecting the overall response rate of the survey.

Related questions should be grouped together in a questionnaire. This facilitates the respondent's train of thought and reduces the amount of time needed to complete the questionnaire. Subheadings similar to what we are using in this book facilitate comprehension. Questions in a pedagogical survey, for example, could be organized under the subheadings of "Teaching philosophy," "Topics," "Methods," "Materials," "Evaluation," and "Grading." Similar questions are grouped together and the subheadings signal the respondent to a subject change. A guiding principle in organizing the questionnaire is to arrange the questions into sections that make the most sense to respondents.

Some researchers suggest that the sequencing of questions is closely related to a subject's willingness to respond. Lin, for example, proposes putting easy and less sensitive questions at the beginning of the questionnaire, since these will "hook" the respondent into answering. Once an individual has answered some of the questions, he or she has made a commitment to respond and the chances of his or her completing the entire questionnaire are improved.[5] Best recommends arranging questions from the general to the specific so that answers proceed logically from little to more depth and difficulty.[6] Other suggestions include using easy but interesting questions at the beginning and at the end of a questionnaire, with the more difficult, less interesting, or sensitive questions sandwiched in the middle. Thus, the respondent receives early incentives to answer and finishes the questionnaire on a positive note.

Whatever your decision concerning sequencing, keep in mind that the organization of the questionnaire should make sense to respondents, should minimize the time, effort, and thought required of them, and should provide incentives for them to complete the entire questionnaire.

Instructions to Respondents. In addition to considering the wording, sequencing, and organizing of questions, the researcher must include in the questionnaire directions or instructions to respondents. The questionnaire should include directions at the beginning, whenever the subject shifts, and whenever the method of answering changes. Initial instructions should convey the importance of answering all applicable questions, should indicate the type of answer desired (*Indicate your first, immediate reaction,* for example), and should explain how answers are to be recorded (*Circle, Check, Place an X, Darken the appropriate line on the answer sheet*).

A simple statement should also be included to orient respondents to a change of subject within the questionnaire. Statements such as the following can be included wherever applicable:

This next section deals with your attitudes toward your supervisor.
The following ten questions relate to your daily communication activities.
Now would you please think about the political advertising you have seen on television.

It is especially important to include additional instructions when the respondent must vary the method of recording answers. If the respondent has been circling the appropriate answers and then comes to a rank-order question that does not include instructions for the method of response, he or she is apt to become confused. A simple statement can clear up misunderstanding: "Please rank (1 = high, 5 = low) the importance of the following skills in your job." Instructions throughout the questionnaire clarify the respondent's task, provide transitions to increase understanding, and maximize respondent cooperation.

Guidelines for Cover Letters and Follow-up Letters

Besides constructing the actual questionnaire, the survey researcher must be skilled at writing cover letters and follow-up letters. The cover letter that accompanies a mail questionnaire must introduce the researcher, explain the purpose of the survey, instruct respondents in the method of answering and returning the questionnaire, and provide the response incentives discussed earlier. Your letter is your main persuasive device to induce respondents to provide the data you need. A survey cover letter should establish rapport with the potential respondent and should answer all the questions he or she may be contemplating. The following information is typically included in a survey cover letter.

1. Introduction. Identify yourself and your institutional affiliation. Using your organization's letterhead stationery will enhance your credibility.
2. Sponsorship. Indicate if your survey is commissioned, sponsored, endorsed, or assisted by a particular individual or group that corresponds to or differs from your institutional affiliation. For example, you may introduce yourself as J. Doe from the Speech-Communication Department at Strivemore University but indicate the survey is sponsored by the Communication Association of America. Make sure the sponsoring organization agrees with the wording of this statement. Two of these authors once had an organization change the wording of our cover letter from "...with the sponsorship of ..." to "...with the assistance of ...," the latter statement indicating a lesser level of support. Being able to affiliate your survey with some well-known, credible group is likely to increase the response rate. Remember, though, that you cannot use an individual's or an organization's name unless they give you permission to do so.
3. Purpose of survey. Give a general overview of your research objective and indicate why the survey is being conducted. You may want to avoid disclosing

the specific research purpose, since such knowledge may bias respondents' answers. Rather than stating a false or disguised purpose, however, state the real purpose in general terms. Surely you can provide some truthful information regarding the survey's purpose without "tipping your hand." In this aspect of the cover letter, you can provide response incentives by showing the significance of the survey, the long-range benefits to potential respondents, or the general positive implications for the social system.

4. Criteria for selection of respondent. A frequent reaction of individuals to a survey is "Why me?, How did you get my name?" The researcher should tell respondents how or why they were selected, whether it be through random sampling, through a certain mailing list, because of their position in an organization or membership in a group, or because they possess a certain characteristic.

5. Uses to be made of the data. Is the study conducted for a thesis or dissertation? Will the results be published? Who will see the data? Will the data be used to make policy decisions? This aspect of the cover letter is akin to the purpose and objectives of the study, but it provides more specific information. Respondents have a right to know how their answers will be used.

6. Confidentiality or anonymity. Many people are reluctant to provide, in writing, information about their attitudes, beliefs, values, or behavior. This is especially true if the survey deals with controversial, sensitive, or private issues. Respondents' answers are anonymous if their names cannot be associated with the information they provide. We suggest that unless you have to know the name of the respondent for some reason, do not ask for it. You most likely will receive a higher response rate if the individual is completely anonymous. If anonymity is part of your survey, point this out in the cover letter. Confidentiality is not the same as anonymity. Confidentiality means that you, as researcher, can associate a respondent's name with his or her answers, but you promise not to reveal that association to anyone else. By emphasizing the promise of confidentiality in the cover letter, you can eliminate a possible reason for not responding.

7. Appeal for cooperation. Although all of these aspects of the cover letter are inducements for cooperation, a direct appeal to respondents also can be included. You can indicate the approximate amount of time the respondent needs to complete the questionnaire, suggest a deadline for returning the questionnaire, briefly explain the method for completing and mailing the questionnaire, and then ask for his or her assistance.

8. Expression of gratitude. Common courtesy would suggest that you thank the respondent for his or her assistance. You also can express your appreciation by promising a copy of the results if you actually intend to distribute those results to respondents.

As indicated in the discussion of response incentives, you may wish to make follow-up contact, after the deadline date, with those individuals who have neglected to respond. This may be accomplished through a telephone call, postcard, or letter. Such follow-up notices must be worded tactfully so that they increase the likelihood of response without alienating the individual. Do not explicitly reprimand or demand. Rather, indicate that you have not yet received the completed questionnaire, acknowledge that they may have misplaced their copy, send a second copy, and politely ask for its completion. Then thank them in advance for their cooperation. Subtle prodding as opposed to obvious pushing in the follow-up notice is likely to generate a significantly higher additional response.

Arranging, Printing, Duplicating, and Disseminating the Questionnaire

The researcher must pay attention to the format and arrangement of the questionnaire to create a credible and professional appearance. As with a resumé, the appearance of the questionnaire sells it. If it looks sloppy, crowded, or confusing, the potential respondent will not even read it. It should have uniform margins, abundant white space, obvious headings, and sufficient space for response. Whenever possible, have questionnaires professionally printed on quality paper. The black ink of stencils is preferable to the purple ink of ditto masters. All copies of the questionnaire should be darkly printed and easily readable. Even the details of folding the questionnaires, placing them in envelopes, and sealing and addressing the envelopes cannot be overemphasized. Any aspect of the survey process that contributes to a sloppy or unprofessional appearance will decrease an individual's desire to respond. In both content and format, the questionnaire, cover letter, and follow-up letter should reflect a dedicated, professional, and considerate descriptive researcher.

INTERVIEWS

The interview method of data collection is similar to the survey in that it gathers information directly from those individuals who possess it. The main difference is that the interview relies on oral contact with respondents. Goyer, Redding, and Rickey define the interview as "two people, one of whom has a distinct purpose, and both of whom speak and listen from time to time."[7] The interview, as a descriptive research tool, may use face-to-face contact or telephone as a means of communication. In either case, an individual acting as interviewer has written a list of questions that he or she orally administers to a second individual who acts as interviewee by orally providing answers to the questions. The interview is a type of oral questionnaire.

In our discussion of the interview as a research technique, we will examine conditions appropriate to conducting interviews, guidelines for choosing interviewees, incentives for inducing interviewee cooperation, mechanics of constructing interview questions, and suggestions for training interviewers. Many of these topics are similar to the consideration involved in administering questionnaires. Since interviews are akin to oral surveys, much of the information from the previous sections of this chapter is applicable here.

When is it Appropriate to Conduct Interviews?

The criteria are the same as suggested to the researcher who is considering a questionnaire: If the interview is the only or the best means of acquiring the information, then use the interview method. Interviews may be preferable to written questionnaires, depending on the research objective, the specific content and types of questions to be included, and the nature of respondents. Under what circumstances is the interview likely to be the most desirable research tool?

If you need complete or detailed answers to questions, the interview would be advantageous. It would also be the preferable method if you need a high response rate; expect respondents to have difficulty in reading, understanding, interpreting, or answering questions; want to insure that respondents do not collaborate with others in answering questions; want spontaneous reactions; or want to observe the respondent's nonverbal behavior.[8] Some researchers prefer the interview when asking sensitive or embarrassing questions, since the interviewer can establish rapport, put the person at ease, or explain the need for such information. Other researchers feel the presence of the interviewer may inhibit the disclosure of such information. Whether an individual is more likely to provide sensitive information in a questionnaire or in an interview has not yet been resolved.

Interviews usually are more costly and more time consuming than questionnaires. Whether they are conducted face to face or by telephone, interviews cost money. The interview researcher frequently incurs long-distance telephone charges and the expenses of interviewer training, travel, and salaries. Although the mail-survey method requires time to distribute questionnaires, wait for replies, make follow-up contact, and wait for additional response, the interview method frequently takes even more time. Interviewers must be trained, they spend time trying to contact potential respondents, interviewers can question only one person at a given time, and they must record, transcribe, or code the interviewee's answers. The interview usually results in more complete, usable data because the interviewer can persuade the respondent to cooperate, allay fears, make sure all questions are answered, and probe for thorough answers. The interview method has its advantages and disadvantages, and the researcher must weigh these in deciding the appropriateness of the interview to his or her research project.

Choosing Interviewees

Occasionally the researcher can interview all the members of a population, as when questioning all the employees of an organization, all the students of a particular course, or all the participants in a certain event. In these cases, the researcher eliminates the task of choosing interviewees. But just as it may be impossible to administer a questionnaire to every member of a population, it may not be feasible to interview all the members of a given population. Thus, the researcher who employs the interview method frequently faces the same issues of sample size and sample representativeness as the researcher using the survey. The researcher can choose interviewees by randomly dialing telephone numbers, visiting homes, or stopping people on the street. Sometimes the researcher wants to reach interviewees who possess certain characteristics relevant to the study. Calling people at random to determine why they buy a certain product, for example, may result in the contacting of hundreds of people who have never heard of the product or do not purchase the product. It may be advantageous for such a researcher to choose interviewees at the grocery store once they have purchased the product.

Some researchers seek to interview a set number of people in various categories. Imagine that you are conducting a study designed to examine the relationship of sex and age to attitudes toward educational television. You might want to interview, say, thirty males between the ages of twenty and forty and thirty males age forty-one to sixty, as well as thirty females in each of these categories. Finding the interviewees who fit these demographic specifications creates additional criteria for the selection of respondents. You would have to ask the potential respondent if he or she fits into the necessary category before proceeding with the interview.

In short, the issues involved in choosing interviewees may include determining appropriate means, methods, or locations for finding respondents, determining whether respondents have the necessary relevant characteristics, deciding on an adequate sample size, and insuring that sampled respondents are representative of the larger population.

Incentives for Inducing Interviewee Cooperation

Many of the same incentives that were suggested for survey research apply to the interview method. Relevance of purpose, interest of topic, and appeals to individual needs can facilitate an interviewee's cooperation. Although the response incentives for the two types of research are the same, the methods of communicating these incentives to subjects differ. Incentives in a survey frequently appear in the cover letter or in the design and format of the questionnaire itself. In the interview method, the interviewer bears the burden of creating response incentives. The appearance that interviewers make, the ways they introduce themselves, the communication climates they create, and their techniques of asking questions all affect interviewees' willingness to cooperate.

When using face-to-face contact, the interviewer should dress similarly to the respondent and should approximate the respondent's vocabulary level. At the same time, however, the interviewer must appear neat, professional, credible, and intelligent. We stress that the interviewer appear somewhat similar to the respondent. This creates identification, trust, and a comfortable climate. Imagine the reaction of a ghetto respondent, for example, to an interviewer who drives up in a Mercedes Benz, wears a suit, and uses language that is foreign to the respondent. This interviewer probably would encounter difficulty gaining admittance into the respondent's home, not to mention problems in getting the respondent to cooperate in answering questions.

The way in which interviewers introduce themselves to respondents is a crucial aspect of gaining cooperation, in both face-to-face and telephone interviews. The interviewer should identify himself or herself, state the organizational affiliation, and discuss the importance of the purpose of the interview. He or she should tell respondents why they were selected, state the approximate amount of time needed to conduct the interview, assure them of anonymity or confidentiality, and ask them to participate. While imparting all of this information, the interviewer also must be establishing rapport with the respondents, reducing their suspicions and creating a climate where they will feel comfortable and so provide honest and thorough answers.

The climate is established even before the interview begins, and it affects the entire interview. Many individuals are suspicious or fearful of a stranger who telephones them, visits them, or stops them on the street to ask questions. The interviewer must allay these fears or suspicions and make the individual feel safe and comfortable in answering all questions. Interviewees must not feel that their answers will be evaluated or that their egos will be threatened.

Once the interviewee agrees to cooperate, the interviewer must ask the questions in an organized, fluent, pleasant, and skilled manner. Otherwise, the respondent will break off the interview or provide superficial or inadequate answers to end the session as quickly as possible. We suggest that interviewers carefully plan and practice response incentives that suit the specific research topic, interview questions, and respondent characteristics.

Constructing the Interview Schedule of Questions

The interview schedule includes the list of questions to be asked and any necessary instructions for the interviewer. As in survey questionnaires, you must be concerned with clarity, objectivity, and the proper sequencing of questions. Most interviews contain either open or closed questions, a combination of the two, or probing questions. Probes are used to stimulate discussion and to obtain additional information. They "motivate the interviewee to communicate more fully so that he or she enlarges, clarifies, or explains reasons underlying responses made previously. Probes allow the interviewer to follow up on superficial responses by directing the thinking of the interviewee to further aspects of the topic."[9] Examples of probing questions include:

Could you elaborate on that answer?
Why is that?
You say that you dislike the product? (*Note:* paraphrasing or mirror responses frequently bring about elaboration from the respondent)

Although clear, easily understood questions are important, should a respondent misunderstand a question, the interviewer will recognize the confusion and can provide the necessary explanation. This does not mean you can overlook the issue of clarity, however. A good interview question should need no explanation. If an interviewer has to explain questions, the interview takes more time, there is more opportunity for biasing responses, and the interviewee is more likely to feel inadequate and frustrated.

Objectivity is a vital concern in the interview process, for the presence of an interviewer orally questioning, listening, and recording responses introduces potential bias into the situation. Questions must be written so as to avoid double-barreled items, negative wording, leading language, and socially desirable responses; moreover, the researcher must insure objectivity in the ways that interviewers ask questions. This issue will be discussed in the next section of this chapter.

Sequencing of questions is also a concern in constructing interview schedules. The interview researcher can control the sequence of questions to a greater extent than the survey researcher can. The interviewer, because he or she is asking the questions, controls the fact that a certain question is answered before or after another. The respondent must answer the questions in the order in which they are asked: the survey respondent can skip questions and return to them later. Like the survey researcher, the interview researcher faces the issues of logical sequencing of questions, reducing inconvenience to respondents, strategically placing sensitive items, and arranging questions in a way that makes the most sense to respondents.

Besides containing the actual questions, the interview schedule frequently includes instructions to the interviewer. Examples of such instructions may include:

Note the respondent's nonverbal communication.
Refer to question 3 before asking this question.

Such instructions should be printed in bold-face type or should be put in parentheses to eliminate any confusion for the interviewer. Just as the novice actor who recites stage directions ruins a performance, the interviewer who reads aloud his or her instructions dooms the interview to failure.

Training Interviewers

Training interviewers is a highly important aspect of the interview method. In large-scale research projects, interviewers frequently are hired assistants who have little understanding, knowledge, interest, or motivation concerning the research project. Without thorough training, interviewers constitute a weak link that undermines a strong chain of research steps. Interviewer training should accomplish three general objectives; it should (1) provide an overview of the total research project, including the interviewer's relationship to other phases of the investigation; (2) motivate the interviewer; and (3) impart communication skills. Training sessions seek to impart the following characteristics to interviewers:[10]

1. Honesty
2. Interest in the work and the topic
3. Ability to follow instructions
4. Adaptability in working with different people

5. A pleasant attitude
6. Communication skills
7. A professional appearance

More specifically, the researcher must train interviewers to develop skills in generating respondent cooperation, standardizing interviews, recording responses, and following ethical responsibilities.

Since interviewers determine whether respondents cooperate, they must understand and must practice techniques of appealing to respondents. Introductions must be rehearsed, yet they still should sound spontaneous and personal. Teaching interviewers how to achieve standardization across interviews is necessary to eliminate bias and to insure the validity of the data. By *standardization,* we mean that all aspects of the interviewer's behavior are as identical as possible from one interview to the next and from one interviewer to the next.

If the same interviewer or two different interviewers behave differently with each respondent, then any differences in the data are apt to reflect variations in interviewer style rather than actual distinctions in individuals' answers. Introductions, the wording of questions, tone of voice, facial expressions, the phrasing of probes, and the details of explanations must be fairly consistent across all interviews. Examine the following feedback responses and imagine the different effects each response would have on the interviewee's subsequent behavior:

"Uh, hum (nonverbal signs of disinterest). Could you elaborate?"
"Yes, I understand (smile and head nod). Could you elaborate?"
"Yes, I agree completely (nonverbal signs of enthusiasm). Could you elaborate?"

Interviewers must be trained to ask questions exactly as they are worded on the interview schedule, to control verbal and nonverbal biasing cues, and to use standard probes and explanations. It is ironic that interviewers must adapt to different interviewees while maintaining consistency in their behavior. Discussion of the importance of standardization will develop in interviewers a sense of consistency. Some actual role-playing practice will develop the skills for maintaining consistency while appearing spontaneous and personable.

The researcher must train interviewers to record answers accurately and thoroughly. Answers may be tape-recorded or hand-transcribed. Although tape recorders provide thorough and accurate representations of answers, their presence may inhibit interviewees. To satisfy legal requirements, a respondent must give permission to have his or her answers recorded on tape. When tape recorders are used, someone—either the interviewer, researcher, or research assistants—then must listen to the tapes and summarize, transcribe, or code answers for data analysis purposes.

When tape recorders are not used, the interviewer writes down the subject's answer as it evolves. Most researchers suggest that the entire answer be written down verbatim in shorthand or using other abbreviation techniques. The interviewer must be skilled at recording the entire answer quickly lest he or she frustrate the respondent by taking a great deal of time between questions. If the interview schedule consists entirely of closed questions, then noting answers is not much of a problem. But when open questions are used, interviewers must be trained in recording responses.

Summarizing a respondent's answer introduces possible bias, for a summary necessarily highlights certain details and omits others. Two interviewers may listen to the same open-ended response and interpret it differently, thereby providing very different summaries. If you plan to employ the summary technique, have interviewers practice summarizing so that their summaries accurately reflect the original information.

Keep in mind that some studies require more specific information than others. The purpose of your research and the intended uses of the data should guide your decision to use tape recording, hand transcribing, or summarizing of interview responses.

A final consideration in training interviewers involves ethical issues. These will not be discussed at length, as Chapter 11 deals with the ethics of research. However, there are certain ethical guidelines that we feel should be discussed during interviewer training sessions. As in any discussion of ethics, the decision to accept or reject these issues lies with the individual. We offer for your consideration this list of interview practices that we consider to be unethical:[11]

1. Interviewers should not add details to incomplete responses because of their failure to probe.
2. Interviewers should not fill in the occasional missing answers.
3. Interviewers should not complete an entire schedule for an imaginary respondent (*Note:* This can happen when interviewer motivation is poor, when salary is low, or when time pressures exist.)
4. Interviewers should not bias responses through tone of voice, facial expressions, verbal feedback, or deviations in wording.
5. Interviewers should not coerce respondents to participate.
6. Interviewers should not violate promises of anonymity or confidentiality.
7. Interviewers should not deceive respondents about their identity, sponsoring organization, or research purposes.

OBSERVATIONS

The third general category of descriptive research involves observation. The observation method gathers data through systematic watching, studying, or interpreting the source of the data. The source may be an individual, a group, or a document.

Within the rubric of observational techniques, we will discuss case studies, content analyses, interaction analyses, relational analyses, network analyses, and naturalistic inquiry. You might question grouping these techniques together, for at first glance they seem more dissimilar than similar. Case studies seem much less systematic than content, interaction, or relational analysis. Content analysis usually examines written documents and is frequently associated with historical rather than descriptive research. Interaction analysis involves the observation of individuals who communicate orally through face-to-face channels. Relational analysis codes sequential messages and determines patterns of relationship control. Network analysis describes a set of relationships among parts of a system, and naturalistic inquiry uses unstructured observations to discover individuals' means of constructing social reality. All these techniques are similar, however, in that they can be used to describe the status quo, and each uses observation.

Case Studies

We will very briefly describe the case study technique, since it involves fewer explicit and standardized procedures than other research tools. A case study is a comprehensive description and explanation of a variety of components of a given social situation. Case study researchers attempt to examine as much data as possible about the subject at hand. They often use heteromethods—a combination of surveys, interviews, and observation. Rather than choosing a large sample of respondents to represent the population, the researcher studies, at great length and through various means, a single idiosyncratic case. Rather than isolating a single or a small number of variables to investigate, the case study researcher examines a large quantity of variables. He or she describes, in great detail, one case. By learning as much as possible about one individual, one group, or one event, the researcher aims to provide insights that may have generalized applicability.[12]

The case study method has been used extensively in psychological, sociological, and educational research. It can generate questions that are subsequently investigated through experimental research methods. Because researchers who conduct case studies do not plan in advance all research procedures, it is impossible for us to provide a step-by-step explanation of this research tool. Instead, we provide an example of the case-study technique to clarify this method.

Imagine that you are interested in describing the conditions within a religious sect. You might join the group to become a participant observer, attending group meetings and participating in group activities, perhaps keeping a diary of your reactions. Your journal entries would document daily events and existing records might provide information on the history of the group. You informally question members and record their answers. By collecting any written materials that the group disseminates, you can later analyze the content of this information. You observe and take notes on the interaction among members. You examine newspaper or magazine articles to find information regarding societal perceptions of the group. You survey nonmembers to learn their perceptions of the group. You use a number of means to collect data that will provide a comprehensive description of the religious sect. Some of these data-gathering techniques are not as sophisticated or as objective as others, but all contribute to an in-depth understanding of the group. Though the researcher uses a variety of research tools, observation is a crucial aspect of the description.

The case-study technique has been used to investigate behavior in concentration camps, adolescent gangs, prisons, mental hospitals, boys' camps, work groups, families, and communities. Educational or psychological research has also examined, through the case study, the behavior of a single individual. Much of the material in Watzlawick, Beavin, and Jackson's classic volume, *The Pragmatics of Human Communication,* is based on case studies. Hennig and Jardim used the case study method in collecting data for *The Managerial Woman.* The researcher who chooses to use this method may want to consult such classic examples of case study re-research as *Management and the Worker,* by F. J. Roethlisberger & W. Dickson, (Cambridge: Harvard University Press, 1947). *Street Corner Society,* by W. H. Whyte, (Chicago: University of Chicago Press, 1965); and *Asylums,* by E. Goffman, (Garden City, N. J.: Doubleday and Company, 1959).

Content Analysis

Content analysis is "a research technique for the objective, systematic, and quantitative description of the manifest content of communication."[13] It is the "systematic reduction of a text to a standard set of statistically manipulated symbols representing the presence, the intensity, or the frequency of some characteristics relevant to social science."[14]

We recommend Berelson's text, *Content Analysis in Communication Research,* to those readers who desire in-depth information on the use of this research tool. He describes three general uses of content analysis and specifies many distinct purposes within these three general heads: (1) to describe the characteristics of the content itself; (2) to make valid inferences from the nature of the content to characteristics of the producers of the content; and (3) to interpret the content so as to reveal something about the nature of its audience or its effects.[15]

Frequently, the speech-communication researcher wishes to describe the characteristics of a speech, a newspaper or magazine article, or some other message. Perhaps the researcher's goal is to discover themes in the message, the frequency of references to a particular person, issue, or event, or the underlying attitudes of the source of the message. The speech-communication researcher may wish to characterize the speaker or the source of the message based on its content. He or she may wish to characterize the receivers of the message based on its content. The following are examples of content analytic research questions that are relevant to speech communication:

1. What words do family-hour television shows use to refer to sexual activities?
2. In what occupations are male and female characters in women's magazines portrayed?
3. What attitudes, as reflected in their speeches, do the current presidential candidates hold toward educational spending?
4. How frequently do job descriptions of business managers include the word *communication?*
5. What is the readability level of basic speech-communication textbooks?

In each of these examples, the researcher observes and analyzes the communication to describe something about that communication. Notice that content analysis can be applied to written or oral messages and can be used in a variety of situations.

Content analysis places information into certain categories. The researcher first must delineate the categories based on the purpose of the study. Then, he or she operationally defines the category—specifies explicit rules for determining what features of the content indicate that it falls into one category rather than another. Consider the question of readability level of speech-communication textbooks. The researcher may wish to classify words as difficult or easy and sentences as long or short. He or she may operationally define a difficult word as one that has four or more syllables and an easy word as having less than four syllables. Similarly, long sentences may be operationally defined as those with twenty or more words and short sentences defined as those with fewer than twenty words. Explicit rules for determining placement of the content into categories makes content analysis an objective research tool.

Once the rules for categorization are clear, the researcher decides whether all or part of the content will be analyzed. Analyzing an entire textbook to determine readability level would prove cumbersome. Instead, the researcher might select samples of the content to represent all of the content. Once this decision is made, the researcher trains coders who actually conduct the content analysis. As in interviewer training, coders must understand their role in the research project, they must be motivated to follow instructions, and they must develop skills in making accurate and consistent interpretations according to explicit coding guidelines.

Sometimes the researcher will refrain from telling coders the specific research hypotheses, for fear that such information might contaminate coding. That is, if coders know what they are expected to find, selective perception will cause them to find data that verify the hypotheses. They should, however, have a general understanding of the nature of the project and a specific understanding of the rules for coding material into categories. Coders usually practice on sample (hypothetical) data until they perfect the skills of accurate observation, judgment, and tallying. If two or more individuals code the same content, the researcher can compare and report their rate of agreement. If you cannot secure multiple coders for the same content, occasional "check coding" can provide indications of coder accuracy. Here, a second coder independently codes a certain percentage of the same content to provide an indication of the degree of agreement between the first and second coders.

Content analysis has advanced of late because of the use of high-speed, large-memory computers to do the actual coding. The researcher still must decide what communication will be observed, the purposes for the observation, and the rules for assigning material to categories, but the actual process of coding is done by the computer. One content-analytic computer program, called the General Inquirer, can be used to analyze not only the occurrence of particular words but also the combination of words that do not have to appear contiguously.[16] If you are planning content-analytic research, we encourage you to check computer facilities at your institution to determine the availability of additional computer programs for content analysis.

Interaction Analysis

Interaction analysis is similar to content analysis in that it codes communication into categories. Interaction analysis, however, is used to observe the ongoing oral communication between two or more individuals. As the name indicates, it is concerned with interaction. Analyzing the content is only one possible use of interaction analysis. In addition, researchers use this tool to analyze the intent of the communicator, the function that statements serve in an interaction, the cultural meanings of statements, the effects of statements, and the relationship of statements to each other over time.[17]

As with content analysis, the researcher is faced with the task of generating relevant categories for describing the interaction and operationally defining those categories. Additional decisions frequently involve the criteria for selecting a sample of the interaction to represent the entire interaction.

Bales' Interaction Process Analysis (IPA) constitutes one of the earliest and most famous attempts at interaction analysis.[18] He used this observational tool to study the socioemotional behavior of individuals in small groups, their approach to problem solving, their roles and status structure, and changes in these over time. Bales coded all verbal and nonverbal communication of interaction groups into one of twelve categories or functions:

1. Shows solidarity
2. Shows tension release
3. Agrees
4. Gives suggestion
5. Gives opinion
6. Gives orientation
7. Asks for orientation
8. Asks for opinion
9. Asks for suggestion
10. Disagrees
11. Shows tension
12. Shows antagonism

Since the classic interaction analytic studies of Bales, interaction analytic techniques have come to enjoy widespread popularity and application in educational, psychological, sociological, and speech-communication research. Because these techniques allow the researcher to analyze the ongoing communication process, they are directly applicable to many of our research purposes.

An interaction analytic scheme called Social Information Processing Analysis (SIPA) has recently been developed by Fisher and his colleagues.[19] The criteria for establishing coding categories in this scheme include:

1. The analytic categories focus on the organization; that is, the relationship of individuals.

2. The analytic categories are content-free in order to discover functions of communication regardless of context or content.
3. The analytical categories focus on the functions of information.
4. The analytical categories reflect a process orientation.

In this scheme, each "act" or uninterrupted verbal comment of a single speaker is coded. The coder uses a speaker's nonverbal communication to assist in deciding how to code verbal acts. Each act receives four separate codings. First, the source of the information is coded into one of four categories: (1) individual; (2) group system; (3) immediately environing system; and (4) environment. The second coding involves the time orientation: (1) past-to-present; (2) present-to-present; (3) future-to-present; and (4) timeless present. Next, the act is coded as to how individuals use the information relative to other information being processed at the same time. There are three categories included in this dimension: (1) generating information; (2) examining information for selection; and (3) retaining information. Finally, the act is coded on a continuum of equivocality reduction. In other words, to what extent does the utterance reduce informational uncertainty? The coder has five options for this dimension: (1) maximum equivocality reduced; (2) moderate equivocality reduced; (3) maintenance of equivocality level; (4) moderate equivocality increased; and (5) maximum equivocality increased.

As in any content-analytic or interaction-analytic scheme, precise definitions are devised for each of these categories. Then coders are trained to make consistent and valid judgments of what kinds of utterances get placed into which categories. With this brief treatment of Bales' IPA and Fisher's SIPA as two representations of interaction analysis, we do not expect the reader to be able to engage in interaction analysis. We offer these two schemes as examples of the technique. This discussion should allow you to understand the general purpose and method of interaction analysis. Interaction analysis is a tool for systematically and objectively reducing a system of communicative acts performed by individual members into simple, understandable categories. It translates or reduces the complexity of communication. Then the researcher reassembles the communication system to discover redundant patterns. Interaction analysis is a reduction process that allows the researcher to identify variables or patterns of interaction that aid in understanding and predicting human behavior.

The schemes discussed here represent just two of the many interaction analytic systems.[20] Rather than presenting other interaction analysis techniques, we will raise some issues that face interaction-analytic researchers:

1. What is the purpose of the interaction analysis? Is it seeking to describe communication-exchange patterns, message characteristics, group structure, interaction phases, or cycles?
2. What is the unit of analysis? Will single communication acts be coded? Will interacts or transacts? Some interaction analytic systems code statements in isolation rather than in relation to previous or subsequent statements. Other systems code reciprocal communication behaviors rather than rating Person

B's statement independently of A's previous statement or C's subsequent statement.

3. What is the size of the unit of analysis? Will each word, each phrase, each simple sentence, or each uninterrupted utterance be coded? The answer to this question depends on the research purpose, though some researchers offer a pragmatic answer: The unit of analysis is whatever amount of behavior provides enough meaning for the observer to make a classification.

4. What will be coded? Will observers code the content of the statement? the function? the intent? Will nonverbal behavior be coded as well as verbal behavior?

5. What sampling methods will be used? What portions of a two-hour interaction will be coded? Will the observer engage in time sampling (recording behavior every specified amount of time) or event sampling (recording every time a certain event occurs)?

6. What number of categories will be used? How simple or complex a scheme will be developed?

7. How much inference (interpretation) will coders make?

This list of issues facing the interaction analytic researcher is not exhaustive. We raise these issues to suggest some of the tasks involved and to demonstrate the complexity of interaction analysis. We suggest that interested researchers consult some of the additional sources listed at the end of the book.

As in interviewing and content analysis, the researcher who uses interaction analysis must conduct extensive training sessions. Coders of interaction must be familiar with the purpose of the analysis, the coding categories, and the rules for coding a piece of behavior into one category rather than another. Since interaction proceeds quickly, with statements occurring in rapid succession, the observer must be especially skilled at making quick but accurate judgments. He or she must be thoroughly familiar with the coding categories and must know the rules for placing behavior into those categories. Frequently, the researcher will videotape the interaction to ease the coding process. Then coders can examine and reexamine the interactants' verbal and nonverbal behavior before making coding decisions.

There exists an interaction-analytic computer program, called PROANA5, to analyze the communication line usage of five-member groups.[21] In this program, the computer tallies the frequency and direction of interaction and the computer printout provides a detailed analysis of communication line usage, balance of participation, clique groups, detrimental clique groups, communication propensity, and degree of leadership, isolation, and dominance.

Relational Analysis

Relational analysis is an observational technique that is similar to interaction analysis. It also utilizes schemes for coding ongoing oral interaction. Relational analysis is innovative, however, in its focus on the exchange of paired sequential messages over time. Most interaction-analytic schemes focus on the utterances of a single speaker. That is, Speaker A's message is coded, then Speaker B's message is coded, and so on. Those schemes take a monadic, or individual, focus. Relational coding schemes focus on communication properties that exist at the dyadic level. Messages that are jointly produced by two communicators are important in relational analysis. The relational analytic researcher studies sequentially linked messages rather than discrete, individual messages. In order to make a judgment concerning Speaker B's message, the coder must interpret that message in light of Speaker A's previous message. These schemes capture the transactional/relational nature of communication.[22]

While interaction analysis concerns *what* is being said, relational analysis concerns *how* it is said. That is, what does the message say about the control, power, or position of the communicators? An example of a relational coding scheme will illustrate and elucidate this observational technique. In 1971 Mark proposed a scheme for coding dyadic communication at the relationship level.[23] He used a three-digit code to designate each message:

First-digit code: (source)	1 = first speaker 2 = second speaker
Second-digit code: (function)	1 = question 2 = assertion 3 = instruction 4 = order 5 = talking over 6 = assertion and question 7 = question and assertion 8 = other
Third-digit code: (relationship of message to preceding message)	1 = agreement 2 = disagreement 3 = extension 4 = answer 5 = disconfirmation 6 = topic change 7 = agreement and extension 8 = disagreement and extension 9 = other 0 = laughter

By determining the relationship of successively paired message exchanges, the researcher can determine patterns of control (dominance-submission) in a dyad. The researcher is not concerned with the content of the communication; rather, the content is coded in order to see what the content says about the relationship. Other relational coding schemes have been developed from Mark's method.[24]

Relational analysis is an offshoot of interaction analysis. Thus, the researcher using relational analysis faces many of the same issues as the interaction-analytic researcher. The tasks of the relational analyst are more complex, however, since contiguous acts (interacts) are coded. The shift from individual message units to paired message units represents more complexity in analysis. The linking of message sequences to patterns of relational control (symmetry and complementarity) is an even more complex endeavor.

Relational analysis, while new and in need of refinement, does provide substantive data. The technique is more commensurate with our definitions of the communication process than are most interaction-analytic techniques. At this point, relational coding schemes are applicable only to the dyadic system. In time, such coding procedures may be applied to triadic or small-group communication. Relational analysis does represent a powerful and increasingly popular tool to aid researchers in studying communication.

Network Analysis

Network analysis is another tool that allows the researcher to describe patterns of interaction. It falls into the category of observational techniques, but it also uses survey methods. It asks questions of subjects and uses the answers to reconstruct the patterns of interaction among those subjects, thereby describing the communication network.

Network analysis stems from a procedure frequently used in sociology and social psychology: sociometry. Sociometry involves having members of a group or community indicate the individuals in the group to whom they are attracted and to whom they are repulsed. For example, students may be asked to indicate whom they would and would not like to sit next to in class. They make sociometric choices indicating attraction and repulsion on a certain dimension (seating). Workers in an organization may report their sociometric choices in terms of most and least preferred work partners. From this information, the researcher can describe patterns of attraction and repulsion among group members on the specific criterion of working together. Network analysis uses sociometric procedures. Specifically, it solicits individuals' choices of communication options within a certain system and uses those data to describe the set of communication relationships among the members of the system.

Imagine a researcher who seeks to determine the communication network within a business organization. The researcher would ask members of the organization to indicate the extent to which they typically communicate with the other members of their unit or department. Subjects could, through free response, write the names of the individuals with whom they communicate or they could check the names of individuals from a list of all unit members supplied by the researcher. A computer analysis of the data would show the links and patterns of the communication network. This actual communication network could be compared with the designated communication network as specified by an organizational chart. This example provides a basic understanding of what network analysis is. Next, let us discuss the purposes of network analysis.

Network analysis allows you to observe and describe the communication flow in a group. It can show who talks to whom, through what channel, and on what topic. Network analysis functions as a diagnostic device to locate communication flow problems. The researcher can use this technique to study any number of networks: task, social, formal, or informal networks. Network analysis can provide information about specific individuals in a group. For example, the amount of communication links an individual has with other individuals in a group can determine whether that individual is an integral group member, an isolate, or a liason between members. The number of links a person has within a group determines the individual's connectedness to the group. Network analysis allows the researcher to evaluate the adequacy of the communication flow and to determine communication overload problems. It can lead to a restructuring of the formal communication network to correspond to the informal communication network. In an organization, network data can provide the basis for changing job descriptions, restructuring organizational charts, or redesigning physical layouts. Network data can be related to data on other variables, such as satisfaction or productivity.

In light of these functions, let us discuss specific procedures for conducting a network analysis. The researcher must first decide the purpose of the analysis. What kind of information is desired? Do you want to determine the frequency of communication, the direction of communication, the importance of communication, or the effectiveness of communication among members of a system, for example? What type of communication do you wish to analyze—communication on work-related matters, communication about policy matters, communication about group innovations, communication on social matters? These issues affect the type of sociometric choices offered to respondents. Next, you must decide if you want the respondent to recall names or choose from a list of names. As in any questionnaire construction, items must be clearly worded and directions for response clearly provided. In addition, you must choose a computer technique for analyzing network data.

Various computer programs exist for analyzing network data.[25] Such programs provide: (1) printouts of operational communication networks, (2) comparisons of actual with expected networks, and (3) identification of group members (individuals whose majority of communication is with each other), liaisons (individuals whose majority of communication is with members of two or more groups but who are not members of any one group), and isolates (individuals who send and receive little communication in a group).[26]

Computer analysis is necessary because of the typical size of the matrix of communication choices in network analysis. Even with a group containing as few as five persons, analysis of the number, direction, and reciprocity of communication links becomes unwieldy without computer assistance.

Network analysis is increasingly being applied by speech-communication researchers, as are some of the other research tools described in this chapter. Organizational communication research is especially likely to see more frequent use of network analysis as a technique for describing patterns of human communication.

Naturalistic Inquiry

The naturalistic approach to inquiry specifies different philosophic assumptions than the scientific approach to inquiry. Research in the scientific tradition follows the assumptions of a philosophy called logical positivism.[27] Because it is based on logical positivism, scientific inquiry searches for causes and effects. The scientific (positivistic) investigator manipulates, defines, and controls phenomena of interest so that logical relationships come into view. Scientific research uses formal logic.

Naturalistic inquiry, in contrast, follows the assumptions of a philosophy called phenomenology.[28] The naturalistic (phenomenological) investigator enters the world of the phenomenon of interest to interpret the phenomenon and its world.[29] He or she does not manipulate or control phenomena, but intrudes as little as possible on the phenomena. Naturalistic inquiry, rather than relying on formal logic, emphasizes logic in use, or individuals' logics of their own actions. That is, people are assumed to be active, planning, purposive, self-monitoring, self-justifying systems whose behavior arises in their pursuit of goals and their making sense of themselves and each other.[30] It is an individual's "sense-making" activity that concerns the naturalistic researcher.

Naturalistic inquiry is a major category encompassing many research methods.[31] To explain further, let us present three common usages of the term: (1) Naturalistic inquiry is sometimes used synonomously with "pretest" or "exploratory" research. It is seen as a method for generating hypotheses rather than testing them. (2) Naturalistic inquiry is sometimes used synonomously with "field" research. It is seen as a method of studying phenomena in their "natural" environment with a minimum of observational intrusion. (3) Naturalistic inquiry is sometimes seen as a means of studying different subject matter than is studied by traditional observational methods. It is often applied to phenomena that exist because people define them as real, for example, definitions of situations, socially constructed meanings, or interpretations of events or social institutions.

While naturalistic inquiry may contain elements of all three of these definitions, the last usage best characterizes the technique. A naturalistic researcher says the knower is inextricably a part of what is known. The naturalistic researcher questions the assumptions that others take for granted; he or she is interested in people's logics of their own constitutive actions; he or she seeks the actor's, not the researcher's, interpretations or meanings.

Let us briefly discuss two types of naturalistic inquiry relevant to the speech-communication discipline: ethnomethodology and discourse analysis.

Ethnomethodology. Unlike the social scientist who assumes one reality and seeks to know or discover that reality, the ethnomethodologist accepts many realities. There is more than one reality because individuals construct their own realities, the ethnomethodologists believe. Ethnomethodology seeks to determine how individuals construct social reality through interaction. It examines the everyday experience of a community of people to learn how those people construct reality. Ethnomethodologists assume people have an elegant knowledge of the workings of social structure. People may not even be aware of this knowledge. It is taken for granted. The ethnomethodologist makes taken-for-granted information explicit. Rather than the researcher imposing reality on the phenomena, the researcher immerses him or herself in the phenomena, so the reality of the phenomena can emerge. The researcher must become a full-time member of the reality to be studied. Each member of a reality can recognize, demonstrate, and make observable the rational character of his or her practices. Ethnomethodology rejects formal logic and accepts logic based on common sense.

The ethnomethodologist uses the following guidelines in the study of practical actions:[32]

1. Any occasion whatsoever can be examined for the feature of choice among alternatives of sense. No inquiries can be excluded no matter where or when they occur, no matter how vast or trivial their scope.
2. Members of an organized arrangement are continually engaging in having to decide, recognize, persuade, or make evident the rational (consistent) character of activities.
3. Any social setting can be viewed as self-organizing. Any setting organizes its activities to make its properties an organized environment of practical activities detectable, reportable, and accountable.

In effect, the ethnomethodologist uses all the available means to understand individuals' social structuring activities: Any fragments, proverbs, passing remarks, rumors, or partial descriptions can help the researcher understand the actors' construction and interpretation of situations. Examples of ethnomethodological studies include the investigation of everyday rule use,[33] analysis of turn taking in conversation,[34] and the study of organizations as a common-sense construct.[35]

Discourse Analysis. Discourse analysis is a method for examining the social coordination that augments linguistic production.[36] It is concerned with the rules by which we organize utterances, sequence utterances, and structure turn taking. The discourse analyst seeks to discover rules of language use in social interaction. Such a researcher would seek rules for discourse from the perspective of the members who use those rules. The goal is to explain how people coordinate speech in interaction.

Discourse analysis would typically proceed as follows: The researcher would first collect and record samples of discourse. Next, he or she would make a verbatim transcript of that discourse, with annotations to reflect nonverbal cues. The researcher, then, would analyze the discourse to determine the function or meaning of each utterance. Note that categories of functions or meanings are not imposed, as in interaction or relational analysis. Instead, the researcher "lets the data speak." Functions of utterances should evolve from the context. Participants in the discourse, perhaps unknowingly, reveal the meanings of utterances by virtue of their subsequent utterances. The discourse analyst lets the actual discourse reveal how people coordinate interaction.

Because there are no specified, a priori steps in discourse analysis, we cannot offer you a detailed plan for using this observational technique. We suggest that you consult the "Additional Sources" at the end of the book. The best way to learn methods of naturalistic inquiry is to read studies employing naturalistic methods and to practice using naturalistic techniques. The naturalistic investigator cannot structure observations, cannot set a priori categories for behavior, cannot impose meanings on situations, and cannot remove communication from its context. Rather, this type of researcher observes and lets a phenomenon speak for itself.

SUMMARY

Descriptive research describes the present state of affairs. Descriptive researchers collect information about events, beliefs, attitudes, values, intentions, preferences, or behaviors. They collect this information through the use of surveys, interviews, or observations.

The survey is a technique of gathering information, in writing, directly from those individuals who hold the information. Survey researchers must determine the appropriateness of the survey method to their research projects by judging the availability of the information through other sources, the time, and the cost of surveying. Sometimes the researcher must consider the issues of size and representativeness of sampling. To insure an adequate response rate, researchers must provide incentives to persuade potential respondents to cooperate. These can include showing the importance of the survey's purpose, emphasizing the significance of the topic, appealing to individual needs, carefully designing and disseminating the questionnaire to minimize inconvenience to respondents, selecting the appropriate time of the year for conducting surveys, and making follow-up contact with nonrespondents.

Specific survey questions should be carefully worded to avoid ambiguity, double-barreled items, negatives, leading language, and socially desirable responses. Questionnaires must be properly sequenced and should include subheadings that signal respondents to a change of topic. Instructions to respondents should appear at the beginning of the questionnaire, whenever the subject shifts, and whenever the method of answering changes.

Survey cover letters should establish rapport with potential respondents, sell the questionnaire, and answer questions that the respondent may be contemplating. Follow-up notices must tactfully prod nonrespondents to reply without reprimanding, demanding, or alienating them. The survey researcher should pay attention to details of arranging, printing, duplicating, and disseminating questionnaires so that they appear neat, professional, and readable.

The interview is a data-collection device in which an interviewer orally administers a set of prepared questions to an interviewee. Availability of data through other means, time, and cost are factors to consider when determining the appropriateness of conducting interviews. The interview is a beneficial tool when you want complete or detailed answers to questions; need a high response rate; expect respondents to have difficulty in reading, understanding, interpreting, or answering questions; want to insure that respondents do not collaborate with others in answering questions; want to receive spontaneous reactions; or wish to observe the respondent's nonverbal behavior.

Interview researchers frequently must determine the appropriate means for finding interviewees, must decide on adequate sample size, and must insure sample representativeness. Interviewers provide response incentives by the appearance they make, the ways they introduce themselves, the communication climates they create, and the skills they use in asking questions.

The interview schedule includes the list of questions and instructions to the interviewer. Questions must be clear, objective, and properly sequenced. Researchers must train interviewers to understand their job, to be motivated to do a good job, and to demonstrate effective communication. Interviewers must know how to generate respondent cooperation, to standardize interviews, to record responses, and to follow ethical guidelines.

Observation is a research tool involving the systematic watching, studying, or interpreting of the source of the data. Observational techniques include case studies, content analyses, and interaction analyses.

A case study is a comprehensive description of a variety of variables within a single, idiosyncratic case. The case study researcher uses any and all methods that help to provide insights that may have generalized applicability. Content analysis is an objective, systematic, and quantitative method of describing communication content. It can be used to describe content, or to provide information about the source, audience, or effect of the communication. Content-analytic researchers must devise the category system, operationally define the categories, arrive at sampling decisions, and train coders. Computer programs exist to aid the content-analytic researcher.

Interaction analysis is a tool to observe and analyze intent, function, meaning, effect, or relationship of statements within an interaction. The interaction analytic researcher must decide upon the purpose of the interaction analysis, the independent or reciprocal nature of the units of analysis, the size of the unit of analysis, the specific behavior to be coded, and the sampling method to be used. Interaction-analytic researchers must train coders to make accurate and consistent judgments when placing segments of behavior into categories. Computer programs can greatly facilitate the use of the interaction-analytic research tool.

Relational analysis employs category schemes for coding sequentially linked messages and uses these messages to determine patterns of relationship control. Network analysis is a technique for soliciting communication choices from members of a system and describing the set of communication relationships within that system. Naturalistic inquiry is a method for observing and reconstructing the logic and meanings individuals use in creating social reality. Ethnomethodology and discourse analysis are two types of naturalistic inquiry.

6

The Experimental Method

Laboratory experiments in the behavioral sciences are designed and executed to provide answers to research questions. They are characterized by precision and control, and they utilize scientific method. Because human subjects are involved, the degree of precision and the level of control is less than is found in such sciences as physics and chemistry.

Invoking the experimental method is one way of generating new knowledge. It is not the only way, nor is it necessarily the optimum method for all research problems. Its limitations are well known, and its use for the study of human beings is sometimes controversial. To provide an initial perspective, we will describe in skeletal form a hypothetical experiment in the speech communication area. At each stage we will provide a brief comment on the nature of laboratory experiments. But, first, this definition of experimentation offered by Cattell:

> *An experiment is a recording of observations, quantitative or qualitative, made by defined and recorded operations and in defined conditions, followed by examination of the data by appropriate statistical and mathematical rules, for the existence of significant relations.*[1]

A HYPOTHETICAL EXPERIMENT

Background Theory and Research

The motivation for conducting an experiment ranges from idle curiosity to the noticing of a knowledge gap existing in a specific theoretical area. The more worthwhile experiments are preceded by a study of relevant theory and of the major previous research in the area under investigation. The area we choose to focus on in our hypothetical experiment is called *communicator credibility theory*—one of the most widely researched theoretical areas in the human communication domain.[2] Contemporary communication scholars have made important contributions in this area via well-designed experiments.

Having decided to conduct research in this general area, our first task is to examine the important books, research monographs, and other kinds of publications that will help us place the "state" of the theoretical area in perspective. A comprehensive scrutiny of this important literature suggests several specific problem areas in need of further research.

Formulating the Research Problem

Having studied and evaluated the literature relevant to our area, communicator credibility, we now move directly to formulating the problem. The number of potential research problems is seemingly infinite and beginning researchers often find it difficult to choose a specific problem area. To narrow the range of possibilities we choose a problem area that has strong theoretical grounding. This implies that the problem grows out of an abundance of theoretical content and that well-established researchers have made important contributions. Historically, the better, more significant experiments have been solidly based in rich theory.[3] Experiments motivated by curiosity alone have contributed far less to the accumulation of knowledge in most research areas.

Existing theory and research leads us to the tentative assumption that a communicator's credentials seem to be positively correlated with his or her effectiveness. That is, the more prestigious communicator is likely to make the greater impact on a given audience. We can reduce the problem we choose to investigate to this question: Are the more prestigious communicators more effective? At this point we need not be concerned with operationalizing the problem with greater precision. That process is involved in the next stage: formulation of a hypothesis.

Deriving Hypotheses

Research problems lead naturally to the formulation of hypotheses.[4] It is not sufficient to ask only if the more prestigious communicators are more effective. At this stage we are obliged to make a statement of prediction based on our knowledge of the research area under investigation. Assume that we narrow our research interest to the area of a communicator's institutional affiliation. Previous research provides indications suggesting that an individual's place of employment—in the case of a university professor, the reputation of the university—is a highly salient factor when the issue is prestige. This finding leads us directly to our research hypothesis: *The more prestigious a communicator's institutional affiliation, the more persuasive will that communicator be.* Note that the hypothesis is a predictive-type statement. The basis of the prediction evolved from our study and evaluation of the relevant literature. As with all predictions we must wait and see if it proves true—in this case, we must await the outcome of our experiment. There are two possible outcomes: the results are consistent with and thereby corroborate the hypothesis; or they are inconsistent and fail to corroborate it. It is inappropriate to use the words *confirmed* or even *supported*. The use of these terms cannot be logically justified. Readers wishing to pursue this issue should consult the definitive work by Popper.[5] Note that, at this point we have stated our hypothesis in general form. To reduce the level of ambiguity, we must state it in a more precise, quantifiable form. Here is one possibility:

H_1: Mean ratings of the concept *capital punishment* will be highest in the high prestige group, next highest in the medium, and lowest in the low prestige group.

Operational Definitions

Hypotheses often contain words and phrases that lack scientific precision or that are otherwise ambiguous. In our research hypothesis statement, two words stand out: *prestigious* and *persuasive*. Can these words be satisfactorily defined? If they cannot, then it makes little sense to proceed with the design of the experiment. We cannot resolve the problem of definition, but we must try. In this particular case we can resort to definition by quantification.

To define by quantification is to invoke the method of *operationism*.[6] An operational definition provides a description of the actual steps, in sequence, that taken together describe the phenomenon in question at a lower level of abstraction. Sometimes it is possible to assign a number, and the numerical value becomes the operational definition. Some examples:

Intelligence: operationally defined as an individual's score on a standardized intelligence test

Creativity: operationally defined as a person's score on a standardized creativity test

Intoxication: operationally defined as a specified percentage of alcohol in the blood

As we have noted, not all operational definitions involve only the assigning of numbers. A recipe is an operational definition of a cake inasmuch as it provides a description of the sequential steps involved in producing the cake. Industrial job descriptions likewise represent attempts to operationally define a job title, for example, a welder. Insofar as possible the writers of the job description provide a comprehensive listing of the things an employee is likely to *do* when he or she assumes the title.

Operational definitions are attempts to reduce the level of ambiguity associated with words. But their use does not guarantee that others will necessarily understand the word or phrase in question or, for that matter, accept the definition as the most appropriate choice. But operational definitions remain the only real option for communicating the nature of scientific terms with minimum ambiguity.

How might we operationally define the word *prestigious* in our hypothesis? One way is to have a group of subjects rate universities on a scale of one to ten. The range of scores would then constitute an operational measure of prestige. The higher the mean score, the more prestigious the university. Lower mean scores would indicate that the university in question carried less prestige, in the opinion of the sample of raters. Can the word *persuasive* be defined in a similar manner? We think so. In this case we could administer attitude tests to our subjects as a key part of the experiment. The higher a group's mean score on the test, the more persuasive we consider the communicator to have been.

In a simplified manner we have operationally defined the two most abstract words in our research-hypothesis statement. Now we can move to the actual design of the study.

The Independent Variable.[7]

Our proposed study seeks to determine if institutional prestige is related to communicator persuasiveness. The independent variable, then, is the communicator's institutional affiliation. It is the central theoretical concern of the experiment. The term *independent variable* is used to refer to that general factor of research interest that we plan to manipulate in the course of the experiment.

Institutional prestige is a variable. There are high-prestige institutions such as Harvard and Yale, and there are medium- and low-prestige institutions. For the purpose of our experiment we choose three levels of prestige: high, medium, and low. We conduct some preliminary research that generates mean prestige scores associated with specific universities. Assume that the prestige ratings by our subjects revealed these scores: Harvard = 9.5, University of Erehwon = 6.5, and Wood State University = 3.5. We can now associate a communicator with one of these universities for each of the experimental groups:

Experimental Group 1: The communicator is affiliated with Harvard (High prestige).

Experimental Group 2: The communicator is affiliated with the University of Erehwon (Medium prestige).

Experimental Group 3: The communicator is affiliated with Wood State University (Low prestige).

To summarize this section, the independent variable is designated *institutional prestige.* The experiment will involve three levels: high, medium, and low.

The Dependent Variable

How shall we measure the effects of our experiment? In scientific experiments measuring instruments are referred to as *dependent variables.* Hence all tests are dependent variables. Strictly speaking, the term evolves from the notion that a subject's test score is dependent on the level of the independent variable to which he or she is exposed.

The selection of one or more dependent variables constitutes one of the more critical choices in experimental research. Much time and reflection should go into choosing them. No experiment should proceed until reliable and relevant measuring instruments have been chosen. For our hypothetical experiment we choose a dependent variable consisting of ten evaluative-type semantic differential scales[8] designed to assess subjects' opinion toward the concept *capital punishment.* The complete set of scales appears in Table 6-1.

Table 6-1   The Ten Evaluative Semantic Differential Scales Used as Dependent Variables in the Hypothetical Experiment.

Concept: Capital Punishment *Scale Items*
1. Valuable - Worthless
2. Fair - Unfair
3. Right - Wrong
4. Just - Unjust
5. Approve - Disapprove
6. Good - Bad
7. Honest - Dishonest
8. Responsible - Irresponsible
9. Intelligent - Stupid
10. Wise - Foolish

To calculate a subject's score on the dependent variable we sum the ten items into a single composite. Semantic differential scales are normally scored 1-7 as follows:

Valuable:_____ : _____ : _____ : _____ : _____ : _____ : _____ :Worthless
              7   6   5   4   3   2   1

End points are consistently weighted 7 or 1 depending on the scale item and the researcher's preferences. With the left end of the scale designated the 7 end on all ten scales, a subject can score a maximum of $7 \times 10 = 70$ and a minimum of $10 \times 1 = 10$.

The Persuasive Communication

Each communicator delivers a fifteen-minute tape-recorded, pro-capital punishment speech. The communication consists of evidence and arguments organized so as to convince the groups that capital punishment is desirable. The higher a subject's composite score on the ten-item dependent variable, the higher the assumed degree of agreement with the position advocated by the communicator.

It is at this point that Cattell's definition of a laboratory experiment takes on meaning. The persuasive communication was created by the researchers to be introduced at strategic, predetermined times and under conditions determined by the researchers. This, then, represents a simple case of manipulation of defined conditions.

Experimental and Control Groups

To test the research hypothesis, we will need three groups of subjects—one for each level of the independent variable: high, medium, and low prestige. We will also need a fourth group of subjects to serve as controls. The control group will be given only the ten-item test, and the mean score will provide a baseline. Each experimental group will be compared both to the control group and to each other. Comparisons of this type are basic in behavioral-science experiments. In general, control groups—when compared with experimental groups—provide information concerning the extent to which influences other than those defined and manipulated by the experimenter have influenced the experiment.

Subjects

From a pool of five hundred college students, we randomly assign two hundred (N = 200) to any one of the three experimental groups or to the control group. This will give us fifty subjects in each of our groups. To insure randomness, we assign subjects to a particular group through the use of a table of random numbers. Most statistics texts contain lists of these numbers.[9] They are simple and efficient and should be routinely used. No other method of assigning subjects to groups can compete with the random-numbers procedure.

Assigning fifty subjects ($n = 50$) to each of the four groups is an arbitrary decision on our part. Precisely how many subjects a study needs can be estimated from *power* tables.[10] If groups contain too few subjects then the study may lack the strength (power) to detect differences arising from the manipulation of the independent variable. Too many subjects can lead to the conclusion that the experimental conditions actually made a difference when in fact the differences were so small that they lacked practical significance.

Experimental Design

Here, then, is our basic experimental design in skeletal form:

1. Problem area: communicator prestige; specifically, the effect of institutional affiliation on communicator persuasiveness.
2. General research hypothesis: the more prestigious a communicator's institutional affiliation, the more persuasive will that communicator be. *Prestigious* and *persuasive* were operationally defined.
3. Independent variable: institutional affiliation designated at three levels of prestige—high (Harvard), medium (University of Erehwon), and low (Wood State University).

4. Dependent variable: a ten-item test—evaluative semantic differential scales.
5. Persuasive communication: a fifteen-minute pro-capital punishment speech.
6. Groups: three experimental groups corresponding to each level of the independent variable, and one control group.
7. Subjects: total N = 200, with n = 50 subjects randomly assigned to each of the four groups.

The Experimental Plan

We will expose each experimental group to an identical fifteen-minute pro-capital punishment speech via tape recording. The independent variable, three levels of institutional affiliation, is set up in this manner: The communicator's general credentials are identical for each of the three experimental groups, with these strategic exceptions: In Experimental Group 1, high prestige, he is designated a Harvard University professor; in Experimental Group 2, medium prestige, a University of Erehwon professor; in Experimental Group 3, low prestige, a Wood State University professor. In effect we are adhering to a classical tenet of science; namely, that all conditions be held constant except those we wish to manipulate experimentally.

Cover Story

Subjects entering an experiment soon devise their own explanations as to the purposes of the experiment unless a realistic explanation is provided by the researchers. Even then the explanation may well be rejected by subjects who feel they are, at a minimum, being duped. A cover story is an explanation—usually untrue—given to subjects so as to enhance the realistic nature of the study. The reasons for providing cover stories include:

1. If subjects knew the real purpose of the study they would not respond "naturally." Some would be overly cooperative; others would be uncooperative.
2. If left to devise their own interpretations of the reasons for the study, each would respond in an idiosyncratic manner—an equally undesirable state.
3. Some behaviors are socially unacceptable. So subjects are not likely to admit to such behaviors if asked directly. Consequently, they must be kept ignorant of "what we are really looking for." An example would be admissions of incestuous behavior.

Cover stories that contain elements of reasonableness and credibility seem to be an essential part of experiments involving human beings. Constructing them is never easy. And unless their effect is throughly pretested on other groups of subjects prior to the main experiment (that is, in a pilot study, explained more fully below), then they are likely to fail.

Procedure

With the experimental plan completed, we proceed to the execution of the experiment. These are the sequential steps we will follow:

1. Obtain four reasonably comparable rooms. Assign subjects randomly to each of the four rooms.
2. Execute the entire experiment at the same hour, rather than at four different hours.
3. Assign one experimental assistant (E) to each of the four conditions. These are the individuals who actually conduct the study—that is, who play the recorded speeches and administer the dependent variables.
4. For each experimental group, have E play the tape-recorded persuasive message.
5. At the conclusion of the recorded message, administer the ten-item dependent variable.
6. In the control group, administer the dependent variable only.
7. At the appropriate time have E debrief the subjects; that is, thank them for their cooperation and inform them as to the nature of the study.

Data Analysis

Experiments in the behavioral sciences are more often than not statistically analyzed. One or more appropriate statistical models are chosen to be applied to the data base. For our experiment one appropriate statistical model is the analysis of variance.[11] It is not necessary that we fully understand the model and its derivation. We need only appreciate the nature of the information it provides. The analysis of variance addresses this basic question: Does at least one pair of group means differ significantly?

We conduct our experiment and obtain the results in Table 6-2. The means are strikingly different. But do they differ in a statistical sense? Applying the analysis of variance model to the data we conclude that at least one pair of means differs significantly. Statistical significance means that the differences are not likely to be the result of chance fluctuations or the accumulation of error. How many pairs of means differ and which are they? The analysis of variance does not provide that kind of specific information. It informs us only that there are some mean differences. To determine the specific pairs of means that might differ we apply a second statistical model to the data base, Tukey's multiple comparison test.[12] This test permits us to examine any or all pairs of means in order to determine which pairs differ significantly.

The results reveal that each experimental group mean differs significantly from the mean of the control group, and that each experimental group mean differs significantly from each of the remaining two experimental group means. The largest group mean is associated with the high-prestige communicator, the next highest with the medium-prestige communicator, and the smallest with the low-prestige communicator.

Table 6-2   Means For the Experimental and Control Groups, Hypothetical Research Example.

Group	Mean
Control	3.61
Experimental #1 (High prestige)	9.52
Experimental #2 (Medium prestige)	7.84
Experimental #3 (Low prestige)	5.59

The results are clear-cut. Our research hypothesis is corroborated by the results: The more prestigious the communicator's institutional affiliation, the more persuasive was that communicator, within the context of the experiment.

Manipulation Check

Experiments whose results corroborate the researcher's hypothesis are normally assumed to be a direct consequence of the independent variable. Error conditions of one kind or another could have influenced the results, but in this case let us assume error was ruled out. We conclude that the high-prestige communicator actually was more persuasive.

What if the results showed the three communicators to be equally effective, the hypothesis failing to be corroborated? Could we then say that institutional prestige was of no importance to the subjects? No, not unless the experiment included a manipulation check. A manipulation check is any procedure that elicits a response from the subjects as to their perception of one or more aspects of the experimental conditions.[13] In our experiment it would include asking subjects to rate the prestige of the institution on, let us say, a seven-point scale, low to high. If means in the three groups differ significantly, then we have positive evidence that the manipulation worked. If the means turn out to be nearly identical, then we have a clear case of manipulation failure, leaving the study essentially uninterpretable. Note that prior to the design of the study, we surveyed another sample of subjects in an effort to establish the differential institutional prestige. And it worked. Subjects rated the three institutions in a significantly different manner. Why, then, include a manipulation check as part of the main experiment?

First, we can assume that institutional prestige was highly salient to subjects in the first sample. Their task was to rate institutions—and nothing else. By comparison, subjects in the experimental groups heard a fifteen-minute taped speech. The designation of the communicator's institutional affiliation took only seconds. It could easily have been missed by inattentive subjects. Second, even if noticed at the outset, it may well have been forgotten as the speech drew to a close. These are but two potential explanations. For these and numerous other reasons we strongly advise the inclusion of a manipulation check in all experiments unless the specific nature of the investigation precludes it.

SCIENTIFIC METHOD AND LABORATORY
EXPERIMENTS

The hypothetical study just described illustrates the essential steps in designing and conducting laboratory experiments on human subjects. The description was brief, hence many details were necessarily omitted. Still, anyone studying the rationale and sequential steps should have a fuller appreciation of how experiments on human subjects typically proceed.

Since experiments employ scientific method it is advantageous to study our hypothetical experiment as an exercise in the utilization of scientific method. What are some of the more fundamental principles and assumptions of scientific method in behavioral research? These we consider fundamental:

1. *There is order in human behavior.* To some extent, human beings are characterized by their unique qualities. They are characterized too by group qualities. Another way of putting it is that there appears to be some degree of regularity in human behavior.[14] Although people are capable of behaving in many different ways under specific conditions, it is a matter of empirical fact that very often they do not. In fact it is amazing how few are the varieties of behavior in many social settings: At funerals, people often say the same kinds of things and behave in essentially the same manner decade after decade. Greeting talk and leave-taking talk is highly predictable within socioeconomic groups. Human beings are capable of assuming an infinite number of bodily postures, but in actuality they engage in only a few. And college student classroom behavior is fairly predictable; the same patterns tend to repeat year after year. Even the most casual observer of human behavior can verify that recurring patterns are the rule rather than the exception. If behavior were completely unique for all humans, experimentation would lead us nowhere and generalization would be impossible.

2. *The notion of the obvious is rejected.* Scientists take nothing for granted. The idea that anything is perfectly obvious is rejected.[15] The history of science contains countless examples of the "obviously true" turning out to be partially, if not totally, false when put to scientific test.

Experimental researchers, after having conducted a study, are sometimes asked, "Didn't we already know that?"—*that* referring to the results of the study. To the questioner the results are intuitively obvious. He or she wonders why it was necessary to spend the time, energy, and resources to research such an obvious phenomenon. To the researcher, however, something becomes "obvious" only after a substantial amount of research provides the basis for a strong generalization.

3. *Hypotheses are generated and tested.* In order to discourage random, unorganized research, scientists have long advocated hypothesis generating and testing as basic to scientific method.[16] Hypothesis generation arises from a careful scrutiny and evaluation of existing theory and research. Experiments can be designed and executed without the testing of hypotheses but we do not recommend it. Strong, viable theories evolve from the execution of systematic research that stems from relevant hypotheses.

4. *A major goal of science is prediction.* Distasteful as it may appear to some, prediction is a major goal of science. Scientists do not look upon experiments as historical events or unique phenomena. Well designed and executed scientific research yields results that, when placed beside other equally well designed studies, form the basis for generalizations and, ultimately, theories. And what purpose do generalizations and theories have? They allow us to predict human behavior—how people are likely to behave under varying sets of circumstances.

5. *Science deals in answerable questions.* Many lay persons are asking *why* scientists are more likely to be asking *how* and for good reason. *Why* questions often border on the metaphysical.[17] Such questions cannot be answered given the present state of science. These are examples of metaphysical questions: Why do humans exist? Is there life after death? Why does a single, undifferentiated egg undergo transformations that produce a human fetus? Why is there human suffering in the world?

Consider the first question, Why do humans exist? It is clearly unanswerable given present methods of inquiry. Not only do scientists not know why humans are here, very few of them have the slightest desire to spend much of their research energy trying to find out.

Scientists are mainly concerned with *how* things occur. Such questions can be answered through the invoking of scientific procedures. These are examples of scientifically answerable questions: How does a given disease lead to the death of the organism? How do people react to a loss of freedom? What ecological conditions tend to be associated with shyness in the individual? In a persuasive communication, are the first or the last statements (primacy-recency) more likely to be remembered longer?

6. *Scientific method involves comparison.* Without comparison, there is no science.[18] To conceive of something one must be able to conceive of its opposite. We cannot test the general hypothesis that high communicator credibility makes a positive difference without comparisons to less-than-high credibility—that is, gradations of high to low credibility.

Early in life humans learn to compare their circumstances with those of others. A college professor earning $35,000 annually may feel good about being in a relatively high income bracket. The elation is short-lived, however, when he finds that garbage collectors in his community are earning $40,000. And so it is, both in ordinary life and in science. The important data are comparative data.

Dependent variable comparison, of course, is a central concern of the behavioral scientist. If two or more experimental conditions actually differ, then that difference must be measurable on a relevant dependent variable. Comparison is the only defensible method of unraveling cause-effect relationships.

7. *Scientists seek to control conditions.*[19] Physical scientists spend endless hours attempting to control atmospheric conditions, temperature, and numerous other critical states. Because of the highly sophisticated instrumentation currently available these scientists are capable of exercising near perfect control. What of behavioral scientists? Are they likewise in a position to exercise near-perfect control?

Clearly they are not; hence, control—or more specifically the lack of it—continues to be a challenge.

Error conditions, if they are known, are minimized, eliminated, or at least accounted for through the utilization of control procedures. Ideally, experiments, such as the hypothetical study described at the beginning of this chapter, are totally controlled. This implies perfectly homogeneous experimental and control groups. It implies also that the conditions of administering the experiment were identical across all groups. These represent but a few of the variables that must be controlled in behavioral experiments. Total control is never possible. All experiments on human beings are compromises with perfect control. But lack of control invites error. Error is always present. It must be recognized, admitted, and its effect evaluated. Researchers must work to isolate and define the important sources of error, or contamination. If known, attempts can be made to minimize them or—in the ideal case—eliminate them. Attempts at controlling error, of course, are often only partially successful. Under such conditions we suggest that the researcher evaluate the extent of the error and make a determination as to the perspective in which the results should be studied.

8. *Science deals in probabilities.* Since scientists can reproduce events in the laboratory at will, we are sometimes tempted to believe that scientific procedures involve dead certainty. They do not. The reasoning surrounding this point of view is beyond the scope of the present discussion. At the heart of the matter is what is called "the problem of induction." In brief, the accumulation of evidence can never lead to certainty, even in the area of the so-called natural laws, for example, of motion. Whether expectations (the sun's rising) will occur in the future is the key question. Since such events cannot be known with certainty, scientists must deal in the realm of probability.[20]

Behavioral scientists likewise describe almost every event in probability terms. Human behavior is characterized by variability; it follows that even homogeneous groups will exhibit variability on any dimension of scientific interest. Regardless of the level of refinement of a theory, the behavioral scientist will never say that identical results will be obtained when an experiment is replicated.

9. *Science is self-correcting.*[21] Scientists use procedures that are open to public scrutiny. There are no secrets. Further, scientists are dedicated to the position that data should be made available to the public.[22] The practical result of this philosophy is that scientific studies can be and very often are repeated. When experiments are repeated (replicated), errors in previous investigations are likely to surface. Errors detected under these conditions are evaluated, and theory is appropriately adjusted or even reformulated. This is the essense of the self-correcting aspect of science. One very important implication of this principle is that little significance is attached to any study whose procedures and data are not made available to the scientific community.

10. *Confirmation comes from replication.* This principle is the work of Tukey,[23] one of the nation's foremost data analysts. It suggests that no single behavioral experiment can, by itself, establish a principle, generalization, or theory. When

large numbers of studies in essentially the same area of inquiry produce similar results—only then does there exist a basis for generalization.

While Tukey's principle is unassailable, in practice it is often ignored. Individual studies are cited as "proving" this or that. What is worse, textbook writers are sometimes the biggest offenders. Far too often authors discuss "principles of communication" that are based on the results of a single experiment. As a result, large percentages of our undergraduate populations develop the questionable habit of drawing strong conclusions from inconclusive findings.

11. *Patience is a prerequisite.* The proper design, execution, and analysis of a behavioral experiment is an enormously time-consuming task. When shortcuts are taken and when haste enters, the results are predictable—a sloppy study that is essentially of no value to science. Some words of advice:

a. Limit the scope of the study. Unless you have a substantial grant, be content with researching a smaller aspect of a larger study.

b. Plan the study. Resist the urge to execute the experiment until the entire study has been designed. Haste inevitably leads to errors and big errors render any study unacceptable. Devise a master checklist that includes every detail. Follow it to the letter.

c. You will need the cooperation of others. Most of them will not have nearly the commitment to your study that you will have. Nor will they move as fast as you would like them to. Some of them will turn out to be unreliable—another instance in which your patience is likely to be taxed.

d. Maintain your composure, especially as the experiment is being executed—at that time you can expect some things to go wrong. Losing your patience and getting angry with people will render you ineffective. If you lose your head you will be incapable of solving the many problems that may surface all at the same time.

12. *Science involves quantification of variables.* Although it is possible to conceive of scientific experiments being conducted without the benefit of quantification, one would have to wonder about the utility of such studies. Comparison of conditions would be awkward, replication by other researchers would approach impossibility, and communicating the nature of the variables would be equally frustrating.

Quantification permits the scientist to work at lower levels of abstraction. To say that one group of subjects is more intelligent than another introduces an element of vagueness. Assigning numerical values to the groups using standardized intelligence tests as a referent provides immediate clarification. Both the groups and the individual subjects constituting them can now be compared through a variety of statistical models.

The objection is sometimes raised that some characteristics or behaviors simply cannot be quantified. If this is indeed true, then those variables cannot be studied scientifically. More and more, however, scientists are taking the position that most of the so-called quality variables are, in reality, capable of quantification. A quality basketball player, for example, can be shown to be superior on the basis of points scored, assists, passing competence, and so forth—all of which can be assigned a number.

13. *Science strives for precise measurement.* Physical scientists are capable of measuring wave lengths, distance, thickness, and other physical properties, with near absolute accuracy, as pointed out in item 7. The accomplishment of landing men on the moon is a testament to this measurement accuracy. Such near perfect measurement is now commonplace.

Behavioral scientists are not so fortunate. Because of the nature of the data, measurement is relatively imprecise and often unreliable. The margin of error is large. Even when measurement is precise it is not always clear exactly what is being measured.[24] Behavioral data measurements, in short, are rough. Now it is one thing to acknowledge the fallibility of one's measurements; that is only realistic. To do nothing to control it, however, would be negligent. Behavioral scientists, in fact, work constantly to improve their tests and other measuring instruments. And it pays off. More standardized tests are available today than ever before, and many of them are characterized by high degrees of reliability.

14. *Science seeks the simplest explanation.* It is called the law of parsimony.[25] It states:

- If something is unnecessary to an explanation, remove it.
  Always prefer the simplest explanation.

Convolution and unnecessary complexity are natural enemies of science. Countless textbook pages and equal numbers of research manuscripts are filled with needlessly complex diagrams, tables, and exposition. Why is there so much unclear, complex writing?

First, the simplest explanation is often far from obvious. Much time and effort may be required to sift through literally pounds of data in order to detect the simple thread uniting the several aspects. Second, some researchers are content only when dealing with the big, surface ideas. Were they to go a few steps beneath the surface, they might find the information that would simplify the entire set of findings. Finally, only a small percentage of behavioral scientists seem to be highly skilled in scientific writing.

15. *Scientists do not reject other modes of knowledge acquisition.* Experiments are designed to answer research questions. Scientific method is employed. It is a powerful mode of inquiry, but it is not the only method. Knowledge can be obtained through a variety of research procedures.

Historical analysis is one such method. The examination of the past in order to gain insights into the future is a well-established procedure. Even the controversial methods of the parapsychologist cannot be dismissed as obvious nonsense. Scientists take this view: Information—knowledge—can come from numerous sources, by investigators employing a wide variety of methods. None can be dismissed as valueless, nor can any of the findings be labeled untrue—unless counterevidence clearly demolishes their authenticity.

16. *Scientists are dedicated to the ultimate elimination of human bias, prejudice, and preference.* Distorted vision, bias, and prejudice are commonplace. In addition, thousands of people prefer one explanation over another on purely personal grounds. Scientific method takes a stand at the opposite end. Steps are constantly being taken to insure unbiased planning and execution of experiments. The same holds for human prejudice and personal preference. If medical scientists determine that a substance in a soft drink is likely to produce cancer cells in humans, then those findings must be made public, regardless of which groups will suffer economically. Pressure is often applied to prevent the dissemination of scientific data; to give in would be the end of science as we presently know it.

Are there areas of human behavior that should not be investigated? We can think of none. Sexual behavior was once considered a taboo research topic. Today it is widely researched, mainly because of the perseverance of large numbers of behavioral scientists. But, in general, there will always be those whose vested interest and personal involvement are considered, by them, to be sufficient to dictate what will be investigated and how the investigation will proceed.

Summary

The principles and assumptions of scientific method outlined above should be studied within the context of our hypothetical experiment. As you do so we hope you are impressed with the fact that experimental research makes heavy demands on the researcher. To conduct an effective experimental research program is a challenge. The pitfalls are many, and it is easy to go wrong. But the payoff can be highly satisfying: The good feeling that comes with discovery and with knowing that one has made a contribution to the world's knowledge.

We end this discussion of scientific method on a note of humility. Recall that immediately before discussing the first characteristic of science we wrote "These we consider fundamental." We chose those words with caution. The last impression we want to put forth is that we know what science really is—especially as it compares with other modes of inquiry. Clearly we do not. To be sure, at the extremes it seems easy enough to detect an unscientific from a scientific approach. But as we move toward the middle, the differences become more and more obscure. We become very reluctant, therefore, to throw the label "unscientific" on another's research endeavors. In this perspective, we find this comment by Mahoney particularly relevant:

At this point in time . . . no acceptable criterion has been established for the demarcation of science from nonscience. We must therefore proceed, if at all, with a humility about our understanding of what it is that constitutes "good scientific research" and show considerable tolerance for statements that convey relativity and tentativeness. Today's science may well be tomorrow's alchemy,...[26]

Testing

With the general principles of experimentation and scientific method before us, we turn to a description of other fundamental principles of experimental research. In this section we focus on the design of experiments in terms of testing—the number of tests, and the point in time at which they are administered.[27] The issue, then, can be resolved to these two considerations. Given that we are to perform an experiment, should the various experimental and control groups be tested before and after the experiment? Or will it be sufficient to test only once, at the conclusion of the experiment? The designs that follow are based essentially on this two-fold consideration.

The Pretest-Posttest Design. In this design subjects are pretested, the experimental treatment is applied, and then another test, the posttest, is given. The second test may be identical to the first, or it may be an equivalent form of it. Posttest scores are subtracted from pretest scores. The difference reflects the power of the experimental treatment.

Schematically:

$$[O_1 \ X \ O_2]$$

O_1 is the pretest, X the experimental treatment, and O_2 the posttest.

Advantages. The pretest-posttest design is simple and easy to execute. Experimental effects can be calculated for each subject showing the precise amount of change from pretest to posttest.

Disadvantages. Strictly speaking, the design requires that the pretest, experimental treatment, and posttest be administered without any time lapses between them. Had we used this design in our hypothetical experiment, we would have had to test the group, play the recorded communication immediately, and give the posttest immediately. This does not pose much of a challenge in some situations, but in others it may well be impractical. For example, subjects may be available for only a few minutes on one occasion and for a longer period of time on a second. On the first occasion enough time may be available to administer the pretest, but not to execute the entire experiment. The experimental treatment and the posttest have to await the second occasion. It is at this point that problems begin to multiply.

Time lapses between pretest, experimental treatment, and posttest tend to contaminate behavioral experiments. How does such contamination occur? To answer this question we must first note the logical model that has been followed in this case. It assumes that any differences between pretest and posttest result from subjects' exposure to the experimental treatment—that is, to the independent variable *and to nothing else.* If other unwanted factors combine with the experimental treatment, the study is said to be confounded. These unwanted sources of error include:[28]

1. Environmental influences. These are the events, happenings, stimuli—anything in the daily stream of life, from being served burned toast to witnessing the attempted assassination of a politician on an evening newscast.
2. Growing older. Commonly referred to as maturation, it amounts to this: People think, feel, and perceive things differently with the passage of time. The magnitude of the change may be simple or profound—but the change is both inevitable and inescapable.

In summary, unless pretest, experimental treatment, and posttest will follow one another without time interruption, then this design cannot be recommended.

The Pretest, Posttest, Control Group Design. This design is an extension of the pretest-posttest design, involving the addition of a control group. The purpose of the control group is to provide a baseline against which experimental groups are compared. Effects detected in the control group are subtracted from experimental group effects. What is left is assumed to be the true effects of the experimental treatment.

Schematically:

$$O_1 \; X \; O_2 \quad \text{EXPERIMENTAL GROUP}$$
$$O_3 \; - \; O_4 \quad \text{CONTROL GROUP}$$

Symbolization is the same as in Design 1. The $-$ indicates the absence of an experimental treatment. Both the experimental and the control groups are tested at the same time. Statistical analysis proceeds as follows: In the experimental group, pretest scores are subtracted from posttest scores. If the mean of O_1 is 15 and the mean of O_2 is 20, then the mean difference is 5. The same procedure is followed for the control group: assume the pretest mean to be 2 and the posttest mean to be 3 with mean difference equal to $3 - 2 = 1$. The final step in the analysis is to determine if the difference means, 5 and 1, themselves differ significantly.

Advantages. This design controls for the major sources of error detailed in the pretest-posttest design. Statistical analysis is straightforward, and interpretation of the results should present no particular problems.

Disadvantages. The design requires much testing—pretests and posttests in both groups.

The Posttest Only, Control Group Design. The design is characterized by an absence of pretests. Experimental and control groups are posttested simultaneously.

Schematically:

$$X \; O_1 \quad \text{EXPERIMENTAL GROUP}$$
$$- \; O_2 \quad \text{CONTROL GROUP}$$

Means are calculated for the two groups and are then tested for statistical significance.

Advantages. This design is the simplest of the three. The number of tests is cut in half and the possibility of a pretest effect is eliminated. Statistical analysis likewise is straightforward. Because of these obvious advantages behavioral scientists have gravitated toward this design so much so that Nunnally refers to it as "the workhorse of evaluation research."[29]

Disadvantages. Since there are no pretests it is not possible to calculate the amount of change subjects underwent. In this same vein, the investigators do not know how subjects might have scored before the experiment was executed. Such information is readily available whenever pretests are employed.

To summarize, the three designs outlined above account for the bulk of research done by behavioral scientists. The pretest-posttest, control group design and the posttest only, control group design are especially popular. Many other designs are available to the experimenter, but all are modifications or combinations of these basic building block designs.

Randomization

A behaviorial scientist would like to do research on two "pure" subjects, if they could be found. They cannot be!" "Pure" subjects are undefined; they do not exist. Any two subjects the scientist could select would have some basic similarities. The problem would lie in the magnitude of their differences. No matter how many pairs of subjects were examined, they would always exhibit heterogeneity. They would never qualify as "pure" or "identical."

What alternative does the behavioral scientist have? Basically only one: Run the experiment on *homogeneous* groups. Groups are defined as homogeneous to the extent that each exhibits about the same amount of any relevant characteristic, such as age, intelligence, values, attitudes, and educational level. How are homogeneous groups obtained? Through the process of *randomization.*

To illustrate, assume that five hundred subjects are available for experimentation purposes. They come from fifty sections of a basic course in human communication. Four groups will be formed: a control group and three experimental groups. If each group is to have fifty subjects, a total of two hundred subjects is required. In the absence of a systematic procedure for assigning subjects to the four groups, a disproportionate number with certain salient characteristics, such as sex or attitude toward serving as a nonvolunteer subject, could end up in one or the other groups. So randomization procedures are employed in assigning subjects to groups. To achieve randomization we assign each of the five hundred subjects a number from one to five hundred. Then we turn to a table of random numbers (found in most statistics texts).[30] A column of such numbers might look like this:

122699
721017
003918
499621
014721

Some tables contain hundreds of thousands of entries, so it is not likely that the researcher will exhaust the possibilities. Any procedure for assigning subjects will do. A simple one is to assign the first fifty relevant numbers to group one, the second fifty to group two, and so on until the two hundred have been selected. Since our highest number is 500 we are concerned only with the first three non-zero digits. In this perspective, the following subjects would be assigned to group one:

S 122	(122699)
S 3	(003918)
S 499	(499621)
S 14	(014721)

Since the first three digits of the second number in the original list, 721017, exceeded the number 500, it was ignored.

It can now be assumed that our four groups are relatively homogeneous. Randomization is not perfect, but no one has yet to devise a better alternative. Among the alternatives to randomization that should be avoided are these:

Drawing names from a hat.
Assigning on the basis of alphabetical order.
Assigning on the basis of seating position.
Assigning on the basis of intuition.

Error

Scientists are at war with error—for good reason. If we are to make valid comparisons between experimental and control groups, then the experiment must be characterized by a high degree of precision. This is another way of saying that all conditions, other than the experimental treatment, must be held constant. Look at it this way: If no other stimuli are present, then we can be confident that resulting differences are due to the effect of the experimental stimulus. But there are always other stimuli, and it is difficult to control them. Schematically, we would prefer this: $[X \rightarrow O]$ where X is the experimental treatment and O is a perfect test, or set of observations. In practice we get this:

$$[(E + X) \rightarrow (E + O)]$$

which translates into: Various kinds of error, E, combine with the experimental treatment, X. The combined $(E + X)$ is then imperfectly measured because O, too, has error associated with it $(E + O)$.

How is error dealt with, or minimized? First, we must recognize the most prevalent sources of error. Then we must exercise ingenuity in dealing with them. In what follows we outline a few of the more damaging varieties of error and offer advice on how to cope with them.

Intersubject Communication. Let us assume that in the hypothetical experiment described earlier we arranged for the four groups to meet at these times on the same day:

Control group at 5:00 P.M.
Experimental Group 1 at 6:00 P.M.
Experimental Group 2 at 7:00 P.M.
Experimental Group 3 at 8:00 P.M.

What are the weaknesses inherent in this procedure? Principally this: subjects coming out of the control group at 5:00 P.M. are in a position to communicate to subjects in Groups 1, 2, and 3. Similarly, Group 1 subjects can communicate with the last two groups; and, finally, Group 2 subjects can communicate with those in Group 3. If such intersubject communication occurs, it can create a bias, mental set, or a new attitude in a subject. In effect, it can destroy the homogeneous characteristic of the groups because *some* subjects in *some* of the groups may now differ substantially in some very important respects. To illustrate: Suppose half the subjects in one group were told "They are trying to get you to change your attitude toward capital punishment." Certainly we could expect this subgroup to have a different mental set as they went into the study. How would this intersubject communication affect the results of the experiment? Since extricating the influence of such a happening is virtually impossible, the experimental results would be rendered essentially uninterpretable. The solution is to execute the entire study at the same hour, for example 7:00 P.M., thus effectively blocking intersubject communication.

Ecological Influences. If an experiment must be conducted at the same hour for all groups, then more than one physical setting must be provided.[31] In our example we must have four rooms—one for the control group and one for each of the three experimental groups. But now a new problem surfaces: If the rooms differ markedly in heat, humidity, adequacy of lighting, comfort of seats, window space, or acoustics, then subjects in the less comfortable rooms could respond to the experiment in qualitatively different ways. The experiment, once again, could be confounded. The solution: Check for comparability. If comparable rooms are not available, consider postponing the study until they are.

Differential Biasing by Instructors. If the experiment involves university students—and many do—another potentially contaminating influence might be at work. Classroom instructors can and do influence the attitudes of research subjects. An instructor telling a class that they are "required to participate in some Mickey Mouse experiment" can spell disaster for the study. College instructors tend to vary in their support of experimentation, some for and others against. A few exhibit an attitude of neutrality. Hence, if students in various sections of a course (fifty sections in our example) are being differentially influenced by their respective instructors, then the experimental team may have a serious problem.

There is no easy solution to this one, but, we suggest you talk with the instructors personally. Explain the study and ask for their cooperation. Provide written instructions for them to read to their classes. Then keep your eyes open. Be alert to the possibility that one or more instructors may attempt to derail your study, and be prepared to adjust the execution of the experiment accordingly.

Experimenter Bias. Few topics have been more researched than that of the influence of the experimenter as a major source of potential error. Space does not permit even a superficial analysis of this topic, but you should be alert to some of the more threatening varieties. Returning to the hypothetical example, since four groups were scheduled at the same hour, we needed four different experimenters. The term *experimenter* refers to that person who is physically present in the room, who greets the subjects, tells them what is in store for them, executes the experimental plan, passes out the testing instrument, and debriefs, thanks, and dismisses the subjects. The experimenter, then, can be a college professor, a graduate student, or an undergraduate. Or it can be anyone of the researcher's choosing.

Unless precautions are taken, a number of problems can arise. To begin with, all four experimenters (Es) should behave in essentially similar ways. For example, it is necessary to avoid having overly friendly Es in two groups with correspondingly stern Es in the other two. Next, we want to keep the level of involvement of E with subjects consistent. This implies, for example, that Es would not interact with subjects in an entertaining manner.

Are sex and physical attractiveness potential problems? Yes. An attractive, blue-eyed, blonde female can influence groups differently than three rather average-looking males of the same age bracket.

The experimenter influence problem cannot be solved. It can only be worked at. But like all problems, the research team must work to keep the influence of these potentially confounding factors to a minimum. Some specific suggestions:

Obtain Es who are roughly comparable in terms of age, physical attractiveness, and grooming.

Avoid Es whose personality factors differ excessively from each other. Reasonably out-going, communicative, friendly individuals should be preferred.

Avoid utilizing Es whose appearance suggests they are members of specific political, social, or religious groups.

Use members of the same sex and ethnic background.

Use Es who are likely to take the experiment seriously and who are likely to follow instructions as provided.

Rehearse procedures until Es are entirely confident as to how they are to proceed. Stress the need for uniformity.

Give Es a checklist to take into the experiment. In addition, provide them with exact wording. Have them read instructions and other information to subjects. Do not ask that they memorize the information. This invites error and promotes nonuniform conditions.

Have Es report any critical deviations from the agreed-upon procedures. Evaluate this information as it relates to the outcome of the study.

Intersubject Bias. Subjects can bias other subjects before they arrive at the experiment. But, equally important, they can bias one another while the experiment is in progress. Consider this event: During the experiment one subject shouts "I think this whole thing is a bunch of baloney"! Another shouts: "I don't think we should be forced to be here if we don't want to"! This is followed by "That's right"! and "I agree"! from other subjects. If you were the director of this study, would you feel the results from this group would be sufficiently error-free to proceed with the overall analysis? Or, at the other extreme, would you be inclined to throw out these results? The situation would have to be evaluated, but our immediate inclination would favor not using this data base; there would simply be too much intersubject error. The solution is to train Es to be firm but friendly. Subjects tend to take advantage of those who project attitudes of weakness or insecurity. If Es, by both their verbal and nonverbal communication, lead subjects to believe that horseplay will not be tolerated, then they are likely to get none. Some other pointers:

Schedule the experiment at a time when the fewest numbers of subjects are likely to resent missing some event—a basketball or hockey game, a rock concert.

Let subjects know how long the session will take and when they can expect to finish.

Ask them to engage in fair play. If reminded, most people will comply.

Be explicit: ask them not to communicate during the experiment.

Do not answer questions. Make your instructions so clear that questions are unnecessary. Opening up a large group to questions invites a loss of control.

Instruct Es to lean on deviants firmly but unobtrusively.

If these suggestions are followed, subjects are likely to have a more positive attitude toward the experience.

Failure to Run a Pilot Study. The design and execution of an experiment is a complex undertaking. Inexperienced researchers sometimes fail to appreciate this, and so execute their studies without the benefit of a pilot. Such a shortcut rarely works. There are just too many ways for a study to fail. *No major study should be undertaken unless it has been preceded by a preliminary, or pilot, study.*[32]

A pilot will reveal trouble areas: defects in the design, execution problems, experimenter mistakes, to mention but a few. A sampling of problems that are likely to be detected in a pilot study:

Subjects did not bring pencils.

One or more of the experimenters failed to appear.

Tape recorder would not operate.

Test pages were stapled out of sequential order. Some pages were missing.

Some subjects could not find the room.
Subjects found the room but a class was occupying it.
Building was locked; subjects could not get in.
Many subjects failed to appear.
Experimenter played the wrong tape.
TV studio piped in the wrong program.
Room acoustics were intolerable. Subjects could not hear.

Does the list sound discouraging? In fact, all of these problems are controllable—if we know what they are. This is the value of the pilot. Over the years experimenters have found that some kinds of pilot studies are more profitable than others. Some principles for devising a pilot:

Devise a detailed checklist. Then work out a time sequence for the items. One way to do this is to imagine yourself to be a subject in one of the groups. Then ask yourself a series of questions. The individual answers will constitute a list of items that must be considered if the experiment is to succeed. Some examples:

The Subject Asks:	*This Implies:*
"How do I know I am to be in an experiment?"	I must communicate dates, times, places.
"What do I do after I get there?"	Experimenter must be fully trained to direct the subject, execute the study, and so on.

This procedure will help you visualize some of the major steps from the subject's point of view. You can expand this list by asking specific questions about each segment of the study. For example, every experiment must have some kind of dependent variable, so these kinds of questions are implied:

Who will obtain the duplicated copies?
Who will check to be sure there are adequate copies, that they have been stapled in the right order, and that they have been properly distributed to experimenters?
What happens if an experimenter runs out of copies during the experiment?
Who will check to be sure all of the above are carried out?

Because the details of running an experiment can seem endless, the sequential "to do" checklist is a must.

Avoid shortcuts. Run the entire experiment with the same number of subjects that will be used in the main experiment. In fact, do everything as you plan to do it in the main study. In effect, then, you conduct two studies. Resist the normal urge to reduce the pilot to a few essential steps. Such shortcut studies are of little value because they are not comparable enough in structure to the main study.

Make detailed observations. Determine what went wrong and what factors were responsible.

Solicit advice. Ask those who helped execute the study for their opinions and recommendations. Interview a few subjects in both the experimental and the control groups. Find out what they considered positive about their experience. More important, ask for negative feedback. If subjects were irritated with the procedures this can translate into additional experiment error.

Analyze the data base. Make all computer runs.

Employ the triple redundancy principle. Assume things will go wrong. Then arrange to have two backups. This applies to materials, locations, and especially to people. Never assume anything will happen precisely as planned.

A well-executed pilot study is one of the strongest factors in combating experiment error. It will not guarantee that the main experiment will be error-free, but it will minimize the probability that the experiment will have to be discarded due to major flaws in design or execution.

In summary, the principles of experimental research outlined above are designed to maximize the *internal validity* of the study. The ultimate criterion for evaluating an experiment is this: Can the results be attributed solely—or, at least, essentially—to the effects of the experimental treatments (the independent variables)? Or are there alternative, rival explanations for the results that are equally plausible and cannot be ruled out? High levels of internal validity, then, mean that the known and important sources of error were controlled or at least minimized. And what of *external validity*, or the generalizability of the study? At this point the most straightforward answer is that the results of most behavioral experiments cannot be widely generalized. If the sample is chosen with care and if it is representative of some larger population, then some generalization is possible. The problem lies with determining if in fact both these conditions have been met. We should emphasize that we are not overly concerned with the generalization issue. As we point out elsewhere, replication is the more important factor. As studies are replicated across experiments, the basis for valid generalization expands.

INDEPENDENT AND DEPENDENT VARIABLES: FURTHER CONSIDERATIONS

The Independent Variable

In our hypothetical experiment we utilized one control group and three experimental groups. The independent variable—the general factor under study—was institutional prestige of the communicator. Three levels of prestige were manipulated: high, medium, and low. Since only one factor was involved, the design is classified as *single factor*. In this case, the factor was decomposed into three levels. But, regardless of the number of levels, the study remains a single-factor design.

Schematically:

Levels of the Factor

	High Prestige: a_1	Medium Prestige: a_2	Low Prestige: a_3
FACTOR A: INSTITUTIONAL AFFILIATION			

Single-factor designs have been widely employed in the past, and for some kinds of research problems, especially basic research, they are still the optimum choice.

Suppose a researcher wants to study a second factor. Must he or she run two single-factor studies? No. Such a procedure would waste time, money, and resources. The solution lies in the idea of *factorial designs*. A two-factor (factorial) design is schematized in Figure 6-1.

Derived from our hypothetical experiment, this study seeks to discover how male and female communicators are related to communicator credibility in terms of persuasiveness. The design is called a 2 × 2 factorial, meaning there are two factors under consideration, each at two levels. Factor A is designated a sex factor. There are two levels of the factor: a_1 = male; a_2 = female. Factor B, credibility, has two levels: high and low. Other characteristics of the design are:

1. Factor A is called the row factor. The two rows are represented by the two levels: a_1 and a_2.
2. Factor B is called the column factor. The two columns are represented by the two levels: b_1 and b_2.

FACTOR *B*: CREDIBILITY

FACTOR *A:* SEX		High b_1	Low b_2
	Male: a_1	Cell 11 n = 50	Cell 12 n = 50
	Female: a_2	Cell 21 n = 50	Cell 22 n = 50

Figure 6-1. A 2 × 2 factorial design.

3. Individual cells are designated by the intersection of a row with a column. In our example, the cell designation for male and high credibility is Row 1, Column 1, or Cell 11.
4. A level of a factor consists of the subjects in that row or column. There are n = 50 subjects in Cell 11. There are also n = 50 in Cell 12. Level a_1, then, consists of n = 100 males. When subjects comprising individual rows or col-

umns are combined into single groups the new configuration is called a *main effect*. Hence the two levels of Factor A constitute the main effect of the sex factor.

Factor B likewise has two main effects associated with it. They are obtained by combining the subjects in Cells 11 and 21 into a single group. Similarly are Cells 12 and 22 combined. The result is the main effect of communicator credibility, high and low.

Factorial designs, as our analysis indicates, can be employed to study the effects of the communicator's sex and the effect of his or her credibility simultaneously. The first research question is: Are the main effects of Factor A significantly different? To understand the concept of main effects more fully let us picture it somewhat differently.

FACTOR A: SEX	Male: a_1	n = 100
	Female: a_2	n = 100

The main effect of A ignores the fact that there is a second factor, B. It simply asks whether males are more persuasive than females, laying aside, temporarily the fact that some are designated high and others low in prestige.

Factor B succumbs to the same line of inquiry. It asks if high-credibility communicators are more persuasive than are low-credibility communicators, irrespective of sex.

FACTOR B: CREDIBILITY	High: b_1	n = 100
	Low: b_2	n = 100

In summary, factorial designs always test the main effects of each factor to determine if they differ significantly.

The final consideration in a 2 × 2 factorial design is whether there exists a significant AB *interaction*. To study the nature of interactions we return to the full 2 × 2 design of Figure 6-1. After studying the design, a researcher might ask these questions:

1. Are male, high credibility communicators more persuasive than any of the three remaining combinations?
2. Are female, high-credibility communicators and male, low-credibility communicators equally persuasive, and are both more persuasive than male-high and female-low communicators? The answer to the first question would be yes if the means for the individual cells looked something like this:

Male
High-credibility
$\overline{X} = 10.00$

Male
Low-credibility
$\overline{X} = 6.00$

Female
High-credibility
$\overline{X} = 6.00$

Female
Low-credibility
$\overline{X} = 6.00$

The male, high-credibility mean is 10.00. The remaining cell means are identical at 6.00. Though the means have not been statistically analyzed, it seems evident that the male, high-credibility communicator was more persuasive than any of the remaining three combinations.

Turning to the second question, a schematic that looked somewhat like the following,

Male
High-credibility
$\overline{X} = 5.00$

Male
Low-credibility
$\overline{X} = 10.00$

Female
High-credibility
$\overline{X} = 10.00$

Female
Low-credibility
$\overline{X} = 5.00$

with the means as indicated, would lead to a clear inference: that female, high-credibility communicators and male, low-credibility communicators are equally persuasive. Second, it would also indicate both are more persuasive than either male, high-credibility or female, low-credibility communicators.

These are two examples of AB interaction analysis. In higher-order designs, such as designs with three and four factors, interpreting interactions becomes increasingly difficult.

Main Effects and Interactions. Experienced researchers know that main effects are easier to interpret than are interactions. To say that males are more persuasive than females is straightforward. It is a simple, parsimonious explanation. And to conclude that high-credibility communicators are more persuasive than their low-credibility counterparts is equally parsimonious. It is not necessary to use the phrase "it depends."

Significant interactions are more complex. In 2 X 2 factorial designs, they are usually interpretable. But interactions are far less parsimonious than are main effects. Indeed the phrase "it depends" describes well what interactions are all about.

How does a researcher interpret a significant interaction when one or more significant main effects also exist? By this rule: *In the presence of a significant interaction main effects are not interpretable.*[33] In other words, if you have an interaction, interpret the interaction and forget about the significant main effects.

Higher-Order Factorial Designs. The 2 X 2 factorial is a classic, easily interpreted design. But designs need not be limited in terms of factors or levels. Note these higher order designs:

2 X 2 X 2:	A three-factor design in which each factor has two levels.
3 X 3:	A two-factor design in which each factor has three levels.
4 X 5 X 6 X 4:	A four-factor design in which Factor A has 4 levels; B has 5 levels; C has 6 levels; and D has 4 levels.

Since the number of factors and levels in a factorial design are limitless, the researcher might think these more complex designs are to be preferred. The opposite is true. Higher-order designs become increasingly more difficult to interpret, especially if interactions result. A handy rule of thumb is to add factors only when absolutely necessary.

The Dependent Variable

The most precisely executed experiment is of questionable value if the dependent variable is found to be weak. For some reason, otherwise competent, thoughtful researchers often spend only a few minutes choosing a relevant, psychometrically sound measuring instrument. The results inevitably turn out badly. We recommend several principles to the behavioral researcher. (For additional details see Chapter 7.)

The dependent variable must be *relevant* to the independent variable. An experiment designed to test the differential ability of high- and low-credibility communicators to persuade subjects as to the value of annual medical checkups must have an instrument capable of measuring attitudes toward that topic. Similarly, a study of political images must have as a dependent variable a test that does in fact measure political images.

Dependent variables must be *reliable*.[34] We define reliability as the ability of the test to obtain consistent results on subsequent occasions. A test that reveals an IQ of 115 on one occasion and 76 on another would be considered unreliable because of an apparent accumulation of random error, sometimes called chance error. Such a test would be of no value to scientific researchers.

Ultimately, the *validity* of a test must be established. Validity is the degree to which a test measures what in fact it purports to measure.[35] Does a high score on a Dogmatism test[36] correlate highly with dogmatic behavior in real life? Put slightly differently, the Dogmatism test is perfectly valid if subjects' true scores (that is, error-free scores) are perfectly correlated with the "dogmatic behavior." This is the classic validity problem. If we cannot demonstrate such relationships, then our experimentation is little more than scientific busy work.

Validity studies pose challenges for several reasons. First, it is extremely difficult to determine if the phenomenon is operating in the nonverbal world. We speak of Machiavellianism,[37] of helplessness,[38] of alienation.[39] Each is a construct, devised and measured by behavioral scientists. So far, so good. But the vital question is: Do these and other constructs have an existence apart from the paper-and-pencil responses of our research subjects? At this point our confidence in these measures is likely to wane. We find some evidence here, a little more there. We conclude that, for some constructs at least, there may be a real-world counterpart.

But the evidence always comes slowly. There are often setbacks. Furthermore, validity studies are expensive.

Another problem: Even if the phenomenon actually exists it is often difficult to obtain a high correlation between behavior on the test and behavior under real-world conditions. It should come as no surprise, then, that most researchers spend more of their time making instruments more reliable than they do in attempting to establish validity—an unfortunate but realistic condition. We can only repeat that validity research cannot be put off indefinitely. Until it has been at least moderately established, the dependent variable in question cannot enjoy high status.

Established tests are preferable to ones designed for a particular research project. Hundreds of tests and measuring instruments are now available to the behavioral researcher. Many have evolved methodically and have adequate reliability coefficients associated with them. Additionally, many have been factor analyzed, and their structure is reasonably well known. Tests that have survived widespread use are distinctly superior research buys.

What are the alternatives? You can devise your own test. We have seen many beginning researchers do this. The results are almost always disappointing. First, to devise an adequate test you must be prepared to work for several months—unless you have a simple instrument in mind. Countless operations are involved, and they eat up the hours. Second, few researchers have the necessary background in psychometric theory to know how to proceed; so the task quickly becomes too complex. You can shortcut the process; many try. In the end the price is paid in the form of unacceptable papers or rejected manuscripts.

When selecting a dependent variable, ask for advice. Most of us do not understand the complex area of test theory very well. That being the case it makes sense to seek the guidance of others. To whom should we turn? Your adviser, others of known reputation in your locality, seasoned researchers, and published researchers who used the test you are considering in their own research. Do not overlook the person most responsible for the development and evolution of the test. Are they famous people who have no time for beginning researchers? Definitely not! If you write or call them, you will be surprised how cooperative they will be.

A final word of advice on dependent variable selection: Do not rush into choosing one. Allow time to study, reflect, evaluate. Do not proceed until you are convinced you have the right test, one that will stand up under the scrutiny of other researchers.

CRITICISMS OF LABORATORY EXPERIMENTS

At the outset of this chapter we suggested that the experimental method was best for some kinds of problems and that its use in behavioral research was controversial. We now examine some of the criticisms of the experimental method. Some are well reasoned, others are based on an ignorance of scientific method generally, and still others seem to stem from pure prejudice or even envy.

Assertion: Laboratory experiments are artificial. Their findings are not relevant to the real world.

Response: Laboratory experiments are artificial to the extent that people are placed in defined situations—often unlike their everyday experiences. This allows for the study of relationships with a precision that is impossible in most naturally occurring life situations. In the real-life situation small but important differences are likely to go unnoticed—to be literally buried with the hundreds of ongoing events. In the laboratory the researcher can observe with greater precision. A principle discovered in an experimental situation can be injected into more natural, real-life situations to test its effect under those conditions. If the principle also operates there, then researchers may suspect it has wider generalizability. If it does not, then researchers can continue to study the phenomenon until the reasons for the failure under natural conditions become clearer.

Scientific laboratory experiments are a logical first step, for we must first establish that something is operating before we can test it on a larger scale.

However, laboratory experiments are totally inappropriate for a variety of research problems. Naturally occurring events, by definition, cannot be duplicated in the laboratory. Knowledge of the conditions surrounding the explosion of Mount St. Helens, for example, must come through other research processes, such as the interview. The same holds for other disasters and important events, such as political conventions. True, we can simulate disasters and conventions. But simulations are not a substitute for the actual event. The knowledge gained is distinctly different.

Assertion: A single experiment does not prove anything.

Response: True, it does not. And seasoned researchers do not claim otherwise. A well-conceived study provides a set of indications that one or more principles may be operating. But only when a number of studies point to essentially the same conclusions can we move toward wider generalization. Researchers, at least the more experienced ones, fully understand the need for large numbers of studies. They are cautious, and they are slow to generalize.

Assertion: People are unique. Their behavior cannot be predicted.

Response: The behavior of large groups of people can be predicted, within limits, on a variety of important variables. One need only glance through the research literature of the past hundred years to verify this claim.

We concur that people are characterized by some unknown degree of individuality. What any single person will do under any given set of conditions is difficult to predict. The point, however, is that most behavioral researchers seek to predict group behavior, rather than individual behavior.

Assertion: Scientists have no right to experiment on people.

Response: Scientists conduct studies to further knowledge of the world we live in. It is difficult to accept the idea that some kinds of investigations are off-limits. Throughout history individuals and groups have demanded an end to this or that kind of research. Science has pressed forward in the face of this opposition.

We are not advocating that anyone be allowed to do whatever he or she wishes in the name of research. Clearly, limits must be established. Our position is this: If scientific research is to be limited, then let those decisions be made at a high level. State and federal governments, as representatives of the citizens, are in the best position to make such decisions. Small subgroups of people scattered throughout the nation rarely reflect public opinion.

Assertion: There is too much error in behavioral experiments.

Response: We agree—there is far too much. Behavioral scientists are not hesitant to admit it. Some published studies have practically no scientific value because of an excess of uncontrolled error. Other studies are exemplary in their apparent success at controlling many of the more obvious types of error. Still, at this point in the development of scientific research on humans, error continues to be the enemy. Worse yet, it appears to be a far greater problem than was originally thought.

One reasonable answer to the error problem has already been discussed: replication. If studies are replicated under a wide variety of experimental designs and conditions, then error will tend to cancel itself out, or become neutralized. Another answer is to design studies in which potentially confounding factors (error) are the independent variable. If we focus directly on these error factors, we will be better able to assess their influence.

Assertion: Behavioral scientists are not sophisticated. Even novice researchers or students in an introduction to graduate studies course can detect errors in published research.

Response: Behavioral scientists have severely limited resources. Only a small percentage manage to get grant money. They are forced to limit the scope of their research. Any study could always have been bigger, more sophisticated, more complex, multivariate rather than univariate. Further, the researcher could have used a better test, kept experimenter error more in check—these and hundreds of other "could haves." But, within the limitations imposed, the researcher probably did the best he or she could. Our job, as consumers of research, is to glean from the study whatever value we can. Perhaps someone concludes that a study is entirely useless. That is their prerogative. But we have found no published study that had absolutely no value. We would advise that you not be too eager to label a study worthless until you have conferred with more experienced researchers.

Some behavioralists in the field of speech communication—and other fields—are not as methodologically sophisticated as we, they, or anyone else might wish. It is simply a fact that we have to live with. If you wonder why researchers in some other domains—for example, psychology—seem to have more research expertise, take a look at the history of our field. For years, the field of speech communication was characterized by courses in voice and diction, public speaking, acting, and the like. Such courses attracted largely students with little if any background or interest in scientific method, mathematics, or statistics, and so there was no demand for coursework in these areas. Only since the 1960s has a pronounced change taken place. Today virtually all graduate programs contain offerings in many kinds of research, including experimental research. Statistical methods courses—both univariate and multivariate—have likewise mushroomed. The result: most researchers in our field are as sophisticated as those in any behavioral field—psychology, social psychology, or educational research.

Assertion: People—especially students—resent serving as guinea pigs in experiments and so purposely set out to sabotage them. Can we place much faith in the results of such studies?

Response: You cannot—not if things really are that bad. It is true, some subjects resent having to participate in an experiment. And some seem to go out of their way to sabotage a study. That is another example of error—in this case, subject error. How do we deal with it?

One effective way is to treat subjects as though they were human beings. When they are dehumanized, they resent it and the experimenter pays the price. In our experience we have run into a variety of negative attitudes, often justified, among subjects. But we have more frequently detected positive attitudes, and the experiments have come off without a flaw. We interviewed a number of subjects with positive attitudes to find out why they seemed so cooperative. On the basis of our investigation we were led to several conclusions. First, as we suspected, we found most subjects to be positive and cooperative to the extent that they felt the research team respected them and acted so as not to rob them of their dignity as human beings. Second, we found that communication failure was the single, most frequently cited reason for subjects' developing negative attitudes. They were not told where to go, when to go, or how long the experiment would take. Often they received conflicting messages, thus adding further to their frustration. Amateurishness ranked next highest in aggravating subjects. Subjects were appalled to witness a study falling apart before their eyes. Some examples: television sets that did not work, experimental assistants who never arrived, room assignments in which a class was in progress—these are a few indicators of amateurishness that make for negative attitudes in subjects. No such breakdowns are necessary. A well-conducted pilot study can catch them before they turn into problems.

PART THREE

SPECIFIC CONCERNS

7

Generating
Quantitative Data

Research involves working with quantifiable data. This is always true of scientific research and typically true of descriptive and survey research. Even historical researchers are increasingly turning to enumeration and measurement for answers to research questions.

Most of the quantitative data generated by speech-communication researchers is likely to result from tests or similar types of measuring instruments administered to one or more groups of research subjects. In the typical research project, subjects fill out the instrument at a time controlled by the researcher. In some investigations the subjects may be observed by a team of researchers who rate, or describe, their behavior against a set of scale items.

The theory associated with the testing of research subjects appears in textbooks under such labels as "psychometric theory,"[1] "measurement and assessment,"[2] and "procedures for observation and measurement."[3] The content is fairly consistent since the problems associated with measurement on human subjects tends to vary little across research studies. In this chapter we confront several classic concerns:

1. The problem of samples and sampling procedures: How should subjects be selected and how large should the sample be?
2. The problem of scaling: What rules govern the assigning of numbers to individual test items?
3. The construct dimension problem: How many qualitatively different constructs (dimensions) does the test measure and how are they determined?
4. The reliability problem: Will successive administrations of the test produce consistent results?
5. The validity problem: Do scores on the test correlate with behavior external to the test itself?

Researchers obtain quantitative data on subjects, but not just on any subjects. The group of subjects used in a research project constitute a sample, and the characteristics of the sample are a basic consideration that must be resolved before the data are collected. Moreover, the number of subjects needed to meet acceptable statistical standards must be estimated. These procedures help to insure that the sample obtained is not inadequate or biased. Sampling theory is complex at the higher levels. Fortunately, a knowledge of the more basic aspects is sufficient for most researchers.

Sampling as a Consideration in the Design of Research Studies

Both survey researchers and experimental researchers are concerned with obtaining a group of subjects (the sample) who are an appropriate representation given the goals of the research. First, the number of subjects needed must be determined. Second, a selection procedure must be adopted. Third, the desired set of characteristics the subjects must display must be considered. Unless all three operations are carefully worked out before the research begins, the investigator runs the risk of obtaining interesting but scientifically irrelevant quantitative data. Those considerations are contained in questions such as these:

1. How many subjects are needed to fulfill the criterion of adequacy—fifty, one hundred, one thousand? What is the minimum number that is acceptable? Is it possible to have too many subjects for a given research project, or is "the more, the better" a reasonable rule?
2. Must the sample be based on randomization principles?
3. What characteristics should the sample members display—similarity in ages, education, socioeconomic status?

Sample Size

Obtaining the subjects needed to conduct an investigation can be a highly frustrating experience. Often you simply cannot find enough subjects. Even when the subjects are available, you may not be able to enlist their participation, for any of several reasons.

First, the pool of potential, qualified subjects at any research location is limited. This seems to be true in industrial organizations, at military installations, and at homes for the aged, to mention but a few. On university campuses the situation may be even more acute. Small colleges may have only two hundred subjects available in a given semester. Even larger educational institutions have trouble maintaining ample subject pools.

Second, some members of a potential sample may object to participating in research. They see such research as an invasion of their privacy, or they look at quantification studies as inherently dehumanizing. Still others may distrust quantitative researchers—some with good reason.

Competition for subjects also depletes the available pool. If four hundred subjects are available and if five research teams each need two hundred subjects, it is clear that some compromises must be made. Is such demand a likely occurrence? Unfortunately it is. Each of the authors of this text witnesses this kind of situation several times a year.

Subject mortality takes its toll. You think you have a commitment from one hundred subjects, but when it is time to execute the study, only forty-six show up. The others forgot, decided they had more interesting things to do, or perhaps lost the slip of paper telling them where to report.

These represent a sampling of the factors contributing to the scarcity of subjects for research projects. The message to researchers is clear: Do not assume adequate numbers of subjects will be made available. The research team must exercise its ingenuity and work hard at recruiting a sufficient number of subjects. Otherwise the result is almost certain to be a sample that by any acceptability criterion is too small.

How many subjects will you need? No precise recommendation is possible, but there are guidelines and a few widely employed rules of thumb.

Sampling procedures have developed to the point where extermely large numbers are no longer required. To determine the current image of a United States senator, a researcher needs a sample of approximately thirteen-hundred American citizens. That is the optimum sample size. A smaller sample is likely to give a distorted view; a larger sample will provide redundant information. And so it is in other research domains. The research age in which we live is characterized by the use of small samples.

For experiments, correlational studies, surveys, and a variety of other research endeavors, it is possible to make reasonable estimates of the number of subjects needed. You simply consult the appropriate "power" table for the needed information.[4] Power tables are designed to take much of the guesswork out of sample size determination. When such tables are used, the research study cannot be criticized for having too few or too many subjects, either of which could pose a threat to the integrity of the research findings.

The statistical model employed and the number of items or questions may dictate the minimum sample size required. This is true for virtually all multivariate models, including the four basic models discussed in Chapter 8. In general, multivariate models imply the use of large samples. Five hundred is considered excellent, though it is frequently not attained.

Some research designs are more efficient than others; consequently, fewer subjects are needed. A class of designs called *repeated measures* represents a case in point. In these designs the same subjects are observed at least twice and often three or more times. Repeated measurement designs are considered to be statistically efficient, for good reason. To illustrate, assume ten subjects are measured over ten trials. In terms of the statistical analysis the study has the equivalent of one hundred subjects. Yet the total sample consisted of but ten.

Factorial designs of the type discussed in Chapter 6 represent another class of efficient designs—efficient, again, in terms of maximum utilization of subjects. Consider again the basic 2 X 2 factorial design, depicted in Figure 7-1. Recall that to compute means for the main effect of *A* requires that cells 11 and 12 be collapsed into a single cell. Likewise cells 21 and 22 are collapsed. Why is a factorial design maximally efficient? Because the identical subjects are used to test for significance of the main effect of *A*, of *B*, and the *AB* interaction. The principle holds for factorial designs of any order.

If an adequate sample is not available, the researcher has at least two options: He or she may wait until sufficient numbers are available or proceed to execute the study anyway. If the latter course is pursued, the basic question will be: How are the results to be interpreted? Cautiously—they will constitute a set of rough indicators at best.

It is possible to obtain statistical significance even if the sample size is inadequate; in fact, the research literature contains numerous examples of this. However, two questions always arise. The first that must be asked is, despite the statistical significance, can the findings be replicated? Or was the set of results a chance happening—a rare occurrence? We never know. What we do know is that significance under conditions of adequate sample size is more likely to render the study replicable. When a small sample is combined with nonsignificant results yet another question must be asked. Was the nonsignificance the result of a lack of statistical power (a sample that was not large enough to detect differences)? Or were there

FACTOR *B*

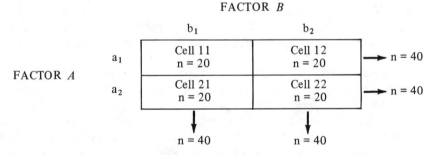

Figure 7-1 A 2 X 2 factorial design illustrating efficient use of subjects.

really no differences among the measurements? The only answer is that there is no way of knowing—one good reason for routinely running a power analysis prior to executing a study.

Randomization

The idea of randomization is basic to behavioral research. Nothing can cast doubt on the integrity of a study faster than an indication that the randomization procedure was not invoked when it would have been appropriate. Despite this truism the behavioral research literature contains studies where randomization was clearly appropriate but was not utilized.

To appreciate the need for randomization procedures it is helpful to look at scientific research in the physical sciences. Suppose a metallurgical team wishes to study the effects of acids on iron. Two slabs of iron are obtained. Each is submerged in acid for a period of one hour. Each slab is then removed and examined. The results reveal that the acids differentially affected the slabs of iron. Furthermore, the differences can be directly attributed to the action of the acids. What conditions made such unequivocal statements possible? Two things. One, the characteristics of the acid were perfectly known. And two, there was virtually no contamination—the acids and the iron were pure, uniform throughout. True, some specks of impurity could be found in both the acids and the iron, but not enough to affect the results of the experiment. In general, both the acids and iron slabs were characterized by high degrees of homogeneity—that is, purity.

Communication researchers, however, work mostly with humans, who tend to vary on a large number of characteristics. No two research samples can ever approach the degree of homogeneity of the acid and the iron slabs. Yet, that is precisely the behavioral researcher's goal: to obtain samples that are homogeneous throughout. The researcher will fail and a compromise will take place. It always has. And it is at this point that the principle of randomization takes on critical significance.

As an example, consider this basic research problem: Subjects are required to read the same poem before a television camera under three different conditions of induced apprehension. The researcher wishes to test the hypothesis that the different experimental conditions produce different group responses. We need not be concerned with the details of the design to appreciate the role randomization plays in the overall design of such an experiment. A causal model is being tested. The induced apprehension is tentatively assumed to be a causal agent. If it is powerful enough, then subjects under the three conditions should be differentially affected. What is needed to carry out this experiment with appropriate scientific rigor is an assurance that the three groups are relatively homogeneous before the experimental conditions are introduced, for if they differ in some important ways prior to the experiment, then we shall be unable to unravel the system of possible causes that contributed to the group differences. Was it the experimental variations? Or were the groups heterogeneous to begin with? Under these latter conditions, the study is said to be confounded. It is, in effect, uninterpretable.

The recommended procedure for achieving the needed homogeneity in this specific instance is randomization. It operates so as to assign subjects to groups solely on the basis of chance. Groups so formed will always exhibit minor variation; that is to be expected. Still, they can be assumed essentially equivalent, except in those rare instances in which randomization fails.

In this experiment assume that two hundred sophomores enrolled in a basic speech-communication course constitute the available subject pool. The researchers estimate that fifty subjects will be needed in each of the three cells. Subjects are randomly assigned to one of the three groups. The recommended procedure is to employ a table of random numbers. There is no viable alternative method for assuring random assignment of the subjects.

There is an important limiting condition of this procedure: We have randomized an available pool of subjects; we have not obtained a random sample of college students. This is a frequently misunderstood aspect of randomization, and a point to which we will return when we discuss generalizability. Finally, we must be careful not to assume that our sample is a truly random sample of 150 Americans. Such a sample would be unbelievably heterogeneous and would be of no scientific value. Our sample can most accurately be described as randomly assigned subjects from an initial pool or population of 200.

Generalizability[5]

Research is conducted to provide the basis for making inferences about a larger class of persons—that is, a population. Otherwise, each study would be akin to a historical event. Something could happen, but it would have little or no application to a research theory. Ideally, then, a single study ought to be generalizable to a larger population. Because generalization is never easy in practice, most researchers err on the side of caution. Either they fail to generalize at all, or they limit their generalizations so severely that other researchers cannot readily understand the kinds of subjects who might be included in the larger population.

Consider another example: Two groups are formed through the random assignment of one hundred university freshmen. A significant difference between means shows the "introvert" group to be more persuasible than the "extrovert" group. To what extent can we generalize? To college freshmen across the country? We think not, for the sample of freshman at the university in question no doubt differs in many essential respects from college freshmen in general. To generalize to all freshmen the research team would have to demonstrate that the sample of one hundred was representative of the population of all college freshmen. They would be hard pressed to demonstrate such similarities. On the other hand, given the money and resources, it would be possible to obtain a sample that could qualify as representative of all college freshmen. Conclusion: Widely representative samples *can* be obtained, but they rarely are. Few researchers have sufficient time, money, manpower, and other needed resources.

The fact that the results of most studies cannot be widely generalized should be of little concern. In the perspective of building meaningful theory in the behavioral sciences, the ability to generalize widely from a single study is less than critical. As we have discussed in other chapters, theory evolves from principles demonstrated on a large number of well designed and executed studies. While the findings of a single study can be misleading, the findings of many will illuminate. We do not advocate reckless, meaningless sample selection. Certainly a more generalizable sample is always to be preferred. We feel only that the "But can you generalize?" argument has been overemphasized.

The College Sophomore Phenomenon. The issue of generalizability sometimes leads to this assertion: "Far too many studies are conducted on college sophomores," or "Our behavioral theories are restricted to theories of college students."

First, the word sophomores is unfortunate. Research in universities is often conducted also on freshmen, juniors, seniors, and even graduate students. The sophomore emphasis probably came about because large sections of some basic courses—for example, the basic course in psychology—is often numbered at the sophomore level. And as any college student soon learns, large sections of basic courses tend to be researched.

The so-called sophomore issue raises basic questions such as these: Are college sophomores representative of people in general? Can knowledge about the behavior of sophomores be extrapolated to any group? To the first question, the answer is no. Sophomores are not representative of people in general—that is, of people from all income groups, ethnic origins, educational levels, and ages. But the answer to the second question is yes. Some of what is learned in research on sophomores will help us predict the behavior of people generally. The reason: Sophomores, too, are human beings, and since all human beings share certain common characteristics, it follows that the behavior of sophomores could suggest patterns that may be found in others. Put differently, suppose researchers feel that a principle of human communication—for example, reciprocity in self-disclosure—is operative in Americans generally. The hypothesis is tested on sophomores. Results reveal a very strong tendency for such reciprocal self-disclosure. The principle is tested on other college students. The results all coincide. Our position is that if the principle is strong enough to surface across many samples of college students, then it ought to have some implications for Americans generally. Note that two conditions were met. The principle was found to operate in later replication studies, and the principle came through strongly in each case.

Biased Samples

Researchers sometimes use a group of subjects simply because they are available. Classic examples are the use of intact classes of some multisectioned course. Suppose, for instance, that Speech 102, Introduction to Speech Communication, is taught by nine different instructors in the college. Students sign up for one section or another depending upon such variables as the instructor's reputation, the time of meeting, and certain other factors. Each class admits fifteen—and only fifteen—students. A researcher wishes to run a study involving three groups. The groups are formed by assigning three classes to Group 1, three to Group 2, and three to Group 3. Each group, then, will contain forty-five subjects. Can subjects be considered to have been randomly assigned to the three groups? Clearly they cannot because they were not formed by randomization procedures. They constitute a biased sample.

The bias stems from the fact that students most likely did not select their classes in a random way. Some chose a section because the instructor was considered easy while others chose it for just the opposite reason. Many reasons may have influenced the selection process. The inescapable conclusion is that the groups are not homogeneous on the characteristics likely to be important to the researcher.

Whatever the research results, they will be confounded with differences already existing in the samples before the research is carried out.

Subjects in the nine sections, however, can be formed into scientifically accept-able samples. All that is necessary is that the total pool of 135 students be assigned to the three groups by recourse to a table of random numbers.[6] Again, the group will not be a random sample. But the total sample of 135 subjects will have been assigned to the three groups via strictly random procedures.

Our general feeling is that intact or otherwise preformed groups should never be utilized as research subjects. *There is no substitute for randomizing.* But having said that, we point to a seeming exception. Consider the example of the sinking of the Titanic. The ship sinks; the survivors form a biased, intact group. Should we not conduct research on these survivors? We should indeed; the information they provide will be of unquestionable value. Note, however, that the research can never qualify as scientific research. First, there is no comparison group. And second, random procedures were not involved. The findings of the research, then, are limited to the particular subjects involved.

SCALING

Tests and other measuring instruments usually consist of ordered collections of scale items or of individual test questions. They are characterized by the presence or absence of certain measurement properties. All provide for subject, or observer, responses. The type of question (or scale item), the method of scoring it, and the relationship of individual items to total test scores—these and similar concerns grow out of an area known as scaling theory.[7]

Types of Measurement Scales

Stevens[8] has presented a rationale for four types of measurement scales: nominal, ordinal, interval, and ratio. This classification scheme has since become a central part of classical measurement theory.

The Nominal Scale. The nominal scale places persons, entities, or things into predesignated categories. A minimum of two categories, is necessary; otherwise, differentiation is not possible. The categories must also be distinct. Classifying people by sex is an exercise in nominal scale usage, in that the two classes are categorically different. Numbers applied to football player jerseys are likewise nominal scales. The numbers do not differentiate the players on the degree to which they demonstrate some characteristic. They do nothing more than differenti-ate each player from the other players.

Although nominal scales would appear to have limited value to the researcher, they can in fact play a major role in studies using such statistical models as multiple regression, canonical correlation, and discriminant analysis. Their popularity derives from the fact that group membership variables are in fact nominal scales. It is possible, for example, to assess the relationship between being a Catholic, Protestant, or Jew and scores on any tests of interest to a researcher. The religious groups are coded 1 if they fall into the category, 0 otherwise:

100 = Catholic
010 = Protestant
001 = Jew

A canonical correlation utilizing the nominal scale categorical system could find, for instance, that Catholics tend to strongly favor the televising of U.S. Senate sessions, while Protestants and Jews favor it only slightly. Regardless of the nature of the research question, any number of groups can be evaluated by transforming their membership into 1 or 0.

The Ordinal Scale. A professor studies the behavior of five students in a speech communication class. She ranks them in terms of their public speaking competence. The most competent is ranked first, the least competent is ranked fifth. In between are the remaining three students. The professor has employed an ordinal scale. Ordinal scales have these characteristics:

1. The *relative* position of a person or entity can be determined.
2. The positioning is based on the characteristic being categorized—in this example, public speaking competence.
3. Any person or entity can be characterized as equal to, greater than, or less than any other person or entity in the group under consideration.
4. Most important, the precise amount separating the levels is thought to be nonuniform, and it is always unknown.

In terms of public speaking competency, it would be helpful if we could state that the student who ranked first was twice as competent as the student ranked second, and so on down to the student ranked fifth. This option is not available. As long as our scale of measurement is defined as ordinal, we cannot make such precise comparisons. We are correct only in stating that they differ.

The Interval Scale. Interval scales have definite advantages over ordinal scales for many research purposes. One deficiency that distinguishes ordinal scales is removed when we utilize interval scales. We can now specify the amount between levels. Moreover, the amounts are equal, no matter which end of the scale one begins at. Had our hypothetical professor employed an interval measurement scale, she could have made this statement: The differences in public speaking competency between Ranks 1 and 2 are equal to the differences between Ranks 4 and 5. This statement demonstrates an important characteristic of interval scales: The interval distances are equal. Distance between one and two is equal to the distance between two and three, which is equal to the distance between three and four, and so on. The principle holds also for the reverse order.

The other special feature of an interval scale is that the zero point is arbitrary. On the public speaking competency test the zero point would presumably represent a state of zero competency—a total lack of competency. But since everyone is thought to have some degree of public speaking competency, the idea of a zero point is essentially meaningless. In this sense, then, the zero point of an interval scale is purely arbitrary.

The Ratio Scale. The desideratum of measurement is the ratio scale. It has all of the positive characteristics of the interval scale, and the added advantage of a zero position that is not arbitrarily determined but can be absolutely determined.

Most of the crucial measurements related to human existence are ratio scales. Time is the most fundamental example. One minute is exactly twice as long as 30 seconds. Equally important, zero time passage is the absolute starting point. Its meaning is universally understood.

To summarize briefly, tests can be described as having nominal, ordinal, interval, or ratio scale properties. A statistical model may be appropriate for interval scale data but inappropriate for ordinal data. Knowledge of a test's scale properties, therefore, is essential to choosing the most suitable model.

VARIABLES AND DIMENSIONS

Speech communication researchers face a problem common to behavioral scientists everywhere: Shall the focus be on individual variables or on constructs? An individual variable, by definition, may consist of a single test (scale) item or a composite formed by summing several items.

Consider an investigation into teaching effectiveness. The subjects, college students, are asked to rate their current professor using the following scale:

Effective:____:____:____:____:____:____:____ : Ineffective
       7   6   5   4   3   2   1

A single scale item constitutes the entire test. The amount of information the researchers can glean from the study is therefore limited. The limitation is the result of a single item being used as the total measuring instrument. The problem here is the relationship of the single item to teacher effectiveness. Can a single item adequately describe a domain of behaviors as large as teaching? If it could then we should have to concede that teaching effectiveness consists of only one dimension and can in fact be measured by that one item. The accumulated research—if it tells us anything—tells us that the teacher effectiveness domain is multidimensional. It cannot be fully explained by a single dimension. This means that to measure it with any degree of comprehensiveness, we must bring into force a large number of scale items, or variables.

Some definitions are in order. What constitutes a dimension? One way of defining it would be to say that a dimension is a construct operationally defined by its variables.[9] This implies that dimensions are the result of a combination of variables. Another stab at defining *dimension* might take this form: A dimension consists of a correlated set of variables that seems to have a common thread running through it.

Consider this set of three individual scales. Each is related to teaching behavior. The instructor is: (a) friendly; (b) interested in students; and (c) accessible in or out of class. What is the larger entity—the construct—that, taken together, the three items define? Or, more specifically, at a higher level of abstraction, how might we label an instructor who seems at once to be friendly, interested in students, and accessible to students? Marsh, Overall, and Kesler chose to label the construct "individual rapport."[10] Note that a dimension is an independent construct, and that in this case it was operationally defined by the variables constituting it. And what about the existence of a common thread? The thread uniting the variables appeared to be "individual rapport," and this thread served as the basis of the label. Consider one more example from the same study: The instructor is perceived as displaying: (a) enthusiasm; (b) energy; (c) humor; and (d) ability to hold interest. Marsh, Overall, and Kesler chose to label this an "instructor enthusiasm" dimension.[11]

Dimensions, as opposed to single variables, are of central concern to the speech communication researcher. The research literature reveals countless examples in which the investigators were either attempting to determine the dimensions of a set of variables or were experimenting with dimensions that had evolved from previous studies. Single variables often represent but a portion of a larger dimension and are therefore of limited interest to most researchers.

In summary, tests and other instruments that involve substantively interesting dimensions are likely to make more significant contributions to the development of theory in any field.

Reliability

If a test or other dependent variable measures a trait or construct perfectly on more than one occasion it is said to be perfectly reliable. Perfect reliability in actual research is, of course, a rare event. Error, in various forms, always influences the outcome.

Unreliable instruments generate useless information; the resulting data are likely to mislead the research community. Researchers should examine the reliability history of any test under consideration. If none is available, or if the figures are clearly too low, then a more reliable instrument should be sought. Written reports of research should include the reliability coefficients for all tests employed in the course of the study. If past and current reliability figures are routinely reported, researchers who follow will be in a position to make more intelligent appraisals of tests they may be considering.

Reliability estimates can be obtained through several well-known procedures, briefly described below. To place the reliability problem in perspective we will describe how these procedures were applied in a research project reported by Hersen and his colleagues.[12] This research team investigated the psychometric properties of the thirty-item Wolpe-Lazarus Assertiveness Scale (WLAS). Assessing the reliability of the WLAS was one of the researchers' goals.

Test-Retest Reliability. A test is administered once, then the same test is later administered to the same sample. Administrations one and two provide the basis for comparison. The extent of agreement is a direct indicator of the reliability of the test.

Test-retest reliability is easily computed. Individual scale items from the two administrations for each subject are put into a Pearson Product-Moment correlational procedure. The result is a single correlation coefficient which, as it turns out, is also the reliability coefficient.

Hersen and his colleagues found the test-retest reliability figures for the WLAS to be .564 for males and .790 for females in their particular samples.[13]

Alternate Forms Reliability. Administering the same test to the same subjects is not without its problems. It is well established, for example, that subjects will score higher on the second administration of an intelligence test. One way of minimizing error of this type is to employ alternative forms of the same test. Subjects are still measured on two different occasions, but first with Form 1 and second with Form 2. The alternative forms must consist of an equal number of items and each item in Form 1 must have a counterpart in Form 2. That is, the pairs of items must be similar in content, length, difficulty, and so on. Reliability is computed in a manner identical to test-retest reliability: scores on the corresponding pairs of items are correlated to produce the reliability figure.

Split-Half Reliability. Whereas the two procedures discussed above require testing on at least two different occasions, the split-half method accomplishes essentially the same end in a single administration. A twenty-item test is divided into ten even-numbered and ten odd-numbered items. (The split-half procedure is also known as the method of internal consistency.) Scores on the first half are correlated with those on the second. The major limitation of the procedure lies with the method of splitting the tests into halves. The obtained reliability tends to be a function of the items selected to form the halves. Since any division of the items is acceptable, an investigator may underestimate or overestimate the true reliability, depending on how the division was made.

Cronbach worked on the problem and devised a formula that produces a coefficient which, in essence, is based on all possible split-half combinations. The obtained figure, Coefficient alpha, is considered to be the mean reliability coefficient. If test items consist of dichotomous responses (for example, right-wrong or true-false), then a special form of alpha known as the Kuder-Richardson Formula 20 (KR-20) may be substituted.[14] Hersen and his colleagues, using KR-20, determined the reliability of the Wolpe-Lazarus test to be .845 for males, .631 for females.[15]

We strongly recommend that reliability be performed and reported whenever a test is utilized for research purposes. As we have shown, there is more than one road to reliability assessment. But one procedure is distinctly superior and should always be computed: Coefficient alpha, or KR-20 if the test items are scored dichotomously. As Nunnally points out, its superiority arises from the fact that the obtained coefficient is an upper limit, meaning that under no conditions can the test be expected to be reliable in excess of that figure.[16] In this perspective, low obtained coefficients serve warning that the test probably is unreliable and that resorting to other methods of estimating reliability are not likely to reveal greater reliability. Churchill is even stronger in his advocacy: "Coefficient alpha *absolutely* should be the first measure one calculates to assess the quality of the instrument."[17]

The question as to what constitutes acceptable reliability varies somewhat depending on the authority consulted. Nunnally suggests that the purpose of the test is the major determining item. For early-stage research .70 is sufficient. For basic research, efforts to increase reliabilities beyond .80 are probably wasteful. But for serious research in applied areas, a minimum of .90 should be the goal.[18]

Computational formulas are provided in most texts on measurement of psychometric theory. We recommend the excellent texts by Nunnally[19] and by Aiken.[20]

Validity

Classical definitions of validity state that a test is valid to the extent that it measures what it purports to measure. In other words, the correlation between the test and the corresponding characteristic should be high. A low score on an articulation test should reflect low levels of articulation competence in the individual. On the other hand, if the test score is high, then we should expect a high level of articulation competence. In general if the relationship between the test score and the actual behavior is high, the test is said to be valid. Departures from this standard suggest that the test is lacking in validity.

Validity comes in several forms:

Predictive Validity. Educational researchers maintain an ongoing search for tests that can predict success in college. If the test correlates highly with some measure of academic success, then it is assumed to be valid, at least to some degree. This, then, is predictive validity. It is a simple method of association, or correlation. If the correlation is high, then the validity of the test is high. If it is not, then the search continues for another test or series of tests that might better predict the performance in question. Tests that successfully predict future performance are also popular in the personnel-selection area. Once we have a measure of successful performance on the job, we then construct tests that might be correlated with that performance. When norms are finally established, we place in a new job only those individuals who score high on the predictor.

Far greater problems exist for behavioral researchers than constructing predictive tests that correlate with job performance. It is not nearly so simple to predict behavior from scores on attitude scales. Consider a test of attitude toward nuclear power plants. Suppose, on the one hand, we have a test of demonstrated reliability. On the other, we have patterns of human behavior. Is there a real-life set of behaviors that could accurately be labeled "antinuclear" behaviors? If so, what might they be? A moment's reflection would suggest the enormity of the task of making such a determination, and so the job of finding a test to correlate with the set of behaviors is likely to be temporarily abandoned.

Construct Validity. In the face of overwhelming and unsolvable problems related to using the predictive schema to assess validity, behavioral scientists have turned to the search for construct validity. Constructs, as we have pointed out above, consist of systems of variables that seem to have a common thread running through them. Constructs are dimensions to which substantive, or theoretical, meaning can be attached.

Assuming a group of variables has been found to describe a construct, how can its validity be assessed? For an example, we choose the construct Machiavellianism[21] (Mach). People characterized as high Machs are thought to be manipulative, questionably open and honest, and relatively unemotional. Those characterized as low Machs are expected to display opposite behaviors: openness, honesty, and interpersonal warmth. Attempts to validate the Mach test can proceed along any of the following paths:

Observer agreement. Subgroups of three observers watch the behavior of small groups over several tasks and occasions. At the conclusion of the study the observers rate each participant on a Mach behavioral scale. At the same time the subjects also complete a Mach test. Agreement between observers' scores and subjects' scores provides empirical evidence in support of the test's validity.

Relationship to other constructs. Assume that research has uncovered a link between Machiavellianism and Dogmatism (Dogm).[22] It is suspected that high Machs are also likely to be essentially dogmatic—close-minded individuals. Since the Dogmatism scale has survived a long evolution it seems plausible to expect that it in fact measures actual dogmatic behavior. This, we stress, is an operating assumption. Subjects are administered both tests and results show a high positive correlation. High Machs are found to be equally high on the Dogm scale. Low Machs are found to be equally low Dogms. We can therefore conclude that the Mach scale relating positively to the Dogm scale constitutes evidence for the validity of the former. As the number of relevant tests found to relate to the Mach scale increases, the assumption of its validity increases.

Other types of validity assessment exist—for example, content validity and face validity. Behavioral researchers, however, are likely to find greater practical value in the construct validity approaches.

TEST CHARACTERISTICS

Communication researchers often work with measures of opinion, attitude, belief, or sentiment. Subjects are asked to respond to any of countless tests. Some are designed to assess amount of self-disclosure, or attitudes toward people, entities, or institutions. Others seek to measure self-concept, rewardingness behavior, or trust in people. Whatever the domain of interest, it seems that someone is working on a set of scale items to measure that phenomenon. The end is nowhere in sight—nor should it necessarily be. Behavioral research as we know it is still in the infant stage, compared to the hard sciences. The next several years will see an even greater proliferation of tests. Some will survive the rigors of science well. Many will make a brief appearance and then disappear. They will fail on the issues of reliability and validity—and for other reasons.

Likert Scales[23]

Named after its inventor, Rensis Likert, these scales are characterized by simplicity. Two elements are needed: a well designed statement and a scale for responding. The second requirement—the scale—poses no challenge. Writing acceptable attitude statements does. Below are some typical statements from Likert scales:

The construction of nuclear power plants should be halted.

Movies showing couples engaged in sexual behavior should be banned.

The energy crisis is a conspiracy on the part of oil companies to make greater profits.

In Table 7-1 we reproduce an eighteen-item Likert-type scale developed by Rosenfeld.[24] Subjects in this study responded by checking one of five possible points for each item:

Almost always	5
Often	4
Sometimes	3
Rarely	2
Almost never	1

A subject's score was computed by assigning a weight of one to five, as shown. Assuming that the eighteen items form a single dimension, a composite score is obtained by simply summing the individual items. A subject, therefore, could score a minimum of 18 by checking "Almost never" consistently or a maximum score of 90 by checking all "Almost always." Most subjects, of course, do not respond in such uniform fashion.

These principles govern the construction of a Likert-type scale:

1. Generate items related to the specific attitude of concern. If the test, as in our example, involves attitudes toward nuclear power plants, then we simply write a number of potential statements—all related, we hope, to that particular social issue. We might choose statements concerning safety, cost, efficiency, value, and long-range capabilities. Two representative items might be:

Nuclear power plants are unsafe.

The cost of constructing nuclear power plants makes their use impractical.

In constructing statements the researcher's concern is homogeneity. The items should all contribute to a single underlying attitude.

Table 7-1 Rosenfeld's 18-item Likert-type Self-Disclosure Avoidance Questionnaire.

1. I can't find the opportunity to self-disclose with this person.
2. If I disclosed I might hurt the other person.
3. If I disclosed I might be evaluating or judging the other person.
4. I cannot think of topics which I would disclose.
5. Self-disclosure would give the other person information which he/she might use against me at some time.
6. If I self-disclose it might cause me to make personal changes.
7. Self-disclosure might threaten relationships I have with people other than the close acquaintance.
8. Self-disclosure is a sign of weakness.
9. If I self-disclose I might lose control over the other person.
10. If I self-disclose I might discover I am less than I wish to be.
11. If I disclose I might project an image I do not want to project.
12 If I disclose, the other person might not understand what I was saying.
13. If I self-disclose, the other person might evaluate me negatively.
14. Self-disclosure in a sign of some emotional disturbance.
15. Self-disclosure might hurt our relationship.
16. I am afraid that self-disclosure might lead to an intimate relationship with the other person.
17. Self-disclosure might threaten my physical safety.
18. If I self-disclose I might give information which makes me appear inconsistent.

2. A next step might be to get initial responses to the statements. Colleagues and a few subjects are administered the test and their reactions are sought. If possible, interviews with these preliminary subjects should be undertaken to determine to what extent the questions and their wording are reasonably comprehensible. Additionally, researchers should be alert to responses that indicate questions that seem extreme or double-barrelled, or that contain preamble bias. For example:

Proponents of nuclear power are emotionally disturbed. (Extreme)

Nuclear power is unsafe and too costly. (Double-barrelled. Is the subject responding to the unsafe issue, the cost issue, or both?)

Nuclear power plants are generally considered unsafe. Do you favor the expansion of nuclear power plants? (Preamble bias)

Semantic purification is often more difficult than most researchers anticipate. A word that subjects find vague or a phrase they find confusing probably seemed totally clear and obvious to the researchers. Poorly constructed statements increase the error factor, and hence, directly influence reliability.

3. Administer the revised set of scales to a sample of at least two hundred. Again, arrange to interview a subset of this sample—say, twenty. Go over each item and look for areas of misunderstanding.

4. Submit the set of scale items to factor analysis.[25] Likert did not call for factor analysis. But with easy programming methods readily available today, it has become almost a routine step. Factor analysis, as presented in Chapter 8, reveals

the number of independent dimensions and the amount of variance contributed by each. If the first dimension (factor) seems to account for most of the variance, then those items that load on that factor can be retained. The remaining items can be discarded. If a researcher begins with fifty scale items, thirty of them might survive the factor analysis.

5. Revise the instrument in view of subject feedback obtained during the interviews and the results of the psychometric analyses. At this point the test should consist of one or more dimensions, each with at least moderately correlated items. This will permit the investigators to sum over the scale items to obtain composite scores for each subject on each dimension.

Issues Related to the Use of Likert Scales

In the past few years an enormous amount of psychometric research has been devoted to studying the properties of scales such as the Likert. We will look at some of the issues that have been raised.

Levels of Endorsement. The Likert technique provided for five levels of endorsement. Other researchers prefer seven; still others nine, eleven, and up. The psychometric question is: How finely can subjects discriminate? For example on an eleven-point scale, can a subject distinguish between the value of position nine versus that of position ten? Some researchers feel they cannot and are inclined to limit choices to not more than five to seven items. That is precisely our feeling. Beyond seven, the discrimination of the subjects may be exceeded.

Positively and Negatively Stated Items. We recommend that about half the items be written in positive format, half in negative. For example:

Capital punishment is *unjust* (negative format).
Capital punishment is *humane* (positive format).

Not everyone would agree. Some researchers believe that negatively worded sentences are harder to understand than positively worded ones. Further, they feel that a subject may be confused by the meaning associated with checking a negative response to a negative question. These criticisms notwithstanding, many psychometricians advocate the positive-negative approach. It tends to make the subject's responses appear more varied than they really are, thereby discouraging subjects from varying their responses for variety's sake. It might also help to hold response sets in check. Response sets occur whenever a subject checks the same response to an entire set of scales. If all items are positively or negatively phrased, response-set behavior is likely to increase.

Weighting the Responses. Two options are available: Add each subject's score on each item, or multiply each subject's scale item score by a weight and then add. The Likert procedure, as originally devised, simply added the subject's responses to the items. The sum (composite) stood as the subject's score on the test. That procedure is still widely employed and highly recommended.

Other weighting schemes have been developed in the belief that some items on a scale are more important than others. If a factor analysis reveals that item 12 is the most heavily loading item on the factor, then it is reasonable to weight that item higher than one loading only half as much. This is the essence of the reasoning. What is the evidence? Little seems to be gained by adopting complex weighting systems.[26] The correlation between simple sums and complex weighting schemes is often found to be very high. And their use in statistical models such as the analysis of variance seems to produce nearly identical results.[27] This being the case we too recommend a simple summing of the scale items.

Appraisal of Likert Scales. Likert-type tests continue to enjoy widespread popularity no doubt due to their ease of construction, administration, and scoring. Because scale items deal with complete ideas, they can be used where other kinds of tests, such as semantic differentials, would be inappropriate. The main problem is that a set of scale items will be used before they have been subjected to a program of psychometric analysis. Our advice, once again, is to use sets of scales that have evolved from well-designed studies.

The Semantic Differential

A second popular rating model is the semantic differential, first introduced into the literature by Osgood, Suci, and Tannenbaum.[28] It is widely employed by researchers in a number of behavioral-science areas. Part of the reason for its widespread acceptance seems to be the apparent ease with which tests can be constructed. In the simplest case, a concept to be rated is chosen, then a series of bipolar adjectives are chosen that—on the surface at any rate—are relevant to the concept chosen. We reproduce in Table 7-2 the semantic differential first presented in Chapter 6. The concept is *Capital Punishment.* The researcher's goal is to assess attitude toward that concept. Consequently, only evaluative scales are chosen. Factor analysis will reveal the number of dimensions. If only a single dimension is uncovered, then the scale items can be summed to a single composite as were the Likert-type scales.

An impressive body of basic theory related to semantic differential scales has been developed. Here we present a few of the more important ideas.

Concepts. Any concept of theoretical or practical interest can be chosen. Some examples from past research include: *Richard Nixon, My Mother, Me, The United Nations, Annual Medical Checkups, Walter Cronkite.* A single word, a phrase, or a complete sentence can be used. The choice is dictated solely by the interests of the researcher.

Bipolar Adjective Choice. The choice of bipolar adjectives is constrained only by relevancy to the concept being rated. The adjectives *good-bad* would seem to be relevant to the concept *nuclear energy,* whereas *thick-thin* would be considered irrelevant. At the early stages of constructing the test, assumed relevancy is a sufficient criterion. If relevant bipolar adjective sets cannot be readily generated, the researcher can turn to the Osgood, Suci, and Tannenbaum book, *The Measurement of Meaning,* for suggestions. The literature of the social and behavioral sciences also contain literally hundreds of potentially rich sources of scales.

Table 7-2 A Ten-item Semantic Differential Designed to Measure Attitude Toward the Concept **Capital Punishment**.

Capital Punishment								
Valuable	7	6	5	4	3	2	X 1	: Worthless
Fair	7	6	5	4	3	X 2	1	: Unfair
Right	7	6	5	4	3	2	X 1	: Wrong
Just	7	6	5	4	3	2	X 1	: Unjust
Approve	7	6	5	4	3	2	X 1	: Disapprove
Bad	X 1	2	3	4	5	6	7	: Good
Dishonest	1	2	3	4	X 5	6	7	: Honest
Irresponsible	1	2	3	4	5	X 6	7	: Responsible
Stupid	X 1	2	3	4	5	6	7	: Intelligent
Foolish	X 1	2	3	4	5	6	7	: Wise

Logical Opposites. Is *good* the logical opposite of *bad?* Most people think so. What are the logical opposites of these adjectives: *animated, sinister,* and *arrogant?* If we were to empirically test them, we might find that each would evoke widely differing opposite adjectives. In one study the modal responses were: *animated-sluggish, sinister-above-board,* and *arrogant-humble.* Because of the wide divergence possible, we suggest that only those bipolar adjectives that have been utilized in previous research be used in the early stages of a study. As we have noted, the sources are plentiful. Using adjectives that invoke widely divergent opposite responses in subjects will introduce additional error into our findings.

Levels of Endorsement. The theory is identical to that of Likert Scales. Choose as many intervals as you wish. Osgood, Suci, and Tannenbaum developed the semantic differential using seven levels, as illustrated in Table 7-2. Seven is not a magic number; there could as easily be five, nine, or eleven. Most researchers using the semantic differential, however, have used seven intervals, and we cannot think of any good reason to advocate another number.

Dimensions. As with any method of measurement the researcher should always determine the number of dimensions by subjecting the data to factor analysis or other appropriate statistical models.

Scoring. If only one dimension surfaces, perhaps a basic evaluative dimension, then scores on the individual scale items can be summed into a single composite for each subject. The ten scale items in Figure 7-2 have been found consistently to produce a single general evaluative dimension. This means the individual items are highly correlated and seem to be measuring the same underlying phenomenon: evaluation of the *capital punishment* concept.

To determine a hypothetical subject's score for the scale in Figure 7-2, we add the weights corresponding to the subject's check marks, coming up with a total of twenty. Note that the positive end of the scale always receives the highest weight and the negative end the lowest. The higher the subject's composite score, the more positive the attitude toward the dimension being measured. Low scores indicate negative attitudes. The highest obtainable score on this particular semantic differential is 70; the lowest is 10.

Semantic differential scales are sometimes randomized on the basis of positive and negative directions:

Valuable:_____:_____:_____:_____:_____:_____:_____:Worthless
Unfair:_____:_____:_____:_____:_____:_____:_____:Fair

The positive end, *valuable,* appears on the left side. This is followed by the negative end, *unfair.* Random positioning of positive and negative ends helps to prevent subjects from speeding through the test in some haphazard, thoughtless manner— at least in theory. In practice, there is no guarantee that the theory works. In fact some researchers feel that random positioning makes matters worse. We subscribe to this latter view. The ten scale items in Figure 7-2 were positioned by putting the positive end of the first five scales on the left and the positive end of the last five on the right. All ten scale items could have been positioned with the positive end on the right or left. Researchers are free to choose their individual styles of visually presenting the scale items.

Test Length. The question of test length arises with predictable frequency. What is the optimal number of items for a semantic differential? Our response is always that the question remains moot. As a rule of thumb, err on the side of many items in the early developmental stages of a test. Factor analysis will tell you how many items are defining each dimension. Certainly no fewer than forty items should be considered at the initial stage. Remember, too, that longer tests are typically associated with higher-reliability coefficients.

Do not be overly concerned with subject fatigue. A typical subject can respond to a fifty-item semantic differential in less than six minutes.

A final word of advice: Semantic differential tests with over one hundred scale items probably contain too many redundant items.

Appraisal of the Semantic Differential.[29] Few measurement procedures have enjoyed the widespread acceptance that the semantic differential has. It is conceptually simple; it is easy to devise and administer. Subject response time is minimal. Moreover, the instrument is easily understood by respondents. The only serious limitation of the semantic differential is that it does not deal with complete ideas; it measures only connotative (psychological) meaning. We can ask people to respond to a statement such as "Senator Smith should be removed from office," via the Likert-type format. The statement expresses a complete idea, and the goal is to get a direct, logical (denotative) response. We could employ a form of the semantic differential with "Senator Smith" as the concept to be rated. However, no matter how well chosen the scales, the results would give a qualitatively different set of responses that might be only obliquely related to Senator Smith's removal. In this instance, Likert scales would be the preferred choice.

Checklists

Likert-type scales and semantic differentials are considered *continuous* scales. This means that each item has three or more response intervals, or levels of endorsement. Scales with only two response intervals are called dichotomous. They provide for two possibilities: The item is either checked or left blank. Checked items are given a score of 1, unchecked items a score of 0. True-false tests are likewise dichotomous in nature.

One class of checklists is referred to as the "adjective checklist."[30] This measurement procedure is widely used and appears in many forms. Although it has found its greatest use in personality assessment, it is so general that it can be modified for use in many research domains, including communication. Some prototypical tests appear below.

In most social situations I am: (Choose one)
_____ (1) Shy
_____ (2) Assertive
_____ (3) Aggressive
_____ (4) Totally silent

Another:

My position as speech therapist is: (Check all relevant responses)
_____ Boring
_____ Rewarding
_____ Unpredictable
_____ Challenging
_____ Dull
_____ Hectic
_____ Fulfilling
_____ Tiring
_____ Dead end

Advantages. Like the semantic differential, checklists are easy to devise, administer, and score. They allow the researcher to gather large amounts of information in a short span of time. Because of their simplicity, subjects rarely have difficulty completing them.

Disadvantages. Aside from the reliability and validity problems that affect all measuring instruments, checklists are unpopular in some quarters because of the dichotomous nature of responses. Critics suggest that too much information is lost when subjects are forced to make dichotomous responses. (Recall that Likert scales traditionally call for five intervals and the semantic differential seven.)

In general, the checklist method of measurement is as psychometrically sound as any. Researchers should consult a detailed reference work on the topic before designing any study involving the use of checklists.

Open-Ended Tests

Likert scales, semantic differentials, and checklists share this common characteristic: They limit the range of subject responses. They are called "forced choice" instruments because the respondent must choose among the limited number of possible responses contained in the test. It is precisely this characteristic that endears them to countless researchers.

However, depending upon the specific goals of the research, forced-choice instruments may be unrealistic. Richer, more freely given responses may be needed. Suppose a research team is considering a study of marital communication. Several forced-choice inventories might be used. But if the team wishes to probe deeply into the communication problems of husbands and wives, then an alternative method must be adopted. It would have to be so designed as to permit couples to reveal as little or as much as they wished. Instruments capable of providing this level of information are called open-ended tests, or tests that permit unstructured responses. We describe two basic varieties.

The Simple Question. Nothing could seem more basic than to ask people to respond to a simple, straightforward question. The procedure is probably as old as the first two human beings to occupy space. The logic: If you want to know something, why not ask? There is no limit on what can be asked. Historically, Americans have been asked to describe their work preference, eating, sleeping, and sex habits, and just about every other conceivable aspect of their lives.

Basic questions take a variety of forms. One type of question seeks a simple answer: "How do you feel when you talk before audiences of, say, one hundred or more people?" "What is your typical response to being interrupted while expressing an opinion?" "What aspect of your personality do you like least?" The goal of these questions is to obtain an expression of feelings. Note that some of the information could be obtained through forced-choice tests but this would limit the possible responses.

A second type of basic question follows this pattern: "Describe your impressions of the typical college debater." "Describe the last fight you had with your wife (husband)." "How would you describe your interpersonal communication style?" Each of the three items calls for a longer, more complex set of responses. The questions call for an overall assessment of a group, person, or some aspect of the self.

Sentence Completion Tests.[31] In another type of open-ended test, a sentence stem is presented, and the respondent is left to complete it in his or her own words:

"Before I will disclose my feelings to another person _____."

All sentence completion tests are constructed according to this basic format. There is no limit on the kinds of sentence stems that can be employed. The technique has been widely used in personality research, to a lesser extent in communication research. Some examples to illustrate its use in different research areas:

1. *Attitude-persuasion*
    "Most political campaign speeches I have heard_____."
    "The thing that irritates me the most with public speakers is_____."
2. *Self-disclosure*
    "My reaction to strangers who tell me their innermost secrets is_____."
    "If a close friend were to ask me to reveal my sexual preferences I would probably_____."
3. *Mass communication*
    "Most network news reporters are_____."
    "The greatest shortcoming of television programming is_____."

Assessment. As we have indicated, open-ended questions remove most of the restrictions that are present in forced-choice instruments. Respondents are free to provide as much detail as they wish, subject only to any limitations imposed by the researcher. The result is richer, more complex sets of responses. Open-ended tests are particularly useful at the exploratory stage, where researchers have little theoretical insight as to what to expect.

The disadvantages are compelling, however. Responses are difficult to score. It is often a challenge to determine the category into which a specific response should be placed. And since the decisions of a single coder are assumed to be unreliable, at least one other trained coder must analyze the entire set of responses. Should the resulting reliability coefficient fall into the unacceptable range, then additional coders will be required or the original coders will have to undergo additional training.

Time is another major problem. Reading, analyzing, coding—these procedures require enormous amounts of time. In fact, so much time is required that many researchers feel that forced choice instruments, with their quick and simple scoring procedures, are more realistic. Our position is that the researchers should use the most appropriate measurement procedure available, when possible. Sometimes the ideal is not possible: Available funds, resources, and auxilliary help limit our options. When conditions warrant, then, the researchers may have to employ a less than optimum assessment procedure.

DEPENDENT VARIABLES: RECOMMENDATIONS

The quality of research is inextricably associated with the quality of dependent variables—our measuring instruments. The most elegantly designed study is of little value if the measurement procedure is found to be faulty or, at best, inappropriate.

The literature of measurement theory seems infinite; the average researcher cannot stay abreast of it. Yet, as we continue our surveillance of the psychometric literature, certain themes recur with regularity. We have reflected upon them; we have evaluated them. At this point we offer in summary form a few of the more important recommendations.

Sources of Tests. Choose a test that has survived use across many previous studies. Christie's Mach II test,[32] Rokeach's Dogmatism Scale,[33] the Social Desirability Scale[34]—these are but three examples of tests that deserve to be labeled classics. They have been utilized in many research studies, and they have survived in the highly critical world of behavioral science. The list of high-quality tests is long. They can be found throughout the relevant research literature.

Resist Devising Your Own Test. Psychometrically sound measuring instruments are the product of years of research. Few can be devised quickly. The steps involved in developing an instrument are many. It is an exhausting, seemingly endless venture. Unless you are prepared to put in the necessary time and energy, we think you should resist putting together home-made dependent variables.

Adhere to the Test Ground Rules. Tests with established track records should be administered, scored, and interpreted according to the instructions set forth by the authors. Consider the Dogmatism scale. If you choose to test subjects on some test items and not others, then your dependent variable is not the Dogmatism scale. It is at best a selection of items from that scale. If in fact you claim the scale as your measuring instrument, then you must administer the complete set of scale items. Likewise, you must score the test as specified by the author. And if the test is to be interpreted in certain specified ways, then you cannot ignore those instructions.

Avoid Single-Item Tests. Beginning researchers wonder why a single-item test is not adequate. There are three important reasons: first, single-item tests have a reputation for unreliability; the error associated with them tends to be high. Second, a single test item can hardly measure a major dimension—construct such as self-disclosure, assertiveness, or any one of hundreds of constructs of interest to communication researchers. Third, reliability assessment is virtually impossible unless multi-item instruments are used.

Reliability Must be Assessed. Regardless of the reputation of the test, reliability estimates must be computed and reported for your specific sample.

Test Validity Cannot be Ignored. As we have argued elsewhere in this volume, the validity issue must be squarely faced. Researchers must become aware of any previous attempts at test validation, and if they plan to continue employing the test, they too must make some effort to contribute to its validity. A lack of validity data implies a questionable relationship between what the test purports to measure and the corresponding presumed set of real-world behaviors.

8

Statistical Models

In this chapter we provide a basic orientation to the world of statistics. In the first section we discuss selected elementary descriptive statistics. Then we move to the topic of statistical inference. Finally we outline the four most popular multivariate statistical models. To do justice to this task would require several volumes. We provide, therefore, an admittedly incomplete discussion. There are many excellent texts in each of the areas discussed and we urge the student to consult those listed in the notes for further details.

DESCRIPTIVE STATISTICS

There are two basic kinds of statistics: descriptive and inferential. In this section we focus on descriptive statistics.[1] As the words connote, descriptive statistics provide summary information about a class of human beings or entities—and it stops at that. Descriptive statistics make no statement as to the value of the information. Nor do they attempt to relate the information to anything else. No assessment is made as to whether the figures differ from those obtained from other samples.

Measures of Central Tendency

Who among us has never heard of the arithmetic average, or the mean? Few things are of greater interest than knowing where "most people" stand with respect to just about anything: intelligence, course grades, income, divorce, sexual preference, almost any trait people display. Knowing the mean, mode, and median provides much information quickly.

The Mean. The mean $(\overline{X})$ is one measure of central tendency. By definition, it is the scores of each individual added together, then divided by the number involved in the computation.

For example, assume that five students receive grades of 10, 10, 20, 45, and 15 on a listening test. The mean is computed:

$$\overline{X} = \frac{10 + 10 + 20 + 45 + 15}{5} \qquad \frac{\text{(The individual scores summed)}}{\text{(The number of scores involved)}}$$

$$\overline{X} = \frac{100}{5}$$

$$\overline{X} = 20$$

The mean is 20, or in statistical notation, $\overline{X} = 20$.

The Mode. The mode is a second measure of central tendency. It tells you which score occurred most often.

Ten applicants for a speech therapist position were given a standard intelligence test. The roster of scores were 95, 96, 99, 99, 101, 115, 115, 115, 121, 142. To calculate the mode we examine the roster in order to determine which score occurred most frequently.

Score	Number of Occurrences
95	1
96	1
99	2
101	1
115	3*
121	1
142	1

Three persons scored 115; therefore, 115 is the mode.

The Median. The median, the third measure of central tendency, is obtained by counting from the lowest score in the direction of the highest until exactly one half the scores lie below and one half above that figure.

Income of eleven graduate teaching assistants was determined to be:

Graduate Teaching Assistant	Income (last year)
1	$2,600.00
2	2,650.00
3	2,680.00
4	2,705.00

Graduate Teaching Assistant	Income (last year)
5	$2,740.00
6 (median)	2,788.00
7	3,000.00
8	3,560.00
9	3,890.00
10	4,000.00
11	4,225.00

The median income of the eleven graduate students was $2,788.00. Exactly half the sample made less money; exactly half made more.

Measures of central tendency have great informational value. Much data is summarized into a single figure. Regardless of the size of the group—ten or ten thousand—we can always compute the three measures simply and quickly now that computers are widely available.

Measures of central tendency suffer from a common shortcoming: Any one of them can present a distorted picture. The mean does not give information about how many scored above and below it. The median fails to reveal how the typical case scored. And the mode tells us only that one score occurred more than all others. To overcome this restriction it is wise to present all three. This will give a more comprehensive picture.

Other Methods of Presenting Data: Variance Statistics

Measures of central tendency leave a fundamental question unanswered; they do not tell us the amount of variance.

Variance statistics provide answers to such questions as:

1. What were the lowest and highest scores?
2. Did the scores vary slightly, moderately, or widely?

The first question is concerned with the *range* of scores. A simple inspection of the data will provide the necessary information. Income for teachers in rural American towns might range from a low of $4,000 to a high of $39,000.

Knowledge of the range per se is often inadequate. The public might want to know how many teachers fall into each of several categories, beginning with the $4,000 low and increasing it in increments of $1,000. It can be seen that as the number of descriptive measures is increased, so is the potential degree of understanding on the part of the consumer.

The second question—the degree of variation in the scores—involves another popular descriptive statistic, the standard deviation (s.d.). As the name indicates, this statistic is a direct indicator of the degree to which all scores deviate from the mean—below the mean and above it. Calculating the standard deviation is a little more complex than deriving the mean. To illustrate the steps, assume we have scores on eleven subjects, as given in Table 8-1. Routinely we calculate the mean by adding the raw scores and dividing by 11; the mean is 63.36. Starting from the bottom and counting up through half the cases, the median score is found to be 61; note that half the scores are above the median score of 61, and half are below. The mode—the most frequently occurring raw score—is 80; it occurred twice in the roster. Finally, it can be seen that the raw score range is 80-45, or 35. The lowest score was 45; the highest 80. Now to the calculation of the standard deviation. The computational formula:[2]

$$s.d. = \sqrt{\frac{\Sigma X^2 - \frac{(\Sigma X)^2}{N}}{N-1}}$$

Σ = the summation (sum).
ΣX^2 = the sum of the scores after each has been squared.
$(\Sigma X)^2$ = the square of the sum of the scores.
N   = the total number of scores entering into the computation.

Table 8-1   Raw Data on 11 Subjects.

Subject	Raw Score
S_1	80
S_2	80
S_3	75
S_4	70
S_5	62
S_6	61
S_7	60
S_8	59
S_9	55
S_{10}	50
S_{11}	45

The calculation, step by step:

1. Sum all 11 scores.

$$80 + 80 \ldots + 45 = 697.$$

The ellipsis (...) indicates that we move through the roster without omitting any scores. The scores 75, 70, 62, 61, 60, 59, 55, and 50 are involved in the calculation even though they are not listed.

2. Square each element and add these squared values.

$$80^2 + 80^2 \ldots + 45^2 = 6400 + 6400 \ldots + 2025 = 45521.$$

3. Square the sum obtained in Step 1. Divide by the number of scores in the roster, 11. The technical name for this figure is the correction term.

$$\frac{(697)^2}{N} = \frac{485809}{11} = 44164.45$$

4. Subtract the Step 3 value from the Step 2 value.

$$45521 - 44164.45 = 1356.55$$

5. Divide the figure calculated in Step 4 by N − 1, the number of subjects in the roster minus 1.

$$\frac{1356.55}{10} = 135.66$$

This figure is the *variance.*

6. The square root of the variance is the standard deviation.

$$\sqrt{135.66} = 11.647 = s.d.$$

Means, Standard Deviations, and Variances

The measures of central tendency outlined all have an important place in descriptive research, in statistical theory, and in the application of scientific method to research problems in the behavioral sciences. Each is straightforward and easily understood. The standard deviation and variance are the only ones requiring somewhat complex calculations. The concept of a mean and its standard deviation/variance should be thoroughly understood before moving to the study of statistical inference. A popular set of statistical models—the analysis of variance—draws heavily upon those two fundamental descriptive statistics.

STATISTICAL INFERENCE

Groups can be described by their means, ranges, and standard deviations. To test hypotheses and contribute to the evolution of theory, however, researchers need more than descriptive statistics. Inferential statistics meet that need.[3] Researchers often pursue some fundamental questions such as these when studying two or more groups:

Do the means of the groups differ?
Assuming the group means differ, is the difference due to chance, or errors in measurement? Or are the differences real and nonchance?

What is the motivation underlying these questions?

To illustrate, assume two groups of n = 10 subjects are given a 20-item test of attitude toward freedom of speech.

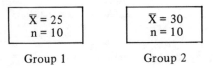

$\overline{X} = 25$		$\overline{X} = 30$
n = 10		n = 10
Group 1		Group 2

The 20 test items are summed to a single composite score. The means are 25 for Group 1 and 30 for Group 2. The researcher is interested in knowing if there are *statistically significant* differences between these two group means. This also is what is meant by the term *real differences*. Note, first that the means are not identical. Clearly they differ. As we have noted, with real-life research data they almost always will differ. So we are pushed on to our second question: Are the differences real; that is, are they statistically significant? The central question can be expressed this way: What is the probability that mean differences this large would occur by chance or the accumulation of error alone? For example the Group 1 $\overline{X}$ = 25, the Group 2 $\overline{X}$ = 30, for a mean difference of 5; is the difference statistically significant?

The t Test[4]

To make this determination, we choose an appropriate statistical model to apply to our data base. One frequently employed model is the *t* test. It is an appropriate way to test whether two means differ significantly. The model computes the means, differences in means, and the amount of error associated with the means. We cannot present the computational algorithm in this chapter. We will present the logical considerations involved in the use of the model and the fundamental procedures involved in interpreting the output. In this example, the question is: Do the means of 25 and 30 differ significantly? The *t* test is computed. The results:

With 19 degrees of freedom, the *t* of 2.861 is statistically significant. The probability associated with this difference is $p < .01$. The null hypothesis is rejected.

Translation:

1. *Degrees of freedom.* A technical term defined in an unnecessarily complicated way in most statistics texts. It is sufficient for our purposes to know that the degrees of freedom (d.f.) are equal to the total number of subjects in the two groups, minus 1: 20 − 1 = 19. The d.f. are needed in order to enter the table of *t* values.
2. The *t* of 2.861. Virtually every univariate statistics text has a table of *t* values. Two items of information are needed to enter the table: d.f. and the obtained value of *t*.

3. The probability associated with a *t* of 2.861 with 19 d.f. is p < .01, as indicated in the table. This is the payoff information. It tells us that, by conventional standards, the mean differences are real, or statistically significant. The probability of a mean difference as large as 5 occurring as a result of error and/or chance is less than 1 in 100, which is thought to be good enough for most research purposes.

4. Rejecting the null hypothesis. The null hypothesis is a part of most statistical model testing. It states simply that the means do not differ in a statistically significant sense. Rejecting the null hypothesis is equivalent to stating that the means do differ significantly.

Why use .01 as a cutoff? Actually most behavioral scientists use .05 as the minimum acceptable probability level. The reason? It's merely a convention, but one that is not likely to change in the near future.

Suppose the *t* test revealed a probability of .10? It would indicate that 10 percent of the time the mean difference would occur by error and/or chance alone. The odds are not good enough. Finally, is it possible that this is one of those 5 times in 100 that could arise by error/chance? We do not know. All that p < .05 tells us is that—in the long run—we can expect that 5 in 100 differences will be significant because of error/chance alone.

Most major statistical model tests are interpreted as in our example. The method of entering the table will vary. But the probability figure always carries the same message. So if you understand the logic of interpreting a *t* test, then you are not likely to experience difficulty with any of the other statistical tables.

The Analysis of Variance[5]

The *t* test is appropriate when two groups are to be compared. When the means on three or more groups are tested for significant group differences, the analysis of variance (ANOVA) is an appropriate statistical model.

Three groups are exposed to three different experimental treatments. With n = 25 subjects in each group, the group means are found to be 51, 65, and 80, respectively.

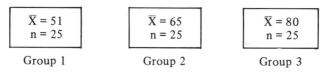

$\bar{X} = 51$	$\bar{X} = 65$	$\bar{X} = 80$
n = 25	n = 25	n = 25
Group 1	Group 2	Group 3

The analysis of variance is designed to indicate if at least one pair of means differs significantly. These are the possibilities:

1. No pair of means may differ significantly.
2. At least one pair of means will differ. Further tests will be needed in order to determine which means differ.

The ANOVA table is called the univariate F distribution. Whereas the *t* test table required that d.f. = one less than the number of subjects, the F table requires two d.f. designations. The first is d.f. between groups. The second is d.f. within groups.

1. d.f. between groups = g − 1, the number of groups minus 1. In our study, with 3 groups, d.f. between groups = 3 − 1 = 2.
2. d.f. within groups = number of subjects minus d.f. between groups, minus 1. In our study 75 − 2 − 1 = 72.
3. d.f., then, = 2/72.

Entering the table with d.f. = 2/72 we find that an F of 4.92 is required for significance at the 1 percent level. Our obtained F of 10.56 greatly exceeds that value. We conclude the F to be significant at $p < .01$. We now know that at least one pair of means differs significantly. Our task is to locate those means that differ through appropriate follow-up tests.

Follow-Up Tests

ANOVA is often referred to as an overall test. It is designed only to give an indication that at least one pair of means differs in a statistically significant sense. Since ANOVA is not designed to pinpoint which specific means differ, it is necessary to employ follow-up tests. There are several possibilities available; we choose to employ a test developed by Newman-Keuls.[6] At a chosen level of significance—.05 or .01—the test permits us to make any and all mean comparisons in order to determine exactly which pairs of means differ. The following pairs of means are compared:

1 and 2
1 and 3
2 and 3

The hypothetical results are that all three comparisons are significant at $p < .01$. The researcher would now normally interpret these group differences in light of the hypothesis, or research questions, enumerated at the start of the study.

Factorial Designs[7]

Factorial designs are also discussed in Chapter 6. Have we emphasized the statistical aspects. Among the terms you should know:

1. *Factor.* A factor is a basic phenomenon of concern to the researcher. These represent a sampling of factors that behavioral researchers have been concerned with: dogmatism, credibility, creativity, self-disclosure, authoritarianism, prejudice, alienation.
2. *Number of factors.* A study of the type illustrated in our hypothetical three-group ANOVA study is called a single-factor design. Only one factor is

being analyzed. The groups can be depicted along a single row. When we add a second factor we are involved with a factorial design. By definition, factorial designs are characterized by a minimum of two factors. Often there are three, four, and even more factors. Each factor represents a separate phenomenon of interest to the researcher.

3. *Levels of a factor.* Factors are decomposed—broken down—into levels. A factor must be broken down into a minimum of two levels to provide a basis for comparison. The number of levels is the researcher's choice. The greater the number of levels, the more complexity is introduced into the design and subsequent analysis.

To illustrate, we will examine a 2 X 2 factorial, the most basic of the factorial design family. The area of investigation is educational theatre. Scientific research in theatre has gained momentum over the past few years. Because of the nature of theatre, scientific research is more difficult to accomplish. The researchers are interested in investigating two factors: Factor A—lighting; and Factor B—background music (see Figure 8-1).

A thirty-minute, one-act play is the basic experimental treatment. The play is presented to four different audiences. Actors strive to keep their performances "identical" for all four presentations. In terms of Factor A, lighting, the researchers wish to test which of two levels of lighting—subdued or bright—increases the audience's evaluation of the play; in terms of Factor B, music, they wish to test which music, classical or modern, increases the rating.

		FACTOR B: MUSIC	
		b_1: classical	b_2: modern
FACTOR A: LIGHTING	a_1: subdued	$a_1 b_1$ $\overline{X} = 10.3$ $n = 30$	$a_1 b_2$ $\overline{X} = 10.4$ $n = 30$
	a_2: bright	$a_2 b_1$ $\overline{X} = 10.1$ $n = 30$	$a_2 b_2$ $\overline{X} = 17.4$ $n = 30$

Figure 8-1   A 2 X 2 Factorial Design.

The dependent variable, the test, is a 10-item rating scale. The higher a subject's score, the higher the evaluation of the play. Each subject's score is obtained by summing the 10 items into a single composite.

Statistical Analysis in a Factorial Design

The analysis of a 2 X 2 factorial design proceeds in this way:

Testing for Main Affects. Collapse all row observation into a single group. The two rows, a_1 and a_2, would treat cells $a_1 b_1$ and $a_1 b_2$ as a single group. It would also treat $a_2 b_1$ and $a_2 b_2$ as a single group:

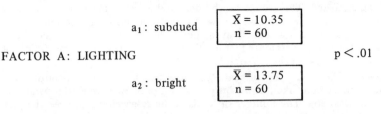

FACTOR A: LIGHTING $\quad\quad\quad\quad\quad\quad\quad\quad\quad\quad\quad\quad$ p $<$ .01

The statistical hypothesis being tested: Is the mean for subdued lighting significantly different than the mean for bright lighting? Note that the main effect,
lighting, disregards the effect of music temporarily. That is why it is designated
main effect. The F ratio in this case is, let us say, 12.54 with d.f. = 1/118, significant at p $<$ .01. Conclusion: Disregarding the level of music, lighting had a
significant effect on evaluations of the play. Specifically, the bright lighting effect
was associated with the highest mean evaluation.

Now to the statistical analysis of the main effect of Factor B, the two levels of
music. Following the same logic described in assessing the main effect of Factor
A, we ask this question: Did the kind of music affect evaluation?

FACTOR B: MUSIC

b_1: classical $\quad\quad\quad\quad$ b_2: modern

$\bar{X} = 10.2$	$\bar{X} = 13.9$
n = 60	n = 60

p $<$ .01

The statistical hypothesis, significant at p $<$ .01: Is the mean for classical music
significantly different from that of modern music? Again, note that the test for the
main effect of B temporarily disregarded the levels of A, lighting. The hypothetical
F of 14.16, with d.f. = 1/118, is found to be also significant at p $<$ .01. Conclusion:
Disregarding the level of lighting, music had a significant effect on evaluations of
the play. Specifically, modern music was associated with the highest mean evaluation. Summarizing the tests of main effects:

Main effect of A, lighting: Significant, p $<$ .01
Main effect of B, music: Significant, p $<$ .01

Testing Interaction Effects. Main effects are easy to understand. They represent
the simplest interpretation of the results. And there is little difficulty in deciding
what they mean. In other words, they represent a parsimonious description of the
results.

Testing for the AB interaction is the final statistical operation in a 2 × 2 factorial
design. Beneath the statistical test for interaction effects is the question: Are the
means of Factor A dependent on the level of Factor B and the means of Factor B

dependent on the level of Factor A? Looking at the four cells in Figure 8-1 once again it is clear that the means are nearly identical except for cell a_2b_2 = 17.4. This is the obvious source of the interaction. In terms of the original research design we conclude that the one-act play under conditions of bright lighting and modern musical background was superior to each of the other three cell conditions. A significant interaction exists at, let us say, p < .005.

Interpreting Main Effects and Interactions

Main effects are easier to interpret than are interactions. Main effects represent straightforward answers to our research questions. As suggested, they are the ultimate in parsimony and simplicity. To summarize:

1. There is no "formula" for interpreting interactions. We cannot consult a table to interpret their meaning.
2. Researchers are compelled to bring to bear their logical, analytical, and intuitive capabilities.
3. As the number of factors and levels increase, so does the difficulty of interpreting an interaction.
4. Interactions render main effects uninterpretable. This is a fundamental characteristic of interactions. In the statistics literature it is often put this way: In the presence of an interaction, main effects are uninterpretable.[8] In our example, the AB interaction renders any discussion of main effects meaningless. In simplest terms, we ignore the main effects and concentrate on the nature of the interaction.

There is one major limitation to the main-effect/interaction problem. If an interaction does not involve a main-effect factor, then both the main effect and the interaction may be interpreted. A three-factor design—3 $\times$ 3 $\times$ 3—results in significant main effects for Factors A, B, and C. The analysis also produces an AC interaction. The interaction is interpretable. So is the main effect of B, because it is not part of the AC interaction. Main effects of A and C cannot be interpreted because both factors are involved in the AC interaction.

Correlational Studies

The analysis of variance designs discussed above are used to discover the extent to which groups differ. A second class of designs asks how one variable relates to a second variable. The statistical model designed to answer such questions is called simple correlation. One specific correlation procedure results in what is called the Pearson *r*—the Pearson product-moment correlation coefficient (PMC).[9] The statistic answers these questions:

How strong is the relationship between these two variables?
In which direction does the relationship lie?

A partial listing of variables that have been subjected to correlational analysis over the years would include:

age-intelligence
creativity-intelligence
dogmatism-socioeconomic class
education-prejudice
sex-shyness

An exhaustive listing would likely fill a good-sized volume. There seems to be no end to the variables that researchers seek to correlate with other variables. Sometimes the correlation is computed out of curiosity alone, but most correlational studies originate from strong theoretical questions.

The steps in computing a PMC are available in most elementary statistics texts.[10] Again—in the perspective of the goals of this volume—we will concentrate on the logic of the model and the basic considerations involved at the interpretation stage. The logic is deceptively simple: Take measurements of any two variables. Then compute the correlation coefficient.

A researcher, after examination of existing theory, concludes that a significant correlation exists between hearing ability and precision in articulation. Tests designed to measure both variables are administered to 100 students with previously diagnosed articulation problems. Another 100 "normal" students in the same age group are also tested. The correlation coefficient, based on N = 200, is computed. The result: A correlation of .88 between the hearing variable and the articulation variable, leading to the conclusion that the better the hearing, the better the articulation, and vice versa. Interpretation proceeds this way:

1. The absolute size, or magnitude, of the coefficient is examined. A correlation of .88 is considered very high, though exactly when a coefficient is high or low is not absolutely certain. Another rule of thumb: Correlations of .10 or less are considered zero correlations. In the behavioral sciences, correlations between important variables are likely to be in the .40 to .80 range. Correlations above .80 occur less frequently.

2. The square of the correlation coefficient is a direct indicator of how much variance the two variables share. To express it another way, it represents the degree to which the two variables can be predicted from one another. In our example, $.88^2 = .77$. The variables share 77 percent common variance.

3. Correlation and causation are separate issues. It is possible that one variable is causing another, but ordinary correlation methods cannot make that determination.[11]

4. The sign of the correlation coefficient indicates the direction of the relationship. A coefficient of zero, or near zero, suggests that the two variables are unre-

lated. A negative sign indicates that the variables tend to covary in opposite directions. In the hearing-articulation example, a coefficient of $-.88$ would tell us that as scores on the hearing test get higher (indicating better hearing), scores on the articulation test get lower. In other words, the better the hearing the worse the articulation (surely an unexpected result). Positive signs indicate that a change in one variable is accompanied by a positive change in the second variable. A correlation of .80 between intelligence and grade point average indicates that the higher the IQ the higher the grade point average.

5. Correlation coefficients can be tested for significance. Just as with the *t* test and the analysis of variance, the statistical significance of a correlation coefficient can be checked by recourse to the appropriate table of r. The designation of the tables differ somewhat. Most contain the words "Pearson Correlation Coefficient." The table is entered with d.f. $= N - 2$. In our example, $200 - 2 = 198$ d.f. Entering the table we find that a correlation of .88 with d.f. $= 198$ is significant at the $p < .001$ level.

6. Correlational studies often have one major shortcoming. The sample is too small. It is a matter of empirical fact that a large amount of error tends to infest correlation studies. This means that they tend to be unreplicable. Two variables yielding correlations of .38 and .87 on separate occasions would certainly leave a researcher wondering which one was closer to the "true" correlation. To overcome the potential error factor, we suggest that a minimum of two hundred subjects be included. Three hundred would be better. Five hundred would be ideal. At the other end, we recommend that the results of any correlational study based on less than one hundred be interpreted with caution.

7. Large numbers of correlations should be handled through more sophisticated multivariate models. Suppose one wanted to intercorrelate twenty variables? The research goal would be to determine how the twenty variables interrelated. Would a series of correlation coefficients represent the most efficient way to proceed? Definitely not. The number of possible relationships would be bewildering—impossible to understand in any parsimonious sense. Two multivariate models would be appropriate: factor analysis and canonical correlation. Both models are described in this chapter.

MULTIVARIATE STATISTICAL MODELS

Introductory Notions

At the higher levels, multivariate theory is exceedingly complex.[12] Further, the number of potential pitfalls is greater than for the univariate models. In this introductory section we present a set of guidelines for the multivariate researcher. Some of the issues have been discussed—at least partially—in previous chapters. It was the decision of the authors, however, that a unified perspective be presented, even at the risk of presenting redundant information.

Multivariate versus Univariate. Univariate statistical models are capable of dealing with single variables only. The analysis of variance and the *t*-test—these are two popular univariate models. If we apply the *t*-test to our data base, two choices are available to us: (1) We can analyze each individual test item separately, or (2) we can sum all of the individual test items and work with a composite score for each subject. In the first case we are analyzing a *single item variable.* In the second, strictly speaking, a *single composite variable* is being subjected to analysis.

When a second dependent variable is added, the data can be analyzed with multivariate models. Regardless of the sophistication of the research design, if the analysis is to be multivariate, a minimum of two dependent variables is required.

The Nature of Dependent Variables. A test is a dependent variable. Intelligence tests, attitude tests, public-opinion questionnaires, spelling tests—these familiar items are classified as dependent variables. Whenever information is recorded or a subject responds in such a way that the data can be analyzed in some manner, we have the makings of a dependent variable.

Dependent variables come in several forms. One class consists of subject responses. An example of this type of dependent variable is the intelligence test. A second class consists of observations made either by the experimenter or by another person. For example, a study of nonverbal behavior might employ judges to observe various movements through a one-way mirror. The resulting ratings of these observers could be treated as dependent measures. Dependent variables may consist of one or several questions, items, or scales. We may test public opinion toward capital punishment by asking a single question: "Do you approve or disapprove of capital punishment?" We may also test public opinion by asking twenty or more questions relating to capital punishment.

Constructs from Variables. A construct is formed by examining variables that are related in order to determine if these variables produce a meaningful larger entity. Often they do; sometimes they don't. As an illustration, consider the following example. Three variables are found to be highly correlated: (1) an assertiveness test; (2) an extroversion test; and (3) verbal fluency. Subjects who score high on one of these tests tend to score high on the other two. Low scores behave similiarly; that is, subjects scoring low on one tend to score low on the other two. In this sense the variables are said to be highly correlated.

If we study the nature of each variable we might find that an underlying thread runs through them. That is, each seems to have something in common with the other two. One approach to the problem of determining if a substantively meaningful construct exists is to ask ourselves what word or phrase most accurately describes a person who has all three characteristics. What, indeed, is the best descriptor of a person who is at once assertive, extroverted, and verbally fluent? Expressive? It may be the best descriptor we can come up with. If so, then we have tentatively identified a construct: *expressivity.* We might go on to say that high scores on the scales are likely to be highly expressive individuals and that lower scorers are likely to be rather unexpressive.

Constructs are the raw material of behavioral researchers. Unlike sciences such as chemistry and physics, which deal mostly with actual matter, the behavioral scientist usually deals with entities that cannot be directly measured. The topics of behavioral research, then, are typically more abstract. Some examples are:

intelligence	job satisfaction
credibility	morale
hate	androgyny
love	authoritarianism
dogmatism	communication appreciation
creativity	

Each is a construct.

Labeling a construct in terms of the variables that constitute it demands knowledge of theory in the relevant areas plus logical and intuitive skills. The first requirement is that the variables be related, be correlated. This provides statistical justification for proceeding with the process.

We next study the variables in terms of the "common thread," if any, that seems to unite them. We may wish to consider several potential labels at this point. As a final step, given these two or three potential labels, our goal is to determine which makes the best theoretical, substantive sense. Only an intimate knowledge of theory in our particular area of inquiry can provide the kind of information we need.

Haste is the enemy of intelligent construct labeling. The variables should be studied and reflected upon. Knowledgeable colleagues and known experts in a given area should be consulted before a final decision is made. We repeat: Check the relevant theoretical and research literature and consult your colleagues before labeling a construct. Every year researchers "discover" constructs that have been around for years.

Constructs versus Single Variables. Behavioral researchers are interested in studying constructs rather than single variables. Although there are some exceptions, history reveals a strong, overriding emphasis on variable systems. Whenever we focus on any one variable, we are likely to be studying at best a portion of a construct.

We think that studying a part of a construct is a questionable practice. The short-term results tend to be misleading. The inevitable, long-term results are hazy theories and studies that are often quite difficult to replicate. To research a construct, multivariate models are needed.

The Interaction of Variables. Univariate analyses of single variables are characterized by a degree of simplicity. We can run an analysis of variance on our data and note whether or not the test leads to statistical significance. It either is or is not significant. Most of us have no trouble understanding either the nature of the statistical test or the results. If we wish, we can even plot the variable and study the resultant distribution of raw scores. Still, there is no problem understanding what is going on in the data. The characteristics of a single variable, in brief, pose little challenge to our analytical and intuitive capabilities.

Adding variables complicates the picture quickly. If we add nine dependent variables to our original variable we will have ten. And if we plot the distribution of scores for each variable in a given study, we will indeed have a great deal to think about. A few possibilities:

Which variables tend to display similar characteristics? Which differ the most from the remaining variables?

Are the variables measuring one underlying phenomenon? More than one? If so, what is the nature of the underlying phenomena (construct)?

Are some variables stronger than others? That is, might some carry more weight than others in terms of separating groups?

Which variables have the highest correlations, and what can we conclude from examining these correlations?

Underlying our attempt to interpret this ten-variable distribution are two inter-related notions: (1) that variables interact in unknown, unpredictable ways; and (2) that our analytical-intuitive capabilities tend to become less trustworthy as the number of variables increase.

Variable interaction is usually not intuitively obvious; therefore, we need statistical models that can summarize complex relationships, that can provide the basis for a parsimonious description and interpretation of the data. Again, we are compelled to turn to multivariate models. Univariate models lack the sophistication; they simply are not up to the task. Multivariate models, then, are optimal when the goal is the simplification of complex variable interactions.

Information Loss. Univariate procedures, by definition, deal with either single-item variables or with single composite variables. One semantic differential scale represents a single-item variable. That scale can be treated by univariate statistics only. In this case, there is no loss of information. The situation changes markedly, however, when we examine a system of variables.

Consider a ten-item test consisting of individual semantic differential scales. If we restrict ourselves to univariate methods of analysis, then we must somehow compress the ten scale items into a single composite score for each subject. A univariate composite score is open to question, however, especially when one considers the potential amount of information loss. The procedure that yields univariate composite scores involves two steps: First, the scores for each of the variables are summed, and then the total is divided by the number of individual variables. Thus, each variable contributes equally to the resulting composite score. Since some of the variables are probably more important than others in the study we may have lost valuable data by treating the variables as if they were equal.

The motivation for analyzing the ten items as a system of intercorrelated variables is to obtain maximum information about individual variable characteristics. This, then, represents our attempt to abstract the maximum amount of information from the data base.

In short, multivariate procedures permit us to work with many dependent variables, with single composites, or with any combination of these. That is our choice.

Univariate procedures offer one, and only one, option: to work with one variable at a time. This limitation, we think, is far too restrictive.

Correlations Among Dependent Variables. Measurements taken on the same person or entity tend to be correlated. If you have strong doubts about this statement, then take several observations on any group of subjects. You might have them respond to such tests as the Dogmatism scale,[13] the Machiavellian scale,[14] and the Rathus Assertiveness Inventory.[15] Compute correlations on all possible combinations. You'll have three correlation coefficients in all. You'll find them to be at least moderately high. And this will probably hold for most tests and situations. Rarely will any two behavioral variables for the same person correlate zero.

If measurements on the same subject tend to be correlated, then our statistical models should take that fact into account, for the answers we get are likely to be quite different—even dramatically different—depending upon our choice of model, univariate or multivariate. Several univariate analyses of a data base rarely approximate a single multivariate analysis of that same data base. The results are predictable: The univariate researcher is likely to draw qualitatively different conclusions than is the multivariate researcher.

Sample Size. How many subjects do you need? If you were running a univariate analysis of variance or a *t* test we could give a fairly accurate estimate.[16] The numbers needed for a multivariate model are far less easily established, even hazy. There simply are no easy answers. The problem is being worked on, but so far the situation is still characterized by indecision. The advice we offer is based on an assessment of the literature combined with our own experiences in conducting multivariate research.

1. Multivariate research requires the use of large samples. This is a fundamental rule. We should spend a portion of our research energies on obtaining subjects. It's rarely easy; subjects are always in short supply, so persistence is required. If we cannot obtain a respectable sample, then we ought to consider delaying our research until adequate numbers are available.

2. As the numbers of dependent variables increases, so should the sample size. At the moment there are no reliable estimates of what that ratio should be. There are opinions only.

3. One hundred subjects should be the beginning point. This should be considered the lower limit, the absolute minimum. Studies employing sample sizes of 23, 36, and 47 can be found in the literature. Except under rare conditions, little faith can be placed in these findings. A respectable study, in our opinion, has an N of at least 200.

Number of Variables. We urge restraint—for many reasons. First, let us state our general position on the issue of the number of variables.

Briefly put, it is possible to have too many variables. Although it isn't easy to decide when that point is reached, we see it as a potential hazard in any research study. Some students of multivariate methods get the idea that because there are no limits on the number of variables that can be included, they can include anything in a given analysis. They are wrong. Throwing any and all variables into an analysis is labeled "shotgun empiricism," an analogy that indicates the nature of the results—inaccurate.

For one thing, we simply do not know what happens to variables when they are involved with large numbers of other variables. Variables, in other words, can become literally buried. Multiple discriminant analysis offers a case in point: As dependent variables are added or deleted the entire variable set of weights changes in value. How and why this happens is clear in terms of the mathematical algorithm. Intuitively, why it should happen is yet another matter.

To some extent we are suggesting that a certain degree of mystery is involved as variables interact. The lesson is simple enough. If we want to be able to make strong inferences, then we shall have to work with fewer variables.

Substantive versus Statistical Findings. Statistical models produce statistical data. The implications of that statement are profound. While it suggests that our statistical models may produce data that in fact make good theoretical sense, it also suggests they may not.

We think there is far too much worshiping of the statistical model and its corresponding output. A researcher runs a study, say, a canonical correlational analysis. The output is studied. Conclusion: The statistical dimensions don't make sense. The study is dropped; no further analysis is made. And why? Because the standard rules for interpreting the output suggested that the findings were nonsensical. Why did the researcher not study the output in the light of what makes theoretical, substantive sense? One reason is that he or she found it difficult to depart from the rules and guidelines associated with the statistical model.

The problem seems to be associated with the way multivariate statistics are taught. Apparently some students are led to believe that statistical output has a strong relationship to the real world—the world of nonstatistics, of human behavior. The facts are these.

1. Statistical output is just that: statistical output. It does not in some miraculous way necessarily conform to real-world behavior. In some cases the fit may be exceptional; in others, dismal. You can prove this for yourself by running several studies and assessing the fit.

2. Scholars who derive multivariate models rarely make excessive claims as to the resemblance of potential findings to the real world. The claims more often than not are made by teachers and practitioners.

3. Statistical output should be treated as a set of potential indications of real-world phenomena. Findings should be poured over, analyzed, reanalyzed— always within the framework of existing theory and research. The ultimate question to be asked is this: Given this body of statistical output and given these alternative explanations and potential interpretations, which is most in harmony with current substantive knowledge?

4. If the statistical output is widely at variance with substantive knowledge, consider halting further consideration of the findings. If, after analysis, the data suggest the existence of strange or otherwise countersubstantive phenomena, it is senseless to force things. The more reasonable course may be to

admit that the research produced nothing theoretically meaningful. Don't abandon hope too soon. But don't err on the side of demanding more than the output can possibly support.

5. The connection between the real world and statistical output is rarely obvious. To be sure, the big, highly salient findings are easily noticed by anyone. But we've found that much escapes the hasty eye. The nonobvious relationships are found not necessarily by exercising our logical, judicial capabilities, but through the use of our intuitive, imaginative competencies. In this respect we advocate a more risky, even daring attitude on the part of researchers. Going out on that famous limb, having the courage to entertain unconventional possibilities—these too have a place in research.

In the remainder of this chapter we describe four of the most basic multivariate statistical models in current use. Mathematical derivations have been omitted and emphasis placed on the logic of the models and how the results may be interpreted.

Factor Analysis[17]

Take several measurements on a group of 500 college students—for example, self-ratings on the 30-item Rathus Assertiveness Scale,[18] a test designed to measure an individual's overall assertiveness quotient. The test requires each student to respond to each question on a scale of +3, "very characteristic of me," to −3, "very uncharacteristic of me."

An interesting research question might be: How are the 30 individual questions (scale items) related to one another? Do they actually measure one central, underlying dimension called *assertiveness?* Or are there several clusters of questions that appear to be measuring different dimensions? Our first inclination might be to correlate each variable with the remaining 29 variables. We could then study the correlations of all possible pairs of variables until we figured out just what was related to what. It would not work. Unless we were blessed with analytical genius we would find the task of assessing the relationships of variables in a 30 X 30 intercorrelation matrix too much for the mind to grasp. At first glance the task appears deceptively simple. The researcher would study the correlation between variables 1 and 2, 1 and 3, 1 and 4, . . . After a few minutes it would become clear that the complexity of the problem had grown enormously. The researcher would surely yield. The lesson learned would be that the human mind is capable of dealing only with a small subset of relationships at any one time.

Factor analysis resolves the problem by *explaining* the 30 X 30 intercorrelation matrix as simply as possible. To illustrate the logic of factor analysis we present the sequential steps using the 30-variable Rathus Assertiveness Scale as an example.

There are several discrete steps in the execution of a typical factor analysis. We give minimal space to all but the final step.

Step 1: Form a 30 X 30 intercorrelation matrix (R). A Pearson product-moment correlation coefficient is run on all possible pairs of variables, 1 and 2, 1 and 3, . . . 29 and 30.

Step 2: Factor the 30 X 30 R matrix. This initial factoring process is a first attempt to suggest the number of dimensions that can be derived from the 30-variable set. The result is called an initial factor matrix.

Step 3: Rotate the initial factor matrix. The dimensions revealed by the initial factor matrix are usually not in their most theoretically meaningful form. The factor analysis algorithm mathematically alters that matrix, resulting in the matrix that is of central concern to the researcher—the *rotated* factor matrix. We report here the results of Karen J. Gritzmacher's[19] factor analysis of the Rathus Assertiveness Scale. Table 8-2 presents the rotated factor matrix.[20]

Interpreting the Rotated Factor Matrix. Factor analysis is concerned with clusters of variables. A cluster is determined by examining the size of the loadings. Variables loading on the same factor, or dimension, are studied in order to determine if a common thread is running through them. If a common thread is found to exist, then the researcher attempts to label it. This is done by looking at the original questions in order to detect similarities among them. In effect, the researcher is checking for the existence of a theoretically meaningful construct.

Gritzmacher's analysis led her to conclude that the 30-item test was in fact measuring two factors, referred to in the table as F1 and F2. The first factor she chose to label *Outspokenness*. Her criterion for inclusion of an item as defining a factor was that it had to load at least .40 on the first factor and not greater than .30 on the second factor. Following this decision rule the first factor was determined by questions 3, 8, 14, 15, 19, 21, 22, 23, 24, 25, 27, 28, and 29. The student

Table 8-2 Rotated Factor Loadings, Rathus Assertiveness Scale.

Item	*F1*	*F2*
1. Most people seem to be more aggressive and assertive than I am.	.08	.55
2. I have hesitated to make or accept dates because of "shyness."	−.20	.55
3. When the food served at a restaurant is not done to my satisfaction, I complain about it to the waiter or waitress.	.42	.04
4. I am careful to avoid hurting other people's feelings, even when I feel that I have been injured.	.25	.06
5. If a salesman has gone to considerable trouble to show me merchandise which is not quite suitable, I have a difficult time saying "NO."	.20	.27
6. When I am asked to do something, I insist upon knowing why.	.20	−.02
7. There are times when I look for a good, vigorous argument.	.21	.08
8. I strive to get ahead as well as most people in my position.	.57	−.02
9. To be honest, people often take advantage of me.	.13	.39
10. I enjoy starting conversations with new acquaintances and strangers.	.00	.48
11. I often don't know what to say to attractive persons of the opposite sex.	−.06	.68
12. I will hesitate to make phone calls to business establishments and institutions.	.08	.49
13. I would rather apply for a job or for admission to a college by writing letters than by going through with personal interviews.	.07	.45
14. I find it embarrassing to return merchandise.	.49	.13
15. If a close and respected relative were annoying me, I would smother my feelings rather than express my annoyance.	.60	.07

16. I have avoided asking questions for fear of sounding stupid.	.13	.56
17. During an argument I am sometimes afraid that I will get so upset that I will shake all over.	.27	.17
18. If a famed and respected lecturer makes a statement which I think is incorrect, I will have the audience hear my point of view as well.	.24	.23
19. I avoid arguing over prices with clerks and salesmen.	.55	−.05
20. When I have done something important and worthwhile, I manage to let others know about it.	.31	−.09
21. I am open and frank about my feelings.	.49	.21
22. If someone has been spreading false and bad stories about me, I see him/her as soon as possible to "have a talk" about it.	.51	.05
23. I often have a hard time saying "NO."	.47	.27
24. I tend to bottle up my emotions rather than make a scene.	.53	.22
25. I complain about poor service in a restaurant and elsewhere.	.65	−.07
26. When I am given a compliment, I sometimes just don't know what to say.	.02	.42
27. If a couple near me in a theater or at a lecture were conversing rather loudly, I would ask them to be quiet or to take their conversation elsewhere.	.59	−.01
28. Anyone attempting to push ahead of me in line is in for a good battle.	.72	−.15
29. I am quick to express an opinion.	.54	.22
30. There are times when I just can't say anything.	.05	.42
Eigenvalue	4.50	3.00
Percentage of Variance	15.00	12.00

Source: Gritzmacher Study. Reprinted with permission of K.J. Gritzmacher and S. A. Rathus.

should verify that these test items seem to be measuring essentially a common, underlying phenomenon *Outspokenness.* As you proceed, however, note that a specific item may be phrased in such a way so as to suggest just the opposite of outspokenness. Question 19 is a case in point: "I avoid arguing over prices with clerks and salesmen." As it stands the item assuredly suggests timidity rather than outspokenness. To resolve this problem, Gritzmacher reversed the scoring on this and similar items so as to give the higher score to subjects who disagreed with the item. Labeling factors has always been controversial. This, then, was Gritzmacher's opinion only.

The second factor was determined by questions 1, 2, 10, 11, 12, 13, 16, 26, and 30. Gritzmacher named that factor *Positive Self Image.*

The table also reveals that some questions were found to be unrelated to either factor. Question 18 is an example. This is to be expected. Factor analyses are run in order to discover those variables that are unrelated to factors as well as those that are related. This analysis suggests that question 18 may be irrelevant to the measurement of assertiveness. If this fact is corroborated in later analyses, the author (Rathus) may wish to remove it from the test.

The table gives some other kinds of information. At the bottom of the table are indicated "Eigenvalue" and "Percentage of Variance." An eigenvalue is a mathematical characteristic of any square matrix. In factor analysis it measures the size of the factor, or—as indicated—the percentage of variance. Factor 1 is said to account for 15.0 percent of the variance. Based on 100 percent, this factor is only moderately large. The second factor accounts for only 10.0 percent of the variance, which is decidedly small. What is the significance of the size of factors and the amount of variance? The psychometric theory relevant to variance is exceedingly complex, so only the most rudimentary explanation can be put forth.

Here is one perspective: The simplest explanation of a test is that it consists of a single factor that accounts for 100 percent of the variance. This would represent the ultimate in parsimony. As the number of factors increases, the complexity of the test also increases. For real tests on real people behavioral scientists rarely find single factors. Rather, they typically find tests that factor analysis shows to consist of two to four factors. Factor analysis of the Rathus Scale produced two factors that accounted for approximately 25 percent of the total variance. This means that about 75 percent of the variance is unaccounted for, clearly an unsatisfactory condition. If the research that follows produces similar results, then the author of the test may well wish to reappraise its adequacy as a measure of assertiveness. We emphasize that a large number of factor analyses as well as other psychometric analyses will be needed before such a conclusion can be drawn.

Summary of Factor Analysis. The motivation for executing a factor analysis varies with the researcher. In our illustration, we have described the most prevalent reason—to determine the structure of a set of variables. The variable set consisted of the 30 questions that make up the Rathus Assertiveness Scale. The question of structure was approached by the application of the factor analytic model to the subjects' responses. The basic issues of structure and the findings were:

1. Structurally, the 30-item test can be described in terms of two factors.
2. The first and largest factor, based on loadings in the rotated factor matrix, was labeled *Outspokenness*. This factor accounted for 15.0 percent of the total variance.
3. The second factor, labeled *Positive Self Image*, accounted for 10.0 percent of the total variance.
4. Some items, for example, question 18, seem to be irrelevant to the measurement of assertiveness in this test.
5. The analysis provides this tentative set of indications, all of which must be researched further via replication studies:
   a. The Rathus Assertiveness Scale is a 2-factor instrument.[21]
   b. The two factors, on the basis of the items loading on them, can be labeled *Outspokenness* and *Positive Self Image*.
   c. Neither factor is particularly strong, as evidenced by the fact that 75 percent of the variance is unaccounted for.

Canonical Correlation[22]

The Pearson product-moment coefficient of correlation has enjoyed great prominence in the field of statistical methods. And well it should, for the relationship existing between two sets of variables is information basic to virtually any major theory.

The statistical relationship between two variables has an obvious built-in limitation—the number of variables whose relationship is sought is, by definition, limited to two. We can, to be sure, execute a very large number of correlations and then study the variables in all possible combinations separately. This possibility was mentioned in our discussion of the factor-analysis model, and we suggested that trying to interpret the relationships of a large set of variables is often too complex for the human mind. What is needed is a statistical model that permits variables to be studied in large numbers and in all possible combinations. The method of canonical correlation *(Rc)* is ideally suited to that task. The characteristics of *Rc* are:

1. Variables are assigned either to Set 1 or to Set 2.
2. There is no limitation on the number of variables that can be placed in either set. Nor need the number of variables in the sets be equal. For example, Set 1 may contain twelve variables, Set 2 three variables.
3. Variables are assigned to the sets on the basis of their theoretical interest. *Rc* reveals the relationships existing between linear combinations of the two variable sets just as ordinary correlation reveals the relationship of two variables.
4. *Rc* provides information about how the variable sets relate at several levels. In other words, multiple relationships exist between the two sets of variables, and the *Rc* model describes exactly both the nature and the strength of those relationships.

The simplest *Rc* analysis involves two variables in each set. As a hypothetical example, assume we wish to test the relationship between subjects' scores on two expressivity tests and two tests of predisposition to emotionality:

Set 1 Variables (Expressivity)

1. *Verbal output index.* The tendency to speak while a member of a problem-solving group.
2. *Opinion index.* The number of opinions expressed per 100 words.

Set 2 Variables (Predisposition to emotionality)

3. *Anger index.* Tendency to exhibit anger toward peers.
4. *Contempt index.* Tendency to verbally express contempt for peers.

Assume these four measurements are taken on 800 university students, while members of small problem-solving groups. What might we hypothesize? Perhaps that a strong relationship exists between the expressivity variables and the emotionality variables such that subjects with high verbal output and a high opinion index tend also to exhibit high degrees of anger and contempt toward their peers.

How the Rc Model Operates

Weights. The computational algorithm in the case of an *Rc* analysis assigns weights to the variables in each set.[23] These weights are then applied to each subject's raw score so that a single composite is formed. With a single composite variable for each set, the next step is to run a simple coefficient of correlation on the composites. *Rc,* then, is the correlation between the two composites. For the example, the *Rc* model may have weighted the variables this way:

Set 1	Set 2
(1) .50	(3) .80
(2) .70	(4) .90

These are the weights used to form the composites. Subject 1, let us say, had the following sets of raw scores:

Set 1	Set 2
(1) 8	(3) 7.5
(2) 9	(4) 6

To form the composite score for Set 1 we multiply the weights X raw scores. This leads to:

$$.50 \times 8 = 4$$
$$.70 \times 9 = \underline{6.3}$$

10.3 = Subject 1's composite score on the Set 1 variables.

and

$$.80 \times 7.5 = 6$$
$$.90 \times 6 = \underline{5.4}$$

13.5 = Subject 1's composite score on the Set 2 variables.

The remaining 799 subjects' composite scores are calculated in precisely the same way. With all 800 sets of two composites the *Rc* model can now derive the coefficient of correlation, which is precisely identical to the canonical correlation coefficient.

Loadings. The key to the interpretation of an *Rc* analysis is contained in the canonical component loadings,[24] often referred to simply as the loadings. Interpretation follows the logic of ordinary correlation. The concern is always with the size of the loading and the direction, positive or negative. In our example, let us assume these canonical component loadings:

Set 1	*Set 2*
(1) .90 (verbal output)	(3) .88 (anger)
(2) .10 (opinion)	(4) .91 (contempt)

Before we decide to interpret the *Rc* output there are two final considerations: the test of statistical significance and the size of the *Rc* coefficient. Hypothetical results:

Rc coefficient = .90
Test of statistical significance = $p < .001$

The size of the Rc, .90, is impressively high. The maximum, as in any correlational model, is 1.0. The test of significance is equally impressive. We conclude that at least one significant relationship exists between the *composites* of the two sets. Interpretation is in order. Studying the loadings we see that in Set 1 the composite is defined solely by the first variable, verbal output, whose loading is .90. The very small loading for variable 2, opinion, means that the variable is essentially unrelated to the composite. Turning to Set 2 it seems clear that the composite is defined nearly equally by the two emotionality variables, anger and contempt. Note that loadings of .88 and .91 are practically identical. Now to the interpretation:

The Set 1 variables, dominated solely by the first variable, appear to be measuring *verbal output*. The Set 2 variables are dominated equally by the *anger* and *contempt* variables. The analysis suggests that students with high verbal output tend also to exhibit high degrees of anger and contempt for their peers. And conversely, students with low verbal output tend to exhibit little anger and contempt. The number of opinions expressed seems unrelated to the other three variables.

Additional Analyses. In the language of canonical correlation, we have examined the variable relationships of the first root. This implies that a second root may provide additional useful information and that is precisely the case. Now a root is a measurement of the amount of variance. Variance is always based on a 100 percent base line. So if 80 percent of the variance is accounted for by the first root, then 20 percent remains to be explained. The number of possible roots is equal to the number of variables in the smaller set or, in this case, two. So we move to an examination of the *Rc* coefficient and the loadings for the second root.

We find the *Rc* coefficient to be .13, not statistically significant. We conclude that only the first root has scientific value. It is not unusual for roots beyond the first to be both practically and statistically significant. The rule of thumb is to consider trivial any root whose *Rc* coefficient is less than .30, whether or not it is statistically significant.

Loadings on roots beyond the first always differ in terms of total configuration. This is to be expected since we are dealing with variance that is not explained by the preceding root. With three roots, a hypothetical set of loadings might look like this:

	Set 1	*Set 2*
Root 1:	(1) .81	(5) .95
	(2) .62	(6) .17
	(3) .11	(7) .21
	(4) .49	
Root 2:	(1) .16	(5) .18
	(2) .73	(6) .52
	(3) .80	(7) .06
	(4) .77	
Root 3:	(1) .22	(5) .52
	(2) .41	(6) .90
	(3) .06	(7) .81
	(4) .18	

Each root is interpreted in the manner described above. Since the loadings shift in absolute value, each composite will be defined differently; and the relationship of the variables across sets will be similarly affected.

Uses of Rc

Relating tests. The relationships of any two tests can be assessed. Individual items of Test 1 constitute the Set 1 variables; items in Test 2 constitute the Set 2 variables.

Psychographic-attitude items. Mass communication scholars especially may be interested in evaluating the relationships among psychographic variables (personality measurements) and attitudes toward consumer products. Such data could provide insights into what types of personalities are attracted to which products.

Repeated measure studies. Any two sets of measurements in time can be studied through an *Rc* analysis. The first measurement would constitute the Set 1 variables; the second measurement the Set 2 variables.

Teacher evaluations. Studies evaluating teachers and professors abound in the literature. Lacking are studies relating student characteristics to their evaluations of instructors. Korth,[25] Pohlman,[26] and Tucker and Hinman[27] have used the *Rc* model to study these relationships. The results have shed considerable light on the kinds of student characteristics most highly associated with certain instructor ratings.

A Research Example. To examine the relationship among assertiveness, manifest anxiety, and self-esteem, Roger N. Conaway[28] utilized the method of canonical correlation. Conaway chose to work with six theoretically relevant dependent variables:

Set One Variables:

1. College Self-Expression Scale[29]
2. Rathus Assertive Schedule[30]
3. Assertiveness Inventory[31]

Set Two Variables:

4. Taylor Manifest Anxiety Scale[32]
5. Self-Esteem Scale[33]
6. Self-Esteem Inventory[34]

Conaway hypothesized that:

1. The three assertiveness variables will positively correlate.
2. The anxiety variable will negatively correlate with the assertiveness measures.
3. The self-esteem variable will positively correlate with the assertiveness measures.
4. The self-esteem variables will negatively correlate with the anxiety variable.

The results (Table 8-3) indicate that only one of the three roots was significant.

An examination of the table reveals that the first root had an *Rc* coefficient of .54. The square of *Rc* = .29 indicates that the composites formed by the two sets contained only 29 percent overlapping information. The relationships of the variable composites, then, can be described as only moderate.

Table 8-3 Canonical correlational analysis of Root 1.

Set One		Set Two	
Variable	Loading	Variable	Loading
1. College Self-Expression Scale	.77	4. Manifest Anxiety (Taylor)	−.80
2. Rathus Assertive Schedule	.86	5. Self-Esteem Scale (Rosenberg)	.79
3. Assertiveness Inventory	.94	6. Self-Esteem Inventory (Coopersmith)	.97

$$Rc = .54$$
$$(Rc)^2 = .29$$
$$\chi^2 = 80.3852 \text{ with d.f.} = 9, p < .0001$$

Source: Conaway Study. Adapted with permission from R.N. Conaway.

The loadings corroborated Conaway's four hypotheses. The three assertiveness variables were all highly related, as evidenced by the loadings of .77, .86, and .94. The self-esteem variables were likewise highly related as evidenced by their loadings of .79 and .97. And, as hypothesized, the Manifest Anxiety variable was negatively related, both to the self-esteem and to the assertiveness variables. In summary, results of the study suggested that: (1) Subjects who score high on one of the assertiveness variables tend to score high on the other two. (2) Subjects who score high on the assertiveness variables also tend to score high on both of the self-esteem variables but low on the manifest anxiety variable. (3) Subjects who score high on the self-esteem variables tend to score low on the manifest anxiety variable.

Canonical Redundancy Analysis. Canonical correlation can also be used to measure the degree of overlap (redundancy)[35] between two *sets* of variables, as opposed to the relationship existing between the linear composites. To illustrate redundancy analysis, we describe a study done by Susan C. Parrish.[36]

According to Parrish, the purpose of the investigation was to examine four constructs—self-disclosure, attraction, homophily, and trust—as they relate to a fifth, uncertainty reduction. The 355 subjects were given packets containing instruments purporting to measure each of the five constructs specified. The data base was subjected to four separate canonical redundancy analyses to determine if the variables of self-disclosure, attraction, homophily, and trust, overlapped (provided redundant information) the uncertainty reduction variable.

Parrish found that when measures of uncertainty reduction were used as the predictor variable set, the analyses indicated redundancy of 4 percent with the self-disclosure set, 23 percent with the attraction set, 15 percent with the homophily set, and 23 percent with the trust set.

When the uncertainty reduction measures were used as the criterion variable set, the analyses indicated redundancy of 2 percent with the self-disclosure set, 8 percent with the attraction set, 3.5 percent with the homophily set, and 5 percent with the trust set.

Parrish concluded that the uncertainty reduction variables were fairly good predictors of attraction and trust, moderate predictors of homophily, and poor predictors of self-disclosure. Further, self-disclosure, attraction, homophily, and trust were poor predictors of uncertainty reduction.

Redundancy analysis appears to be a viable method for studying the degree of overlap between any two sets of variables. The procedures for computing the analysis are straightforward, and the results are usually easy to interpret. Students desiring to conduct such an analysis are referred to the chapter by Tucker and Chase in *Multivariate Techniques,* by Monge and Capella.[37]

Multivariate Analysis of Variance

Earlier in this chapter we presented the rudiments of ANOVA—the univariate analysis of variance. As pointed out, ANOVA is appropriate whenever the goal is to test the capability of a single dependent variable to separate three or more groups. The multivariate analogue of ANOVA is MANOVA—the multivariate analysis of variance.

MANOVA always involves a minimum of two dependent variables. The test is whether the set of correlated variables significantly separates the groups. As in ANOVA, rejection of the null hypothesis constitutes evidence that at least two groups differ in terms of the dependent variable set.

An Illustration. A single-factor MANOVA at four levels, employing four dependent variables, is schematicized in this way:

Freshmen	*Sophomores*	*Juniors*	*Seniors*
Group 1	Group 2	Group 3	Group 4
n = 100	n = 100	n = 100	n = 100

The dependent variables are:

DV_1: Articulation test
DV_2: Fluency test
DV_3: Hearing acuity test
DV_4: Vocal resonance test

The subjects, 400 students representing 100 from each class at a major university, are assigned at random to the groups. The research goal is to evaluate significantly different profiles, if they are found to exist, among the four classes.

Since four dependent variables and four groups are involved, MANOVA is an appropriate statistical model. The program is executed and the null hypothesis is rejected at $p < .001$. The vector of four dependent variables, it is concluded, differs significantly among the four groups. Which variables were most responsible for this group separation? We have the option of looking at the univariate Fs for each variable. If only a few variables are involved—as in this example—this is an entirely appropriate procedure.[38] Suppose the univariate Fs were found to be:

DV_1: 6.66, $p < .01$
DV_2: 7.29, $p < .01$
DV_3: 2.21, not significant
DV_4: 1.14, not significant

The first two variables are significant; the last two are not. A reasonable inference would be that DVs 1 and 2 were predominantly responsible for the group separation. Univariate follow-up tests could pinpoint precisely which groups were most affected by these variables.

Research Example

Tucker and Dierks-Stewart[39] designed a study to investigate the effect of the experimenter and other unwanted sources of influence in the typical persuasion experiment. An identical communication on the topic of annual medical checkups was presented to six different groups of subjects with n = 50 per group. The independent variable was the individual experimenter. The experiment was executed at the same hour for all six groups. The researchers sought to determine how the groups would differ, if at all, on the several dependent variables of interest.

Subjects, after exposure to the persuasive communication, responded to five dependent variables:

DV_1: Attitude toward annual medical checkups.

DV_2: Evaluation of the experimenter (the person conducting the study who was physically present in the room).

DV_3: Attitude toward the source (the person delivering the taped persuasive communication).

DV_4: Attitude toward being a non-volunteer in the research study.

DV_5: Evaluation apprehension as a result of being in the study.

Tucker and Dierks-Stewart hypothesized that the groups would not differ on the five dependent variables. If group separation were to result, then suspicion might be cast on the wisdom of employing multiple experimenters as is the practice in some persuasion experiments.

With five dependent variables and six groups, MANOVA was an appropriate statistical model. The results:

The MANOVA was significant, indicating that the groups differed on the set of five dependent variables. The multivariate F, with d.f. = 25/1078.8040, was 4.7916, $p < .0001$. To pinpoint those variables contributing most to group differences, univariate Fs were conducted with the following results:

DV_1: Significant, $p < .04$

DV_2: Significant, $p < .0001$

DV_3: Significant, $p < .002$

DV_4: Not significant

DV_5: Not significant

The univariate Fs indicated that some of the variables separated the groups, and others did not. Specifically, when each variable was analyzed separately, the most discriminating variable was DV_2, evaluation of the experimenter. Almost as discriminating was DV_3, attitude toward the source. DV_1, attitude toward annual medical checkups, was next most discriminating with $p < .04$. The two remaining variables, DV_4 and DV_5, did not reach statistical significance at the .05 level.

Tucker and Dierks-Stewart analyzed the results of the MANOVA and the univariate follow-up tests and concluded that—to the extent the results of the study were generalizable—the use of multiple experimenters poses a threat to both the internal and the external validity of the typical persuasion experiment.

MANOVA may be used any time at least three groups are involved. There is no theoretical limit as to the number of dependent variables that can be employed, although there are practical limitations. Our recommendation: A maximum of five.

For variables in excess of that number we recommend multiple discriminant analysis.

Multiple Discriminant Analysis[40]

In some important ways, multiple discriminant analysis (MULDIS) is similar to MANOVA. Both may be used when the goal is the assessment of group separation. But MULDIS goes several steps further. It indicates which variables in the set are most responsible for group separation, and—like MANOVA—it takes into consideration the correlations existing among the several dependent variables. How MULDIS accomplishes this can be more fully appreciated by referring back to the hypothetical example used to illustrate MANOVA. With four groups and four dependent variables, MULDIS may be employed to assess group differences. Interest centers upon the number of significant roots and the nature of the discriminant function loadings for the variables. Hypothetical results:

Root 1

DV_1:	Articulation	.80*
DV_2:	Fluency	.10
DV_3:	Hearing	.85*
DV_4:	Vocal resonance	.16

A straightforward interpretation is possible because in this artificial case there are two very high and two very low loadings. The loadings indicate that, *as a correlated set of dependent variables,* the articulation and hearing variables are the best separators of the groups. In contrast, the fluency and vocal resonance variables are relatively weak separators. As in *Rc* analysis, the researcher is interested in labeling the construct formed by the combination of the articulation and hearing variables. Were this actual research we would check the literature of speech disorders for clues as to what an appropriate label might be. For our purposes an arbitrary label might be "expressive-receptive competency."

As indicated, MULDIS and canonical correlation exhibit similar properties. Both provide weights that are applied to the subjects' raw scores to compute composites. In MULDIS, these composites are called *discriminant function scores.* Likewise, as with the *Rc* analysis, weights are distinctly different from loadings. In MULDIS, weights are used to form group centroids (means of the discriminant function scores). Loadings are used to label the centroids.

Additional Roots. MULDIS is yet another statistical model that provides more than one level of information through the examination of individual roots. The number of roots is equal to the number of dependent variables or the number of groups minus one—whichever is smaller. In our example there are three roots. Each root provides a different configuration of loadings. So again, as in the case of *Rc,* the centroids defined by each root will represent a different construct. Hypothetical loadings for the second root:

Root 2

DV$_1$:   Articulation   .13
DV$_2$:   Fluency   .94*
DV$_3$:   Hearing   .19
DV$_4$:   Vocal resonance   .89*

Clearly the loadings are qualitatively different from those of Root 1. Again the interpretation poses no problem—two very large and two very small loadings. Maximum group separation can be attributed, for the most part, to the combined effects of DV$_2$ and DV$_4$. The construct so defined might be labeled "vocal expression."

The third root is interpreted in the same manner. Another way to think about roots is to see them as representing another perspective on the data. Simply put, in multivariate analysis there are always multiple ways of looking at the results.

A fundamental question involves the number of roots a researcher may choose to interpret. The first criterion ought to be the test of significance. If a root is not significant, then this constitutes ample grounds for ignoring it. Beyond that, there is only rule-of-thumb advice—that is, the first two roots usually contain most of the important information in most discriminant analyses.

Plotting the Centroids. The purpose of running a multiple discriminant analysis is to determine the extent to which a set of correlated variables separates the groups. One effective method of displaying the results is to plot the centroids in Cartesian coordinate space. For our four-group problem we present these hypothetical results in Figure 8-2. Interpretation of the study is made by visually examining the relative position of the centroids:

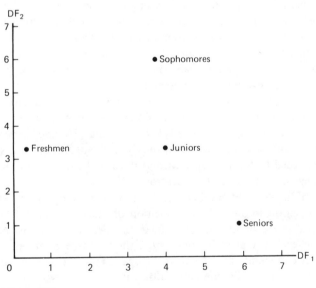

Figure 8-2

1. Discriminant Function I, DF_1, representing the information contained in Root 1, is interpreted by noting the position of the centroids on the horizontal scale. Recalling that the centroid was labeled "expressive-receptive competency," it is evident that the largest group separation occurs between freshmen and seniors, with the senior group possessing more of the trait. Sophomores and juniors have identical centroids and seem to fall midway between the freshmen and the seniors. The general impression one receives from examining the first function is that after the freshman year expressive-receptive competency improves notably. No increase in competency occurs from the sophomore to the junior years, but in the senior year this communication skill again increases.

2. Discriminant Function II, labeled "vocal expression," is evaluated by reference to the vertical axis. Here sophomores and seniors are maximally differentiated, with sophomores scoring highest. Freshmen and juniors occupy an intermediate position. Overall, it appears that vocal expression competence increases following the freshman year. After that, the trend is distinctly downward.

3. Additional insights are obtained by studying the groups on the two discriminant functions simultaneously. In this perspective we might wish to examine the group centroids one at a time. For instance, directing our attention to seniors only, note that this group is highest on expressive-receptive competency (DF_1). It is lowest on vocal expression (DF_2). Juniors, on the other hand, are at the midpoint relative to the other three groups on both discriminant functions.

With only four groups, the problem of interpretation is straightforward. As the number of groups increases, the difficulty of interpretation also increases. For this reason, restraint is again suggested.

A question frequently asked is: Are there significance tests among group centroids? There are none. Discriminant analysis is based on the premise that a rejection of the null hypothesis implies significant group separation. It does not say which—of all possible centroids—is different. Interpretation is strictly a visual operation.

Research Example. Multiple discriminant analysis was employed by Tucker[41] to assess the relative abilities of three college instructors as lecturers. The design involved student evaluations of three instructors in different sections of the same basic course. All were graduate teaching assistants.

The dependent variable consisted of five instructor-rating items taken from Korth's[42] study:

DV_1: The lectures were generally very good.

DV_2: The lectures were organized so that I could see what was being developed.

DV_3: The way that the instructor spoke kept me interested.

DV_4: The instructor provided plenty of review and summary.

DV_5: I understood the instructor's explanations all the time.

With five dependent variables and three groups, a multiple discriminant analysis was an appropriate statistical model to apply to the data base. The results are displayed in Figure 8-3 and Table 8-4.

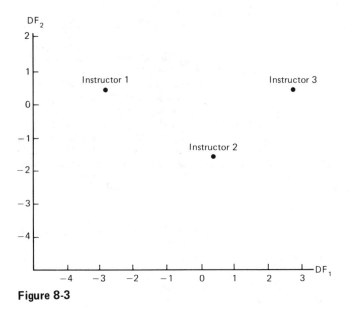

Figure 8-3

Table 8-4 Statistical Summary of Multiple Discriminant Analysis, Tucker Lecture Competence Study.

	Centroid Values	
	DF_1	DF_2
Instructor 1:	−2.94733	.57363
Instructor 2:	.27486	−1.34451
Instructor 3:	2.67287	.77088
	Weights (Standardized)	
DV_1:	− .89484	.54599
DV_2:	1.51613	.54667
DV_3:	− .15133	−1.06720
DV_4:	−2.27170	− .40132
DV_5:	1.95723	− .20386
	Loadings	
DV_1:	.43	.26
DV_2:	.04	.07
DV_3:	.24	.62
DV_4:	.10	.25
DV_5:	.20	.28
	Test of Significance	
Root 1:	$\chi^2 = 177.97$ with d.f. = 10, p < .0001	
Root 2:	$\chi^2 = 46.686$ with d.f. = 4, p < .0001	

Univariate F Tests (with d.f. = 2/72)

DV_1:	39.54	p < .0001
DV_2:	.5020	p < .6074
DV_3:	24.66	p < .0001
DV_4:	4.401	p < .0157
DV_5:	10.99	p < .0001

Turning first to the tests of significance we find that both roots are highly significant at $p < .0001$. This indicates that there are two different ways of assessing group differences.

The centroids confirm the fact that the three instructors were clearly differentiated by their classes. What constructs do the respective centroids represent? To answer that question we study the loadings. DF_1 is clearly dominated by DV_1 and to a lesser extent by DVs 3 and 5. Referring back to these test items we might call this "generalized ability to lecture." On this first function, Instructor 3 is evaluated highest and Instructor 1 lowest. Instructor 2 occupies a midposition.

The second discriminant function is defined almost exclusively by DV_3. The loading of .62, as contrasted to the remaining four small loadings, means the centroid can be labeled in terms of this variable only. In this perspective it is clear that the centroid might be appropriately labeled "Delivery." The figure shows clearly that Instructors 1 and 3 are nearly identical, with Instructor 2 receiving clearly lower evaluations.

The table of univariate Fs presents additional useful information. Note that, taken by itself, DV_5 is a powerful separator of the groups with $p < .0001$. When the analysis involves a correlated set, however, as in the case of multiple discriminant analysis, its contribution to group separation is minimal as evidenced by the loadings of .20 and .28 on Discriminant Functions 1 and 2, respectively.

STATISTICS AND THE FUTURE

In this chapter we have presented brief accounts of basic univariate and multivariate statistical models. Students who take the time to understand them will gain a valuable perspective on the direction of research in the behavioral sciences, including speech communication, insofar as data analysis is concerned. This will be a beginning, an initial effort. Real proficiency in statistical usage will require obtaining a comprehensive foundation. If your basic mathematics is rusty, enroll in a refresher course and then in the basic descriptive statistics course and follow up with courses in statistical inference. Finally, learn the fundamentals of multivariate data analysis. A knowledge of basic multivariate models will be your greatest asset as you prepare for a career that is almost certain to include research of some kind.

Research:

Presentation and Evaluation

Research is being reported in record amounts. Within any single discipline the output far exceeds the professional's ability to absorb. On the surface most of it looks impressive, and much of it is. Some of it, however, is clearly unsatisfactory. Both researchers and consumers of research, then, must be able to differentiate the acceptable from the unacceptable. In this chapter we present a set of criteria that can be applied to most research products, whether they be of the experimental type, descriptive, or historical-critical. Additionally, we offer guidelines for the presentation and writing of research reports.

GENERAL CONSIDERATIONS

Does the Research Derive from a Theoretical Base?[1] Theory-derived research implies a support for the main-stream issues within a discipline. Main-stream issues are so classified because they reflect the work of numerous investigators, each dedicated to unravelling some of the mystery surrounding a given phenomenon. This is most rapidly accomplished by large numbers of researchers working in areas of theoretical importance.

Is the Research Worthwhile? Whether a given study is worthwhile or not is often a matter of opinion. What follows is ours.

We think some inferior research is conducted, and some of it gets into print. What makes it inferior? We mentioned one of the reasons—lack of a theoretical base. In the remainder of this chapter we detail many of the characteristics of "good" and "poor" research. But for now let us take a quick look at some "odds-and-ends" factors that tend to spell success or failure for a study.

One of the most damning observations on a research study is contained in the words *So what?* or *Who cares?* Its implication is that the research is trite and unrelated to anything important.

Second, many studies could have survived the above question had the researcher been less hurried. The study was significant in a larger sense. The problem was that the researcher focused on only a trivial aspect of a larger problem, simply because he or she was in a hurry. And what was the reason for hurrying? He or she had to get "something" published for some professional or economic reason. This meant that the original investigation had to be cut drastically in scope and time allocation. The result is a study so severely limited as to be of virtually no significance. A study originally intended to investigate the influence of dress and clothing on persuasiveness could qualify as worthwhile research. If only the color of neckties is considered because the researcher feels pressed for time, the significance is highly suspect. Good research is time-consuming. If sufficient time is not available we suggest waiting until it is.

Haste operates to produce other negative outcomes. Designing studies, choosing acceptable measuring instruments—these and countless other elements in the research process are enormous time-eaters. The urge to compromise is always present. Researchers who succumb may find themselves involved in:

Adopting a dependent variable that, superficially at any rate, looks suitable; or throwing some hand-made scales together in a matter of minutes.

Hurried designs in which the choice of independent variable, levels, time and place of study, and execution are based on instant analysis.

In historical research, choosing sources because they just happen to be on the library shelf.

Rushing into the analysis stage without establishing and recording a strong, documented factual base.

Finally, there is the issue of analysis of data: True data analysis—whether of the behavioral, library, or historical-critical type—cannot be rushed. The data must be pored over.[2] It must be reflected, and it must be incubated. By that we mean that it should be "slept on" for one, two, three, or more nights. We have found that conclusions based on immediate analysis differ in many important ways from those characterized by greater periods of incubation. Often the meager, unsophisticated findings resulting from the "instant" analysis lead the reader directly to the conclusion that the study was not worthwhile, that it lacked either theoretical or practical significance—or both.

PROBLEM DESCRIPTION

What Precisely Is the Problem? A clear problem statement is needed.[3] It must be communicated in a relatively few words. Complex problem descriptions rarely get across to the reader. Again, parsimony is the key. This implies that considerable writing and rewriting may be necessary, for problem statements must often turn a complex area into one that is conceptually simple and is within the grasp of the typical scholar in a particular field.

Is the Problem Important? As with the question of "Is it worthwhile?" the researcher must document the potential importance of the problem early in the manuscript. On the surface it may appear that judgments as to the importance of a problem are totally subjective. They are not. Subjective opinion figures in; but the ability of the researcher to reveal a tie-in with existing theory and research figures prominently also. The researcher does this by documenting issues, points, and findings from the literature.

The response of scholars to potential research problems falls roughly into three categories: first, at the highest level, the feeling that the solution to the problem would tend to further knowledge in a given discipline sufficiently; second, that a solution to the problem would be of interest only to a few specialists; and finally, that the problem as stated is either vague, lacking in meaning, or in its present form incapable of being solved.

Has Previous Research Been Taken into Account? Avoid "private universe" research. Such research is characterized by a failure to note and feed into the relevant and important previous research.[4] Significant problems are derived from previous research, and the researcher must demonstrate how that research forms part of the basis for the current problem. How do you deal with previous research? We suggest some guidelines.

First, the trend in published research is to streamline the literature review. In the past, some researchers have been guilty of beating the literature to death, leaving the reader hopelessly bogged down and confused. Brevity is now the rule—intelligent brevity.

Second, all literature appraisals should include a discussion of the most relevant classic and contemporary studies. The criterion for selection is that these studies—more than any others—relate to the topic in the most straightforward way. That relationship is usually along a content dimension. At least one of the studies discussed should have employed the method to be used in the current study. This is especially important if the proposed method has not enjoyed widespread use in the past.[5]

Additionally, the discussion must include recent research. The researcher cannot rely on monthly abstracts to provide information on the latest research; such publications may be as much as a year behind. The current periodical shelf must be checked. In the typical case this involves looking through some twenty to fifty recent issues.

Summarizations are desirable when a large number of research studies are to be discussed. They may even be included in table form if this will make for a smoother presentation.

Literature relevant to the problem may be scarce or even nonexistent. If so, the most relevant research—even though not directly related—should be used, and care should be taken to make its relationship to the problem especially clear. A word of caution. It is crucial that the literature be surveyed with great care before concluding that no relevant research exists. We have yet to find a research problem of any significance that did not have a literature base, though it may have been a small one.

Finally, the literature review must be integrated. The reader will be asking throughout, "How are these studies related to the problem?" The answer should be evident.

Are Objectives, Hypotheses, or Research Questions Clearly Stated? One of the most devestating observations on a manuscript is that it is hard to determine exactly what the researchers were trying to do. If such questions arise it is probable that the objectives of the study have been confused.

Hypotheses must be enumerated in such a way that their relationship to the general problem stands out in bold relief. There must, in other words, be an obvious connection between the two. If research questions rather than hypotheses are used, the same expectation holds. Interrelationships must be demonstrated at every stage of the research process. Nowhere is that statement more applicable than in the relationship between problem and research hypotheses (questions).

METHOD

The procedures by which the research was carried out constitute the design and method.[6] At this stage of the report it is the obligation of the researchers to spell out in sufficient detail precisely how the research was executed. In doing so they must be guided at once by parsimony and comprehensiveness. The test of a well-conceived methods section is that the study can be replicated by another researcher essentially on the basis of the information presented.

Is the Method Appropriate? Some space must be devoted to presenting a logical and reasonable justification for the method used. Uppermost in the mind of the reader will be the question "Can the problem in fact be solved by this method?" If the conclusion of knowledgeable scholars is that it cannot be, then no amount of sophisticated data analysis can salvage the project.

Inappropriate methods abound. Journal editors make frequent reference to this unfortunate state of affairs.[7] A problem best solvable through application of the method of canonical correlation, for example, must utilize that statistical model. Inappropriate models will produce qualitatively different results.

Is the Method Adequately Described? A quick perusal of a journal article may leave the impression that the methods employed are quite clear. Scrutinizing the same article with a highly critical eye may—and sometimes does—lead to the opposite conclusion. Many studies leave readers wondering exactly what the sequence of steps was that constituted the overall design of the study. At a minimum these items must be included: what unit was being researched, that is, speeches, people, or historical documents; how many there were; how they were selected, and how they were analyzed.

Scientific research makes additional demands. Unless the following items are discussed, the research report will necessarily be labeled inadequate:[8]

1. The independent variables and the number of levels of each. Example: a 2 X 2 X 2 factorial design.
2. The nature of the dependent variable and a logical justification for its choice.
3. The total number of subjects in each group and how they were assigned. If not assigned through randomization procedures, the method used must be justified.
4. Source of subjects and their demographic characteristics.
5. Control measures. In addition to the use of appropriate control groups, researchers must communicate how they dealt with:
   (a) Experimenter bias. The differential effects on subjects arising from the influence of the experimenter(s).
   (b) Ecological bias. The effects of differences in environments (heat, light, humidity, and acoustics, for example) if more than one room was used for the research.
   (c) Cover-story incredulity. Today's sophisticated subjects are wary of most kinds of behavioral research. Unless the cover story (if any) is checked for credulity the entire research project may be rendered suspect.
   (d) Volunteer or nonvolunteer effects. Volunteers are thought to respond differently from nonvolunteers under a variety of research conditions.
   (e) Nonsimultaneity of study execution. Ideally, all aspects of a study are executed at the same time. This prevents a variety of uncontrolled and unwanted influences from contaminating the data. In practice it is admittedly difficult to accomplish, but if it is not accomplished a reasonable explanation must be offered.

A large percentage of studies could be rejected by master's and doctoral committees, and journal editors, on the grounds that the study was inadequately controlled. The more important problems of control cannot be ignored. They must be addressed in the manuscript if the reader is to have a reasonable basis for appraisal.

DATA COLLECTION AND ANALYSIS

The payoff in research is the acquiring of a data base. That data may be a content analysis of Hitler's early speeches, the number of times a group agreed with a proposition, or a set of experimental findings. Readers have a right to know the extent to which the data were collected and analyzed in an unbiased manner, according to acceptable principles of research.

What Are the Characteristics of the Dependent Variable? In historical or library research there may not be a dependent variable as such. Studies conducted on human beings almost always involve some kind of measuring instrument. It may be tailor-made[9] for the specific study or chosen among many available in the literature.[10] If the measuring instrument has not been published, these procedures should be followed:

Refer to @ Tøldhaber for a discussion of the ICA comm audit

1. Give the reader a few representative items so that its general flavor can be appreciated.
2. Describe the essential steps involved in constructing the test.[11]
3. Indicate the degree to which the test has been utilized in previous research, including any pilot studies that you may have run.
4. Provide all available indications that the test has acceptable psychometric properties: validity, reliability, construct validity.
5. Describe administration procedures: average time required for subjects to complete the test, problems that have arisen, reactions to the test.
6. If coders rather than subjects scored the test, provide intercoder reliability coefficients.

Are the Data Adequately Organized and Presented? Researchers find themselves immersed in large bodies of data. What should be reported and how it should be reported are two decisions that often lead to either a superior or to a mediocre course assignment, research article, thesis, or dissertation. The key is good organization and presentation. How is this accomplished?

First decide what is trivial, interesting, and of highest priority. Check current journals, theses, dissertations, term projects for insights into how contemporary researchers in your area handle their data. Space is always limited; sometimes a maximum number of pages is specified. The conclusion is inescapable: You must be selective about what to include.

Next, data must be organized so that the flow is natural, given the nature of the research. Historical-critical research offers a good case in point. To haphazardly present data from various time segments would be unthinkable. Good historical researchers always present information in time sequence unless there is good reason to utilize an alternative plan.

Behavioral scientists cannot follow a time sequence as such. Their decisions as to what to present and where and when to present it must be based on other criteria. We recommend that researchers consider several possible plans for organizing their data. After reflecting upon each, they should seek the opinion of knowledgeable colleagues, friends, and consultants.

When appropriate, include plots, diagrams, drawings, pictures, and other graphic aids. The expression "One picture is worth a thousand words" remains true.[12] This is aptly illustrated in the case of the multivariate statistical model known as multiple discriminant analysis (see Chapter 8). Researchers using this procedure often plot "centroids" on two geometric axes. Strictly speaking this visual display is not mandatory—the research could be reported without it. Its value lies in its high visual impact. Readers can make immediate visual checks to determine how the groups separated. They can also refer to the centroid values per se. But the visual display is always quickly decipherable.

In our opinion much research errs by including too little graphic matter. We urge you to reflect on which portions of your results might better be presented with something to supplement the words.

A note of caution: An amateurish appearance can ruin a visual presentation. These are some of the underlying reasons for a poor appearance:

1. *Haste.* Rushing through something that by its nature cannot be rushed. Artwork and visual aids cannot be thrown together hastily. Ask any artist what the probable results would be.
2. *Poor spacing.* The amount of data that will fit in a given space without overcrowding can be determined. Often, too much is crammed into too little space. Readers tend to skip over unattractive, hard-to-read visual presentations.
3. *Inaccuracies.* Many visual presentations involve plotting of lines that correspond to data points. A random check of published articles will reveal that the lines on a visual display may not precisely coincide with the data points. Such errors can be detected, before publication, by researchers who closely scrutinize the presentation—and ask other competent researchers to do likewise.
4. *Lack of artistic skill.* Most of us are not endowed with the ability to draw beautiful plots—or even straight lines. If you are among this majority we urge you to consider turning the job over to someone with greater skill. Art students are normally available for a modest fee.

    Never present amateurish appearing visual material to a professor, research committee, journal, or book editor.

DISCUSSION AND CONCLUSIONS

A study that is subjected to the best principles of data analysis should lead to theoretically relevant conclusions. This is true in all areas of communication research: historical, library, behavioral. Over the years certain principles for reporting conclusions have evolved. As a first step we once again suggest that researchers study publications in their area of interest. Note how scholars of proven reputation handle the presentation of conclusions, how they deal with the thorny problem of generalization and with the assessment of error.

Again, we suggest some guidelines, questions that should be reflected on before the final draft is submitted.

Is the Discussion Relevant to the Findings? Relevancy is fundamental. Digressions, guesses, and wild speculations, should be ruthlessly deleted. Nothing marks the researcher as unsophisticated and naive faster than engaging in displays of irrelevant exposition. Readers expect the researcher to stick to the data.

Relevant discussions follow one or more of these paths.

1. The findings are discussed. The researcher explains what they mean within the context of the study.
2. Findings are evaluated in terms of current theory. Is there a good fit between the two? If not, what are the plausible explanations?
3. Findings are evaluated in the light of previous research. In what ways do they corroborate or fail to corroborate previous research? How do you account for these differences?

4. Results that are at variance with well-established theory and/or the contemporary research classics present additional problems. Effort must be directed to the task of explaining this phenomenon.

In the end, your conclusions will be what is left after all plausible, rival explanations have been ruled out. This is the essence of scholarly research.[13]

Have Minor Findings Been Capitalized upon? The typical set of results is permeated with slight indications, trends, and tendencies. They are, in effect, weak indicators. They do not provide a basis for strong inference.[14] If the researchers are not careful they may find themselves elevating the status of these minor findings, especially if the main hypotheses or research questions were not corroborated. A slight difference in male-female responses, for example, may be mentioned briefly, but to capitalize on this slight difference is unacceptable. Whether these sex differences are important should be left to future research.

Behavioral researchers sometimes refer to a finding as "approaching significance" or as "just short of significance at the .05 level." Such statements are meaningless. They violate the principle of statistical probability usage, which is: Choose an appropriate level of significance, then report tests as either meeting that criterion or as not meeting it.[15]

GENERALIZATION

The goal of research is to provide sets of findings that can contribute to theories and that provide a basis for generalization beyond the confines of the study itself. A study whose findings relate only to the specific persons, entities, or elements contained in that study is of minimal value. Some degree of generalization is the goal. Unfortunately, the status of generalization theory is imprecise. We know what we would like. The problem is we do not know how far we can go in any specific instance. Readers are alert to unwarranted generalizations, so researchers are justifiably reluctant to go out on that shaky limb.

Our opinion, once again, is best stated in answer to a number of questions that should be considered by all researchers.

Are the Conditions of the Study Conducive to Generalization? Readers must first be assured that the study was conducted under conditions of relative precision and control. If all of the major principles of good research in the researcher's domain of interest are met, then the basis for some generalization is enhanced.

Next, the selection of subjects or entities figures heavily. A historical-critical researcher wishing to establish that public speeches followed certain themes during a particular period would have to assure the reader that the speeches chosen for study were representative of a larger body of speeches given during that time period. Behavioral researchers face the same problem. Subjects must be representative of some larger population of interest.

Is Generalization Reasonable? An adequate generalization might be to extend conclusions to include undergraduate students in midwestern universities. A reckless generalization would extend them to American college students generally. A few heavily financed studies—such as public opinion polls—are in a position to make broad, nationwide generalizations. The typical researcher cannot and should not attempt it.

Generalization should be reasonable. It should fit the scope of the study. Limited generalizations form the backbone of research. As they accumulate, theory evolves.

If Generalization Is not Possible, Can Publication of the Findings be Justified? Studies which offer little hope of generalization may sometimes provide information of theoretical interest. Showing the value of such information is difficult, but if the investigators can provide a suitable rationale, then some editors may be interested. The fact that something happened may be of dramatic interest in its own right. Future research can study the phenomenon further under more generalizable conditions.

YIELD

Yield is a fundamental criterion to be applied to all research. These items are relevant to the notion of yield.

Does the Research Survive the "So What" Question? In the critical age in which we live, *so what* appears to be on the tip of every reader's tongue! Unless the study has demonstrated significance and value, then critics are likely to refer to it as a useful research exercise only, implying that the researchers may have learned something from conducting the research—but the world profited little thereby. Theoretical and practical significance should both be made specific in the manuscript.

Is the Solution to the Problem Definite? The most valuable pieces of research result in visible, clear solutions to the problems that were put forth at the beginning of the study. Elegantly designed and executed studies are not a substitute for strong findings. In the end research is evaluated on *results*, not on the hopes and dreams of the researchers. A critical appraisal of a manuscript, therefore, will always include an evaluation of yield—how much did we learn and of what value is it?

TECHNICAL DETAILS

The research process is a demanding one. Design, execution, analysis, interpretation—these are but a few of the more fundamental demands made on the researcher. As if these were not enough, there is the final task of writing the drafts. In evaluating the technical details of manuscript presentation we offer these guidelines:

Do Tables Agree with Textual Explanations? Research reports must be models of exposition. There is literally no room for error. Manuscripts are looked upon with grave suspicion whenever there is an obvious discrepancy between what the running commentary indicates and what the figures or tables reveal. Readers, not knowing which is correct, tend to give up trying.

Are Words, Phrases, or Sentences Incomplete or Missing? Examples of missing information—sentences that have no ending, words that are not there—these and other sins of omission constitute additional grounds for considering a manuscript to be the product of haste.

Are Bibliographic Entries Accurate? Judging from published research, some authors do not spend enough of their allocated time checking sources and bibliographic entries. Potential error number one is failing to include in the bibliography a work that is cited in the text. The second potential downfall is failing to provide correct names of authors, article or book names, publishers, dates, and pages.

Is the Typing Perfect? A mark of scholarship is perfect typing of manuscripts, in the style of and according to the instructions set down by the professor, journal, or book publisher. Perfect typing produces a manuscript with heavy and clear type that is free of errors, mark-overs, or general shoddiness. Since few researchers have that level of typing skill, we suggest that professional typists be employed.

PRESENTATION AND EVALUATION OF RESEARCH: A CHECKLIST

The listing that follows is intended as a guide to the researcher and to the reader of research. Most of the items have been discussed throughout this chapter. Since the number of potential pitfalls is large we advocate checking each item for compliance before forwarding a manuscript to one's professor, editor or publisher.

A. Appropriateness[16]

_____ 1. Is the article appropriate to the target journal? Does it relate to the main stream of articles as evidenced by a perusal of back issues?

_____ 2. Is the level of sophistication of the article equal to the bulk of those previously published?

B. Sources

_____ 1. Are primary sources utilized to the fullest extent?

_____ 2. If secondary sources are used, is there a justification for using them rather than primary sources?

_____ 3. Is the genuineness or authenticity of texts, entities, and events reasonably established?

C. The Problem

_____ 1. Is the problem stated in a clear and unambiguous manner?
_____ 2. Is the problem significant?
_____ 3. Is the problem appropriately limited in scope?
_____ 4. Can the problem be solved by currently available research methods?

D. Related Research

_____ 1. Has the classic research been appropriately considered?
_____ 2. Is the latest research (within the last six months) included in the literature review?
_____ 3. Is the literature used to show the evolution of the research problem?
_____ 4. Are large bulks of research appropriately summarized?
_____ 5. Are the important studies evaluated against established principles of research?
_____ 6. Has at least one relevant methodological study been described and evaluated?
_____ 7. Is previous literature used to establish a theoretical base for the study?
_____ 8. Are studies contrary to the researcher's hypotheses described and evaluated?

E. The Hypotheses (or Research Questions)

_____ 1. Are the hypotheses (research questions) clearly stated?
_____ 2. Do the hypotheses (research questions) flow logically from the problem statement and literature review?
_____ 3. Is the source of the hypotheses (research questions) evident?
_____ 4. Are the hypotheses (research questions) reasonable in light of previous research?

F. The Dependent Variable[17]

_____ 1. Is the dependent variable logically related to the independent variable?
_____ 2. Is the choice of dependent variable reasonably justified?
_____ 3. Is the use of a single dependent variable (as opposed to multiple dependent variables) justified?
_____ 4. Was the dependent variable developed by the researcher? If so, is the evolution of the test construction described?
_____ 5. Are known psychometric properties of the dependent variable included? (Reliability, validity, factor structure).

G. Method

_____ 1. Is there sufficient information on method to permit another investigator to carry out a replication?

_____ 2. Was the method used appropriate to the problem to be solved?

_____ 3. Are demographic characteristics of the sample included?

_____ 4. Was the sample characterized by homogeneity?

_____ 5. Were subjects randomized? By what method?

_____ 6. Were subjects volunteers or nonvolunteers? Were they paid?

_____ 7. How was experimenter bias controlled?

_____ 8. What were the other sources of potential contamination? How were they controlled?

_____ 9. Was a cover story used? If so, did the evidence indicate subjects believed it?

_____ 10. Were control groups employed where needed?

_____ 11. Did control groups receive identical treatment with the exception of the experimental variable?

_____ 12. Was a power analysis computed in order to determine the optimum number of subjects needed?

_____ 13. Was there a description of the nature of the independent variable, the apparatus, and other pertinent factors?

_____ 14. Were the experimental conditions sufficiently natural as to be representative of conditions outside the confines of the study?

H. Data Analysis

_____ 1. Is there evidence that the results were comprehensively analyzed?

_____ 2. Did the analysis go beyond simple significance testing?

_____ 3. Were the statistical models appropriate choices for the data base?

_____ 4. Were there violations of assumptions in the use of the statistical models?

_____ 5. Was there an excessive number of statistical comparisons?

_____ 6. Was statistical significance measured against practical, or common-sense, significance?

I. Presentation of Results

_____ 1. Are results presented in a logical, orderly manner?

_____ 2. Are figures and tables instantly intelligible?

_____ 3. Is data presentation in its simplest, most parsimonious form?

_____ 4. Have charts, graphs, and other pictorial representations been used to maximum advantage?

_____ 5. Are graphs and figures accurate? Scaled properly?

_____ 6. Does textual explanation agree with tables and graphs?

J. Discussion-Interpretation

_____ 1. Are the findings interpreted against theory, the study's hypotheses, and previous research?[18]

_____ 2. Is the interpretation reasonable in light of the findings?

_____ 3. Are findings that are inconsistent with previous research adequately explained?

_____ 4. Are generalizations appropriately restrained?

_____ 5. Is the interpretation limited to the actual body of findings?

_____ 6. Is the interpretation comprehensive, yet parsimonious?

_____ 7. Have alternative explanations for the findings been ruled out?

_____ 8. Is there a capitalization on minor results?

K. Sources of Error

_____ 1. Have flaws that might have influenced the results been admitted?

_____ 2. Has the role of error in the study been taken into consideration?

L. Recommendations

_____ 1. Are recommendations made for future research in the area?

_____ 2. Do the recommendations result from reflection as opposed to superficial analysis?

_____ 3. Is there advice given to future researchers concerning potential pitfalls?

M. Technical Details

_____ 1. Is the manuscript typed perfectly?

_____ 2. Is the recommended style manual followed to the letter?[19]

_____ 3. Are special instructions of the individual professor or editor complied with?

_____ 4. Are drawings, graphs, and other visual aids of professional quality?

N. Miscellaneous

_____ 1. Have instructions concerning the number of copies, provision for returning the manuscript, identity of author(s), and other details been followed?

_____ 2. Are revisions made promptly and returned to the professor or editor?

NONBEHAVIORAL RESEARCH

The above checklist is relevant to the research process in general. All researchers are equally concerned with theory presentation, literature review, presentation of results, and interpretation. Still, historical-critical and documentary-type researchers, may find some of the above recommendations irrelevant to their purposes. We recognize this. We chose to present one comprehensive taxonomy rather than several since the factors common to all research far outnumber those that apply only to specific areas.

*A Final Note on the Presentation and Evaluation
of Research*

The most prevalent attitude toward a research report is often one of criticalness. This attitude is especially common to graduate students. Research is considered of no value in some cases unless it is flawless. We think this is an extreme attitude— extreme because the flawless study is an impossibility. First, researchers are limited by their content and methodological competence. Relatively few researchers are highly sophisticated methodologists. They work with the research tools they understand. Sometimes they make weak choices and perform inappropriate analyses. Second, everyone is limited by resources. Research is expensive. Time, energy, money—these are but a few of the costs. Researchers would often like to do a study of wider scope, with all of the steps executed properly. It is hard to accomplish this.

All research, then, is flawed in some way. Compromise with the ideal is the realistic position researchers are forced to accept.

How, then, should we evaluate our own research and that of our colleagues?

1. Read with an open mind. Study the report carefully before concluding that it is or is not acceptable.
2. Evaluate it against our suggested checklist. Use other criteria as well.
3. Avoid the tendency to halo the research as good simply because some particular aspect of it fascinates you.
4. Do not be easily impressed, either positively or negatively.
5. Recognize that something can be learned from the study. We know of no research that is completely without value.
6. Above all, do not expect perfection.

10

Writing and Publishing

When you think of a writer, or someone who has published, what is your first impression of the person? Do you think of an older person, fairly well-established in the field, who may have been teaching or researching for several years? Often, the writer is placed on a pedestal or viewed in awe—someone you hope to emulate. Writing and publishing is a goal, a hope, or a dream for the future. Nonsense. Most of you who are reading this book can be writers and can get published. That those who write are older, well-established teachers or researchers is a myth. Most who fit these descriptions have been writing for many years. They began early in their career—many while still in graduate school.

The purpose of this chapter is to make the process of writing and publishing clear—to wash away the myths and misperceptions. We will first explain some of the reasons why people write and publish. We will then focus on graduate research: seminar papers, prospectuses, theses, and dissertations. Next we will look at writing style, style manuals, and the need to be careful in the area of style, then provide hints for the writer. Once a manuscript is completed, we need to know where and how to disseminate it. We will not only examine how to prepare a manuscript for publication but provide several outlets for conveying ideas to others. We discuss the characteristics of a successful writer. In the final section we take a brief look at the copyright laws and how they affect the article writer.

WHY WRITE AND PUBLISH?

Perhaps the first question to consider is why write and publish? What difference does it make? Who cares? You may not be expected to write or publish; you may think you can get through a graduate program while avoiding this troublesome area. If so, this chapter may change your viewpoint.

It would be impossible to detail all the reasons why people write and publish, and many are private and personal reasons. We can, however, comment on some of the major ones.

First and most important is pleasure. Some writers enjoy writing and publishing. It provides self-satisfaction and an outlet for their creative talent. It is also a way to communicate ideas to a large population. It is a way to play with, manipulate, and mold ideas. For these reasons it can be fun and exciting.

Second, and also a strong motivating force for writing and publishing, is to help move the field forward. Many writers hope that an insight an idea, a theory, or an approach they have will help others to see things more clearly, in new ways or ways that have never been seen. To contribute to our field is to help our discipline and profession.

A third motivating force that we feel is natural and logical is to improve teaching effectiveness. Most, but certainly not all, writers in our field are also teachers. Often, there is a close connection between their writing and publishing interests and their teaching specialty. Writing and publishing causes us to seek out new information and materials, to question present methods and approaches. It keeps us alert to changes. We feel that effective teaching means active writing and publishing; they are not separate activities, but rather they support and reinforce each other.

Writing and publishing is likely to have the same effect on whatever profession one enters. The M.A. (or M.S.) and Ph.D. degrees are research degrees. To pursue advanced degrees not only says something about one's intent but also reveals to others something about one's interests. Every profession today has outlets for those who want to write and publish. To have published is likely to improve on-the-job effectiveness as well as visibility.

A fourth reason for writing and publishing, closely tied to the third reason, is simply to gain information—that is, to keep up with the field. Without question, personal pursuit of information has professional results. To push the frontiers of knowledge, one must know where the line of demarcation lies: Where is the frontier now?

These are not the only reasons people write, nor are they necessarily the most important. Other motives exist. Some writers simply enjoy the prestige. They like seeing their name in print and enjoy some of the fame and notoriety that accompanies success in writing and publishing. But this should be a byproduct, not a primary motive.

Some write and publish because they want to leave a record. To be published is to make a mark—as slight as it may be—in the records of history. This is their way of being remembered forever—their eternity.

Some writers write because they must. *Required* to write? Some colleges and universities make it clear that merit, tenure, and promotion depend upon evidence of success in writing and publishing. On a college and university level publication may mean more money, job security, or greater prestige or university visibility through higher rank. Few professional journals that cater to the academic community pay the author for articles they publish; thus, monitary reimbursement for time and effort spent on article writing comes through merit and promotion.

Writing also has inherent benefits: writing for writing's sake. How can writing help you?

1. Writing helps clarify ideas.
2. Writing makes ideas specific; it helps to narrow the focus.
3. Writing causes you to think in a more concentrated manner. It pushes you to think more deeply on an issue.
4. Writing may force you to think more formally, logically, or in a more organized fashion, it sometimes has the effect of structuring facts and ideas.
5. Writing demands that you find support for ideas. Through writing you broaden your base of expertise and credibility.
6. Causes you to think of ideas that may not have been present previously. It creates alternatives and contingencies; thus, it may help to eliminate some initial bias.
7. Writing may cause you to see outcomes or applications of theory that were not previously present. Most writing and publishing is stimulated by a problem. But having completed the investigation, one often sees other applications for one's results—applications beyond the problem area that evoked the original concern or thought.

In writing and publishing, this is often the *heuristic* part of the manuscript: that part when the writer or investigator suggests to the reader other lines of research that would further the investigation.

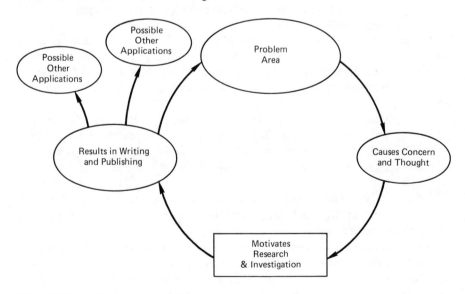

Figure 10-1 Motivation for Writing

One final point: Writing helps make you a better writer. The more writing experience you get, the more your writing will improve. More writing is also likely to bring success, and that first success serves as part of the driving force toward the next success. Just as failure often dampens the spirit, success lifts up and bolsters the spirit. The sooner this strengthening of the spirit is allowed to begin, the sooner the success cycle illustrated in Figure 10-2 can begin.

GRADUATE RESEARCH

Too often graduate students overlook opportunities to write and publish because of attitude, point of view, or oversight. They might feel that the seminar papers and class projects required in graduate school are simply class projects, exercises, or busy work. Their attitude must be changed. Each paper, project, or exercise, as noted in Chapter 3, can and should be viewed as an opportunity to publish.

Graduate students should assume that they have something worthwhile to say. They need not wait until they are older and more experienced or until they write their thesis or dissertation to say it. Most graduate students bring to the field fresh new insights. Creativity is not necessarily coming up with brand new ideas; it is rearranging and recombining ideas already known. As one is exposed to new information in massive doses—as occurs in graduate school—one should not only allow the creative juices to flow but also capture the results of that creative energy in some more formal manner.

In addition to problems in attitude and point of view, graduate students sometimes forget to utilize all their experience. They just do not think to write their papers, or even their theses and dissertations, with the goal of publication. You might wonder how to turn writing done as a class project into writing suitable for a particular journal. Below are suggestions to bring class writing closer to that appropriate for professional journals.

1. Examine particular journals for style and approach before writing the paper; the style and approach of the class paper can be as close as possible to the one appropriate for the journal.
2. Think and converse about the topic more broadly—with a wider range of people. Much classwork is performed independently of others. We are not suggesting group projects; we are recommending wide consultation.
3. Investigate the problem more intensively; do a more complete review of the literature. This should result in a paper that reveals greater depth and thoroughness.
4. Pay strict attention to style, grammar, and form in the writing of the paper.
5. Gain feedback on the paper from as many people as possible—not just from the person who assigned the project.

Theses and dissertations, for the most part, do not achieve publication beyond microfilming and the reproduction of a summary in *Dissertation Abstracts.* It is not

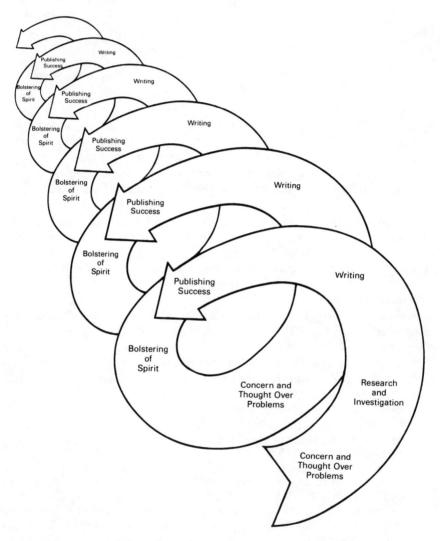

Figure 10-2   The Success Spiral

because the findings do not merit publication; it is because the author does not take the time to incorporate the findings in the professional literature. Two major reasons seem to account for this: The first is lack of motivation. The personal goal of completing the dissertation has been achieved; publication has little more to offer. The second reason is that revision for publication is a distasteful task. After revising the manuscript so many times to get the dissertation approved, the writer often gets tired of the material.

The graduate student should consider the faculty-professional time he or she has taken in preparing the thesis or dissertation. This debt to society can be partially repaid by making the findings part of the body of professional knowledge. Otherwise time is lost; later students may unknowingly repeat the work—a major waste of time to the discipline as well as to those involved in the work.

Graduate students should begin to guide their early professional careers with direction and foresight. Pursue each writing project as if it were an integral and essential component of professional life. Consider graduate school as a part of rather than a step toward your career. The kinds of activities and the type of discipline required vary little. The additional work is compensated for by the early professional gains that are possible.

WRITING THE PROSPECTUS

An essential step in thesis and dissertation writing is the preparation of a prospectus. A well-planned and prepared prospectus provides a thorough outline or guide for *any* research project. Prospectuses also have value elsewhere in our work. A prospectus sets forth the exact nature of what we are investigating and provides a detailed account of the methods we plan to employ. It usually contains material that supports the significance of the topic we have selected and the appropriateness of the methods we will employ.

A prospectus serves three important functions:

1. *As a means of communication,* it conveys a clear picture of our research plans to others—teachers, consultants, or advisors. In work on a thesis or dissertation, the prospectus is the primary resource used by the student's committee to judge the value and contribution of the planned research. The quality and economy of the advice will often hinge on the clarity and thoroughness of the prospectus.

2. *As a plan of action,* it serves as a step-by-step guide for the planned research. It gives the student an opportunity to thoroughly and carefully anticipate problems. It sets contingent courses of action to help insure against oversight and ill-considered choices that might occur when executing the investigation. It provides teachers, consultants, and advisors with evidence that the researcher has engaged in careful and systematic preplanning. To those who will use the research, it offers the qualitative basis on which the research can be judged. That is, the acceptability of results is judged on the basis of the methods employed in making, recording, and interpreting the observations. The prospectus must include a clear and thorough plan for observations and the accompanying supporting arguments and expectations.

3. *As a contract,* once approved, it provides a formalized agreement between student and advisors. Implicit in the approved prospectus is the statement that if this research is conducted carefully and competently, it should provide the basis for a report that meets the agreed-upon standards of acceptability. Changes in the prospectus should be made only with the full knowledge and agreement of all involved parties, and major changes should be accompanied by supporting evidence or arguments. Seldom if ever should a prospectus be revised after the collection of data has begun.[1]

Now that we know why we write a prospectus, the next obvious question is, how do we do it? Unfortunately, there are no universal rules or guidelines. There are, however, regulations that govern the form and content of the *final* report. Since the prospectus should set forth a plan that will result in a report that conforms to specific regulations, it is important to know their nature before writing the prospectus. Sometimes these regulations are specified by the department, sometimes by the university or college; sometimes they are determined informally by the advisor or committee; sometimes all or some of the above influence the final report. As we mentioned in Chapter 3, the student should discover the various governing policies before planning and pursuing any research activity.

We will suggest some essential areas that should be covered in a prospectus, but you should remember some important overall standards of writing that should be employed. Every prospectus—every manuscript for that matter—should reflect simplicity, clarity, and parsimony. The document must be easily and correctly understood; thus, the student should make certain that it is presented in terse, well-edited prose. The final goal of the prospectus should be kept in mind at all times: to inform readers quickly and accurately.[2]

A strong and effective prospectus can with some adaptation become part of the final report; a thorough job here can save time later. It can assume as much as half of the final report—under ideal conditions. With changes in verbs and connectives between major headings, the prospectus can convert into the opening chapters of the final product. This simply reinforces the need for quality and precision in the early stages of work.

One final note: An effective, high-quality prospectus adds to your own credibility. Since you are judged by the work you can do, sloppiness here may cause concern and delay. Those reading your work may ask for further proof, more research, or clearer methodology. This may cause you to delay the actual investigation and may cause those judging your work to look at it more critically.

Format of the Prospectus

The following outline is suggested as a possible format for the prospectus. Remember, again, there are *no* universal guidelines. Your prospectus must be adapted to your topic, as well as to university or college, department, or committee regulations. The guidelines should be known before the prospectus is prepared. Also, it is recommended that all steps be planned before the actual project is undertaken. Here, then, is a list of essential considerations to be used as a guide:

Guidelines for the Prospectus

  I. The Problem

    A. Offer a clear, brief statement of the problem, defining concepts where necessary.

    B. Show that the problem is limited enough to be treated or tested.

    C. Describe the significance of the problem with reference to one or more of the following criteria:

      1. Timeliness
      2. Relates to a practical problem
      3. Relates to a wide population
      4. Relates to an influential or critical population
      5. Fills a research gap
      6. Permits generalization to broader principles of social interaction or general theory
      7. Sharpens the definition of an important concept or relationship
      8. Has implications for a wide range of practical problems
      9. May create or improve an instrument for observing and analyzing data
      10. Provides possibility for a fruitful exploration

(The questions to answer are: What is the need for the study? or What is its potential contribution?)

  II. The Theoretical Framework

    A. Describe the relationship of the problem to a theoretical framework.

    B. Demonstrate the relationship of the problem to previous research. (This includes the brief review of the literature.)

    C. Present alternate hypotheses considered feasible within the framework of the theory.

  III. The Hypotheses

    A. Clearly state the hypotheses selected. (Null and alternate hypotheses should be stated.)

    B. Indicate the significance of the hypotheses to the advancement of research and theory.

    C. Define concepts of variables.

(In an experimental study, independent and dependent variables should be distinguished, and the scale upon which variables are to be measured should be specified: quantitative, semiquantitative, or qualitative.)

    D. Describe possible mistakes and their consequences.

    E. Note seriousness of possible mistakes.

  IV. The Design

    A. Describe the design of the study with special attention to potential interfering variables.

    B. Describe the stimuli, subjects, environment, or properties necessary for specification. Also, describe how interfering variables will be controlled.

(In an experimental study, specify statistical tests to be used, including dummy tables for each test and levels of confidence desired.)

V. Sampling Procedures

A. Describe the population to which the hypotheses are relevant.

B. Explain the determination of size and type of sample.

C. Specify the method used for drawing or selecting the sample.

(In an experimental study, describe the experimental and control samples under A; describe the importance of Type I and Type II Error and estimate the relative costs of the various sizes and types of samples allowed by the theory under C.)

VI. The Methods of Gathering Data

A. Describe measures of quantitative variables, showing reliability and validity when these are known. Describe means of identifying qualitative variables. How will bias be avoided?

B. Include the following in the description of questionnaires or schedules, if they are used:

1. Approximate number of questions to be asked of each respondent.

2. Approximate time needed for the interview.

3. The schedule as it has been constructed to this time.

4. Preliminary testing of interview and results.

C. Include the following in the description of interview procedure, if this is used:

1. Means of obtaining information, for example, by direct interview, completely or partly by mail, telephone, or other means.

2. Particular characteristics interviewers must have or special training they must be given.

D. Describe the use to be made of pilot studies, pretests, or trial runs. What is the importance of, and means for, coping with unavailables, refusals, and response error?

VII. The Working Guide

Prepare a working guide with the time and budget estimates, including all or some of the following:

A. Planning

B. Pilot study and pretests

C. Drawing sample

D. Preparing observational materials

E. Selection and training

F. Trial plan

G. Revising plans

H. Collecting data

I. Processing data

J. Preparing final report

VIII. Analysis of Results

In specifying the method of analysis, the use that will be made of tables, calculator, sorter, computer, graphic techniques, and such should be clarified.

IX. Interpretation of Results

Discuss how conclusions will be fed back into theory.

X. Bibliography

It should cover the essential points of the proposed study. It need not be exhaustive at this point.[3]

Sometimes the categories for a prospectus fall into such traditional headings as background, importance, review of literature, methodology, definitions, and limitations. Certain prospectuses will demand changes in the order of presentation, emphasis on particular aspects or categories, or inclusion of tasks not covered in the material outlined above. The investigator must be sensitive, alert, and flexible. To adhere to rigid, personal predispositions will inhibit the process and may create unnecessary hurdles. It is, however, better to err on the side of too much information than not enough. Seldom are complaints made because a student did more work than what was expected!

PREPARING COPY FOR PUBLICATION

As William Strunk, Jr., and E. B. White state in *The Elements of Style,* "Who can confidently say what ignites a certain combination of words, causing them to explode in the mind?"[4] We know, however, that we want our words to have that effect: impact. And we should write with that thought in mind.

If what we have said thus far in this chapter has had an impact, then you should realize that preparation of the final copy should not be left to the last minute. Keeping the ultimate goal of publication in your mind, you will want to prepare final copy that will require little revising and polishing. Your words cannot be left to chance; your style and form should be correct. You should take care of all details.

It is important at this juncture to understand the theory of the weakest link. That is, a piece of writing or research is likely to be judged on the basis of its weakest link. Visualize a chain—a chain that is as strong as its weakest part, and you get the idea. You want all the links to be strong: no weaknesses. What are the links in the final copy? It is impossible to list them all, but the most obvious include:

1. Strong content
2. Impressive style
3. Correct grammar and punctuation
4. Accurate documentation
5. Proper form in footnotes and bibliography
6. Suitable physical appearance (a well-prepared manuscript)

A submitted manuscript should look professional. Anything that is distracting—or weak—will call attention to itself. It may also lead the evaluator to look more closely at all other elements. It is unfortunate that poor grammar or incorrect punctuation affects content, but it does. Graduate students who ask upon the

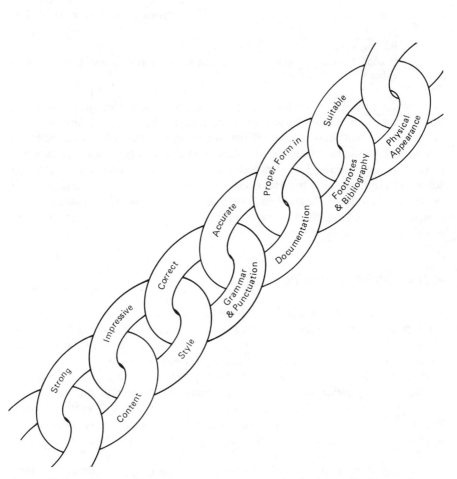

Figure 10-3   The strength of a manuscript may lie in the strength of its weakest link.

submission of a paper, "Are you going to look at the grammar and spelling?" are naive. Manuscripts are evaluated as a gestalt—based on the impression of all factors as they make up the whole. The weakest link calls attention to itself—distracts from the whole—and may become the focus of the evaluator's or reviewer's attention. If one link is weak, the others are also suspect.

Many manuals and handbooks are available to assist you with the mechanics of writing and the form of the manuscript. It would be a waste of space for us to repeat the suggestions they make here. However, we would make two important recommendations:

1. Purchase one of the manuals or handbooks.
2. Follow it religiously. Do not use a variety of styles, and do not follow the

manual only when the mood inspires you. A seat-of-the pants style will call attention to itself as a weak link because of glaring errors and, most importantly, inconsistencies.

The three manuals or handbooks we would recommend are: The most recent edition of *Publication Manual of the American Psychological Association*,[5] the most recent edition of *MLA Handbook For Writers of Research Papers, Theses, and Dissertations*,[6] and the most recent edition of Kate L. Turabian, *A Manual for Writers of Term Papers, Theses, and Dissertations.*[7] An excellent source for information on the fundamentals of writing style is a brief book referred to earlier: Strunk and White's *The Elements of Style.*[8] It is, in our mind, a book to buy, study, and enjoy.

DISSEMINATING AND PUBLISHING THE MANUSCRIPT

Always write with a specific audience, or editor, in mind. In that way, throughout manuscript production you will have followed all the basic requisites of a specific journal so that your form and style are correct. As we move through the steps of submitting copy for publication, remember two things: Think big, and think positive.

Make a habit of submitting articles to the best journals first. Although this approach may increase the chance of a rejection, you will never know if what you wrote was good enough for the best unless you try them. If they reject your article, simply aim at the next journal in line. Set up your own hierarchy, but always aim for the top first.

Think positive. Assume that your article will be accepted. Sometimes articles are returned with suggestions for rewriting. Accept the comments, do the revision, and resubmit the manuscript. Do not view your words and ideas as sacred—unalterable—*if* you want to be published. One fellow refused to rewrite, convinced the editor did not know what he was talking about. To this date the fellow has not been published. Positive thinking is best accomplished if you view the whole process of writing and publishing as a learning experience. We can all improve.

You must also be realistic. At times you will feel like the person looking for that first job: All employers want a person with experience, but this person must first get a job before an experience base can be established. It seems to be a vicious cycle. Publishing is easier once you acquire some experience. The overall, guiding principle is perserverance—stick-to-it-tiveness!

Understanding a couple of things about publishing may help you maintain a realistic perspective. First, it is a competitive business. Less than ten per cent—usually far, far less—of the manuscripts submitted get published. Thus, the likelihood of getting published on a first effort is very small. Not nil—just small.

Second, toughen your hide. Nobody likes to be rejected, but the competitive nature of publishing almost assures you of a rejection. If you are active, you can expect a fair number of rejections. This is not a rejection of you as a person; do not let editors destroy your will to continue. Rejections are a fact of life in publishing. Chin up—move on.

One way to brace yourself against rejections is to keep several manuscripts in circulation. Diversify. The best advice we ever received was to always be working on something. At times, three or four manuscripts might be under consideration by different journals. But notice we did not say the *same* manuscript would be sent simultaneously to several journals. This is unethical in article publishing. Even when several manuscripts were being considered we were still working and developing others. When several articles are being considered, it takes the weight off any one of them.

Another reason for not pinning your hopes on a single article—submitting one manuscript and doing nothing else until it sees publication—is that the process of publishing takes time. A wait of from one to two years is not uncommon. The normal length of time from submission to publication is between nine and twelve months, but the length of time varies dramatically, and there is no standard.

Submitting Manuscripts

You have prepared a clean, neat manuscript, followed closely the suggestions of the style manuals and handbooks, and now you want to submit it. Prepare a cover sheet for your manuscript that includes the title of your paper—centered and slightly above the center of the page. Place your name, centered, several spaces below the title. Some journals call for an abstract of the article. This can also be placed on the cover sheet if sufficient space exists. The date should be placed one inch above the bottom of the page again centered. Your name should appear on *no* other pages of the manuscript, either front or back. Most manuscripts are submitted blind (with no name) to associate editors for their response. Thus, no identifying marks or labels should appear in the manuscript.

Two other mechanical aspects of submitting papers: Number pages chronologically, beginning with the page where the content (actual writing) begins. Do not include the cover sheet in the numbering. Place numbers one inch from the top of the page, either centered or at the right margin. The first page should include the title—*especially* since the cover sheet will not be sent to readers or associate editors. Since this is the first page, it need *not* be numbered, and the title can be centered one inch down from the top. Then skip five lines to begin copy. This allows space for the insertion of the author's name *if* the manuscript is accepted for publication.

A cover letter should accompany the manuscript. Most cover letters are simple and to the point. They need to contain little more than: "Enclosed, please find a manuscript entitled, "(name of article)." Please consider this manuscript for publication in (name of journal). Thank you for your consideration." If you are submitting copies as well as the original, note that in the opening sentence. A return, self-addressed, stamped mailing envelope is appreciated by all editors. It is not the sign of an expected return; it is a courtesy. Also, if you want the editor to contact you at an address other than the one on your letterhead stationary, be certain to call attention to it. You might, for example, place your home address below your name in the signature of the letter, and add a postscript instructing the editor to please forward all future correspondence to your home address.

The editor of the journal will often acknowledge the receipt of your manuscript, usually stating how long the editorial review of your manuscript is likely to take. This may range from several weeks to several months. Editors would like to inform authors about the disposition of their manuscript within sixty days. Do not get impatient; editors are as anxious to let you know the situation as you are to find out. Wait for their response—unless, of course, the time becomes excessive. What is an excessive amount of time is hard to determine, but if six months goes by and you have heard nothing, a follow-up letter would be appropriate. In this letter, the writer should simply request information concerning the status of the manuscript. Make sure you mention the title of the work and its number, if it was assigned a number by the editor of the journal upon its initial receipt.

The editor of the journal may read all the material submitted, but he or she seldom makes any unilateral editorial judgment about its publishability. He or she will number or code the manuscript, remove all traces of author identification, retain one copy, and send it out to readers—usually two associate editors. These editors will try to read the manuscript within the prescribed time (two to three weeks) or, if for any reason are unable to do so, will suggest an alternative reviewer. The editor is somewhat at the mercy of his or her editorial board. A competent board makes the editor's job easier and more efficient. The author must remember that the editor is, in one sense, a mediator between author and reviewer. In the end, however, the editor is the final arbiter.

The associate editor's job is to evaluate the manuscript with respect to the quality of the essential idea and the materials used to develop it. If these are worthwhile, he or she can suggest improvement in the organization, the style, or any other aspect of manuscript development or presentation. He or she then makes a recommendation for each manuscript. The author may or may not see these, depending on the discretion of the editor. The overall recommendation will usually fall into one of the following categories: (a) publish, (b) publish if space is plentiful, (c) publish with minor revisions, (d) publish with major revisions, (e) revise and resubmit, and (f) reject.

The editor of the journal receives the manuscript with comments and recommendation from the associate editor, makes a decision, and informs the author. The author seldom, if ever, knows the name of the associate editors who have evaluated his or her manuscript. In some cases the author receives the associate editor's comments and recommendation; in other cases, the editor synthesizes comments from associate editors and passes them on as a total recommendation from the editorial board.[9]

Where to Submit Manuscripts. The field of speech communication has a number of journals that regularly publish submitted manuscripts. Our suggestion, once again, is to examine the journal to which you wish to submit your manuscript.

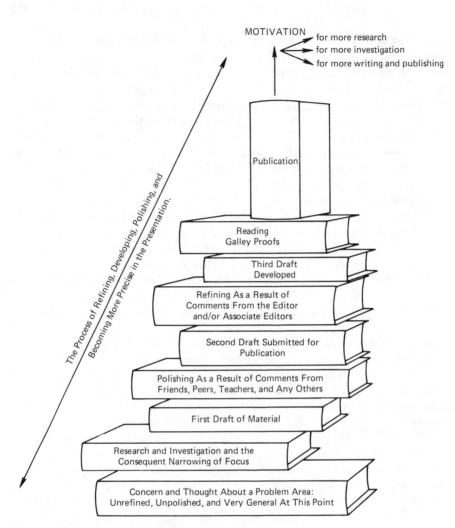

MOTIVATION
- for more research
- for more investigation
- for more writing and publishing

Publication

Reading
Galley Proofs

Third Draft
Developed

Refining As a Result of
Comments From the Editor
and/or Associate Editors

Second Draft Submitted for
Publication

Polishing As a Result of Comments From
Friends, Peers, Teachers, and Any Others

First Draft of Material

Research and Investigation and the
Consequent Narrowing of Focus

Concern and Thought About a Problem Area:
Unrefined, Unpolished, and Very General At This Point

The Process of Refining, Developing, Polishing, and
Becoming More Precise in the Presentation.

Figure 10-4   Typical Building Blocks To Publication

Do not assume you know editorial policy, types of content, or recommended style and form. Do not even assume that because you know one, you know the others. Examine a copy—or several copies. Avoid submitting copy openly to "Dear Editor." Current copies contain the name of the editor. Use that name. If editors are being changed, the former editor will forward your manuscript to the new editor and will notify you of this action. A change of editors is usually noted in one or several preceding issues.

Editors of certain journals are predisposed to specific kinds of material. For example, *The Quarterly Journal of Speech* (often referred to as *QJS*) is rhetorically oriented; *Communication Monographs (CM)* is behaviorally oriented; *Communica-*

tion Education (CE) is pedagogically oriented. A pedagogically-oriented manuscript submitted to *QJS* will almost surely be rejected. Check each journal for the nature of the content, and compare it with what you want to submit. Some appropriate planning on your part will lessen the chance of a rejection notice.

The three journals mentioned above are publications of the Speech Communication Association and emanate from its national office.[10] There are in addition four regional journals sponsored by the four major regional speech associations. *The Western Journal of Speech Communication* is sponsored by the Western Speech Communication Association. The Southern Speech Communication Association publishes *The Southern Speech Communication Journal;* The Central States Speech Association publishes *Central States Speech Journal;* and the Eastern Communication Association publishes *Communication Quarterly.* The content of these journals varies widely, and a writer would profit from examining them closely before deciding to submit material.

The International Communication Association (ICA) publishes *Human Communication Research,* a behaviorally oriented journal. It also publishes the *Journal of Communication,* concerned with communication theory, practice, and policy. As stated on the title page of the journal, "It is addressed to those in every field who are interested in research and policy developments and in the public impact of communication studies." Numerous state associations also sponsor their own journals, and one should not overlook these outlets when submitting manuscripts.

Still another source for publication is the Educational Resources Information Center (ERIC) Clearinghouse on Reading and Communication Skills sponsored by the National Institute of Education. This was mentioned in Chapter 3. The ERIC Clearinghouse collects, analyzes, evaluates, and disseminates information relevant to reading, English, journalism, and speech sciences. Manuscripts should be submitted to ERIC, care of SCA, 5105 Backlick Rd., Annandale, Va. 22003, in the same form as for any other journal—typed on white paper or, carbon or xeroxed copies only (no dittos). Notification of manuscript receipt is sent, and if the manuscript is selected, a further notification of when it will appear in RIE *(Resources in Education)* and a microfiche copy of the article will be forwarded. RIE is simply a catalogue of titles in the ERIC data base along with an annotation of the article and an ED number. The ED number is necessary if someone wishes to order a copy of your paper. To get the ED number, you must check the RIE for the month you were informed your article would appear. Material is catalogued under both author and subject.

In 1977-1978, the Speech Communication Module of ERIC located and evaluated 764 documents, and selected and processed 377 of these documents for input into RIE.[11] That gives your article almost a 50 percent chance of acceptance. These articles are not copyrighted; when submitted to ERIC they can be submitted or published elsewhere at any time, and ideas lodged there can be borrowed for use by others.

We tend to be provincial when it comes to considering journals for possible future publication. We think only of those in our own field. Communication, by its very nature, is interdisciplinary. It touches all other disciplines: history, education, business, psychology, and sociology to name a few. Do not overlook these areas and their journals. Provincialism limits the markets for your productivity.

When deciding where to submit your manuscript, do not depend on your own judgment alone. Ask colleagues for their opinion. Check out the age of the journal; older ones are generally more stable and have had longer to establish a reputation. Determine the size of the journal's circulation; generally, the larger the readership, the higher the journal's quality. It may be useful, too, to determine ownership. Some journals are owned by nonprofit associations; some are published by organizations that want to earn a profit. Much of this information can be found at the end of the last issue in each volume. Our point is that it is wise to be informed.

Outlets other than journals, are also available for your writing efforts. Professional conventions, conferences, and honors seminars also offer a forum for your ideas. In general, as a member of one of the professional associations, you will receive announcements of these events through the mail. Convention presentations offer an opportunity to test ideas before professional colleagues before sending material out for publication.

One should not overlook the value of friends and teachers in the profession as resources and consultants. It is wise to allow as many people as possible to read your material before submitting it. They may be able to spot weak links that have gone unnoticed.

Why are writers unwilling to allow others to read their material? The answers are not surprising, and they reveal some very human worries:

1. They question the value, asking, "Could another person *really* help me?
2. They do not want to take the time. Perhaps they are too eager to enter "the big time." They may not realize that if they take a bit more time—slow down and be patient—they may improve their chances of an early acceptance.
3. They fear the possibility of criticism. They fear rejection—appearing unworthy, inadequate, or unqualified in the eyes of teachers and colleagues. It requires risk—the willingness to take a chance.
4. They are skeptical about the strength of their ideas and approach. Perhaps they suspect weaknesses and would prefer that friends or others not discover them. Few ideas are perfectly and fully developed and few ideas could not be approached or developed differently either by you at another time or by someone else.
5. They feel they do not have the knowledge or credibility to be engaging in such an enterprise. This is an unfortunate stereotype. Since manuscripts are read blind, if the ideas and content are strong, the manuscript has a chance. Friends, peers, and others can help catch oversights that might undermine the knowledge base or the credibility. Depend on them to help put your ideas and content in the best possible light.

Getting an article published can involve months and months of work, waiting, pressures, and deadlines. Patience is essential. A typical article may be accepted for publication with minor revisions, or it may have to be fully revised. Your seriousness as an author is quickly revealed. Do you *really* want your material published? Can you undertake most if not all of the changes requested? Are you willing to work on it *now?* Can you spare the time? If your answers are yes, you should begin work at once.

A second submission does not guarantee acceptance. A different associate editor is likely to read the manuscript and request further changes. More work and yet another submission—more waiting. You may be unable to fulfill all the requests for changes. Do the best you can; where you cannot fulfill a request, provide the editor with a justification. He or she *does* retain a copy of comments made, and your response to the requested changes is checked both by the editor and possibly by the associate editor who made them.

After the article is accepted, you may have yet another opportunity to see your material. Most editors will send you your copy of galley proofs—long sheets of type that have not yet been divided into journal-length pages. You are asked to correct typographical errors, transpositions, spelling errors, and other minor errors. No major changes in content or organization can be made at this point. This is your final look at the manuscript before it goes to press. Many breathe a sigh of relief because they have seen enough of it by this time.

When the article is published, the editor will send you six or more copies of the article. Prior to final publication, you will usually receive an order form and may request as many copies as you desire of the final, published article. For these, a set fee is charged.

CHARACTERISTICS OF THE SUCCESSFUL WRITER

Some characteristics typical of the successful writer are personal, character traits that we have little control over. But many are not. Many are flexible, variable, and changeable. If you were to list the traits most valuable to a successful writer, the following would probably be basic:

1. *Discipline.* Time management is crucial. To be a successful writer make and protect time for writing, refusing to be distracted by things going on around you. Make out a schedule; this will help insure your future time. You will suceed if you will only make time to work on your plan. Remind yourself that you will certainly fail if you do not block out the time and start working.

2. *Curiosity.* The successful writer raises questions, expresses doubts, and challenges vested authority. Unwilling to accept even the obvious, he or she is seldom if ever without something to write about. Rather, time cannot be found to write all that he or she wants.

3. *Enthusiasm.* Enthusiasm is an asset that cannot be underestimated. The will to continue, the drive to do well, and the stimulation to meet goals all relate to basic motivational level. Writing is often a personal, selfish process—one you must do by yourself. Seldom does the spark for continuing to write come from others; rather, others often prove to be distractions or annoyances. Enthusiasm that is

sufficient to overcome the obstacles—to lure you away from the bait of distractions—is what results in accomplishment.

4. *Intensity.* A deep commitment—a passionate concern—in one's effort, potential contribution, and method of working is important. Following a formal, systematic, and objective line of inquiry and analysis challenges some of the best researchers and writers. A deep concern for answers—wanting to answer a question or solve a problem—can be a driving force for the successful writer.

5. *Decisiveness.* When action is needed, the successful writer takes that action rather than procrastinating. He or she learns to use judgment but can find the middle ground between impulsive action and delaying a decision until he or she has passed the critical point.

6. *Precision.* The successful writer demands accuracy; it is an overriding goal. He or she wants accurate observation, verification, and description as well as accurate presentation. He or she is willing to persist in following through on even the smallest details in a careful and controlled quest for precision.

7. *A broad background.* Ideas come from all sources, whether they be history, business, philosophy, current events, or the classics. The more ideas the writer has, the more he or she has to draw upon and the more his or her creativity can be exercised. Being widely read is a trait of the successful writer.

8. *Patience.* Research and writing is rarely spectacular. The successful writer goes about the task steadily—prepared to accept disappointment and discouragement and realistic about both the chances of publication and the potential impact of the ideas.

9. *Courage.* Many important insights are made despite the opposition of others. The successful writer must be willing to undergo violent criticism at times from those whose personal convictions, experiences, or observations run counter to those of the writer.

10. *Organizational ability.* Presenting ideas clearly and succinctly requires organization, just as getting published follows an organized process. Those who are successful have a feeling for the logic inherent in it.

11. *Productivity.* The successful writer produces a great deal of material. How much he or she writes is hard to suggest, but most successful writers are involved in a number of projects—seldom just one. The more writing one does, the easier and more natural it becomes.

We have found that productivity breeds productivity. When we are writing, we not only feel like writing more, but do. Our productivity is not limited to our immediate concern; rather, the urge expands to many other ideas and projects. It becomes a positive reinforcing cycle.

12. *Imagination.* This characteristic is an obvious one. The successful writer uses his or her mind. Inspiration most often comes through perspiration. Do not sit back and wait for inspiration. Get involved, and the ideas will start to flow.

13. *Positive attitude.* Expect exciting things to happen. This bolsters self-confidence, productivity, and enthusiasm. Believe that you can go anywhere from where you are, and you begin to believe that you will succeed. Activate positive

ideas by writing them down and then doing something about them. Do not give up! You may have to adjust a time schedule, scale down the size of your plans, rearrange your resources, or trim your sails—but do not quit!

14. *Experience.* Talk to your colleagues, students, and teachers. Getting out among people helps get information. Experience widely. Do not become a recluse. People help keep your life balanced; they give you perspective. They are also a valuable resource and provide an opportunity for rebounding ideas. The successful writer also travels, explores, discovers nature, and reads widely. He or she is an adventurer in life and is willing to experience because of its value and rewards.

15. *Persistence.* Those who are successful are persevering, steadfast, and unfailing in their devotion to the overall goal. Rejection should be seen as part of the learning experience. It is simply one more step in the process of getting published or getting results.

These are ideal traits but, surprisingly, most successful writers exhibit all of them at one time or another. We lapse or falter—nobody's perfect—but we can all strive for these characteristics. They are not unrealistic and all can be met, at least to some degree. They are worth the effort.

THE COPYRIGHT LAWS

The copyright laws are guides imposed on us as writers and publishers in the form of laws handed down by the government. In this section, we will examine those copyright laws that most directly affect the writer and publisher.

A copyright is a form of legal protection given by the United States to the author of literary, dramatic, musical, artistic, or other intellectual works. When you own a copyright, you are granted by law the right to:

1. Print, reprint, or copy the work
2. Sell or distribute copies of the work
3. Transform or revise the work by means of dramatization, translation, musical arrangement, or the like
4. Record the work
5. Perform the work publicly, if it is a literary, dramatic, or musical work

Although copyright can be obtained on unpublished works, our concern is with those works that have been made available to the public in some way—usually by the sale or by public distribution of copies. The law covers the material from the earliest date when copies of the first authorized edition were placed on sale or publicly distributed. Most journal editors copyright the material published in their journals. When an article you write is published, it is covered by the copyright laws. From January 1978 forward, this copyright runs for the life of the author plus an additional fifty years after the author's death.[12]

Copyright laws protect the words in which ideas are expressed, not the ideas themselves. The author may borrow ideas from other authors, courteously acknowledging the source of course, but he or she may not legally quote passages without the permission of the copyright owner. Any thing published before 1906 is in the public domain and may be taken without permission. Brief quotations fall under the "fair use" interpretation of the law. There is, however, no definitive legal interpretation as to the exact number of lines or words that may be quoted from a source without penalty. In a court, the guiding principle appears to be whether the commercial sale of or demand for the original work has been reduced by the quotation of the material. When used for scholarly purposes, direct quotation of any passage of a reasonable length (one or two paragraphs) is generally regarded as acceptable. In some instances, paraphrases may constitute infringement.

Plagiarism is defined as passing off as one's own the words or ideas of another. It is blatantly dishonest. This is why scholars carefully acknowledge their debt to those who have supplied them with information and ideas. They expect their own contributions to the work of others to be rightfully acknowledged as well.[13]

The law covers material that you choose to use that is copyrighted in another author's name or by a journal. In most articles written for professional journals, which are generally not written for pay, use of others' material can be covered by proper footnoting. As the author of a scholarly study, you would seldom need permission to quote copyrighted materials. If, however, the completed study were published for profit, you might need permission to avoid being sued for encroaching on the property rights of another author. You should secure copyright permission from the owner before publication for profit occurs.

Because books are written for profit, permissions must be sought for extensive use of another's material when it will be used in a book. Often, a royalty (compensation) is paid for such use. Most book companies provide the author with detailed instructions on permission procedure.

It would be wise to investigate the copyright laws governing literary works if you intend to write for profit. When writing for professional journals such concerns are not as important. Copyright infringement generally becomes a factor only when profits are at stake. Information on how to secure a copyright, the fees, forms, and addresses, is readily available.[14]

SUMMARY

We have discussed writing and publishing from the point of view of the first-time writer. Why should you be concerned about it? Why should you begin at once? Many reasons were listed as possible motivations. One that was not mentioned and that is, nevertheless, important, is simply "that's what educated people with M.A.s and Ph.Ds do." You are entering a profession where publication is expected. A master's or doctor's degree tells others you are a writer and publisher. A graduate degree is a research degree.

Graduate school is a prime time for beginning your academic and scholarly pursuit just because it is a time when you are barraged with new and sometimes stimulating ideas. You are being asked to write by your teachers, and our point is simply for you to capitalize on what is already expected of you to make it pay off both personally and professionally.

The prospectus is one important step in the writing and publishing process. Theses and dissertations, to which prospectuses often lead, should be viewed as springboards for articles. No opportunity—whether it be a seminar paper or group project—should be overlooked as a potential, publishable work. If you have written something that you want to publish, we offer you ideas for disseminating and publishing the manuscript.

One underlying assumption in this chapter is that you have decided that you have something worthwhile to say. We have assumed that you have high-quality content. It is a waste of time—yours and those who must read your material—to submit content that fails to meet the highest standards of rigor and correctness. Rather than discouraging you, this should challenge you to find the very best ideas, then research and develop them to the best of your ability, and present them as effectively as you know how.

Writing and publishing can be an exciting, challenging, and rewarding enterprise. The specific rewards are implicit in the reasons why people publish—outlined toward the beginning of this chapter. Now, full of your beliefs, sustained and elevated by the power of purpose, armed with the mechanics of the process, you are ready for exposure.

General Suggestions
for the Researcher

Information is recorded on note cards, then assembled into some coherent whole; observations are written down, then generalizations are drawn from them; or data are punched into cards, coded, computerized, then processed by machines. All sound like research, but what is missing is the part the researcher plays in this process and the effect he or she can have on the results. No matter which methodology or combination of methodologies you choose to use, no matter how you transcribe or record the raw data, no matter how you interpret the material, and no matter what your research results are or how you apply them, there are fundamental and transcendent ideas that make the job of the researcher more efficient and thus more rewarding. These are ideas that have proved valuable and worthwhile because of excessive use. Most often, they result from experience, not from reading them or learning them beforehand. But familiarity with them *can* help you avoid some common researcher-oriented weaknesses. If understood early, they can become habitual practices that will yield positive benefits over and over again.

The purpose of this chapter is to outline and explain several transcendent ideas that will help the researcher, no matter what topic he or she investigates, what approach he or she chooses to attack the topic, or what area of specialty he or she identifies with. We will first discuss the value of immersing yourself in the field. We will then relate creativity and research and show what it means to engage in the creative process. To provide the reader with specific goals, we will develop several characteristics of a successful researcher. Finally, we will consider the ethics of research through an examination of both personal and professional ethical responsibilities.

Often, we feel that the researcher who discovers a new idea or a new combination of ideas is just lucky, at the right place at the right time, or patient enough to wait until it was bound to happen. Serendipity, making desirable but unsought discoveries by accident, does occur in research, and its benefits should not be underestimated. But serendipity and startling discoveries seldom occur outside a research-based context. You could just be sitting in church one Sunday and think of the answer to a problem about which you had little knowledge and for which you had done little investigation—but it is highly unlikely. The startling discovery, as well as the serendipitous finding, grows out of a knowledgeable base. To take this one step further, both are likely to be encouraged proportionally with the increase in the substantive base. The more research and knowledge, the better the chance for these occurrences.

But why, you might wonder, would we tend to believe that the answer to a research question or the solution to an investigative problem could occur out of thin air? Sometimes this belief is encouraged through popularized accounts of famous researchers. Spontaneous discoveries have been sensationalized. For example, it is said that Archimedes discovered the idea of specific gravity while taking a bath, that Descartes discovered his best ideas while in bed on cold mornings, that Newton discovered the law of gravity while resting under an apple tree, or that Edison would lie down for a nap and creative new ideas would begin to pop into his head. What we tend to forget is that all of these people were prepared; all had a foundation from which to draw their insight. There is no substitute for thorough preparation. We will discuss this again later in this chapter.

There are more advantages to becoming immersed in one's field than simply preparing the way for spontaneous insight or serendipity. Immersion in your subject means that you *know* what you are talking about. It gives you a base for asking intelligent questions. Immersion also opens a wider range of approaches. The biased person is often the person who has little knowledge; he or she wears blinders. The larger your base of information, the more likely you will discover alternative methods; you are not limited because of limited information.

Immersion channels your energies. Ernest Hemingway labeled this characteristic one of crap detecting.[1] Visualize hunting an animal with either a shotgun or a high-powered rifle. Although either approach may succeed in bringing in the game, imagine how much shot is wasted in the scattering of the shotgun blast. Notice the efficiency and streamlined nature of the rifle shot. Knowing your subject matter allows you to choose the weapon that will get to the heart of the matter in the most direct and efficient manner.

A thorough immersion in your field also compels you to think more deeply and comprehensively. Again, the better the base, the more essential ingredients you will have to draw upon. Not only can you spend more time amassing the specific details for in-depth investigation, but you can also draw from the more general perimeters that have been defined.

Still another important benefit can result from immersion in the subject matter. If, indeed, you have chosen a topic that is timely, relates to a practical problem, relates to a wide or critical population, fills a research gap, has many implications, and concerns you deeply, the result is likely to be passionate commitment to and engagement in your work. The benefit is that such commitment and engagement will enable you to summon the energy for intense and prolonged effort and concentration. Many enter the research arena without an understanding of the demands, both physical and mental. One can become sapped as easily from mental fatigue as from physical. We like easy answers, and society encourages short attention spans and a certain amount of restlessness; these characteristics often run counter to the demands made on the researcher. This is not an attempt to scare off the would-be researcher but to portray the realities of research. To be successful, you must not take your research lightly.

Becoming immersed in a field is like deliberately hunting for inspiration. You are going into a subject-matter area where you are most likely to find something to inspire you; you are constantly on the alert for it. What you are doing is enlarging the stock of ideas in your mind and multiplying your observations; thus, the chances that inspiration will come are increased. Also, the chances increase when you know what you want to find. George A. Miller, in an interview reported in *Psychology Today,* stated: "I truly believe that's the way the mind works. You have your conclusion to begin with, and you're very clever at searching for evidence that either directly—or indirectly, by arguments you cleverly invent—leads to your conclusion."[2]

Immersion could be synonymous with driving power. Here quantity often generates quality. The driving power is the effort necessary to pile up opportunities and helpful accidents—serendipity. If any luck is associated with the overall research effort, it is likely to be a by-product of the effort you exert. Inspiration is unlikely to come without perspiration: The perspiration is the immersion in the field. Immersion will help you overcome those times of frustration and depression when negative results, tiredness, or conflicting demands on your time wear heavily.

ENGAGE IN THE CREATIVE PROCESS

In a methodology book such as this, one can be lead to thinking that to do research means to follow a prescribed set of behaviors with little deviation—little flexibility. Some think of science and discovery as classified knowledge or classifying knowledge. Some think that research tends to put on the blinders; you must see things like *this,* rather than opening your eyes to new discoveries. Actually, there is a little of both in research. The blinders of research—harmful if carried to an extreme —keep our attention on the process used to get efficiently from a beginning point to an end point. Without them we might be inclined to use a shotgun rather than a rifle. But we cannot let these methodological blinders keep us from seeing the creative aspects of research and discovery. After all, where does knowledge—

classified or not—come from? Where else but from people's hunches, from their ability to conjure up alternatives, and from their dreaming of new ways and unique devices for testing ideas, guesses, and those hunches.

Creativity is, indeed, the process of doing or making something new or different. In this chapter we will think of it as the process of recombining elements to produce more valuable or satisfying ideas in the mind of the thinker.[3] Imagination is the means by which this more valuable or satisfying idea is created; that is, our

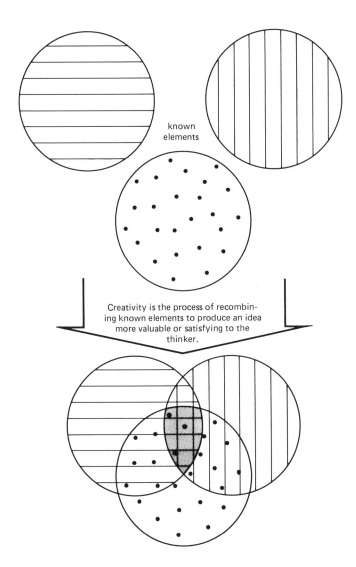

Figure 11-1

imagination helps us order, arrange, and synthesize the parts and put them together in some meaningful form. If it were not for creativity and imagination, research would be a dull, boring, lifeless task.

Before going further, we should warn against applying the metaphor of blinders too rigidly. One cannot really gain total control over one's imagination. Given a stimulus, our imagination is likely to act. It begins selecting and trying out alternatives and plans of action at the introduction of the stimulus. This is often how flaws, conflicts, undesirable effects, and dangers are avoided. Through this selecting, testing, and experimenting, intelligent choice and action is determined.[4] Despite following a rather specific and well-defined methodology, one's imagination is unlikely to be stifled and boxed in.

But, you might wonder, what about the other side of the coin? Why does a researcher even need a measure of creativity? At many points in the research process, researchers operate in hazy and confusing situations. From an atmosphere murky with misunderstanding, they are expected to emerge with some kind of order and logic. The human factor must be retained in any effective research effort. It is the researcher who must conceptualize, organize, and direct the research effort. It is also he or she who must determine how much and when to rely on strict methodology, how much and when to implement new procedures, how much and when to suggest new lines of investigation, how much and when to apply findings to practical situations, populations, and other hypotheses.

"How much and when" is dependent on how many bits and pieces are stored away in the researcher's mind. Bits and pieces of information are combined and recombined in endless combinations, but the number of combinations in any situation are, in part, dependent on mental capacity. The more experience the researcher has, the more ideas his or her imagination can generate by combining and recombining the bits and pieces to come up with both new and useful ideas. The bits and pieces are part of the material of creativity.

In this section on the creative process we will do three things. First, we will discuss the basics for creative behavior. Second, we will present some of the benefits of creative behavior. Finally, we will present the step-by-step process that represents most creative behavior.

The Basis for Creative Behavior

Creative behavior results first from activity and energy. The lazy, or inactive mind, is unlikely to reveal the creative spark. That is why this chapter opened with the challenge to get immersed in the field. Immersion will help provide the stimulus for effort, no matter what the subject. Idea people in all areas—whether industrial, economic, artistic, social, scientific, or educational—are people who think, invent, and create. They are the ones who get the rewards and recognition.

These people, too, are ones who can break out from inhibitions. Educational processes are often so rigid and inhibiting that normal behavior is repressed. Memorization and coercive control is substituted. Teachers may even punish a child for having different ideas or for experimenting with other ways of doing things. To exercise self-growth and to free oneself from the chains of the norm—encouraging one's talent and ability—requires effort. It is not likely to occur naturally because of years and years of contrary training.[5]

It should be clear that creative behavior represents many learned skills. Some limitations may be set on these skills by heredity and by the extensiveness of the contrary training, but through learning and experience, one can extend these creative skills. That is, creative talent *can be* deliberately nurtured. It requires practice.

Thus, activity, freedom, and practice are essential basics. Their opposites—laziness or indifference, tight structure or incompetence, and lack of opportunity to exercise one's abilities or mental inertia—can be stultifying. They can so restrict or impinge that one becomes imprisoned. Such imprisonment can cause the beginning of a negative self-fulfilling prophecy with the concomitant excuse, "I can't do it," the proof being failure in early efforts. Research has proven that one can learn to recognize and deliberately call on one's creative abilities.[6]

The point of the discussion thus far is that the practice of creativity—at the most basic level—must begin with yourself. It depends in large part on the time and thought you invest in making more and better use of the talent you now possess. You begin by becoming more sensitive to the problems around you. You start to use each problem as an opportunity to exercise, develop, and test your skill.

Problem areas are more available than you might imagine. Frustration, boredom, anxiety, anger, or helplessness are signals of problems. Look for the problem at the root of these responses and proceed to work on it. If you find the problem impossible to solve, begin with some smaller subproblem. The exercise of creativity and creative imagination need not be only an academic process; when you begin to expand your talents, you can directly affect the quality of your life.[7] Practicing creativity as an everyday activity is valuable because it allows you to rationalize, to accept, and over a period of time, to expect small miracles of yourself. It sets a pattern that can easily be transferred to all other aspects of your life.

The Benefits of Creative Behavior

Sometimes we need a challenge or stimulus to encourage us to engage in a new behavior. We often ask, "What's in it for me?" This could be as true in the area of creativity as in other areas. What are the benefits? Why should I be concerned about the creative process? The benefits are numerous.

1. It increases sensitivity to problems, needs, and opportunities. As you begin to exercise and extend your talents and abilities you will increase your power to observe and perceive. You will look at things from new and different angles, going beyond mere observation to deeper insight. As you see things from different points of view, you will break out of habitual behavior patterns. The creative process will help you escape from stereotypical thinking, rehashing old ideas, and operating in mundane, expected ways.

2. It helps you discard habitual ways of doing things. Because your mind is

pushed toward seeing new alternatives and contingencies, discarding old programs and attitudes is easier. When established habits are no longer appropriate, it is wise to drop them and move on toward thinking that is not as categorized and expected. By multiplying your alternatives you are able to make choices that enhance and nourish you, rather than deplete you. Thus, the scope of your life is broadened.

3. It releases you from rigidity and staleness in your routine and habit. It causes you to think beyond, to avoid the cut and dried, to shun the safe and sure, to refrain from the tried and tested. Using creative imagination will, likely, make you dissatisfied with conventional thinking.

4. It enlarges your capacity to look for new, different, and more effective ways to solve problems. Getting to the heart of problems becomes easier, and thinking up good ideas and solving them becomes less difficult or painful.

5. It helps you become more self-reliant and self-trusting. You have more ability to mobilize your own resources. In this way, then, you are more likely to extend, expand, develop, and express your true potential.

6. Creativity revitalizes you through the development of a new spirit of exploration and adventure. It encourages an awareness of the excitement and challenge in life. Because your curiosity is stimulated, you experience a renewed enthusiasm and appetite for rewarding new experiences.

7. It challenges you to think ahead, to project your thoughts into the future. It thrusts you boldly and directly forward.

8. It reawakens your spirit for play and experimentation. It helps you recapture and reexpress those childlike qualities of vitality, freshness, and a sense of wonder.

9. It gives you a sense of accomplishment, well-being, and purpose. It makes work easier, more interesting, and more successful.[8]

10. It assists you in fitting into the professional community. Those who are most active in the area of research and development, those whose ideas are most sought after, those who enjoy the rewards of merit, promotion, and tenure, are those who are able to utilize their capacities and express their true potential in a creative way.

11. Finally, creativity invigorates your psychological health. There is a relationship between your mental health and your creative expression. Whatever enhances and reinforces your creativity has a similar effect on your psychological health; when your psychological health is enhanced and reinforced, so is your creativity. One reason for this reciprocal and also cyclical relationship is the close association of both creativity *and* psychological health with such things as positive action, integration, self-knowledge, commitment, enthusiasm, self-fulfillment, goal direction, and personal involvement.[9]

One other benefit may be too far removed from your immediate situation to concern you now, but it can have vital and long-range implications: the value of creative behavior to your adjustment in old age. The experts agree, the surest predictor of a happy old age is a happy youth and middle age. The adventuresome spirit that is revealed in the eager pursuit of knowledge may have lasting benefits.[10]

The point of this discussion of the benefits of creative behavior is to provide a personal challenge. The benefits of creative endeavor are not simply manifest in the results, implications, or applications of research—even though they can be. The benefits touch the very roots of our personality. The philosopher William James, at the turn of the century, postulated that healthy, productive people function at 10 percent or less of their capacity. More recently, this figure has been revised downward. In 1966 the late Margaret Mead, the anthropologist, suggested it is more like 6 percent. Still more recently, Herbert Otto, the humanistic psychologist, placed it closer to 4 percent. The point is that we use only a fraction of our potential, and if we want to develop all of our capacity, we have a long way to go.[11] To make better use of our potential is a personal challenge.

The Process of Creative Behavior

In outlining the process of creative behavior, we are not suggesting that the steps are either universally recognized or accepted. We are not suggesting that they are followed by everyone—or even by creative people all the time. The point in presenting the process in a step-by-step manner is to increase our recognition and understanding of it, to help clarify it. At several points in the process we might be inclined to do something destructive or harmful to our product, ourselves, or the potential outcome if we did not understand that what was happening was normal and to be expected. Explaining the step-by-step process allows us to explain some "typical" behaviors—things to watch out for as the process unfolds. It also identifies some of the normal and expected occurrences, problems, or junctures in getting from a beginning point to an end point in creative thinking.

The impulse to create is the most fundamental step in the process. It precedes even immersion in the field, for how can one even get immersed if one does not *want* to? This is, perhaps, the grayest, least defined, most amorphous of the steps to be identified, simply because it is an internal process and varies from one person to the next. Ask yourself, what is the driving force that gets you involved? That results in your commitment to a project? That makes you give a damn?

We must be receptive to the continual wonder of life and to the joy of being alive. The creative person is immersed in life, tries to get everything out of it. This is an attack on laziness. There are so many distractions, so many pathways that lead to the vast wastelands of our minds. What is happening now is important: Tune in, do not put off experiencing. Life itself, so rich in resources, supplies much of the material of creativity.

Preparation is the second step in the creative process. There is, unfortunately, no escape from the need to gather material and investigate methods of handling it. All work and experience benefit if you are able to bring more to them; the better the preparation, the better the results are likely to be. The preparation phase is not a short, easy step. It can be better characterized as a conscious preparatory period of baffled struggle. It is not easy to capture in words the strain or labor involved because it varies dramatically from researcher to researcher and from problem to problem. It is not like trying to put round pegs in square holes; it is more like trying to put pegs of undefined sizes into holes of undefined shapes. The preparation process is so important to the whole creative process that if done inadequately or incompletely, the other steps of the creative process are unlikely to follow. If they do, they may be incorrect.

Incubation is the third phrase of the creative process. During this period the researcher seems to make no progress toward the goal. The impact of this phase can be so great that the researcher gives up the task, sets it aside, develops dislike or anger toward the task, or experiences feelings of defeat or worthlessness. The preparation stage is a conscious one; the incubation stage is not. We do not know why this period is necessary, but it is likely that the subconscious mind needs time to incubate the idea.

This step has some serious implications that should be considered by the conscientious researcher. For example, one reason some problems do not get solved may be that we do not allow enough time for the incubation of ideas or solutions. The researcher, if he or she is normal, is likely to come to an impasse—often just about halfway through the work. No amount of effort will solve the problem; no amount of thinking will get him or her unstuck. The incubation stage has been set in motion.

There is some sort of subconscious mental process that works in important and profound matters. Most answers to such concerns come not while grappling directly with the problem, but only after it has been allowed to drop into the pit of the unconscious and incubate until ready to pop out.

The implication here is that "sleeping" on a problem may be a more constructive and realistic approach than taking action. Our society, however, considers being busy and active "doing something" a high virtue. Unfortunately, much of this busyness and activity is merely sound and fury; it signifies nothing and may even be a substitute for thought. These flurries of motion stir up the air but fail to move the researcher nearer to the goal.

Learning to relax, to let go, to give a problem or concern a chance to incubate, is to give time its adequate role in problem solving. Too often, we force ourselves to make premature decisions because we succumb to the hectic, time-dominated social order. When we are ignorant or impatient of the incubation process, when we attack problems as they confront us, we often find that satisfactory solutions elude us—even after hours of grim, but wasted, concentration.[12] To recognize *and* utilize the incubation phase of creative behavior will increase our efficiency.

A *period of insight, or flash of insight,* follows or emerges from this reduced state of activity. The idea that creativity of a genius comes in a flash is popular partly because, as mentioned previously, insights frequently spring upon us suddenly and effortlessly.

One of the authors of this book experienced such an insight. Before going to bed, she placed paper and pen on the night stand. Suddenly and unexpectedly in the middle of the night, a topic for the dissertation came to her mind. Sitting up and turning on the light, she transcribed the topic on the sheet of paper, turned off the light, and returned to sleep. In the morning, as she dressed, writing on the paper caught her attention. What she read became her dissertation, yet to this day she does not remember waking up or writing down the topic. It had evolved from both her growing concern about the problem and the research she had done to support papers in several of her graduate classes.

Our coauthor is not alone in this occurrence. Part of the mythology of creativity has resulted from the publicity given to just such insights and that these flashes of brilliance have helped change the world. We mentioned some examples at the opening of this chapter. Another example is James Watt, inventor of the steam engine, who is said to have thought it up on a Sunday afternoon while taking a walk. Sir William Rowan Hamilton, in describing his discovery of quaternions (a linear algebra consisting of four-dimensional vectors whose coordinates are any real numbers), stated that his solution came to him as he approached the Brougham Bridge while walking with Lady Hamilton to Dublin.[13] Charles Darwin wrote in his autobiography, "I can remember the very spot in the road, whilst in my carriage, when to my joy the solution [to the evolution of species] occurred to me."

This flash of insight, often blinding and unexpected, will come with such certitude that a logical statement of it can be prepared. It requires, however, that the researcher be receptive to it. One must carry paper and pen to capture these insights. Receptivity is the key. How open are you to insight?

Revision is the final stage in this five-step creative process. This involves working to state an idea or ideas in the clearest and most attractive form. The problem with insights is that they occur spontaneously and often in a form that needs further work: They might need elaboration—further development and explication; they might need alteration—change or transformation to make them more intelligible or clear; or they might need correction—improvement in the accuracy or precision with which they are stated. Many insights are not perceived by others as such because they are poorly supported, badly stated, or slightly inaccurate.

Society forces us to move quickly. Because of time and deadline pressures, often we neglect this final phase. We omit the process of refining, unwilling to take the time to make our effort recognizable as a product of creativity.

One more item is important when speaking of creativity, an item that is lost when we suggest that creativity is a step-by-step process or when we treat those who exhibit creative behavior as a group of normal similar individuals. Just as it is often the defective oyster—the one that is irregular in shape or stunted in growth—that produces the pearl, it is sometimes those people who do not fit into well-defined pigeonholes who make most of the contributions.

In defining the regular contours of the creative individual and creative behavior in general, we make it look as if creative people behave more or less like everyone else. But it is likely that a kind of irritation within them causes them to be different from the rest of us. It may be that their type of irritation produces the pearl. It may also be that if the creators, innovators, and visionaries were more like the rest of us, there might have been no one to discover the first pearl.

It is worth being different; it is worth deviating from the norm. There are immediate outcomes that result from engaging in the creative process. Anyone who has experienced the satisfaction of creative endeavor usually discovers that the satisfaction alone motivates further creative efforts. Satisfaction, in this context, is almost synonymous with self-confidence. Pleasure and happiness do result from research efforts. It is not all grim concentration, painful strain, and gruesome struggle.

CHARACTERISTICS OF A CREATIVE RESEARCHER

Just as there is no rigid structure for the dynamic and on-going process of creative behavior, there is no rigid set of characteristics that defines all successful researchers in all situations. The characteristics are fluid and flexible. But just as there are ideal characteristics of the successful writer and publisher, there are ideal characteristics of the successful researcher—and certainly some of these overlap.

We have added another dimension to these characteristics that ties them more directly to creativity. Several sources list "attributes of creativity."[14] A number of sources, too suggest characteristics of researchers.[15] In the following list of items, we have combined these approaches. Our list, thus, is labeled "Characteristics of the Creative-Researcher" and it should provide guidelines for growth, development, and change.

1. *Sensitivity to problems.* Since research is directed toward the solution of problems, the researcher must have insight into problem situations and perceive possibilities of their solution. In attempting to answer questions, the researcher must also be sensitive to significant materials and elements in the situation that may lead to a solution.

2. *Ability to generate ideas.* The more creative a person is, the more alternatives he or she has. This includes ways to tackle problems and methods for responding to situations. Because research emphasizes the development of generalizations, principles, and theories, and because research usually goes beyond the specific objects, groups, or situations investigated, the more information the researcher has to draw on, the more fluid his or her ideas.

3. *Flexibility.* Although research demands accuracy, careful design, and rigorous analysis, the researcher must be able to adapt or change quickly in the formative stages of research and also as he or she examines the data. Shifting from one explanation or approach to another, and not being bound by a few stereotyped methods, is the key to surging forward.

In this regard too, and within the confines of objectivity and sound logic, the creative researcher is able to apply every possible test to validate the procedures employed, the data collected, and the conclusions reached. Also, he or she has the ability to see objects as potentially filling functions different from the usual. It is an ability to redefine and rearrange as well as to use things in new ways.

4. *Originality.* Although he or she knows what is already known about the problem, has searched the related literature carefully, is thoroughly grounded in the terminology, the concepts, and the technical skills necessary to understand and

analyze the data, he or she may still be prone to the uncommon response. The creative researcher can transcend the conventional or conforming response.

5. *Ability to analyze and abstract.* Although creativity and research may at times appear random and unsystematic, the creative researcher can differentiate among elements, discover details, and take situations apart to discover parts and meanings. He or she is capable of applying rigorous analysis.

6. *Ability to synthesize.* Research involves gathering information from primary or first-hand sources or using existing data for a new purpose. It is up to the researcher to put all of these parts, formerly unrelated, together into a new whole. Closure is the researcher's ability to visualize and speculate on how the elements will go together before the details have been worked out. This process is that of trying to see the whole picture.

7. *Organizational ability.* He or she can draw elements together harmoniously, so they fit together economically. As the research is recorded, terms are defined, limiting factors are recognized, procedures are described, references are documented, results are recorded, and conclusions are presented with scholarly caution and restraint, disparate elements are reshaped or eliminated. The result is an organized whole that is recognized as consistent and belonging together.

8. *Patience.* The care and organization required must be carried on in an unhurried manner. The opportunity for additional insights and for unexpected relationships must be allowed. Research is rarely spectacular. The creative researcher must expect disappointment and discouragement as he or she pursues answers to difficult questions.[16]

Having explained these attributes, you might wonder what conditions would most likely encourage their development. Two major conditions seem to be psychological safety and freedom. When individuals feel they are of worth, that others have faith in their efforts, they learn to be whatever they can be without sham or facade. With the security of these feelings, they have less need of rigidity, they can discover what it means to be themselves, and they can try to actualize themselves in new and spontaneous ways. They are moving toward creativity.

Another condition that fosters psychological safety, hence creativity, is the absence of evaluation. You may think that it is impossible to go through the research process without evaluation, that since evaluation is inherent in the process, our creativity must always suffer. Not true. We should make a clear distinction between evaluation and reaction. We are not suggesting that a researcher should, or needs to, receive less reaction. Rather, we are concerned with the *kind* of reaction received. The kind of evaluation that is threatening and that creates a need for defensiveness is that which measures the product against external (someone else's) standards of right and wrong or goodness and badness. When a person says, "I don't like your idea," this is a reaction—not an evaluation. This can be clearly differentiated from a comment such as, "What you are doing is bad." A reaction allows creative researchers psychological safety, for it is not condemnation from an outside source, and it still permits them to make their own evaluation. When an evaluator praises or condemns, it puts researchers at the mercy of outside forces.

It is more difficult—even impossible—under an evaluation response for the research-er to ask: Is this a valid expression of *me?*

Psychological safety, thus, results when external judgments are not made. Creative researchers can then be more open to their own experience. They can recognize their own likes and dislikes. They can respond more sharply and sensi-tively to the nature of their materials and even to their own reactions to them. When the locus of evaluation is within the creative researchers themselves, they are moving toward creativity.

Finally, psychological safety also results from empathic understanding. When we have shared our ideas with others, and when those others see us and what we are feeling and doing from *our* point of view, they enter our private world and see it as it appears to us—as far as that is possible. When they do this and still accept us, we have the ultimate in psychological safety. It is from this climate that our real self will emerge and we can begin to express ourselves in varied and novel ways.

In our experience there is also an element of freedom connected with fostering creative development. When we are permitted complete freedom of symbolic expression, creativity is likely to result. It is just such permissiveness that gives us complete freedom to think, to feel, and to be. It is this freedom of symbolic expression, too, that fosters openness, the playful and spontaneous juggling of perceptions, concepts, meanings, and ideas—all a part of the role of the creative researcher.

One note of caution: The freedom being advocated is neither softness nor in-dulgence. It is permission to be *free*—which also means that one is responsible. As one writer on creativity stated it:

> The individual is as free to be afraid of a new venture as to be eager for it; free to bear the consequences of his mistakes as well as of his achievements. It is this type of freedom responsibly to be onself which fosters the development of a secure locus of evaluation within oneself, and hence tends to bring about the inner conditions of constructive creativity.[17]

In the following section we will attempt to clarify some of those responsibilities. No matter how much freedom is exercised by the creative researcher, he or she must accept certain well-defined limits or restrictions that are commonly accepted as ethical behavior in the academic marketplace. These limits, as shall be made clear, tend to be wide, external perimeters that tend not to hinder creative productivity—when recognized. The arena they define is large enough to allow the freedom of movement and exploration that is an inner condition of creativity.

THE ETHICS OF RESEARCH

Two major areas of ethical responsiblity must concern the researcher. The first is a personal responsibility that operates as a direct link between the researcher and his or her information and findings. It begins as the researcher begins the

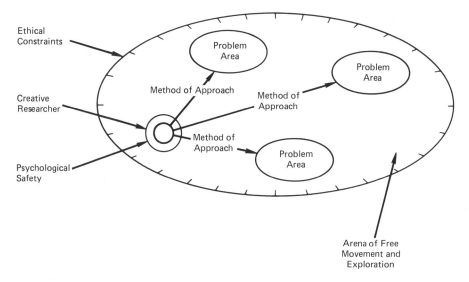

Figure 11-2 The relationship of ethics to freedom and psychological safety.

investigation by building up his or her own knowledge base and ends as the conclusions to the investigation are presented in proper perspective. We could add that this personal, ethical responsibility also extends to the manner in which the information is dispersed to the reading public. This step-by-step development and the underlying ethical concerns will be treated briefly.

The second ethical responsibility has emerged more recently (the former having existed since the beginning of research investigations). This one concerns the researcher's cognizance and protection of the rights and welfare of the subjects used in human experimentation. We will also discuss this important area of responsibility in some detail.

Personal Ethical Responsibility

There are ethical responsibilities that we fill, or attempt to fill, as we initiate *any* research investigation. To say this another way: Any information we plan to share with a wider audience must reflect certain properties. These are properties to which we, as responsible investigators, must give our attention. As our information becomes public, it must reflect a thorough knowledge of the subjects, a sensitivity to relevant issues and their implications, and an awareness of the essential and trustworthy opinions and facts. Our first personal responsibility, then, is to build competence through knowledge.

Closely aligned with competence and knowledge is the fair selection and presentation of the material we discover. Most of us do not intentionally distort or conceal data; at least, we would contend that we do not begin our research with such a motive. But as professionals in any field will attest, initial motives can be a faint shadow of what can result. What happens in the interim? What can cause researchers to intentionally distort or misrepresent information? We certainly do not have all the answers; however, some of them are obvious:

1. The pressures of time
2. The quest for prestige
3. The need for merit, tenure, or promotion
4. The desire for accomplishment—to show progress
5. The need to have a result (publication) for the time and the effort invested
6. The demand that we publish (the familiar "publish or perish" syndrome)

It is important for the researcher to follow all the rigors that fairness in selecting and presenting the data demands. There are *no* legitimate excuses or reasons for unfairness.

Another area that causes concern in our personal ethical responsibility is documentation. Two major problems occur in this area. The least important of the two is accuracy. Inaccuracy may reflect on your competence and thus on your credibility as a researcher. But inaccuracy also has other disadvantages: (1) it may lead other researchers astray; (2) it may waste valuable time; and (3) it may not give others their fair and just attribution or credit.

That last point is more important than a quick reading may indicate. If we are relying on the information and ideas of others, we should be willing not only to indicate our debt but to do it accurately and responsibly. This is both an ethical and an academic responsibility.

The second problem with respect to documentation is more important: It is unethical to use the words or ideas of another person without giving credit. We discussed this in Chapter 10 under the copyright laws. A neophyte researcher might ask, "Why do it? Why would you use the words or ideas of another person without giving credit?" Of course, it may not be intentional. Notes taken early in the course of research may not be documented. Notes may come from a class or from someone else. You may happen to find undocumented material in your files or in lecture material on a subject you have chosen to investigate. As responsible, ethical researchers we must take great care in the information we use. We must check it closely. If, indeed, it is undocumented and the source cannot be discovered through careful and tedious searching, then it is better *not* to use it, or to paraphrase it *very* loosely and to footnote the reference to the best of your ability.

We may also select a piece of information from another author whom we feel has said it better than we think we could or who has structured the information in a way that pleases or satisfies us. Hoping that the source is obscure, we choose to use it as our own to strengthen our case or to make us look better. Most people are familiar with this feeling. Again, whatever the motive, the result is unethical, and we must take great pains to avoid any such temptation.

Put yourself in the place of the other. Think first about creativity—how much challenging, probing, and questioning it sometimes requires to come up with a new idea or with a new recombination of ideas. Think, second, about the task of writing and publishing. It is an arduous, involved process that requires both perspiration and inspiration, and even with that, success may still elude the most persevering. When a researcher has made a contribution to the literature, he or she would appreciate receiving the just reward: the acknowledgement that his or her ideas have contributed to the expansion of the frontiers.

Another area that may cause concern is the issue of selective perception. We tend to undertake research with a bias. We often like to believe that we are not biased or take precautions to minimize the bias, but it exists nevertheless. The question becomes, to what extent can we allow and encourage the diversity of ideas and opinions despite our biases? To what extent, to phrase it somewhat differently, can we compromise and yield when we find material contrary to our biases? Certainly, we are not asking for sacrifice; a researcher should be able to face conflict without having to accept total appeasement. But a researcher's results suggest honesty, openness, and objectivity. They suggest that the researcher has not only reported contrary evidence but that he or she has respected and appreciated that evidence as well. The ethical point is simply, can researchers admit the force of opposing evidence and still legitimately advocate a position that represents their convictions?

There is another issue that we will label "scholarly restraint." Sometimes the enthusiasm for research, the impressiveness of results, or the joy of reporting so affects the researcher that he or she will overstate, exaggerate, or fail to limit the conclusions for a study. The researcher should have a sufficient understanding of the philosophical and social issues underlying the problem. He or she should have a grasp of both the problem and the limitations underlying the findings so that the conclusions can be seen in their proper perspective. In the presentation of findings, care must be taken against misrepresentation. For example, when we use university and college students as subjects, we do not have a cross section of all Americans. When we have bitten away part of the problem, it is unlikely that we have solved the whole problem. When we have surveyed administrators or analyzed university or college department chairpersons, we cannot act as though our evidence would apply to real-world business administrators or real-world business departments and offices. Scholarly restraint is reflected in deliberate cautiousness. We are not the keepers of the public conscience, however, and it is true that knowledge is preferred to ignorance. Balance and perspective must be maintained.

One final personal ethical responsibility that should be mentioned concerns making the results of research known through publication. It is customary in speech communication to send manuscripts to only one journal at a time. Unwritten ethical law prevents the researcher from sending a manuscript to several journals at the same time. He or she must wait for a rejection slip before sending it to another journal. In textbook writing, a prospectus for a book may be sent to any number of publishers at the same time; this is not true in article writing. Although the authors of this book disagree with this unwritten law governing manuscript submission, we not only follow it, but we strongly recommend that others do so. If it is determined that an author is sending a manuscript to several sources, there can be professional repercussions that may make the publication of the manuscript more difficult or may affect the reputation of the researcher.

Personal ethical responsibilities place many expectations on the shoulders of the researcher. Outside expectations regarding freedom from bias, objectivity, and honesty force the researcher to be concerned about ethics. Is the knowledge base sufficient? Is the selection and presentation of materials clear and fair? Are the sources used well documented and available? And finally, has the researcher adequately allowed for the diversity of ideas and opinions in the investigation? These are by no means the end of any ethical concern, but they do make up a good part of it.

Professional Ethical Responsibility

We could label this "public" ethical responsibility, as opposed to "personal" responsibility, because the concern here is for the rights and welfare of human subjects used in experimentation. "What is your responsibility, as researcher, for the human subjects you use in your research investigation?" As a researcher, you have definite responsibilities. These are clearly delineated, and any researcher who plans to use human subjects should investigate them. Some of the responsibilities have been enacted by legislatures, some by codes such as the American Psychological Association's guidelines,[18] and some remain unsolved issues. The APA's code of ethics defines the responsibility of the researcher to the profession, to the client, and to the sponsoring agency.

At this point you may wonder what the problem is. Why the fuss? Perhaps, *the* major concern in doing research with human beings is the subject's constitutional rights, particularly his or her right to privacy.[19] Thus, the conflict boils down to one between two sets of highly esteemed values: (1) the right of all to the dignity and freedom guaranteed in the Constitution, and (2) society's (or the individual's) right to discovery as the basis for social progress and advancement. The sacrifice of certain minor rights is generally thought of as acceptable if they are sacrificed on behalf of other human beings.

It may be difficult to understand the problem of professional ethical responsibility without having a research problem at hand. Consider, for example, the problem of doing research on the nonverbal indicators of cues involved in either lying or the perception of lying. To discover the cues, subjects must be deceived—lied to. Unethical? Certainly; lying is wrong. But to tell the subjects beforehand that the experiment involved deception would preclude getting results. Whose rights come first? The subject's right to know (*informed consent* is consent freely given, based on the subject's understanding of the purposes of the study, the nature of the commitment, including full freedom to withdraw at any time, the use to be made of the data, and an adequate degree of confidentiality) or the investigator's freedom to carry out his or her obligation to society? Studying the nonverbal indicators that reveal lying is an example of research where deception is unavoidable—and there are many similar examples. In this case the investigator must provide debriefing to counteract the negative effects of deception. Debriefing is not a universal remedy, however. There is no justification for engaging in the practices that reveal marginal ethical responsibility and relying on debriefing to automatically rectify the situation. One of the obligations of the researcher is to find meaningful ways to conduct research into significant problems without resorting to violations of subjects' integrity or unwarranted invasion of their privacy.

The following principles for protecting human subjects are intended to serve as a general guideline. The principles are the same for all types of research, but some are more generally recognized than others. Because of the variety of sources for such principles, we suggest that the researcher investigate those that most directly affect his or her study.[20]

1. *Value.* To what extent is the researcher contributing to the advancement of human knowledge? If the research has no value, it should not be done.

2. *Responsibility for subjects.* To what extent has the researcher made an effort to protect the subjects? If human subjects are involved, the researcher should seek the advice and consultation of peers, review committees, and supervisors. He or she should not depend on personal knowledge alone to determine ethical responsibility. If, for example, a researcher attempts to find out what kind of intrapersonal communication occurs when one makes brand decisions in a supermarket—a seemingly innocuous investigation—to what extent should he or she take precautions to make certain the subjects' rights are protected?

    a. What if the subject chooses not to participate?
    b. What if the subject does not want the brand decision made to be public knowledge?
    c. What if the subject considers your investigation of his or her intrapersonal communication to be an invasion of privacy?
    d. What if the subject does not want to reveal the way he or she makes such decisions?
    e. What if the subject chooses to back out, in the middle of the interview?

The researcher has a responsibility for each of these possibilities. Assuming such responsibility must involve elaborate preplanning and precautions. Such decisions cannot be left to a response such as, "We'll cross *that* bridge when we come to it," a response that reflects an escape from responsibility rather than a move toward it. The responsibility, however, does not end with preplanning. Ethical responsibility is an inherent part of every phase of the research investigation.

3. *Responsibility for self and aides.* To what extent has the researcher taken responsibility for his or her self and for his or her aides? Just because one uses other assistants—perhaps graduate-student colleagues—in his or her research, and just because they may be trained to perform in certain ways, does not free the

researcher from responsibility for the protection of the rights of subjects. The researcher is still in charge and is still responsible.

A researcher is responsible for an assistant who gives misinformation, who mistreats subjects, or who deceives them. Using assistants does not free us from responsibility; rather, it increases and compounds the responsibility we already have. The biggest added responsibility is to make certain that we have good aides.

Because of the responsibility the researcher assumes for the behavior of assistants within the experimental situation, the choice of assistants demands thought and consideration. For help with a research project, one should not randomly or thoughtlessly pull any passerby off the street, especially when one knows nothing about the person.

4. *Informed consent.* To what extent have subjects been given all the information they need about the study to make a decision about participating? Have subjects been misled? Of course, as mentioned previously, in certain cases full information cannot be provided because certain types of investigation would be impossible if subjects knew everything about the experiment beforehand. Another problem is subjects who decide to leave an experiment once they find out the purpose of the study. If enough were to leave, the remaining group might no longer be representative. Thus, there are reasons for not getting informed consent when certain types of meaningful research is the goal. In such cases, the guidelines would indicate providing as much information as can be given without ruining the experiment. However, when full disclosure has not been made, the weight of the researcher's responsibility to protect the subject's welfare and rights during the investigation and after is increased. Researchers should give subjects any information withheld at the earliest opportunity.

5. *Protection from danger.* To what extent has the researcher assumed responsibility for any harm or discomfort that might come to a subject? Despite getting informed consent, the researcher is still responsible for what may happen as a result of the experiment. For example, if a researcher is doing a study of the self-fulfilling prophecy and decides to feed subjects negative information—ideas that might have an adverse effect on the student's self-concept—the researcher has an ethical responsibility to remove the effects of this information after the study is completed.

6. *Confidentiality.* To what extent has the researcher protected the anonymity of the participants? They have a right to insist on anonymity, and they should be assured that they will not be identified by their performance or by the nature of their participation. The researcher can accomplish this by using numbers to identify subjects and by analyzing group rather than individual data.

7. *Freedom.* To what extent have the subjects been coerced to participate in the research? Subjects must be given freedom; the choice to participate or not to participate must be theirs.

8. *Final responsibility.* To what extent has the researcher assumed responsibility toward the subjects after the completion of the experimental procedures? What are these responsibilities? The researcher should correct misinformation; remove

any effects that may have changed the subjects' state of being; allay any anxiety that may have been created; and make certain the welfare of the subjects, their rights, health, *and* comfort was protected throughout.[21]

SUMMARY

To attempt to make research a realistic, practical, and attainable enterprise, we have tried to put it into its proper framework. Certainly, what we have said should help you to prepare yourself—to shore up the spirit and courage necessary—so that you can begin with intelligence and direction.

We explained at the outset of the chapter the need to become immersed in the subject field and listed some of the advantages of such immersion. Perhaps the most important one is inspiration and energy. Passionate involvement is necessary to gain the momentum for deep and concentrated work. Now that you have the chapter in perspective, you can see that it is from immersion that the creative spark is kindled.

We presented the process of creative behavior to clarify its workings. It is easy to become boxed-in by standardized, routine ways of doing things; our purpose was *not* to provide just one more set of pigeonholes. We outlined some of the recognized, typical behaviors, in an attempt to identify some of the normal and expected occurrences, problems, and junctures. This may help you to recognize when you are on a creative binge. To suggest that creative people follow a set of prescribed behaviors is to define creativity rigidly; it is contradictory to the very essence of the word itself. We tried to make it clear that not all research is grim concentration, painful strain, and gruesome struggle.

It is our hope that the researcher will understand his or her part in the research process. We often think of research as dry and boring—the process of classifying knowledge. We forget about the role the researcher can and does play in the whole process—the personalization of research. We have attempted to link research and creativity, to show that creative power is essential to research. More often than not, it is the creative, innovative, and imaginative researcher who rises above the others and distinguishes himself or herself in a field. From start to finish, creativity plays an indispensable and important role in every research effort. It may, indeed, be the ingredient that causes a research effort to surpass the ordinary, to be recognized as superior, or to become the backbone and guide for further creative endeavor.

Speech-Communication Research: Current Status and Trends

As a student of communication, you have probably been asked by a skeptical parent, friend, or potential employer, "Communication? What does it mean to have a degree in communication? What will you do with it after you graduate?" Even though you may believe that effective communication is necessary for most careers, you may still have difficulty explaining and justifying speech communication as an academic field. While the study of speech communication dates back to classical Greek times, the discipline is in its infancy as a distinct academic area. This relative newness coupled with its kinship to the disciplines of philosophy, history, political science, English, linguistics, psychology, and sociology has led to identity problems. Because of our newness, speech-communication scholars still debate definitions, views of the field, and research methodologies.

In this chapter we will survey some of the arguments on these issues. Since the field of speech communication will not stand still while we describe its status quo, we offer you a very tentative, necessarily incomplete picture of the discipline. We will present some current definitions of communication and indicate their implications for speech-communication research. We will characterize speech-communication research in terms of paradigmatic affiliations, theoretical development, and methodological issues. Then we will explain three popular approaches to speech-communication inquiry (covering laws, rules, and systems) and introduce some of the debate surrounding these approaches. Finally, this chapter will include some statements concerning the future of speech-communication research.

By specifically relating much of the information in preceding chapters to the speech-communication discipline, we aim to accomplish two objectives: (1) to reduce abstract information concerning research methods into crystalized, concrete, and usable statements, and (2) to facilitate your development of a professional identity through an understanding of the speech-communication research community. The practical research skills and a perspective on the field, as well as confidence and enthusiasm, should provide the *rite de passage* that enables you to become a contributing member of the community of speech-communication researchers.

DEFINING COMMUNICATION

Ask five communication scholars to define communication and you are likely to receive five different definitions. A survey of the communication literature indicates various definitions. Shannon and Weaver define communication "to include all of the procedures by which one mind may affect another."[1] Dance defines communication as "the eliciting of a response through verbal symbols."[2] Cherry sees communication as "the establishment of a social unit from individuals by the use of language and signs."[3] Berelson and Steiner posit that communication is the "process of transmitting information, ideas, emotion, skills, etc. by the use of symbols."[4] Miller and Steinberg stipulate that "communication involves an intentional, transactional, symbolic process of influencing another's behavior to produce physical, social, and economic rewards."[5]

These definitions do not exhaust all the possibilities. Several of the components of the various contemporary definitions of communication have implications for research. For example, communication is thought to be a process. Since the publication of Berlo's landmark volume, *The Process Of Communication,*[6] the concept of communication as process has been widely adopted. A process is a continuous interaction of a large number of factors, with each factor affecting every other factor, all at the same time. A process approach views events and relationships as dynamic, ongoing, ever-changing, and continuous. A process is not a fixed sequence of events having a beginning and end. The process approach says that communication does not consist of absolute actions or factors with well-defined boundaries. The notion of process is antithetical to the idea of stasis, permanence, and simple cause-and-effect relationships.

This view of communication has serious implications for our research. When doing research, we typically rely on the assumption of linear causality. We try to discover and validate cause-and-effect relationships. Scheidel observed that we pay lip service to the idea of process and speculate more about process rather than engage in process analysis.[7] Smith argues that our assumptions about communication and our methods of doing research in communication are contradictory. By defining communication as process, we negate the assumption of linear causality of events. Smith suggests that we more realistically investigate the communication process through correlational designs, factor analyses, research without hypotheses, descriptive studies, ethnomethodological studies, interaction analyses, and participant observation.[8] Perhaps in response to the same criticisms, Hawes has proposed a model for communication processes that assumes mutual causality.[9]

A second component of various definitions is that communication is relational or transactional. It involves mutual impact or influence, with all parties simultaneously influencing all other parties. The transactional approach emphasizes the reciprocal, mutually dependent nature of communication. The individuals in any communication situation constitute one interdependent unit. It is not sufficient to examine how one's message affects another individual. Instead, it is more useful to ask how each person's message affects the other and how those messages characterize the relationship between the two parties. The relational component of communication can be illustrated by examining contemporary views of the power variable. The relational approach to communication posits that power does not reside within an individual but within the relationship between those individuals. Person A cannot have power over Person B without B giving it to A or allowing A to exercise it. The relational approach also presumes a mutual dependence between leaders and followers. There cannot be one without the other. Such is also the case with the pair terms dominant-submissive or talkative-quiet. They are inherently transactional concepts.

The idea that communication is transactional or relational has implications for research. It invalidates the one-way, stimulus-response, linear causality assumptions of many research models. Several writers charge that much of our research is conducted according to a unidirectional or individualistic focus rather than a transactional/relational focus. Morton, Alexander, and Altman elaborate: "While many speak of interpersonal and social processes, the literature in this field has really focused on the individual participant as the unit of analysis and then only inferred to the level of the mutual relationship between people."[10] They suggest that we need to examine the reciprocal nature of communication, that we should study intact, real relationships as well as contrived laboratory situations, and that we need to adopt a more longitudinal perspective to follow relationship histories as they progress through time. Fortunately, some researchers are beginning to propose models, frameworks, or methods for conducting research according to a transactional/relational perspective.[11]

A third component of some definitions of communication is intentionality. This poses additional problems to researchers. As Watzlawick, Beavin, and Jackson suggest, it is impossible for us to see the mind at work. We are limited to observing the outward manifestations of mental processes. Because we cannot get into the "black box" of the mind to determine such intangibles as motive and intention, we must satisfy ourselves with studying the function of behavior.[12] This means that our research cannot be consonant with a definition of communication as intentional behavior, since there is no way to directly observe intention. As researchers, we attempt to measure internal, cognitive processes such as intention by paper-and-pencil self-report tests. That is, we ask subjects to report their motives to us, and we assume the subject is both aware of motive and honest in disclosing that motive. We do not mean to condemn self-report measures. We raise this issue to indicate the potential discrepancy between the conceptual definition of communication as intentional behavior and the limited operational definitions of intentionality. This may make our research problematic.

If we accept the components of process, transactional/relational, and intentional into our conceptual definitions of communication, then we must realize the implications for our research. In effect, we must question whether the assumptions of our research methods are congruent with the assumptions inherent in the conceptualizations of the phenomena we study.

STATE OF THE ART IN SPEECH-COMMUNICATION RESEARCH

Humanistic or Behavioristic Approaches

As a scholar in speech communication, albeit possibly a new member of the field, you may have noticed a polarization in the discipline. Some members of your department who pursue the study of rhetoric may look askance at the "rat runners" or "computer freaks" who study communication. Similarly, the communication people may flaunt statistical jargon and charge that the rhetoricians do nothing more than "dig up obscure dead orators to study." We do not want to make light of this controversy, to offend anyone, or to unnecessarily stir up a sensitive issue. Rather, we believe that if this apparent dichotomy is to be overcome, one must understand the issues between rhetorical and communication scholars.

The competition between a number of supposedly distinct views of the field (rhetoric versus communication; speech communication as art versus speech communication as science) is not unique to our discipline. This polarity may exist in a number of the social sciences. It essentially involves a difference between humanistic and behavioristic approaches to inquiry. Borden and Stone provide a succinct comparison of the underlying assumptions of these views of human nature.[13] Some of the characteristics frequently associated with each paradigm include the following.

Behavioristic Approach	*Humanistic Approach*
1. A mechanistic learning model	1. A cognitive emotional model
2. Behavior is externally controlled by the environment	2. Behavior is internally controlled by the person
3. Behavior is predictable because of environmental conditioning	3. Behavior is unpredictable because of freedom of choice
4. Skinnerian approach	4. Rogerian approach
5. Speech communication as science/communication	5. Speech communication as art/rhetoric
6. Descriptive/Empirical/Experimental methodologies	6. Descriptive/Historical-Critical methodologies

The debate on the relative merits of humanistic and behavioristic approaches to speech communication represents a longstanding philosophic argument. Numerous writers in the last several years have criticized the extremism surrounding this dichotomy. They have tried to provide a compromise by showing that both approaches are similar, complementary, necessary, and useful in our quest for knowledge. Let us examine several of these compromise positions.

First, Williams sees rhetoric and communication as complementary and offers a human science of communication that incorporates the best of both.[14] A human science of communication would emphasize *meanings* as the central concern of inquiry. It would seek not causes of behavior but reasons and purposes inherent in a person's capacity to understand. Further, it would advocate participant observation and naturalistic procedures as methodological stances.

Second, Miller sheds light on the humanistic/scientific controversy. He charges that the debate between humanistic and scientific (behavioristic) approaches to speech communication are characterized by "acrimonious rivalry, exaggerated claims and counterclaims, mutual lack of understanding, and absence of much real, substantive stocktaking."[15] He sees the distinctions between approaches as illustrative of the complexity of the phenomena we study. The key distinction between the two approaches, according to Miller, lies not in methodology but in motive for inquiry. He proposes this main difference in objective.

Humanistic	*Scientific*[16]
deals with the particular; aims to understand events of historical significance; aims to draw factual conclusions and make ethical/aesthetic judgments of specific communication phenomena	deals with the general; aims to predict similar future events; aims to develop empirical statements with generalized predictive and/or explanatory validity

Third, Pearce contends that "the difference between the 'chi squares' and the 'green-eye-shades' are better discussed in terms of their criteria for useful knowledge than in their preferences for newsprint or statistics."[17] Additionally, Delia sees a problem in trying to define our relationship to humanistic and scientific scholarship. He offers this solution: Rather than seemingly drifting between each, "we need to make it clear that we use diverse methods, that some of us creatively employ methods that cannot clearly be pigeonholed as either scientific or critical, that many of us use multiple methods."[18]

It is not possible to legislate compromise between the humanists/artists and behaviorists/scientists. Nor can we force the unification of rhetoric and communication or demand ecumenicalism in the social sciences. Such writers, however, provide the valuable services of illuminating faulty assumptions and unfounded charges of both groups. We anticipate that the gulf between the two schools of thought will lessen as a result of examining the controversy. Speech communication scholars are beginning to realize that the various approaches to inquiry are not dichotomized. They are not mutually exclusive but quite compatible and necessary. We are now seeing empirical studies of contemporary rhetorical artifacts and rhetorical analyses of so called communication variables. Along this line, the Wingspread Conference of 1970 called for a broadening of rhetoric to include the discursive and the nondiscursive, the verbal and the nonverbal, the intentional and the nonintentional.[19] The New Orleans Conference of 1967 recommended the use of heteromethods or multimethods in the study of speech communication.[20] In short, we must ask a variety of questions, pursue a number of goals, use diverse methods, and investigate a host of relevant variables to facilitate our understanding of human communication.

Theoretical Development

Recall from Chapter 1 that a paradigm is a view of a field or an approach to research that specifies assumptions, variables, and methods for the research process. The humanistic and behavioristic approaches to speech-communication research can be seen as paradigms. Each approach states certain assumptions about human behavior that lead to the investigation of certain variables by specific research methods.

Equally important to the progress of research in an academic field and closely related to the concept of paradigm is the level of theoretical development characterizing a discipline. There is frequent confusion between what a paradigm is and what theory is. This is because the two concepts are closely related. Since a paradigm is a world view or an over-riding way of looking at things, it is bound to affect our views of phenomena—that is, theories. Think of a theory as being subsumed by a paradigm. We have already explained that researchers use existing theory to justify and guide their investigations. They also compare research results with that theory to further develop and articulate the theory. The level of theoretical development of an academic field is an index to that field's sophistication and maturity. Recall that Kuhn describes an immature discipline as one in which there is competition among paradigms, a lack of integrated body of theory, and more or less random fact gathering. Ziman's explanation of the stages of research parallels this description.

At this point, we can ask where on the maturity continuum the speech-communication field lies? We know that the longstanding debate between the humanistic and behavioristic paradigm proponents continues. Where do we stand, though, in terms of theoretical development in relation to the choice of a paradigm? Do we have integrated, well-developed, and clearly articulated theories to explain and predict human communication behavior? This very question is the subject of much recent discussion in the speech-communication literature. It is a frequently asked question that generates much soul-searching and numerous self-critical statements. Let us examine some of the recent statements on the issue of theory construction in speech communication.

Bloom observed that "communication scholars lack a consistent critical perspective under which communication inquiry may be shaped and through which it may be evaluated."[21] By "critical perspective" Bloom may be referring more to the absence of a guiding paradigm than to the lack of theory. His comment, though, inevitably points to both the lack of a consistent paradigm, and consequently, to the lack of a body of theory. He argues that we should opt for the pragmatic perspective because it allows a plurality of possible methods of knowing. He concludes, "no one point of view, no one methodological technique, no one theory can claim to be unique and definitive in the codification of a given body of knowledge."[22] So Bloom simultaneously laments our lack of a critical perspective and advocates the adoption of a paradigm that allows multitheories and multimethods.

Rossiter has characterized the speech-communication field and speculated on its future.[23] Agreeing that the adoption of a paradigm is one sign that a discipline is moving from an immature to a mature state, he warns that an aparadigmatic field will produce a plethora of research publications that are not cumulative. He characterizes speech communication as "an emerging discipline with a developing scientific community that is moving from the aparadigmatic stage to the preparadigmatic."[24] Rossiter believes that we are abandoning the humanistic paradigm in favor of the scientific (behavioristic). He sees the frequent disagreements within the scientific community as evidence that we will soon unite around the scientific approach to speech-communication inquiry.

Rossiter's comments on our paradigmatic allegiances indirectly address the issue of theoretical development in speech-communication. If we are approaching the resolution of our paradigm debate by adopting the scientific perspective, then we would be in a better position to articulate the overriding relationships among phenomena (theories) that allow research results to be cumulative rather than isolated and disconnected. That is, agreement about a guiding paradigm would facilitate theory construction. Monge also points to the very fact that we are disagreeing about perspectives as evidence that we are approaching the critical stage of self-examination that precedes the shift to a new paradigm.[25]

According to Dance's commentary on human communication theory, we have no grand theories, a number of partial theories, and many particularistic theoretical bits and pieces.[26] He posits many reasons for this lack of theoretical development: (1) the processual nature of communication, which precludes prediction; (2) the omnipresent and ubiquitous nature of communication, which makes explanation difficult; (3) the fact that communication is both the instrument and the object of our study; (4) the rigidity and condemnation that results from paradigmatic debates, and (5) the competitiveness among related disciplines. Dance concludes that it would be neither possible nor desirable to suppress the disagreement within our discipline. He advocates multiple approaches to theory construction.

Berger presents a more optimistic view of the speech-communication field's progress in theory construction.[27] He admits that while we have traditionally depended upon theories from sociology, psychology, political science, and linguistics, we are beginning to engage in our own theory building and testing. As examples of attempts to develop speech-communication theory, he cites Miller and Steinberg's new perspective on interpersonal communication, the rules theories of various researchers, Berger and Calabrese's axiomatic theory of initial interaction, and Park's axiomatic theory of relational communication.[28] Berger agrees that multiple approaches to speech-communication inquiry are necessary. Yet he criticizes the debate that surrounds the existence of multiple perspectives. He suggests that we should not argue about which approach is the best for theory construction. Instead, we should attempt to clarify the range of phenomena that can best explain each of the approaches.

In reading these commentaries concerning paradigm choice and theory construction in speech communication, you may be confused or frustrated. On the one hand, you read that it is desirable to have a single paradigm and a consistent, unified body of theory that has emerged from research conducted according to that paradigm. Various communication scholars observe that we have neither a governing paradigm nor a clear theoretical orientation. That would mean that the speech-communication discipline is immature, fragmented, and at the early research stages of conjecture or discovery. We have, according to many observers, a long way to go in our quest for a single paradigm that unites us. We have an equally demanding task of constructing a body of theory to guide our research investigations.

On the other hand, however, both Bloom and Dance contend that debate is healthy and that *multiple* paradigms and *multiple* theories are preferable. In addition, Toulmin claims that no single mode of explaining phenomena will suffice.[29] Krippendorf believes that an integrated theory of communication process is necessarily either futile or unfeasible.[30] Delia clearly advocates multiple perspectivism at the community level and theoretical development at the individual level. He praises our field for its multiple perspectives. "We can be justly proud of the multiple perspectivism and metamethodological sophistication that our discipline inculcates and of the quality of our best recent scholarship."[31] He believes that having a diversity of competing views makes it more likely that we will find some paradigm that can give coherence and order to our work and therefore win allegiance of a large number of researchers. The individual researcher, however, should not have multiple perspectives, according to Delia. Rather, he or she should be developing, utilizing, and defending a coherent theoretical system.[32] If a multiplicity of perspectives and theories are beneficial to an academic community and desirable even by mature disciplines, then speech communication receives a clean bill of health. Thus, where speech communication stands in terms of its level of maturity and sophistication really depends on which set of criteria are applied.

Let us attempt to resolve these discrepant statements by offering this position. Multiple paradigms are useful in that they can provide varying perspectives on the same phenomena. Since a paradigm necessarily influences what we see and what we do not see (and even what we look for), let us use different paradigms as a way of broadening our perspectives on human communication. Perhaps we need to use different paradigms to research the same phenomena. If similar results were obtained from different paradigm-governed research, then we could place great confidence in those results.

In terms of theoretical development, multiple theories do not mean atheoreticalism. A discipline that has little or no theoretical base is necessarily weak. Theory and research go hand in hand. Theories are worked out in concrete research activity. Atheoretical research must be equated with unsound research. Without theory, specific research investigations cannot be justified. Research results, then, cannot cumulate into an understanding, explanation, and prediction of human communication behavior. Commentaries on the state of speech-communication research do not criticize the existence of multiple theories. Rather, they charge atheoreticalism—the existence of no theories. We would agree with Berger that theory building does occur in speech-communication research. We also will echo Delia's concern that we need to emphasize theoretical development. We need to insure that our investigations are grounded in existing theory, we need to test inconsistent theories in an attempt to compare their relative explanatory and predictive power, and we need to articulate integrated, organized, and useful theoretical positions.

The discussion thus far has painted a rather bleak picture of the speech-communication field, we fear. We find that definitions vary, and that those definitions are not always consonant with research investigations. There is competition between humanistic and behavioristic approaches to inquiry. Many writers charge that we lack sufficient theory to guide research. We do not want these statements to disillusion or discourage you from speech-communication research.

Recall from Chapter 1 Kuhn's discussion of the evolution of knowledge in a new academic community. Early on in the development of a discipline, there is competition, debate, borrowing from established fields, and insufficient theoretical development. We must keep in mind that speech communication has recently entered the realm of scientific research. Let us offer some comments by Delia that provide a more positive view of our disciplinary progress so far.

Delia admits that our youth as an academic field is responsible for our sharp and rapid shifts in areas and methods of inquiry. He points to our increasing strength and maturity. "Even the most cursory examination of national journal issues randomly picked from across the years of their publication will convince one that our work is steadily maturing."[33] So we ask you to realize that critical statements of the field by researchers in the field are healthy and necessary. With this realization in mind, you can now appreciate additional evaluations of the status of speech-communication research.

Methodological Issues

We have examined numerous statements concerning allegiances to paradigms and the desirability of single versus multiple perspectives. We also have presented several commentaries regarding the level of theoretical development in speech communication. In addition to characterizing our discipline in terms of paradigmatic affiliations and theory construction, let us also discuss some common methodological issues affecting speech-communication research. What follows are some frequently heard methodological criticisms about research in our field. We caution that because paradigms, theories, and methodologies are so highly interrelated, there will be some repetition of points already made. Methodologically, how does speech-communication measure up? To answer this question, let us examine four methodological concerns: (1) methodological worship; (2) overreliance on experimentation; (3) emphasizing method over theory; and (4) inconsistencies between conceptual and operational definitions.

Methodological Worship. Several writers have discussed our tendency toward engaging in methodological worship or jumping on the methodological bandwagon. That is, we may apply a certain methodology or certain tools not because of their appropriateness to the research question but because that method and its tools are conventional, popular, or in vogue. Kaplan coined the term "law of the instrument" to refer to the tendency of researchers to inflict an available methodology on phenomena, regardless of the appropriateness of that methodology. Kaplan explains, "Give a small boy a hammer and he will find that everything he encounters needs pounding."[34] Hewes compares the speech-communication researcher to the little boy with the hammer. "Methodological conventionality has been allowed to dictate theoretical moves and observational strategies in ways which are detrimental to the study of interpersonal communication."[35] Bloom makes a similar charge concerning speech-communication inquiry. "Teach a student statistics and communication is meaningful only if it is quantifiable. Teach a student canonical rhetoric and all utterance must be analyzed in terms of invention, disposition, elocution, memory, and delivery."[36]

These comments remind one of the authors of a prime example of this methodological worship. When she questioned a doctoral student about the student's proposed dissertation topic, she received this answer from the enterprising but misguided doctoral researcher: "I am going to do a canonical correlation study, but I am not yet sure of the specific topic." We can only speculate as to whether this example is typical. In an attempt to justify speech-communication to colleagues from other fields or to enhance the respectability or legitimacy of our research, we must not apply methodologies because they are impressive or sophisticated. This strategy can only hurt our reputations, both at the individual and community levels. Sound research is legitimate and respectable. Sound research follows the sequence of steps presented in Chapter 2—research question or hypothesis determines methodology, not vice versa!

Overreliance on Experimentation. Closely related to and perhaps a subpoint of the charge of methodological worship is the criticism that speech-communication researchers rely too heavily on experimentation. Currently, the experimental method is very popular in speech-communication research. We do not see this as a temporary fad. The experimental method is here to stay. It allows us to answer some questions that cannot be attacked as well by other methods. But this is also true of historical/critical and descriptive methods. Each provides its unique contribution. Nearly all speech-communication scholars would agree in principle that each methodology serves its purpose and that no one method is inherently better than any other. Many researchers, however, either openly or unwittingly favor the experimental method regardless of the specific research question. We do not endorse such an obvious practice of methodological worship.

Why an emphasis on experimentation? First, using the experimental method to investigate communication behavior is a rather new phenomenon in our discipline. Experimental studies of speech communication have emerged in approximately the last twenty years. As with anything new, this method is initially attractive because of its novelty. As it becomes more popular, it generates bandwagon followers. We in speech communication may still be enthralled and enamored with the experimental method.

Second, the New Orleans Conference on Research and Instructional Development, held in 1967, called for the use of scientific approaches in speech-communication research.[37] The report of this conference recommended that we stress scientific approaches in research, insure that our concepts are capable of operational definition, apply scientific approaches to traditionally nonscientific areas, and create scientifically based instructional programs. These recommendations must be examined in light of the times when they were outlined. Since few experimental studies were conducted in our field prior to the mid-sixties, conferees may have been seeking to swing the research pendulum away from an overreliance on historical-critical studies. It is fair to observe that our discipline traditionally has favored historical-critical methods. The predominance of that method certainly influenced the kinds of research questions asked. By viewing the recommendations in the context of the times, we can interpret them as an attempt to restore balance to the field.

A third explanation for reliance on the experimental method relates to the concern for professional survival. Those who perceive a future—or perhaps a present—where only research projects that employ the experimental method will be acknowledged and rewarded see no choice but to opt for experimentation. Of course, the more that people believe this and disregard the appropriateness of the experimental method to the research purpose, the more that methodological worship takes place.

A final possible reason for an emphasis on the experimental method is the mystique it has for those who are unfamiliar with the techniques and perhaps frightened by the jargon of experimentation. Additionally, the notions of "control," "manipulation," and "statistical significance" give rise to an elitist view that the experimental method is more rigorous and, therefore, somehow more valid than other methods. Hawes makes this very point when he contends that "social scientists wishing to answer 'what' questions with descriptive analysis or 'how' questions with interpretive analysis are made to feel like second-class citizens in the social science community."[38] He advocates that we answer "what" questions by describing behavior, "how" questions by interpreting behavior, and "why" questions by experimenting with causes of behavior. Thus, we should employ and have equal respect for all methodologies. Delia, among others, stresses that we ought to affirm no particular methodological approach to the exclusion of others.[39]

Emphasizing Method over Theory. Besides the alleged methodological worship and overreliance on experimentation, another issue concerns our possible preference for hypothesis testing rather than theory building. The issue was addressed at length in the section on theoretical development, but we mention it here because it does represent a methodological problem. Several writers have charged that our priorities are misguided, that is, that we show more concern for data collection as an end in itself rather than as a step toward theory construction. O'Keefe charges that we neglect the analysis of conceptual foundations and theoretical approaches in our effort to increase the "confused and unconnected empirical findings."[40] He claims that communication researchers seem "obsessed with 'doing studies' at the expense of theoretical explication and analysis." Somehow we think that "more research" will provide the answer to our confusions and inconsistencies. Berger offers an explanation for what he also sees as our emphasis on tests of hypotheses.[41] Testing hypotheses, he says, is a relatively low-risk activity whereas theory building is a high-risk activity. The theory builder offers an explanation of reality and may be threatened by the risk of being wrong; one who tests hypotheses derived from someone else's theory engages in a less threatening endeavor. Knutson feels that critics of speech-communication research frequently emphasize methodological issues at the expense of theoretical issues.[42] Miller echoes this same concern and Seibold crystallizes the problem when he says, "Within the positivistic confines of variable-by-variable stockpiling of findings, too little effort has been devoted to critical assessment of these findings, of their finders, or of the foundling communication science."[43]

Since numerous state-of-the-art observations of the speech-communication discipline point to deficiencies in the area of theory building, we must give some credence to this criticism. We must beware the tendency to assume that our investigation is complete when we have confirmed or disconfirmed the hypothesis. The researcher has the additional obligation of relating the results of the hypothesis test to existing knowledge. Why was the hypothesis verified? Theory should help explain why the predicted outcome held true. After all, theory is what allowed the researcher to make that prediction in the first place. Why was the hypothesis not confirmed? Does this indicate some difficulty with the predictive accuracy of the theory? Have the findings of other research investigations cast doubt on the theory? Does the theory need to be revised? Obviously, if the researcher is following the stages in the research process, then he or she is not finished when the results of the hypothesis test are in. To merely report research results indicates a lack of concern with appropriate research methods. Interpreting or discussing the findings means relating the results to theoretical material. In this sense, we are all theory builders.

Additionally, an academic community needs individuals who will, apart from conducting specific investigations, organize existing knowledge, resolve inconsistent findings, and relate new information to existing information—in other words, engage in theory building. Speech communication needs individual researchers who will ground their studies in theory and relate their findings to theory as well as "theoreticians" who will provide some "think pieces" that organize, synthesize, and comment on accumulated research results.

Inconsistencies between Conceptual and Operational Definitions. The final methodological issue that we will discuss relates to definitions of communication.

We conceive of communication as transactional or relational, with a mutual dependence among interactants, yet much of our research focuses on the individual communicator. It is only recently that research methods have been proposed to investigate the reciprocal nature of communication. We have already noted the many scholars who indicate the inconsistencies between conceptual definitions and operational definitions (research techniques). Let us add Berger's suggestions concerning the topics and methods of our research.[44] He points to communicator style, communication competence, and social influence studies as examples of research that focuses on the individual. He contends that we need to find, develop, and employ methods to investigate relationship messages of control, complementarity and symmetry, the sequential structure of interaction, and communication as it develops over time. The issue is both a definitional problem that affects research and a methodological problem that influences what research questions we are capable of answering. A definition that cannot be adhered to within research studies is an unworkable definition. Why hold a certain assumption about communication when we necessarily must violate that assumption in research? Until recently, we had no techniques for conducting research according to the reciprocal nature of communication. This methodological-definitional dilemma is being resolved, however, with the use of interactional units of observation, relational coding, and stochastic modeling, techniques that allow research in communication to be congruent with definitions of communication.

THREE APPROACHES TO SPEECH COMMUNICATION INQUIRY

Currently in the field of speech communication, there is debate among the proponents of the covering-laws, rules, and systems approaches to research. Let us briefly explain these approaches and introduce the controversy surrounding them. Since volumes have been written on each of these approaches to inquiry, our treatment of these perspectives is necessarily limited. For additional coverage of these topics, we suggest the "Additional Sources" at the end of this book.

Covering-Laws Perspective

To understand the notion of covering laws, one must examine the epistemological assumptions of this approach to research. Epistemology is the philosophy of the origins, nature, methods, and limits of human knowledge. Since the goal of research is to generate knowledge, researchers must conduct investigations according to certain epistemological assumptions. The covering-laws perspective is linked to the assumptions of logical positivism, also known as logical empiricism. Logical positivism says there are only two ways of knowing: (1) direct verification through sensory data; and (2) discovery through logic. Thus, if we cannot observe a phenomenon (if it does not have an empirical referent), or if its existence cannot be derived through logic, we can never *know* that the phenomenon exists. According to logical positivism, there are regularities in nature that can be observed or discovered. There is an underlying deterministic order to these regularities that can be accounted for by causal relations. Laws are simply the articulation of regularities in nature.

What does all this have to do with speech-communication research? Speech-communication research typically has been conducted according to the covering-laws perspective. Because of its association with logical positivism, the covering-laws perspective characterizes our research according to these features:

1. The search for causality—discover the antecedent conditions that will inevitably trigger the consequent conditions.
2. The assumption of reductionism—analyze reality in terms of smallest units; isolate and manipulate specific components.
3. The goal of prediction—use knowledge of antecedent conditions to predict future conditions; construct if-then statements.
4. The desire to generalize—predict relationships that hold across situations; create invariant predictions (laws) that cover all occurrences of the phenomenon.

These four characteristics should sound familiar considering what you now know about the experimental method of research. Chapter 6 explains the techniques of discovering antecedent and consequent conditions, isolating and manipulating variables, constructing if-then hypotheses, and generalizing experimental results. The experimental researcher in speech communication, and in any discipline for that matter, traditionally has operated by the covering-laws perspective. This approach leads the researcher to locate lawlike regularities in human behavior.

With this rather basic explanation of the covering-laws approach, let us turn to some of the controversy surrounding the search for covering laws in speech communication. Cushman sums up many of the criticisms of this perspective when he claims ". . . staunch advocates of the laws perspective in the behavioral sciences have been diminishing in numbers over the past ten years. One reason for this decline in support has been the failure of the social scientists to locate regularities which have the same degree of generality, necessity, and strong empirical support as the lawful regularities discovered in the natural sciences."[45]

In short, it may be futile to search for lawlike generalizations in human behavior since human beings have free will, often are unique and idiosyncratic, and engage in culture-bound communication. The advocates and critics of the covering-laws approach may be debating the even larger issue of paradigm choice. The covering-laws approach follows a behavioristic paradigm; critics of the covering-laws approach may operate by the assumptions of the humanistic paradigm.

Bloom sees the logical positivists' emphasis on empirical, observable referents for the method of knowing as inappropriate to the study of communication. "If scholars allowed only those hypotheses which are open to direct observation, communication inquiry as we know it would be severely limited. . . . Constructs such as 'attitude,' 'listening,' and 'credibility' would be meaningless due to our inability to observe them directly. Most of rhetorical theory embodied in public address and its criticism would also be meaningless, according to the positivistic criterion of meaning and knowledge."[46]

Monge claims that researchers frequently violate the assumption of the covering-laws model, yet they continue to use this model in research. He contends that the assumption of generalization or universality makes the model unusable by communication researchers. A law specifies that a relationship will hold throughout time and space. Yet it is impossible to examine all future cases to see if the relationship will be invariant. More important for speech communication research, the assumption that communication is culture-bound, rule-governed, and characterized by choice automatically violates tenets of the covering-law perspective.[47]

Miller and Berger defend the covering-laws model against these criticisms.[48] They see the critics of the covering laws approach engaging in this syllogistic reasoning, which they label as fallacious:

Logical positivism champions the covering-laws model of explanation.
, . . The covering-laws model demands universal, invariant generalizations.
. . . No such generalizations have been discovered in communication.
. . . Therefore, the covering-laws model and logical positivism are inappropriate to the study of communication.

The problem with this reasoning, according to Miller and Berger, is the first assumption, equating logical positivism with the covering-laws model. They contend that the claim that covering laws constitute the sole acceptable means of scientific explanation does not exist in the literature of logical positivism. Berger additionally finds fault with the argument that says it is impossible to establish laws because communication is culturally bound. He claims that laws *do* have boundary conditions.

As in any debate, arguments are proposed, counterarguments are offered, and a third party evaluates the merits of each to judge the outcome of the debate. There is no official judge for this debate, however. Each researcher must decide for him or herself where to stand in this controversy.

Rules Perspectives

Instead of viewing all behavior as causally determined, proponents of the rules perspectives say that behavior can be intentional and guided by rules. Rules are consensually shared expectations about appropriate behavior in particular contexts. Rules are not universally embraced. Rather, they represent regularities in behavior. Rules are necessarily contingent because people and situations vary. Proponents of rules approaches assume two classes of behavior: (1) Some of our behavior involves stimulus-response. This class of behavior is inevitable or governed by deterministic force. Stimulus-response behavior can be explained and predicted through covering laws. (2) Some of our behavior, however, is purposeful, intentional, and governed by free choice. It is this second class of behavior that is guided by rules. That is, individuals can willfully violate a rule. Rules researchers admit the possibility of rules violation. In fact, those who study rules may seek to determine why there is variability in compliance to rules. This possibility for falsification accounts for the unique character of rules research.

We refer to rules perspectives because there is no one rules approach. There are various types of rules that fulfill different functions. For example, rules can allow us to interpret social actions, coordinate actions to accomplish some task, or develop a grammar of interaction. Though the various rules approaches are distinct and have different epistemological frameworks, they are often linked together or confused.

Let us explain and contrast two common rules perspectives: the coordinative approach and the interpretative approach.[49] The coordinative approach sees rules as allowing individuals to coordinate their actions. It examines how people use rules to coordinate meanings to accomplish goals. If two communicators have a common set of rules, then each can predict how the other will react to certain behavior. The more obligatory or compelling the rules, the more one can accurately predict what the reactions to his or her behaviors will be. The coordinative approach tries to establish how a set of rules explain, predict, and control human behavior so as to allow us to coordinate goal achievement.

The interpretive approach sees rules as allowing individuals to make sense of conversation. Rules affect how we sequence and interpret talk. This approach attempts to describe how conversations are structured according to certain rules. It looks retrospectively at conversation and describes how the conversation was created.

Rules-based approaches to communication appear to be growing. Supporters of these perspectives favor the assumption that human communication is not always law-governed but often rule-governed. They prefer to abandon a mechanistic, deterministic, covering-laws approach and adopt an approach that admits human beings make rule-guided choices of behavioral alternatives. As Harré and Secord suggest, behavioral scientists should stop examining variables and their causal relationships with each other and begin to study rules that guide behavior.[50]

Because they allow the existence of free will, rules-based approaches are consonant with the definition of communication as intentional behavior. Interactants have the choice to follow or disobey rules. They may intentionally choose to violate a rule. Thus, communicators are seen as proactive rather than reactive. Some rules are shared by the social group; others are unique to individual relationships. Some rules are activated; that is, they have been used repeatedly and need only to be called forth. Other rules are constructed, or amended from general rules to fit a specific situation.

Despite a growing number of supporters, rules approaches also have critics. For example, Berger links rules with description and covering laws with explanation. He questions whether we should be satisfied to know what the rules are (description) without knowing why some rules are selected over others (explanation).[51] Similarly, Pearce shows concern with rules approaches when he says it is not enough that we identify rules. Additionally, we must describe contracts, which consist of sets of rules, metarules or rules about rules, and switching cues, which signal which set of rules is to be salient at a particular time.[52]

Cushman and Pearce, two leading proponents of applying rules theories to human communication, admit that rules perspectives are, as yet, poorly articulated and not well supported by a powerful set of research procedures. This may be a result, in their opinion, of different researchers separately trying to develop rules theories.[53] Bochner reviews rules-based research and arrives at a pessimistic conclusion thus far. He cautions against jumping on the rules bandwagon. Rules exist hierarchically. There are not only rules, but rules about making rules and rules about how to follow rules. Researching a hierarchy of rules is an inherently complex and elusive endeavor. Bochner criticizes that we have been able to discover only very trivial, obvious, and unimportant rules. He concludes, "Research conducted under the rules framework has been disappointing. Methodological and procedural details are frequently absent and the issues chosen for study have been, at worst, trivial, or, at best, insufficient to justify unabashed enthusiasm."[54]

So much for the explanation, advantages, and problems with rules perspectives for research. The debate continues, and we introduce a third framework for speech-communication research—the systems approach.

Systems Perspective

The systems approach to research also emerges from recent dissatisfaction with applying the logical positivism, covering-laws approach to human communication. The systems approach views nature in terms of interlinked sets of components, hierarchically organized into structural wholes that interact through time and space, are self-regulating, yet capable of structural change.[55] A theory of human communication according to this perspective consists of a set of elements, a set of propositions expressing the relationship between all the elements, and a calculus for drawing implications from the system.[56]

To understand the idea of systems, think of an individual as a component of a family system, the family as part of the community, the community as a component of the state, and the state as a subsystem of the nation. Looking at the family system, we see that individual members are interdependent. The family has rules to regulate itself and is capable of change. The family is more than just the sum of individual members. The family is a changing, dynamic, adaptive entity. Members mutually affect one another, and a change in one component of the family system affects the entire family system. These are just a few characteristics of a system. Systems theorists attempt to explain the pattern of relationships among parts of systems. They assume that the nature of an entity changes as a function of the system of which it is a part. Thus, systems theorists focus on the ongoing, changing behavioral sequences over time and admit the simultaneous, mutual, and multiple causes of events.

Like the different schools of thought concerning rules theories, there are at least two groups of systems theorists: general systems theorists and systems modelers.

General Systems Theorists. General systems theorists believe there exist regularities of organization (systems) which can be discovered and articulated as laws. These laws could unify the diverse areas of human knowledge—that is, they could be interdisciplinary. Thus, general systems theorists seek to discover a rather all-encompassing set of principles that can be applied to many kinds of phenomena and can be used by members of diverse disciplines. Like probability theory, it could be applied to many fields. Note the epistemological assumptions of general systems theory are similar to those of the law theorists.

Systems Modelers. Systems modelers deny that regularities of organization (systems) exist in nature. Rather, they assert that systems are artificial creations that serve as useful models for reality. Systems are *conceived* by the researcher rather than merely *observed* by the researcher.

The systems approach(es) also has both proponents and critics. Monge contends that a systems approach allows us to ask a number of useful questions about communication and to look at different variables from what we normally investigate. It is an explanatory model sufficiently complex to account for the complexity of communication. Monge further contends that the systems approach allows us to integrate existing research findings.[57] Cushman and Craig claim that we can best understand communication by understanding the systems in which communication takes place. They conceive of human civilization as one great communication system comprised of cultural, social, organizational, and interpersonal subsystems. They see the systems perspective of communication as more of a relationship focus than an individualistic focus.[58]

One criticism of the systems approach is that it is too encompassing. The definition of a system may be so all-embracing as to be meaningless. If everything is a system, nothing is a system.[59] Fisher explains that research with the systems perspective is recent and rather sparse. This perspective is in the process of being theoretically and empirically developed.[60] Cushman and Pearce claim that "systems theory provides a rigorous and flexible method of discovery and verification, yet has produced relatively little significant research or theory construction in communication. . . . There are more staunch advocates of the systems perspective than producers of theory or research."[61]

While the assumptions of the systems approach are theoretically sound and match our conceptual definitions of communication, research within the systems approach is necessarily difficult. When a phenomenon is complex, simultaneously changing and stable, and composed of interdependent parts, investigating that phenomenon is no easy task. Research according to the systems perspective is further frustrated by our lack of tools to investigate mutual rather than linear causality.

Thus, we see advantages and disadvantages of the covering-laws, rules, and systems approaches to speech-communication inquiry. We regret that we cannot offer definitive conclusions to this debate. Kuhn indicates that methods, theories, models, and paradigms cannot be legislated by a research community. An approach to inquiry will win supporters and the debate surrounding the approach will die a natural death when that approach proves to better explain phenomena, better resolve the puzzle, and better contribute to our quest for knowledge. Bochner explains, "The superiority of one perspective over another cannot be proven merely by rhetorically countering one argument against another. The ultimate test will always lie in the advocate's ability to show that one perspective does a better job than another in explaining observable communicative phenomena. And that demands substantive research."[62] He suggests that we suspend polemical discourse and start doing substantive research.

Each of these approaches allows the researcher to generate different questions and use alternative principles of explanation, prediction, and control. Each rests on diverse criteria of proof. In short, each is based on different philosophic assumptions. Let us address the assumption of "necessity," which is an inherent part of any theory. By doing so, we will see that laws, rules, and systems approaches are based on different types of necessity.[63]

In Chapter 1, we defined a theory as a set of interrelated concepts that presents a systematic view of phenomena by specifying relationships for the purpose of explaining and predicting phenomena. *Necessity* means the phenomena accounted for by the theory must possess some knowable characteristics that make the occurrence of regularities expected and interpretable.[64] That is, there must be some specifiable force to the relationship stated by the theory. Three types of necessity may be identified, and each has a different type of force associated with it.

Nomic necessity states that there is some knowable characteristic of nature such that the proposed relationship must occur. If there is a causal relationship between two phenomena, then their relationship is a predetermined and inevitable one— subject to observation. Nomic necessity depends on certain observable antecedent conditions yielding or causing certain consequent conditions. The covering-laws approach claims nomic necessity.

Logical necessity states that there is a network of relationships such that a change in one requires a change in the others. If there is a logical relationship between two phenomena, then their relationship can be expected or known by definitional force. Logical necessity depends on maintaining the logic of the system as defined. The systems approach claims logical necessity.

Practical necessity states that normative force affects performance of given activities. If two phenomena are linked normatively, then their relationship can be expected or known through normative force. Practical necessity depends on the power of normative pressures. The rules approach claims practical necessity.

Thus, if covering laws are based on nomic necessity, systems on logical necessity, and rules on practical necessity, then each approach rests on different epistemological assumptions. On the basis of this fundamental philosophical difference, the choice of which approach is most useful for human communication research does not depend on contentions or evidence of its usefulness. Instead, one must examine philosophical assumptions, decide on an epistemological approach, and affiliate with the perspective (laws, rules, systems) that matches one's philosophical underpinnings.

Each approach, therefore, can help explain phenomena, resolve the puzzle, and contribute to a quest for knowledge. The resolution of the debate among proponents of each approach depends on a resolution of philosophic differences. An individual's answer to the question, "What is knowledge?" necessarily affects that individual's choice of approach for generating knowledge.

DIRECTIONS FOR FUTURE RESEARCH

Critical statements about the status of research in a discipline indirectly provide suggestions for future directions of that field. Critics of the status quo frequently offer solutions to the problems they illuminate. This chapter includes a synthesis of statements from various speech-communication scholars about future directions for research in speech communication. Some statements are predictive; that is, they point to current trends that are likely to shape the future. Other statements are prescriptive. Those comment on what directions speech-communication research ought to take. Let us first present predictions for the future of speech-communication research.

1. Increasingly, researchers will investigate the transactional/relational aspects of communication.
2. There will be less debate between humanists and behaviorists as both groups realize each others' contributions.
3. Speech-communication researchers will continue to develop and utilize research methods that are consonant with the definitions of communication as processual, relational/transactional, and intentional.
4. We will continue to conduct research according to the covering-laws, rules, and systems approaches until one approach proves itself consonant with philosophic assumptions and more useful in providing knowledge of speech-communication phenomena.

Next we offer prescriptions for the future of speech-communication research.

1. We should make sure that the assumptions of our definitions match the assumptions of our research tools.
2. We should develop and utilize research models that investigate mutual causality of human behavior.
3. We should use different paradigms to research the same phenomena, pursue multiple approaches to theory construction, employ heteromethods, and have equal respect for all research methodologies.
4. We should be less concerned with hypothesis testing and more concerned with theory construction.
5. We should regard research methods as tools and apply those tools only as they are appropriate to our research questions.

SUMMARY

This chapter surveyed the numerous definitions of communication and discussed their implications for speech-communication research. Although communication is frequently seen as processual, relational/transactional, and intentional, these assumptions tend to be violated in our research. Current definitions of communication assume mutual causality of behavior; current research models investigate linear causality. Research methods must be developed that are isomorphic with conceptual definitions.

We discussed the paradigmatic affiliations of speech-communication scholars and illuminated the debate between advocates of the humanistic and behavioristic paradigms. It was suggested that debate is unnecessary since paradigm choice cannot be legislated. Yet, controversy can lead to an understanding and respect for different viewpoints. Humanistic and in behavioristic approaches complement each other, each allows us to answer certain questions, and each is valid and necessary in furthering knowledge of human behavior.

The attempt to characterize the theoretical development of the speech-communication field showed some inconsistent findings. Some scholars criticize that we have no unified body of theory in speech-communication. Others claim that we can never have definitive theory. We examined some of the debate concerning the relative merits of single versus multiple perspectives. Some observers note that we are engaging in theory construction while others lament that we sacrifice theoretical orientations in our quest to test hypotheses. Whatever the current appraisal, in the future, speech-communication researchers must ground their investigations in theory and must test and articulate theoretical positions.

Speech-communication research seems to be characterized by several methodological problems, including methodological worship, overreliance on experimentation, emphasis on hypothesis testing, and inconsistencies between conceptual and operational definitions. We may be guilty of choosing a research method before deciding on the research question. We must beware using certain techniques because they are in vogue. The emphasis on experimentation in speech communication may be because of the novelty of the method, our attempts to become more scientific, beliefs that professional advancement is dependent on doing experimental studies, or the elitist view that the experimental method is better than other methods. Whatever the reason for the worship of experimentation, overreliance on any one method is restricting.

We explained the covering-laws, rules, and systems approaches to speech-communication inquiry. The covering-laws approach is based on the tenets of logical positivism. It aims to predict human behavior through the discovery of lawlike generalizations. The rules approach seeks to understand people's choice of rules that typically guide behavior. The systems approach focuses on complex and changing behavior over time. Advantages and disadvantages were discussed concerning these three approaches and epistemological assumptions of each were explained.

Finally, from the commentaries on communication definitions, paradigmatic affiliations, theoretical development, methodological issues, and contemporary approaches to inquiry, we provided a list of predictions and prescriptions concerning future directions of speech-communication research.

In a society of rapidly accelerating change, social science research becomes increasingly important. Specifically, the understanding of human communication assumes a special relevance. For those of us in the field of speech communication, it is imperative that we understand our contributions, acquire the skills of analyzing and monitoring our behavior within the research community, and develop the tools to create a future in which, through research, we can better understand human communication.

Appendix

I. The Problem
  A. Statement
     To identify a consistent pattern of moves and countermoves made during negotiations between Marathon Oil Company representatives and Teamsters Local 273 representatives on an existing contract.
  B. Definitions
     1. *moves* and *countermoves* (an operational definition): offers (demands), counteroffers (counterdemands), acceptances, rejections, threats and promises (hereafter "thromises"), and information seeking. Each of these elements will be considered in more detail in the methodology section.
     2. *negotiation* (Rubin and Brown, 1975, p. 18):
        a. At least two parties are involved.
        b. The parties have a conflict of interest with respect to one or more different issues.
        c. Regardless of the existence of prior experience or acquaintance with one another, the parties are at least temporarily joined together in a special kind of voluntary relationship.
        d. Activity in the relationship concerns: (1) the division or exchange of one or more specific resources, and/or (2) the resolution of one or more intangible issues among the parties or among those they represent.

This material was prepared by Andrew Powell in connection with a course entitled "Introduction to Graduate Studies" (Speech 597) at Bowling Green State University. It also served as a basis for the thesis he wrote for the completion of his Master's Degree.

e. The activity usually involves the presentation of demands or proposals by one party, evaluation of these by the other, followed by concessions and counterproposals. The activity is thus sequential rather than simultaneous.

3. *existing contract,* other than first-time negotiations: "The techniques for an employer bargaining with a union for the first time are quite different from those employed when labor agreements are being renegotiated" (Morse, p. 47).

C. Testability

This study will be limited to the years 1973 through 1979 for three reasons:

1. Those are the years for which primary documents are currently available.

2. The negotiations in this period involve the same union—the Teamsters.

3. Each party is represented by the same chief negotiators during this period.

D. Significance and Justification

1. Rubin and Brown undertook the monumental task of reviewing all of the experimental research on negotiations and bargaining available previous to 1975. They concluded that most research relevant to bargaining has been laboratory experimentation utilizing game-theoretic paradigms. Very few studies have been conducted on real people over real issues. It is only by getting into the field that we can arrive at a true understanding of the bargaining process (Rubin and Brown, p. 298).

2. There is an information gap between the writings of professional negotiators and the writings of experimental researchers. Institutional and descriptive literature concerning collective bargaining has largely ignored the theories of bargaining and game-paradigm research. In this bargaining and paradigm research, references to collective bargaining are parenthetical statements that only suggest that a comparison can be made (Stevens, p. xii). This paper does not claim to fill this gap, only to acknowledge that such a gap exists. By maintaining this awareness, however, some steps may be taken to bridge this chasm.

3. Since this paper will focus on patterns of interaction, some justification for this convergence is necessary. Patchen explains that ". . . most bargaining theorists do not, in their informal models, treat the actions of each side as being in part a reaction to the previous actions of the other. In other words, most theories of bargaining do not give direct and explicit attention to the process of interaction between the parties. And yet it is the interaction process, rather than separate characteristics of the parties which may be crucial to the outcomes in a social relationship" (Patchen, p. 389-407).

II. The Theoretical Framework

A. Stevens (p. v) points out a need for a theoretical framework more specialized to collective bargaining and to industrial relations systems. By analyzing transcripts from actual negotiations this specialization will be achieved. If the results of this thesis affirm its hypothesis, we will have a tool with which to analyze patterns of interaction in other professional settings. This, of course, is not the entire framework. However, we can surmise from what Patchen (1970) has said about understanding of the interaction patterns in bargaining relationships that it is a key factor in developing such a framework.

B. Literature Review

Because of the schism between the two theoretical approaches to bargaining behavior (institutional and experimental), the author plans to give considerable attention to both. This prospectus will consider bargaining patterns from both areas. The institutional literature will be reviewed first, followed by the experimental literature.

1. Institutional literature

Morse mentions some things to look for in any procedural analysis of a bargaining relationship. "As time goes on you will 'knock off' the relatively unimportant issues first. Real bargaining customarily does not begin until about ten days before the expiration date or deadline set by the parties" (Morse, p. 55). He emphasizes the importance of the interactive process in that deadline period when he states, "Even the 'final' proposal near the end of the negotiations should hold back one or two minimum concessions you would be inclined to give rather than take a strike" (p. 65).

2. Experimental literature

a. The numerous experimental studies of bargaining behavior have dealt much more than the other with patterns of behavior. They too recognize that there is a dependence between the two parties for interaction. One 'move and countermove' strategy that has been studied is the rate of concession making. Druckman, Zechmeister, and Solomon felt that their results indicated that the buyers were more responsive to seller concession-rate strategies than to other cues in the experimental situation. This supports the characterization of the two-person bargaining process in terms of behavioral interdependence (1972). The way in which this paper will consider concession making will be explained in the methodology section.

b. Gruder and Duslak (1973) found that subjects who were highly competitive or highly cooperative were much less likely to reach agreement than were those who employed a "tit for tat" strategy (return a competitive move with a competitive move and a cooperative move with a cooperative move).

c. Oskamp (1970) concluded that those subjects who began by making only competitive choices and then later switched to only cooperative choices (reformed sinner), reached agreement more often than did those subjects who were competitive throughout. He also found that those who were put into a "free play" situation arrived at agreement less frequently than those in any of the other situations. If we are to believe that this occurs consistently in the field, then we would conclude that there is not much hope for successful negotiations.

C. Literature Review Summary

It is apparent that all of this literature points to an interactive dependence between parties. Each member of the relationship has an impact on the others' behavior. Wyer explains this impact in more detail. O's behavior is likely to influence subjects' responses in any of three ways: by providing them with good (or bad) outcomes, and thus inducing them to reciprocate by acting in O's behalf (or against O's behalf); by providing them with information about how the magnitude of their own outcomes will be affected by their behavior; and by providing a cue as to what behavior is generally appropriate in the game-playing situation, independent of the outcomes available—i.e., imitative behavior in a novel situation (1971).

D. Alternative Hypotheses

1. A 'free play' bargaining situation leads to cooperative behaviors.
2. The frequency of agreement will increase as the deadline date approaches.
3. The frequency of rejection will decrease as the deadline date approaches.
4. The frequency of offers and demands will increase as the deadline date approaches.

III. Hypothesis

There is an identifiable pattern of moves and countermoves in the bargaining relationship between Marathon Oil Company and Teamsters Local 273. Null: No identifiable pattern of moves and countermoves exists in the bargaining relationship between Marathon Oil Company and Teamsters Local 273.

IV. The Design

This study will employ a historical-critical methodology.

V. The Data

The data for this study will be primary documents in the form of transcribed minutes recorded by persons present during negotiations. This author has learned that the transcriptions were made by the same individuals who took the minutes.

VI. The Methodology

A. Most experimental research talks about the frequency of cooperative moves versus competitive moves and at what point in negotiation relationships they are most likely to occur. Field analysis, however, does not lend itself to such clear distinctions. This author is looking for "patterns" of moves and countermoves, which does not require the establishment of these distinctions. To identify these patterns (or their absence) the following will be considered.

1. Frequencies of offers and demands (counteroffers and counterdemands)
2. Frequencies of rejections
3. Frequencies of agreements
4. Change in variance of offers from initial positions
5. Frequencies of "thromises" (threats and promises)

B. Operational Definitions

offer: a statement of position that is presented for acceptance or rejection.

demand: same as offer, the only difference is the manner in which the position is stated.

counteroffer: a statement of position that is presented for acceptance or rejection in response to an offer or demand.

counterdemand: same as counteroffer; the only difference is the manner in which the position is stated.

agreement: acceptance by both parties of the solution to an issue.

rejection: refusal of one party to accept an offer, demand, counteroffer, or counterdemand made by the other party.

thromise: a combination of *threat* and *promise* because of similarity in form.

threat: a statement in which the source indicates his or her intention to provide the target with a reinforcing consequence that the source anticipates the target will evaluate as noxious, unpleasant, or punishing.

promise: same as threat, except that the reinforcing consequences are thought to be pleasant, positive, or rewarding.

VII. The Working Guide

A. January 15:   Prospectus presentation and defense

B. January 30:   Completion of literature review
Finalization of methodology
Verify validity of documents
Final limiting of area of consideration

C. May 31:   Analysis of data and processing
Reevaluation of methodology
Reevaluation of documents

D. July 15:   Final review of literature
Final draft of thesis and submission

E. July 16:   Thesis defense

VIII. Analysis and Interpretation of Results

A. The results of this study will be analyzed to see if there are comparisons which can be made to bargaining strategies studied by experimental researchers. If this study supports its hypothesis, then we will have a tool with which to analyze other bargaining relationships.

B. With some adaptation, this author believes that we may also use this tool to search for patterns of interactions in other institutional settings as diverse as legislatures and families.

C. Another advantage, if this study affirms its hypothesis, is that we will have a clearer understanding of real-life negotiations. The benefit from this would be two-fold:

1. We would be better able to replicate real-life negotiations in the laboratory.

2. When in the laboratory, we will be able to ask better questions about what we are looking for.

IX. Bibliography

Cross, J.G. *The economics of bargaining.* New York: Basic Books, Inc., 1969.

Druckman, D., Zechmeister, K., and **Solomon, D.** Determinants of bargaining behavior in a bilateral monopoly situation: Opponents concession rate and relative defensibility. *Behavioral Science,* 1972, *17,* 514-531.

Fouraker, L.E., and **Siegel, S.** *Bargaining behavior.* New York: McGraw-Hill Book Co., Inc., 1963.

Froman, L.A., and **Cohen, M.D.** Compromise and logroll: Comparing the efficiency of two bargaining processes. *Behavioral Science,* 1970, *15,* 180-183.

Gruder, C.L., and **Duslak, R.J.** Elicitation of cooperation by retaliatory and nonretaliatory strategies in a mixed motive game. *Journal of Conflict Resolution,* 1973, *17,* 162-174.

Karrass, C.L. *The negotiating game.* New York: World Publishing Co., Inc., 1970.

Kelley, H.H., and **Thibaut, J.W.** *Interpersonal relations: A theory of interdependence.* New York: John Wiley & Sons, 1978.

Morse, B. *How to negotiate the labor agreement.* Southfield, Mich.: Trends Publishing Co., 1977.

Nierenberg, G.I. *Fundamentals of negotiating.* New York: Hawthorne Books, 1973.

Nothdurft, K.H. *The complete guide to successful business negotiation.* London: Leviathan House, 1974.

Oskamp, S. Effects of programmed initial strategies in a prisoner's dilemma game. *Psychonomic Science,* 1970, *19,* 195-196.

Patchen, M. Models of cooperation and conflict: A critical review. *Journal of Conflict Resolution,* 1970, *14,* 389-407.

Rubin, J.Z., and **Brown, B.R.** *The social psychology of bargaining and negotiation.* New York: Academic Press, 1975.

Stevens, C.M. *Strategy and collective bargaining negotiation.* New York: McGraw-Hill Book Co., Inc., 1963.

Walton, R.E., and **McKersie, R.B.** *A behavioral theory of labor negotiations: An analysis of a social interaction system.* St. Louis: McGraw-Hill Book Co., 1965.

Wyer, R.S. Effects of outcome matrix and partner's behavior in two-person games. *Journal of Experimental Social Psychology,* 1971, *7,* 190-210.

Notes
and Additional Sources

CHAPTER 1

[1] Joseph Luft, *Group Process: Introduction to Group Dynamics* (Palo Alto, Calif.: National Press Books. 1970).

[2] Alvin Toffler, *Future Shock* (New York: Bantam Books, Inc. 1971).

[3] John Dewey, *How We Think* (Boston: D.C. Heath & Co., 1910).

[4] Robert K. Merton, *Social Theory and Social Structure* (New York: Free Press, 1957), pp. 543-545.

[5] Fred N. Kerlinger, *Foundations of Behavioral Research* (New York: Holt, Rinehart & Winston, Inc., 1973), p. 9.

[6] John Ziman, *Public Knowledge: The Social Dimension of Science* (Cambridge: Cambridge University Press, 1968), pp. 51-52.

[7] Thomas Kuhn, *The Structure of Scientific Revolutions* (Chicago: University of Chicago Press, 1970).

[8] Charles M. Rossiter, "Models of Paradigmatic Change," *Communication Quarterly,* 25 (1977), pp. 69-73.

[9] See, for example: Jesse G. Delia, "Alternative Perspectives for the Study of Human Communication: Critique and Response," *Communication Quarterly,* 25 (1977), pp. 46-62.; B. Aubrey Fisher, "Evidence Varies with Theoretical Perspective," *Western Speech,* 41 (1977), pp. 9-19.

[10] Nwankwo, "Communication as Symbolic Interaction," appears in *Journal of Communication,* 23 (1973), 195-216; Seibold, "Communication Research," in *Human Communication Research,* 2 (1975), 3-32; Mortensen, "Small Group Research," in *Quarterly Journal of Speech,* 56, (1970), 304-309; Kraus, "Mass Communication and Political Socialization," in *Quarterly Journal of Speech,* 59 (1973), 390-400; and Bochner, "Conceptual Frontiers" in *Human Communication Research,* 2 (1976), 381-397.

[11] Watson, "Conflicts and Directions," appears in *Journal of Communication,* 22 (1972), 443-459; Bormann, "Small Group Research," in *Speech Monographs,* 37 (1970), 211-217; Frentz, "A Psycholinguistic Analysis of Metaphor," in *Quarterly Journal of Speech,* 60 (1974), 125-133; Erlich, "Populist Rhetoric Reassessed," in *Quarterly Journal of Speech,* 63 (1977), 140-151; and Hovland, "Reconciling Conflicting Results," in *American Psychologist,* 14 (1959), 8-17.

[12]Kenneth Burke, *Language as Symbolic Action: Essays on Life, Literature, and Method* (Berkeley: University of California Press, 1966).

[13]Turner, "Comic Strips," appears in *Central States Speech Journal*, 28 (1977), 24-35; Weiher, "American History on Stage," in *Quarterly Journal of Speech*, 63 (1977), 405-412; Lane, "Communication Behavior and Biological Rhythms," in *Speech Teacher*, 20 (1971), 16-20; Phillips, "Rhetoric and Its Alternatives" in *Communication Quarterly*, 24 (1976), 11-23; and Weaver, ' Role Playing," in *Today's Speech*, 19 (1971), 35-39.

[14]George C. Homans, *Social Behavior: Its Elementary Forms* (New York: Harcourt Brace Jovanovich, 1961).

[15]Kenneth L. Villard and Leland J. Whipple, *Beginnings in Relational Communication* (New York: John Wiley & Sons, Inc., 1976), pp. 141-168.

[16]Burgoon, "Unwillingness to Communicate," appears in *Central States Speech Journal*, 28 (1977), 122-133; Berger and Calabrese, "Toward a Developmental Theory," in *Human Communication Research*, 1 (1975), 99-112; Harrison and Knapp, "Nonverbal Communication Systems," *Journal for Communication*, 22 (1972), 339-352; Enholm, "Rhetoric as an Instrument for Understanding and Improving Human Relations," in *Southern Speech Communication Journal*, XLI (Spring 1976), 223-236; and Monge, "The Systems Perspective," in *Communication Quarterly*, 25 (1977), 19-29.

[17]Fred P. Barnes, "We Are All Researchers," *The Instructor* 69 (1960), 6-7.

[18]Scott and Wheeless, "Three Types of Communication Apprehension," appears in *Southern Speech Communication Journal*, 42 (1977, 246-255; McGuire, "Rethinking the Public Address Curriculum," in *Communication Education*, 27 (1978), 65-68; Hayes, "Measure of Speech Experience," in *Central States Speech Journal*, 29 (1978), 20-24; Golden and Berquist, "Rhetoric of Western Thought" in *Communication Education*, 27 (1978), 153-158; and Thomas, "Teaching Stagecraft Through Models," in *Communication Education*, 27 (1978), 165-169.

[19]Applbaum and Phillips, "Subject Selection" appears in *Communication Quarterly*, 25 (1977), 18-22; Tucker and Mack, "Speech as Process," in *Speech Monographs*, 28 (1971), 341-349; Alexander, "Image and Method of Measurement," *Journal of Communication*, 21 (1971), 170-178; Hahn and Gonchan, "Studying Social Movements," in *Speech Teacher*, XX (1971), 44-52; and Fletcher, "Semantic Differential Type Scales," in *Western Speech*, XXXVI (1972), 269-275.

[20]Neil Postman and Charles Weingartner, *Teaching as a Subversive Activity* (New York: Delacorte Press, 1969).

ADDITIONAL SOURCES

Achinstein, P., Law and Explanation. Oxford: Clarendon Press, 1971.

Barzun, Jacques, and Henry F. Graff, *The Modern Researcher*. New York: Harcourt Brace Jovanovich, Inc., 1977.

Blalock, H. M., Jr., *An Introduction to Social Research*. Englewood Cliffs, N. J.: Prentice-Hall, Inc., 1970.

Bowers, John Waite, *Designing the Communication Experiment*. New York: Random House, Inc., 1970.

Crane, Diana, *Invisible Colleges*. Chicago: University of Chicago Press, 1972.

Dubin, R., *Theory Building*. New York: Academic Press, Inc., 1969.

Fisher, B. Aubrey, *Perspectives on Human Communication*. New York: Macmillan, Inc., 1978.

Hagstrom, W. O., *The Scientific Community*. New York: Basic Books, Inc., 1965.

Hawes, Leonard, *Analoguing: Theory and Model Construction in Communication*. Reading, Mass.: Addison-Wesley Publishing Co., Inc., 1975.

Hempel, Carl, *Philosophy of Natural Science*. Englewood Cliffs, N. J.: Prentice-Hall, Inc., 1966.

Kaplan, Abraham, *The Conduct of Inquiry*. Harper & Row Publishers, Inc., 1964.

Larabee, Harold, *Reliable Knowledge: Scientific Methods in the Social Studies*. Boston: Houghton Mifflin Co., 1964.

Merton, Robert K., *The Sociology of Science*. Chicago: University of Chicago Press, 1973.

Nagel, Ernest, *The Structure of Science*. New York: Harcourt Brace Jovanovich, 1961.

Nagi, Saad Z., and Ronald G. Corwin, *The Social Contexts of Research*. New York: John Wiley & Sons, Inc., 1972.

Popper, Karl R., *The Logic of Scientific Discovery*. New York: Harper & Row Publishers, Inc., 1959.

Ravitz, J. R., *Scientific Knowledge and its Social Problems*. Oxford: Clarendon Press, 1971.

Ruben, Brent D., and John M. Weimann, "The Diffusion of Scientific Information in the Communication Discipline: Conceptualization and Propositions," *Communication Quarterly*, 27 (1979), 47-53.

Rudner, Richard, *Philosophy of Social Science*. Englewood Cliffs, N. J.: Prentice-Hall, Inc., 1966.

Stinchombe, Arthur, *Constructing Social Theories*. New York: Harcourt Brace Jovanovich, 1968.

Tullock, Gordon, *The Organization of Inquiry*. Durham, N. C.: Duke University Press, 1966.

Van Dalen, Deobold B., *Understanding Educational Research*. New York: McGraw-Hill Book Company, 1979.

CHAPTER 2

[1]Carter V. Good, "Criteria for Selection of the Research Problem," *Peabody Journal of Education*, 19 (1942), 242-256.

ADDITIONAL SOURCES

Allen, George R., *The Graduate Student's Guide to Theses and Dissertations*. San Francisco: Jossey-Bass, Inc. Publishers, 1974.

Best, John, *Research in Education*. Englewood Cliffs, N. J.: Prentice-Hall, Inc., 1977.

Jones, Ralph H., *Methods and Techniques of Educational Research*. Danville, Ill.: The Interstate Printers & Publishers, Inc., 1973.

Leathers, Dale G., *Modcom Modules in Speech Communication: Orientations to Researching Communication*. Chicago: Science Research Associates, Inc., 1978.

Lin, Nan, *Foundations of Social Research*. New York: McGraw-Hill Book Company, 1976.

Lin, Nan, Ronald S. Burt, and John Vaughn, *Conducting Social Research*. New York: McGraw-Hill Book Company, 1976.

Mason, Emanuel J., and William J. Bramble, *Understanding and Conducting Research/Application in Education and the Behavioral Sciences*. New York: McGraw-Hill Book Company, 1978.

Skager, Rodney W., and Carl Weinberg, *Fundamentals of Educational Research*. Glenview, Ill.: Scott, Foresman & Company, 1971.

CHAPTER 3

[1]Virginia Clark, "Teaching Students To Use the Library: Whose Responsibility?" *College and Research Libraries*, 21 (September 1960), 369-372.

[2]Robert B. Downs and Clara D. Keller, *How To Do Library Research*, 2nd ed. (Urbana: University of Illinois Press, 1975), p. 1.

[3]Ibid. pp. 1-2.

[4]Kenneth Whittaker, *Using Libraries* (New York: Philosophical Library, Inc., 1963), p. 112.

[5]Tyrus Hillway, *Handbook of Educational Research: A Guide to Methods and Materials* (Boston: Houghton Mifflin Company, 1969), p. 43.

[6]Published monthly by the H. W. Wilson Company.

[7]Published by the Speech Communication Association. One can order a copy of this publication by writing: Speech Communication Association, 5105 Backlick Rd., Annandale, Va. 22003.

[8]Published by Sage Publications, 275 South Beverly Drive, Beverly Hills, Calif. 90212.

[9]Published monthly by Macmillan Information, a division of Macmillan Publishing Co., Inc.

[10]Until 1967, ERIC was the acronym for Education Research Information Center.

[11]Marilyn Halpern, *Guide to ERIC*, rev. ed., Bibliographic Series No. 73 (Bowling Green, Ohio: Bowling Green State University Libraries, 1978), p. 3.

[12]Published by H. W. Wilson Company, New York.

[13]Published by the American Psychological Association, Inc., 1200 Seventeenth Street, N. W., Washington, D. C. 20036.

[14]Published by Sociological Abstracts, P. O. Box 22206, San Diego, Calif. 92122.

[15]Published by the New York Times Company, 229 West 43rd Street, New York, N. Y. 10036.

[16]Published by Newspaper Archive Developments Limited, Holybrook House, Castle Street, Reading, RG 1 7SN, England.

[17]Published by H. W. Wilson Company, 950 University Avenue, Bronx, N. Y. 10452.

[18]*Books in Print,* published by R. R. Bowker Company, 1180 Avenue of the Americas, New York, N. Y. 10036, produces a complete listing, compiled from information received on an on-going basis directly from publishers, to all scholarly, popular, adult, juvenile, reprint, and all other types of books covering all subjects provided they are published or exclusively distributed in the United States and are available to the trade or to the general public.

[19]*Forthcoming Books, Subject Guide to Forthcoming Books,* and *Publishers Weekly,* are all published by the R. R. Bowker Company. Most of the foreign editions of books in print are either published by or distributed by the R. R. Bowker Company as well.

[20]Published by the Library of Congress, Washington, D.C.

[21]Margaret G. Cook, *The New Library Key*, 3rd ed. (New York: The H. W. Wilson Company, 1975), pp. 74-75.

[22]*The MLA Style Sheet,* 2nd ed. (New York: The Modern Language Association of America, 1970). Copies of this publication may be obtained from the Publications Center, Modern Language Association, 62 Fifth Ave., New York, N.Y. 10011. *Publication Manual of the American Psychological Association,* 2nd ed. (Washington, D.C.: American Psychological Association, 1974). Copies may be ordered from Publication Sales, American Psychological Association, 1200 Seventeenth Street, N.W., Washington, D.C. 20036.

[23]J. Jeffery Auer, *An Introduction to Research in Speech* (New York: Harper & Row, Publishers, 1959), p. 89.

[24]Tyrus Hillway, *Handbook of Educational Research: A Guide to Methods and Materials* (Boston: Houghton Mifflin Company, 1969), pp. 16-17.

ADDITIONAL SOURCES

Auer, J. Jeffery, *An Introduction to Research in Speech.* New York: Harper & Row, Publishers, 1959. See especially Chap. 1-4.

Barzun, Jacques and Henry F. Graff, *The Modern Researcher,* 3rd ed. New York: Harcourt Brace Jovanovich, Inc., 1977.

Brooks, P. C., *Research in Archives: The Use of Unpublished Primary Sources.* Chicago: The University of Chicago Press, 1969.

Cook, Margaret G., *The New Library Key,* 3rd ed. New York: The H. W. Wilson Company, 1975. The best guide to library usage discovered.

Downs, Robert B. and Clara D. Keller, *How To Do Library Research,* 2nd ed. Urbana: University of Illinois Press, 1975.

Galin, S. and P. Spielberg, *Reference Books: How to Select and Use Them.* New York: Random House, 1969.

Gates, Jean Key, *Guide to the Use of Books and Libraries,* 2nd ed. New York: McGraw-Hill Book Company, 1969.

Hillway, Tyrus, *Handbook of Educational Research: A Guide to Methods and Materials.* Boston: Houghton Mifflin Company, 1969. Chapters 1-4 are especially pertinent.

Kent, Allen, *Textbook on Mechanized Information Retrieval,* 2nd ed. New York: John Wiley & Sons, Inc. (Interscience Publishers), 1966.

Poulton, Helen J., *The Historian's Handbook: A Descriptive Guide to Reference Works.* Norman, Okla.: University of Oklahoma Press, 1972.

Rivers, W. L., *Finding Facts: Interviewing, Observing, Using Reference Sources.* Englewood Cliffs, N.J.: Prentice-Hall, Inc., 1975.

Whittaker, Kenneth. *Using Libraries.* New York: Philosophical Library, Inc., 1963.

CHAPTER 4

[1]Wood Gray, *Historian's Handbook: A Key To the Study and Writing of History*, 2nd ed. (Boston: Houghton Mifflin Company, 1964), pp. 5-6.

[2]Emanuel J. Mason and William J. Bramble, *Understanding and Conducting Research/ Applications in Education and the Behavioral Sciences* (New York: McGraw-Hill Book Company, 1978), p. 28.

[3]Deobold B. Van Dalen, *Understanding Educational Research: An Introduction*, 3rd ed. (New York: McGraw-Hill Book Company, 1973), pp. 159-160.

[4]Stephen Isaac and William B. Michael, *Handbook in Research and Evaluation: A Collection of Principles, Methods, and Strategies Useful in the Planning, Design, and Evaluation of Studies in Education and the Behavioral Sciences* (San Diego: Robert R. Knapp, Publisher, 1971), p. 17.

[5]William J. Lucey, *History: Methods and Interpretation* (Chicago: Loyola University Press, 1958), p. 22.

[6]Van Dalen, *Understanding Educational Research*, p. 161.

[7]Isaac and Michael, *Handbook in Research*, pp. 17-25.

[8]Clyde W. Dow, ed., *An Introduction to Graduate Study in Speech and Theatre* (East Lansing: Michigan State University Press, 1961), p. 53.

[9]Volumes I and II edited by William Norwood Brigance (New York: Russell & Russell, Inc., 1943). Volume III edited by Marie Kathryn Hochmuth (New York: Russell & Russell, Inc., 1955).

[10]Herbert W. Simons, "Changing Notions About Social Movements," *Quarterly Journal of Speech*, 62 (December 1976), 425.

[11]Dow, *An Introduction to Graduate Study*, pp. 55-56.

[12]Wayne N. Thompson, "Barbara Jordan's Keynote Address: Fulfilling Dual and Conflicting Purposes," *Central States Speech Journal*, 30 (Fall 1979), 272-277.

[13]Robert L. Heath, "A Time for Silence: Booker T. Washington in Atlanta," *Quarterly Journal of Speech*, 64 (December 1978), 385-399.

[14]Roderick P. Hart, "An Unquiet Desperation: Rhetorical Aspects of 'Popular' Atheism in the United States," *Quarterly Journal of Speech*, 64 (February 1978), 33-46.

[15]Barnet Baskerville, "Must We All Be 'Rhetorical Critics'?" *Quarterly Journal of Speech*, 63 (April 1977), 115.

[16]Robert L. Scott and Bernard L. Brock, *Methods of Rhetorical Criticism: A Twentieth Century Perspective* (New York: Harper & Row, Publishers, 1972), pp. 8-9.

[17]Craig R. Smith, "The Republican Keynote Address of 1968: Adaptive Rhetoric for the Multiple Audience," *Western Speech*, 39 (Winter 1975), 32-39.

[18]Wayne N. Thompson, "Barbara Jordan's Keynote Address: The Juxtaposition of Contradictory Values," *Southern Speech Communication Journal*, 44 (Spring 1979), 223-232.

[19]Bruce E. Gronbeck, "The Rhetoric of Political Corruption: Sociolinguistic, Dialectical, and Ceremonial Processes," *Quarterly Journal of Speech*, 64 (1978), 155-172.

[20]Martha Solomon, "Jimmy Carter and *Playboy*: A Sociolinguist Perspective on Style, *Quarterly Journal of Speech*, 64 (1978), 173-182.

[21]Loren Reid, "John Bright: Spokesman For America," *Western Speech*, 38 (Fall 1974), 233-243.

[22]Ronald H. Carpenter, "Frederick Jackson Turner and the Rhetorical Impact of the Frontier Thesis," *Quarterly Journal of Speech*, 63 (April 1977), 117-129.

[23]Ernest G. Bormann, "Fetching Good Out of Evil: A Rhetorical Use of Calamity," *Quarterly Journal of Speech*, 63 (April 1977), 130-139.

[24]Scott and Brock, *Methods of Rhetorical Criticsm*, p. 10.

[25]Scott and Brock, *Methods of Rhetorical Criticism,* pp. 9-10.

[26]Michael C. McGee, "The Fall of Wellington: A Case Study of the Relationship Between Theory, Practice and Rhetoric in History," *Quarterly Journal of Speech* 63 (February 1977), 28-42.

[27]Gerard G. LeCoat, "Music and the Three Appeals of Classical Rhetoric," *Quarterly Journal of Speech,* 62 (April 1976), 157-166.

[28]Jesse G. Delia, "Constructivism and the Study of Human Communication," *Quarterly Journal of Speech,* 63 (February 1977), 83.

[29]For a comprehensive overview on Kenneth Burke, see William Rueckert, ed., *Critical Responses to Kenneth Burke* (Minneapolis: University of Minnesota Press, 1969), Burke's major works include *Counter-Statement* (New York: Harcourt, Brace and Company. 1931); *Permanence and Change* (New York: New Republic, 1935); *Attitudes Toward History* (New York: New Republic, 1937); *The Philosophy of Literary Form* (Baton Rouge: Louisiana State University, 1941); *A Grammar of Motives* (New York: Prentice-Hall, 1945); *A Rhetoric of Motives* (New York: Prentice-Hall, 1950); *A Rhetoric of Religion* (Boston: Beacon Press, 1961); *Language as Symbolic Action* (Berkeley: University of California Press, 1966).

[30]The analogy of the balance scale is developed by Dow, *An Introduction to Graduate Study,* p. 88ff.

[31]Edwin Black has criticized this approach in *Rhetorical Criticism: A Study in Method* (New York: Macmillan, Inc., 1965). See Karlyn Kohrs Campbell, *Critiques of Contemporary Rhetoric* (Belmont, Calif.: Wadsworth Publishing Co., Inc., 1972), pp. 24-38, for more information on each of these approaches.

[32]See Kenneth Burke, *A Grammar of Motives* and *A Rhetoric of Motives* (New York: Meridian Books, 1962).

[33]J. Jeffery Auer, *An Introduction to Research in Speech* (New York: Harper & Row Publishers, 1959), pp. 140-141.

[34]Robert M. W. Travers, *An Introduction to Educational Research,* 4th ed. (New York: Macmillan Inc., 1978), pp. 382-383.

[35]Dow, *An Introduction to Graduate Study,* pp. 64-67.

[36]Kurt H. Wolff and Barrington Moore, Jr., eds., *The Critical Spirit: Essays in Honor of Herbert Marcuse* (Boston: Beacon Press, 1967), pp. 110-111.

[37]George J. Mouly, *Educational Research: The Art and Science of Investigation* (Boston: Allyn & Bacon, Inc., 1978), p. 166.

[38]John W. Burgess, "The Methods of Historical Study and Research in Columbia College," in G. Stanley Hall, ed., *Methods of Teaching History* (Boston, 1885), 218.

[39]Albert B. Hart, *Studies in American Education* (New York: n.p., 1895), p. 76.

[40]Oscar Handlin et al., *Harvard Guide to American History* (Cambridge, Mass.: Harvard University Press, 1954), pp. 5 and 6.

[41]Joseph T. Klapper, *The Effects of Mass Communication* (Glencoe, Ill.: The Free Press, 1960), pp. 15-49.

[42]Dow, *An Introduction to Graduate Study,* pp. 69-77. For an excellent analysis of the problems in historiography, developed from a writer's perspective, see Barbara Tuchman, *A Distant Mirror: The Calamitous 14th Century* (New York: Alfred A. Knopf, Inc., 1978), especially her "Foreward: The Period, the Protagonist, the Hazards," pp. xiii-xx.

ADDITIONAL SOURCES

Critical Methodology

Baird, Albert Craig, Lester Thonssen, and Waldo W. Braden, *Speech Criticism,* 2nd ed. New York: Ronald Press Company, 1970.

Campbell, Karlyn Kohrs, *Critiques of Contemporary Rhetoric.* Belmont, Calif.: Wadsworth Publishing Company, Inc., 1972.

Scott, Robert Lee, and Bernard L. Brock, *Methods of Rhetorical Criticism: A Twentieth-Century Perspective.* New York: Harper & Row, 1972.

Historical Research

Auer, J. Jeffery. *An Introduction to Research in Speech.* New York: Harper & Row, Publishers, 1959. See especially Chapter 5, "The Historical Method," pp. 118-146.

Barzun, Jacques, and Henry F. Graff, *The Modern Researcher,* 3rd ed. New York: Harcourt Brace Jovanovich, Inc., 1977.

Benson, Lee, *Toward the Scientific Study of History.* Philadelphia, Pa.: J. B. Lippincott Company, 1972.

Best, John W., *Research in Education,* 3rd ed. Englewood Cliffs, N.J.: Prentice-Hall, Inc., 1977.

Blankenship, Jane, and Hermann G. Stelzner, eds., *Rhetoric and Communication: Studies in the University of Illinois Tradition.* Urbana, Ill.: University Press, 1976.

Brooks, P. C., *Research in Archives: The Use of Unpublished Primary Sources.* Chicago: The University of Chicago Press, 1969.

Cantor, Norman F. and Richard I. Schneider, *How to Study History.* New York: Thomas Y. Crowell, 1967.

Carr, Edward H., *What Is History?* New York: Alfred A. Knopf, Inc., 1962.

Clark, G. Kitson, *Guide for Research Students Working on Historical Subjects.* Cambridge: Cambridge University Press, 1958.

Dow, Clyde W., ed. *An Introduction to Graduate Study in Speech and Theatre.* East Lansing: Michigan State University Press, 1961. See especially Chapter 4, Gregg Phifer, "The Historical Approach," pp. 52-80, and Chapter 5, Elton S. Carter and Iline Fife, "The Critical Approach," pp. 81-103.

Garraghan, Gilbert J.. *A Guide to Historical Method.* Westport, Conn.: Greenwood Press, 1946.

Gottschalk, Louis R., *Understanding History.* New York: Alfred A. Knopf, Inc. 1950.

Gottschalk, Louis R., C. Kluckhohn, and R. Angell, *The Use of Personal Documents in History, Anthropology, and Sociology: Bulletin No. 53.* New York: Social Science Research Council.

Gray, Wood, *Historian's Handbook: A Key to the Study and Writing of History,* 2nd ed. Boston: Houghton Mifflin Company, 1964.

Hockett, Homer Carey, *Introduction to Research in American History.* New York: Macmillan, Inc., 1948.

Hockett, Homer Carey., *The Critical Method in Historical Research and Writing.* New York: Macmillian Co., 1967.

Hughes, H. Stuart, "The Historian and the Social Scientist," *American History Review,* 66 (1960) 20-46.

Li, Tze-Chung, *Social Science Reference Sources: A Pratical Guide.* Westport, Conn.: Greenwood Press, 1980.

Marsak, Leonard M., *The Nature of Historical Inquiry.* New York: Holt, Rinehart, and Winston, 1970.

Mason, Elizabeth B., and Louis M. Starr, eds., *The Oral History Collection.* New York: Columbia University Press, 1979.

Neuenschwander, John A., *Oral History: As A Teaching Approach.* Washington, D.C.: National Education Association, 1976.

Nevins, Allan, *The Gateway to History,* rev. ed. Boston: Raytheon Education Company, 1962.

Shafer, Robert Jones, ed., *A Guide to Historical Method.* Homewood, Ill.: The Dorsey Press, 1974.

Shorter, Edward, *The Historian and the Computer: A Practical Guide.* Englewood Cliffs, N.J.: Prentice-Hall, Inc., 1971.

Swierenga, Robert P., ed., *Quantification in American History: Theory and Research.* New York: Atheneum, 1970.

Thompson, Paul, *The Voice of the Past: Oral History.* Oxford: Oxford University Press, 1978.

Wallace, Karl R., ed., *History of Speech Education in America.* New York: Appleton-Century-Crofts, Inc., 1954.

Wilson, John R. M., *Research Guide in History.* Morristown, N.J.: General Learning Press, 1974.

Winks, Robin W., ed., *The Historian as Detective: Essays on Evidence.* New York: Harper & Row, Publishers, 1968.

CHAPTER 5

[1]John W. Best, *Research in Education,* 3rd ed. (Englewood Cliffs, N.J.: Prentice-Hall, Inc., 1977), p. 116.

[2]Keith V. Erickson, T. Richard Cheatham, and William J. Jordan, "Demographic Characteristics of Nonrespondents to Speech Communication Survey Research," *Communication Quarterly,* 26 (Spring 1978), 35-40.

[3]Raymond L. Gorden, *Inverviewing: Strategy, Techniques, and Tactics* (Homewood, Ill.: Dorsey Press, 1975), pp. 123-137.

[4]Nan Lin, *Foundations of Social Research* (New York: McGraw-Hill Book Company, 1976), p. 241.

[5]Lin, *Social Research,* p. 224.

[6]Best, *Research in Education,* pp. 166-167.

[7]Robert S. Goyer, W. Charles Redding, and John T. Rickey, *Interviewing Principles and Techniques: A Project Text* (Dubuque, Iowa: William C. Brown Co., Publishers, 1964).

[8]Gorden, *Interviewing,* pp. 76-78.

[9]Garry M. Richetto and Joseph P. Zima, *Fundamentals of Interviewing* (Chicago: Science Research Associates, Inc., 1976), p. 16.

[10]C. A. Moser and G. Kalton, *Survey Methods in Social Investigation,* 2nd ed. (New York: Basic Books, 1972), pp. 282-287.

[11]Gorden, *Interviewing,* pp. 142-174.

[12]Earl R. Babbie, *Survey Research Methods* (Belmont, Calif.: Wadsworth Publishing Company, Inc., 1973).

[13]Bernard Berelson, *Content Analysis in Communication Research* (New York: Free Press, 1952), p. 18.

[14]John Markoff, Gilbert Shapiro, and Sasha R. Weitman, "Toward the Integration of Content Analysis and General Methodology," in David R. Heise, ed., *Sociological Methodology 1975* (San Francisco: Jossey-Bass, Inc., Publishers, 1974), pp. 1-58.

[15]Berelson, *Content Analysis,* pp. 26-113.

[16]Philip J. Stone et al., *The General Inquirer: A Computer Approach to Content Analysis* (Cambridge, Mass.: MIT Press, 1966).

[17]Karl E. Weick, "Systematic Observational Methods," in Gardner Lindzey and Elliot Aronson, eds., *Handbook of Social Psychology,* 2nd ed. (Reading, Mass.: Addison-Wesley Publishing Co., Inc., 1968), p. 425.

[18]Robert F. Bales, *Interaction Process Analysis* (Reading, Mass.: Addison-Wesley Publishing Co., Inc., 1950).

[19]B. Aubrey Fisher, G. Lloyd Drecksel, and Wayne S. Werbel, "Social Information Processing Analysis (SIPA): Coding Ongoing Human Communication," *Small Group Behavior,* 10 (1979), 3-21.

[20]For a review of selected interaction analytic techniques, see L. Edna Rogers and Richard V. Farace, "Analysis of Relational Communication in Dyads: New Measurement Procedures," *Human Communication Research,* 1 (1975), 222-239.

[21]Edward Bodaken, William Lashbrook, and Marie Champagne, "PROANA5: A Computerized Technique for the Analysis of Small Group Interaction," *Western Speech,* 35 (1971), 112-115.

[22]For a detailed discussion of the transactional/relational nature of communication, see Chapter 12.

[23]Robert A. Mark, "Coding Communication at the Relationship Level," *Journal of Communication,* 21 (1971), 221-232.

[24]See Rogers and Farace, "Analysis of Relational Communication." 1975.

[25]For a description of various network analysis computer programs, see William D. Richards, "Network Analysis Methods: Conceptual and Operational Approaches." Paper presented at the Fourth Annual Colloquium on Social Networks, Social Sciences, and Linguistics Institute, University of Hawaii, December 1977.

[26]Gerald M. Goldhaber, *Organizational Communication* (Dubuque, Iowa: William C. Brown Co., Publishers, 1979).

[27]For a detailed discussion of logical positivism, see Chapter 12.

[28]For a discussion of phenomenology, see: Joseph K. Kockelmans, ed., *Phenomenology* (New York: Doubleday & Co., Inc., 1967); Alfred Schutz, *The Phenomenology of the Social*

World (Evanston, Ill.: Northwestern University Press, 1967); George Psathas, *Phenomenological Sociology* (New York: John Wiley & Sons, 1973).

[29]Leonard C. Hawes, "Toward a Hermeneutic Phenomenology of Communication," *Communication Quarterly*, 25 (1977), 30-41.

[30]Rom Harre, "Some Remarks on 'Rule' as a Scientific Concept," in Theodore Mischel, ed., *Understanding Other Persons* (Totowa, N.J.: Rowman and Littlefield, 1974), pp. 148-149.

[31]W. Barnett Pearce, "Naturalistic Study of Communication: Its Function and Form," *Communication Quarterly*, 25 (1977), 51-56.

[32]Harold Garfinkel, *Studies in Ethnomethodology* (Englewood Cliffs, N.J.: Prentice-Hall, Inc., 1967).

[33]Robert M. Emerson, *Judging Delinquents* (Chicago: Aldine Publishing Co., 1969).

[34]Harvey Sacks, Emmanual Schegloff, and Gail Jefferson, "A Simplest Systematics for the Analysis of Turn-Taking in Conversation," *Language*, 50 (1974), 696-735.

[35]Egon Bittner, "The Concept of Organization," Ralph H. Turner, ed., *Ethnomethodology* (Baltimore: Penquin Books, 1974).

[36]See Elaine M. Litton-Hawes, "A Foundation for the Study of Everyday Talk," *Communication Quarterly*, 25 (1977), 2-11; Robert E. Nofsinger, Jr., "A Peek at Conversational Analysis," *Communication Quarterly*, 25 (1977), 12-20.

ADDITIONAL SOURCES

Banaka, William H., *Training in Depth Interviewing*. New York: Harper & Row Publishers, Inc., 1971.

Bruyn, Severyn T., *The Human Perspective in Sociology*. Englewood Cliffs, N.J.: Prentice-Hall, Inc., 1966.

Bruyn, Severyn T., "The New Empiricists: Participant Observer and Phenomenologist," *Sociology and Social Research*, 51 (1967), 317-322.

Budd, Richard, Robert Thorpe, and Lewis Donohew, *Content Analysis of Communications*. New York: Macmillan, Inc., 1967.

Cappella, Joseph N., "Talk-Silence Sequences in Informal Conversations, I," *Human Communication Research*, 6 (1979), 3-17.

Chavers, Pasqual D., "Social Structure and the Diffusion of Innovations: A Network Analysis." Unpublished doctoral dissertation, Stanford University, 1976.

Crano, W., and M. Brewer, *Principles of Research in Social Psychology*. New York: McGraw-Hill Book Company, 1973.

Ellis, Don G., "Relational Control in Two Group Systems," *Communication Monographs*, 46 (1979), 153-166.

Farace, Richard V., Peter R. Monge, and Hamish M. Russell, *Communicating and Organizing*. Reading, Mass.: Addison-Wesley Publishing Co., Inc., 1977.

Festinger, Leon, and Daniel Katz, eds., *Research Methods in the Behavioral Sciences*. New York: Holt, Rinehart & Winston, 1966.

Fisher, B. Aubrey, "Current Status of Interaction Analysis Research." Paper presented at the Speech Communication Association Convention, Minneapolis, 1978.

Fisher, B. Aubrey, "Decision Emergence: Phases in Group Decision Making," *Speech Monographs*, 37 (1970), 53-60.

Frentz, Thomas S., and Thomas B. Farrell, "Language-Action: A Paradigm for Communication," *Quarterly Journal of Speech*, 62 (1976), 333-349.

Granovetter, Mark, "Network Sampling: Some First Steps," *American Journal of Sociology*, 81 (1976), 1287-1303.

Gumperz, John J., and Dell Hymes, eds., *Directions in Sociolinguistics: The Ethnography of Communication*. New York: Holt, Rinehart & Winston, 1972.

Hawes, Leonard, "Conversation Analysis: Accomplishing an Incumbency Reversal." Paper presented at Speech Communication Association, Minneapolis, 1978.

Hawes, Leonard C., "How Writing is Used in Talk: A Study of Communicative Logic-In-Use," *Quarterly Journal of Speech*, 62 (1976), 350-360.

Holsti, Ole R., *Content Analysis for the Social Sciences and Humanities*. Reading, Mass.: Addison-Wesley Publishing Co., Inc., 1969.

Hymes, Dell, *Foundations in Sociolinguistics: An Ethnographic Approach.* Philadelphia: University of Pennsylvania Press, 1974.

Jurick, Donna M., "The Enactment of Returning: A Naturalistic Study of Talk," *Communication Quarterly,* 25 (1977), 21-29.

Lesniak, R., M. Yates, Gerald Goldhaber, and William Richards, "NETPLOT: An Original Computer Program for Interpreting NEGOPY." Paper presented at International Communication Association Convention, Berlin, Germany, 1977.

Litton-Hawes, Elaine M., "A Discourse Analysis of Topic Co-selection in Medical Interviews." Unpublished doctoral dissertation, Ohio State University, 1976.

Lofland, John, *Analyzing Social Settings: A Guide to Qualitative Observation and Analysis.* Belmont, Calif.: Wadsworth Publishing Co., Inc., 1971.

Mabry, Edward A., "An Instrument for Assessing Content Themes in Group Interaction," *Speech Monographs,* 42 (1975), 291.

Mabry, Edward A., "Sequential Structure of Interaction in Encounter Groups," *Human Communication Research,* 1 (1975), 222-239.

McCall, George J., and J. L. Simmons, *Issues in Participant Observation.* Reading, Mass.: Addison-Wesley Publishing Co., Inc., 1969.

Meehan, Hugh, and Houston Wood, *The Reality of Ethnomethodology.* New York: John Wiley & Sons, 1975.

Nofsinger, Robert E., "The Demand Ticket: A Conversational Device for Getting the Floor," *Speech Monographs,* 42 (1975), 1-9.

Nofsinger, Robert E., "On Answering Questions Indirectly: Some Rules in the Grammar of Doing Conversation," *Human Communication Research,* 2 (1976), 172-181.

Parks, Malcolm R., "Relational Communication: Theory and Research," *Human Communication Research,* 3 (1977), 372-381.

Philipsen, Gerry, "Linearity of Research Design in Ethnographic Studies of Speaking," *Communication Quarterly,* 25 (1977), 42-50.

Richards, William, *A Manual for Network Analysis: Using the NEGOPY Network Analysis Program.* Palo Alto, Calif.: Institute for Communication Research, Stanford University, 1975.

Schatzman, Leonard, and Anselm L. Strauss, *Field Research: Strategies for a Natural Sociology.* Englewood Cliffs, N.J.: Prentice-Hall, Inc., 1973.

Speier, Matthew, *How to Observe Face-to-Face Communication: A Sociological Introduction.* Santa Monica, Calif.: Goodyear Publishing Co., Inc., 1973.

CHAPTER 6

[1]R. B. Cattell, *The Scientific Use of Factor Analysis in Behavioral and Life Sciences* (New York: Plenum Publishing Corporation, 1978). Italics in the original. The experimental method is discussed in detail in several other excellent texts also. For example, Clair Selltiz, Lawrence S. Wrightsman, and Stuart W. Cook, *Research Methods in Social Relations,* 3rd ed. (New York: Holt, Rinehart & Winston, 1976), Chap. 5.

[2]Some examples: J. C. McCroskey, P. R. Hamilton, and A. N. Weiner, "The Effect of Interaction Behavior on Source Credibility, Homophily, and Interpersonal Attraction," *Human Communication Research,* 1 (1974), 42-52; R. F. Applbaum and K. W. Anatol, "The Factor Structure of Source Credibility as a Function of the Speaking Situation," *Speech Monographs,* 39 (1972), 216-222; and D. K. Berlo, J. B. Lemert, and R. Mertz, "Dimension for Evaluating the Acceptability of Message Sources," *Public Opinion Quarterly,* 33 (1969), 563-576.

[3]Mahoney appropriately refers to this characteristic as theoretical validity. See Michael J. Mahoney, "Experimental Methods and Outcome Evaluation," *Journal of Consulting and Clinical Psychology,* 46 (1978), 600-672.

[4]Alternately, research questions may be posited if the study is exploratory.

[5]K. R. Popper, *The Logic of Scientific Discovery* (New York: Harper & Row, Publishers, Inc., 1959).

[6]P. W. Bridgman, *The Logic of Modern Physics* (New York: Macmillan, 1927).

[7]For additional details on the nature of independent variables, see any standard textbook

on experimental design. Example: F. J. McGuigan, *Experimental Psychology,* 3rd ed. (Englewood Cliffs, N.J.; Prentice-Hall, Inc., 1978).

[8]C. F. Osgood, G. J. Suci, and P. H. Tannenbaum, *The Measurement of Meaning* (Urbana, Ill.: University of Illinois Press, 1957).

[9]Roger E. Kirk, *Experimental Design: Procedures for the Behavioral Sciences* (Belmont, Calif.: Brooks/Cole, Publishing Co., 1968).

[10]Jacob Cohen, *Statistical Power Analysis for the Behavioral Sciences,* rev. ed. (New York: Academic Press, Inc., 1977).

[11]A standard topic in most inferential statistics texts. See, for example, Kirk, *Experimental Design.*

[12]John W. Tukey, "Comparing Individual Means in the Analysis of Variance," *Biometrics,* 5 (1949), 99-114.

[13]Manipulation checks are illustrated effectively in John A. Daly, Virginia P. Richmond, and Steven Leth, "Social Communicative Anxiety and the Personnel Selection Process: Testing the Similarity Effect in Selection Decisions," *Human Communication Research,* 6 (1979), 18-32.

[14]Albert E. Scheflen, "Communication and Regulation in Psychotherapy," *Psychiatry,* 26 (1963). See also John Stuart Mill, *A System of Logic* (London: Longman, 1967).

[15]Gustav Ichheiser, *Appearances and Realities* (San Francisco: Jossey-Bass, Inc., Publishers, 1970). See especially Chap. 1.

[16]Popper, *Scientific Discovery.*

[17]For comments on the relationship of science to metaphysics, see Barry Hindess, *Philosophy and Methodology in the Social Sciences* (Atlantic Highlands, N.J.: Humanities Press, Inc., 1977).

[18]Mahoney, "Experimental Methods," pp. 661-662.

[19]Fred N. Kerlinger, *Foundations of Behavioral Research,* 2nd ed. (New York: Holt, Rinehart & Winston, 1973), Chap. 1.

[20]See Popper, *Scientific Discovery;* I. Lakatos, "Changes in the Problem of Inductive Logic," in I. Lakatos, ed., *The Problem of Inductive Logic* (Amsterdam: North-Holland Publishing Co., 1968).

[21]Walter B. Weimer, *Notes on the Methodology of Scientific Research* (Hillsdale, N.J.: Lawrence Erlbaum Associates, Publishers, 1979). See especially Chap. 4.

[22]L. Wolin, "Responsibility for Raw Data," *American Psychologist,* 17 (1962), 657-658.

[23]John W. Tukey, "Analyzing Data: Sanctification or Detective Work?" *American Psychologist,* 24 (1969) 83-91.

[24]For a fuller perspective see the excellent article: Gilbert A. Churchill, Jr. "A Paradigm for Developing Better Measures of Marketing Constructs," *Journal of Marketing Research,* 26 (1979), 64-73.

[25]McGuigan, *Experimental Psychology,* 484.

[26]Mahoney, "Experimental Methods," pp. 660-661.

[27]The classic discussion is that of Campbell and Stanley. See Donald T. Campbell and Julian C. Stanley, *Experimental and Quasi-Experimental Designs for Research* (Chicago: Rand McNally & Company, 1963).

[28]Discussed in Campbell and Stanley, *Experimental Designs.*

[29]Jum C. Nunnally, "The Study of Change in Evaluation Research: Principles Concerning Measurement, Experimental Design, and Analysis," in E. L. Struening and M. Guttentag, eds., *Handbook of Evaluation Research, Vol. 1* (Beverly Hills, Calif.: Sage Publications, Inc., 1975), p. 123.

[30]Kirk, *Experimental Design.*

[31]Unless the experimental treatments are confined to, for example, instructional booklets. In such cases all subjects can be tested in the same room while the different conditions (booklets) are randomly distributed.

[32]Discussed fully in Murray Sidman, *Tactics of Scientific Research* (New York: Basic Books, Inc., Publishers, 1960), Chap. 7.

[33]Discussed in R. Darrell Bock, *Multivariate Statistical Methods in Behavioral Research* (New York: McGraw-Hill Book Company, 1975).

[34]For a comprehensive discussion, see Jum C. Nunnally, *Psychometric Theory,* 2nd ed. (New York: McGraw-Hill Book Company, 1978), Chap. 7.

[35]See Nunnally, *Psychometric Theory,* Chap. 3.

[36]The Dogmatism construct is, for the most part, the work of Rokeach. See Milton Rokeach, *The Open and Closed Mind: Investigations into the Nature of Belief Systems and Personality Systems* (New York: Basic Books, Inc., Publishers, 1960).

[37]R. Christie and F. Geis, *Studies in Machiavellianism* (New York: Academic Press, Inc. 1970).

[38]W. Gamson, "The Flouridation Dialogue: Is It an Ideological Conflict?" *Public Opinion Quarterly,* 25 (1961), 526-537.

[39]R. Middleton, "Alienation, Race, and Education," *American Sociological Review,* 28 (1963), 973-977.

ADDITIONAL SOURCES

American Psychological Association, *Ethical Principles in the Conduct of Research with Human Participants.* Washington, D.C.: American Psychological Association, 1973.

Bellack, Alan S., and Hersen, Michel, eds., *Research and Practice in Social Skills Training.* New York: Plenum Press, 1979.

Hersen, Michel, and Bellack, Alan S., eds., *Behavioral Assessment: A Practical Handbook.* Oxford, England: Pergamon Press, 1976.

Isaac, Stephen, and Michael, William B., *Handbook in Research and Evaluation.* San Diego: EDITS Publishers, 1971.

CHAPTER 7

[1]Jum C. Nunnally, *Psychometric Theory,* 2nd ed. (New York: McGraw-Hill, 1978).

[2]Dean K. Whitla, ed., *Handbook of Measurement and Assessment in Behavioral Sciences* (Reading, Mass.: Addison-Wesley Publishing Col, Inc., 1968).

[3]Bruce W. Tuckman, *Conducting Educational Research,* 2nd ed. (New York: Harcourt Brace Jovanovich, Inc., 1978), Chap. 8.

[4]Jacob Cohen, *Statistical Power Analysis for the Behavioral Sciences,* rev. ed. (New York: Academic Press, Inc., 1977). See also Lawrence J. Chase and Raymond K. Tucker, "Statistical Power: Derivation, Development, and Data-Analytic Implications," *The Psychological Record,* 26 (1976), 473-486.

[5]The generalizability problem is discussed in Donald T. Campbell and Julian C. Stanley, *Experimental and Quasi-Experimental Designs for Research* (Chicago: Rand McNally & Company, 1963).

[6]Found in most statistics texts. See, for example, Richard A. Zeller and Edward G. Carmines, *Statistical Analysis of Social Data* (Chicago: Rand McNally College Publishing Company, 1978).

[7]See Nunnally, *Psychometric Theory,* especially Chaps. 1 and 2.

[8]S. S. Stevens, "Problems and Methods of Psychophysics," *Psychological Bulletin,* 55 (1958), 177-196.

[9]Raymond B. Cattell, *The Scientific Use of Factor Analysis in Behavioral and Life Sciences* (New York: Plenum Publishing Corporation, 1978).

[10]Herbert W. Marsh, Jesse U. Overall, and Steven P. Kesler, "Class Size, Students' Evaluations, and Instructional Effectiveness," *American Educational Research Journal,* 16 (1979), 57-70.

[11]Ibid. 62.

[12]Michel Hersen, Alan S. Bellack, Samuel M. Turner, Martin T. Williams, Kaylee Harper, and John G. Watts, "Psychometric Properties of the Wolpe-Lazarus Assertiveness Scale," *Behavior Research and Therapy,* 17 (1979), 63-9.

[13]Hersen et al., "Psychometric Properties" 65.

[14]See, for additional details, J. Paul Peter, "Reliability: A Review of Psychometric Basics and Recent Marketing Practices," *Journal of Marketing Research,* 16 (1979), 6-17.

[15]Hersen et al., "Psychometric Properties" 65.

[16]Nunnally, *Psychometric Theory,* Chap. 7.

[17]Gilbert A. Churchill Jr., "A Paradigm for Developing Better Measures of Marketing Constructs," *Journal of Marketing Research* 16 (1979), 68 (italics in the original).

[18]Nunnally, *Psychometric Theory,* Chap. 7.

[19]Nunnally, *Psychometric Theory.*

[20]Lewis R. Aiken, *Psychological Testing and Assessment,* 3rd ed., (Boston: Allyn & Bacon, Inc., 1979).

[21]Richard Christie and Florence L. Geis, *Studies in Machiavellianism,* (New York: Academic Press, Inc., 1970).

[22]Milton Rokeach, *The Open and Closed Mind* (New York: Basic Books, Inc., Publishers, 1960).

[23]Rensis Likert, "A Technique for the Measurement of Attitudes," *Archives of Psychology,* 140 (1932).

[24]Lawrence R. Rosenfeld, "Self-Disclosure Avoidance: Why I Am Afraid To Tell You Who I Am," *Communication Monographs,* 46 (1979), 63-74.

[25]Nunnally, *Psychometric Theory,* pp. 606-607.

[26]Richard L. Gorsuch, *Factor Analysis* (Philadelphia: W. B. Saunders Company, 1974), p. 245.

[27]Desmonde F. Laux and Raymond K. Tucker, "The Effects of Differentially Computed Factor Scores on Statistical Decisions," *The Psychological Record,* 29 (1979), 501-516.

[28]Charles Osgood, George Suci, and Percy Tannenbaum, *The Measurement of Meaning* (Urbana, Ill.: University of Illinois Press, 1957).

[29]Kerlinger has an excellent chapter devoted to the semantic differential. See Fred N. Kerlinger, *Foundations of Behavioral Research,* 2nd ed. (New York: Holt, Rinehart & Winston, Inc., 1973), Chap. 33.

[30]H. G. Gough, "The Adjective Checklist as a Personality Assessment Research Technique," *Psychological Reports,* 6 (1960), 107-122. See also H. G. Gough and A. B. Heilbrun, Jr., *The Adjective Checklist Manual* (Palo Alto, Calif.: Consulting Psychologists Press, 1965).

[31]The classic work on sentence completion is Amanda R. Rohde, *The Sentence Completion Method: Its Diagnostic and Clinical Application to Mental Disorders* (New York: Ronald Press, 1957).

[32]Christie and Geis, *Machiavellianism.*

[33]Rokeach, *Open and Closed Mind.*

[34]D. Crowne and D. Marlowe, *The Approval Motive* (New York: John Wiley & Sons, 1964).

ADDITIONAL SOURCES

Cochran, W. G., *Sampling Techniques,* 2nd ed. New York: John Wiley & Sons, Inc., 1963.

Coombs, C. H., *A Theory of Data.* New York: John Wiley and Sons, Inc., 1964.

Cronbach, Lee J., *Essentials of Psychological Testing,* 3rd ed. New York: Harper & Row Publishers, Inc., 1970.

Dick, W., and Hagerty, N., *Topics in Measurement.* New York: McGraw-Hill Book Company, 1971.

Ghiselli, E. E., *Theory of Psychological Measurement.* New York: McGraw-Hill Book Company, 1964.

CHAPTER 8

[1]For additional information see: Jum C. Nunnally, *Introduction to Statistics for Psychology and Education* (New York: McGraw-Hill Book Company, 1975).

[2]For additional information see any standard descriptive statistics text.

[3]For additional information see: William L. Hays, *Statistics for the Social Sciences,* 2nd ed. (New York: Holt, Rinehart & Winston, 1973); and Benjamin J. Winer, *Statistical Principles in Experimental Design,* 2nd ed. (New York: McGraw-Hill Book Company, 1971).

[4]For details see Hays, *Statistics,* or Winer, *Statistical Principles.*

[5]An excellent text on the topic is Roger E. Kirk, *Experimental Design: Procedures for the Behavioral Sciences* (Belmont, Calif.: Brooks/Cole Publishing Co., 1968).

[6]See Kirk, *Experimental Design,* Chap. 3.

[7]See Kirk, *Experimental Design,* Chaps. 6-11.

[8]For a fuller discussion, see Kirk, *Experimental Design,* Chap. 7.

[9]A comprehensive discussion may be found in Jum C. Nunnally, *Psychometric Theory,* 2nd ed. (New York: McGraw-Hill Book Company, 1978).

[10]For example, Nunnally, *Introduction to Statistics,* Chap. 7.

[11]For further details on the nature of causation, see the excellent text by David R. Heise, *Causal Analysis* (New York: John Wiley & Sons, 1975).

[12]The text by T. W. Anderson *Introduction to Multivariate Statistical Analysis* (New York, John Wiley and Sons, 1958), is a high-level treatment illustrating how complex multivariate analysis can become. A text by Monge and Cappella, however, can be readily understood by the typical graduate student in speech communication. See Peter Monge and Joseph Cappella, *Multivariate Techniques in Human Communication Research* (New York, Academic Press, Inc., 1980). Another, in preparation, is by Tucker. See Raymond K. Tucker *Basic Multivariate Research Models* (Houston: College Hill Press, in preparation).

[13]Milton Rokeach, *The Open and Closed Mind* (New York: Basic Books, Inc., Publishers, 1960).

[14]Richard Christie and Florence Geis, *Studies in Machiavellianism* (New York: Academic Press, Inc., 1970).

[15]S. A. Rathus, "A 30-Item Schedule for Assessing Assertive Behavior," *Behavior Therapy,* 4 (1973), 398-406.

[16]See Lawrence J. Chase and Raymond K. Tucker, "Statistical Power: Derivation, Development, and Data-Analytic Implications," *The Psychological Record,* 26 (1976), 473-486.

[17]A summary of the issues and controversies surrounding factor analysis can be found in Raymond K. Tucker and Lawrence J. Chase, "Factor Analysis in Human Communication Research" (paper presented at the annual convention of the International Communication Association, Chicago, 1975). Several excellent texts are currently on the market. Examples: Richard Gorsuch, *Factor Analysis* (Philadelphia: W. B. Saunders Company, 1974); and R. J. Rummel, *Applied Factor Analysis* (Evanston, Ill.: Northwestern University Press, 1970).

[18]Rathus, "A 30-Item Schedule."

[19]Karen J. Gritzmacher, "A Multivariate Investigation of Selected Assertiveness Instruments," (unpublished Ph.D. Dissertation, Bowling Green State University, 1978).

[20]There are two basic methods for rotating an initial factor matrix: orthogonal and oblique. Gritzmacher employed one of the oblique methods, specifically the direct oblimin method.

[21]Again, we emphasize that these are the results of a single study and may not hold up under replication.

[22]An overview of canonical correlation may be found in Raymond K. Tucker and Lawrence J. Chase, "Canonical Correlation in Human Communication Research," *Human Communication Research,* 3 (1976), 86-96. See also Raymond K. Tucker and Lawrence J. Chase, "Canonical Correlation," in Monge and Cappella, *Multivariate Techniques.*

[23]A simplified account may be found in Donald J. Veldman, *Fortran Programming for the Behavioral Sciences* (New York: Holt, Rinehart & Winston, 1967), Chap. 11.

[24]For additional background on the topic of canonical component loadings see Robert M. Thorndike and David J. Weiss, "A Study of the Stability of Canonical Correlations and Canonical Components," *Educational and Psychological Measurement,* 33 (1973), 123-134.

[25]Bruce Korth, "Relationship of Extraneous Variables to Student Ratings of Instructors," *Journal of Educational Measurement,* 16 (1979), 27-37.

[26]J. T. Pohlmann, "A Multivariate Analysis of Selected Class Characteristics and Student Ratings of Instruction," *Multivariate Behavioral Research,* 10 (1975), 81-91.

[27]See the Tucker and Chase chapter in Monge and Cappella, *Multivariate Techniques.*

[28]Roger N. Conaway, "An Examination of the Relationship Among Assertiveness, Manifest Anxiety, and Self-Esteem" (unpublished doctoral dissertation, Bowling Green State University, 1978).

[29]J. P. Galassi, J. S. Delo, M. D. Galassi, and S. Bastien, "The College Self-Expression Scale: A Measure of Assertiveness," *Behavior Therapy,* 5 (1974), 165-171.

[30]Rathus, "A 30-Item Schedule."

[31]R. E. Alberti and M. L. Emmons, *Your Perfect Right: A Guide to Assertive Behavior* (San Luis Obispo, Calif.: Impact Publishers, 1974).

[32]Janet A. Taylor, "A Personality Scale of Manifest Anxiety," *Journal of Abnormal and Social Psychology,* 48 (1953), 285-290.

[33]M. Rosenberg, *Society and the Adolescent Self-Image* (Princeton, N.J.: Princeton University Press, 1965).

[34]S. Coopersmith, *The Antecedents of Self-Esteem* (San Francisco: W. H. Freeman & Company Publishers, 1967).

[35]D. Stewart and W. Love, "A General Canonical Correlation Index," *Psychological Bulletin,* 70 (1968), 160-163. See also Robert M. Thorndike, *Correlational Procedures for Research* (New York: Gardner Press, Inc., 1978).

[36]Susan C. Parrish, "The Relation of Self-Disclosure, Attraction, Homophily, and Trust to Uncertainty Reduction" (unpublished master's thesis, Bowling Green State University, 1979).

[37]Monge and Cappella, *Multivariate Techniques.*

[38]T. J. Hummel and J. R. Sligo, "Empirical Comparison of Univariate and Multivariate Analysis of Variance Procedures," *Psychological Bulletin,* 76 (1971), 49-57.

[39]Raymond K. Tucker and Kathi Dierks-Stewart, "Multiple Experimenters—Uninterpretable Results" (unpublished research, Bowling Green State University, 1978).

[40]For an understandable treatment, see Thorndike, *Correlational Procedures,* Chap. 8.

[41]Raymond K. Tucker (unpublished research, Bowling Green State University, 1980).

[42]Korth, "Extraneous Variables," p. 33.

ADDITIONAL SOURCES

Child, Dennis, *The Essentials of Factor Analysis.* London: Holt, Rinehart, and Winston, 1970.

Tatsuoka, Maurice, *Multivariate Analysis: Techniques for Educational and Psychological Research.* New York: John Wiley & Sons, Inc., 1971.

Thorndike, Robert M., *Correlational Procedures for Research.* New York: Garden Press, 1978.

Van De Geer, J. P., *Introduction to Multivariate Analysis for the Social Sciences.* San Francisco: W. H. Freeman & Co., Publishers, 1971.

CHAPTER 9

[1]A powerful discussion of the role of theory is presented in Raymond B. Cattell and Ralph M. Dreger, eds. *Handbook of Modern Personality Theory* (New York: John Wiley & Sons, 1977), Chap. 1.

[2]Dr. John Tukey is the current revolutionary in data analysis. See, for example, John W. Tukey, *Exploratory Data Analysis* (Reading, Mass.: Addison-Wesley Publishing Co., Inc., 1977).

[3]For additional perspectives see Claire Selltiz, Lawrence S. Wrightsman, and Stuart W. Cook, *Research Methods in Social Relations,* 3rd ed. (New York: Holt, Rinehart & Winston, 1976), Chap. 3.

[4]The term is usually attributed to Raymond Cattell. He discussed the nature of private universe research in, for example, Raymond B. Cattell, ed., *Handbook of Multivariate Experimental Psychology* (Chicago: Rand McNally & Company, 1966).

[5]For instance, flowgraph analysis has not been widely employed in speech communication research; hence, it would seem reasonable to discuss, at least briefly, how it was used in a previous study. Flowgraph analysis is discussed in David R. Heise, *Causal Analysis* (New York: John Wiley & Sons, 1975), Chap. 2.

[6]See, for example, any current text on experimental design.

[7]A representative case is that of Brendan A. Maher, editor of the *Journal of Consulting and Clinical Psychology.* See Brendan A. Maher, "Preface," *Journal of Consulting and Clinical Psychology,* 46 (1978), 595.

[8]For additional details, see Selltiz, Wrightsman, and Cook, *Research Methods.* See also the classic by Donald T. Campbell and Julian C. Stanley, *Experimental and Quasi-Experimental Designs for Research* (Chicago: Rand McNally & Company, 1963).

[9]We suggest that tailor-made instruments be used only as a last resort. See Chap. 7 for details.

[10]A representative publication containing many such instruments is John P. Robinson and Phillip R. Shaver, *Measures of Social Psychological Attitudes,* rev. ed. (Ann Arbor, Mich.: Survey Research Center, Institute for Social Research, 1973).

[11]An excellent example is Eileen M. Redden, "A Multivariate Investigation of Group Norms." (unpublished doctoral dissertation, Bowling Green State University, 1979).

[12]See John W. Tukey, *Exploratory Data Analysis* (Reading, Mass.: Addison-Wesley Publishing Co., Inc., 1977).

[13]For a fuller discussion see, for example, Campbell and Stanley, *Designs.*

[14]John Platt, "Strong Inference," *Science,* 146 (1964), 347-353.

[15]See any textbook on statistical inference, such as Roger E. Kirk, *Experimental Design: Procedures for the Behavioral Sciences* (Belmont, Calif.: Brooks/Cole Publishing Co., 1968).

[16]The first pages of most scholarly journals contain information concerning the types of manuscripts that might be appropriate.

[17]See Chapter 7 for a discussion of dependent variables.

[18]Additional insights are contained in T. C. Chamberlin, "The Method of Multiple Working Hypotheses," *Science,* 148 (1965), 754-759.

[19]Since style varies considerably, it is wise to study the current issue of the journal before submitting a manuscript.

ADDITIONAL SOURCES

Debakey, L., ed., *The Scientific Journal: Editorial Policies and Practices.* St. Louis: C. V. Mosby Company, 1976.

Flesch, R. F., *How to Test Readability.* New York: Harper & Row, Publishers, Inc., 1951.

Lester, J. D., *Writing Research Papers: A Complete Guide* rev. ed. Glenview, Illinois: Scott, Foresman, & Company, 1971.

Woodford, F. P., ed., *Scientific Writing for Graduate Students: A Manual on the Teaching of Scientific Writing.* New York: Rockefeller University Press, 1968.

Zeisel, H., *Say it With Figures* 5th ed. New York: Harper & Row, Publishers, Inc., 1968.

CHAPTER 10

[1]Lawrence F. Locke and Waneen Wyrick Spirduso, *Proposals that Work: A Guide for Planning Research* (Columbia University: Teachers College Press, 1976), pp. 1-2.

[2]Locke and Spirduso, *Proposals,* p. 3.

[3]Delbert C. Miller, *Handbook of Research Design and Social Measurement* (New York: David McKay Co., Inc., 1977), pp. 3-5.

[4]William Strunk, Jr., and E. B. White, *The Elements of Style,* 3rd ed. (New York: Macmillan Publishing Co., Inc., 1972), p 66.

[5]You may order your copy by writing: American Psychological Association, 1200 Seventeenth Street N. W., Washington, D.C., 20036.

[6]You may order your copy by writing: Publications Center, Modern Language Association, 62 Fifth Avenue, New York, N.Y. 100-11.

[7]You may order your copy by writing: University of Chicago Press, 5801 Ellis Avenue, Chicago, Ill. 60637.

[8]You may order your copy by writing: Macmillan Publishing Co., Inc., 866 Third Avenue, New York, N.Y. 10022.

[9]Adapted from "Notes to the Editorial Board on Reviewing Manuscripts for *Communication Education,"* distributed by Dr. Gustav W. Friedrich, Editor, *Communication Education,* 1979-1981.

[10]The Speech Communication Association has its national office at: 5105 Backlick Rd., Annandale, Pa. 22003. For journal or membership information, write Dr. William Work, Executive Secretary of the SCA.

[11]Mollie Haines, ed., "ERIC Reports," *Spectra,* 14 (August 1978), 9.

[12]*General Information on Copyright, Circular 1 and Circular R99—Highlights of the New*

Copyright Law, publications of the Copyright Office, Library of Congress, Washington, D.C. 20559 (Washington, D.C.: U.S. Government Printing Office, 1976).

For more information on Copyright Laws and their implications write: Publications of the Copyright Office, Copyright Office, c/o Register of Copyrights, Library of Congress, Washington, D.C. 20559.

[13]Tyrus Hillway, *Handbook of Educational Research* (Boston: Houghton Mifflin Company, 1969), pp. 70-72.

[14]See footnote 13. Most local libraries retain information on copyright laws as well.

ADDITIONAL SOURCES

A Manual of Style (12th ed.). Chicago: The University of Chicago Press, 1969.

Barzun, Jacques, and Henry F. Graff, *The Modern Researcher,* 3rd ed. New York: Harcourt Brace Jovanovich, Inc., 1977. See especially Part 3, "Writing," pp. 209-323.

Best, John W., *Research in Education,* 3rd ed. Englewood Cliffs, N.J.: Prentice-Hall, Inc., 1977. See especially Chapter 2, "Selecting a Problem and Preparing a Research Proposal," pp. 18-35. See also Chapter 9, "The Research Report," pp. 309-339.

Etzold, T. H., "Writing for Publication: The Art of the Article," *Phi Delta Kappan,* 57 (1976), 614-615.

Hillway, Tyrus, *Handbook of Educational Research.* Boston: Houghton Mifflin Company, 1969.

Isaac, Stephen, and William B. Michael, *Handbook in Research and Evaluation.* San Diego: Robert R. Knapp, 1971.

Locke, Lawrence F., and Waneen Wyrick Spirduso, *Proposals That Work: A Guide For Planning Research.* New York (Columbia University): Teachers College Press, 1976. See especially Parts I and II, pp. 1-43, which cover the function and development of a proposal.

Mason, Emanuel J., and William J. Bramble, *Understanding and Conducting Research/Applications in Education and the Behavioral Sciences.* New York: McGraw-Hill Book Company, 1978. See especially Chapter 12, "Guidelines for Conducting Research," pp. 309-326.

Miller, Delbert C., *Handbook of Research Design and Social Measurement,* 3rd ed. New York: David McKay Company, Inc., 1977. See especially Part 1, pp. 1-61, "General Description of the Guides to Research Design and Sampling."

Mouly, George J., *Educational Research: The Art and Science of Investigation.* Boston: Allyn & Bacon, Inc., 1978. See especially Appendix A, "The Research Report," pp. 325-342.

Mullins, Carolyn J., *A Guide to Writing and Publishing in the Social and Behavioral Sciences.* New York: John Wiley & Sons, 1977.

Travers, Robert M. W., *An Introduction to Educational Research,* 4th ed. New York: Macmillan Publishing Co., Inc., 1978. See especially material on "Writing the Report," pp. 410-420.

CHAPTER 11

[1]Neil Postman and Charles Weingartner, *Teaching as a Subversive Activity* (New York: Delacorte Press, 1969), pp. 2-3.

[2]Elizabeth Hall, "Giving Away Psychology in the 80's," *Psychology Today,* 13 (January 1980), 49.

[3]Sidney J. Parnes, *Creative Behavior Workbook* (New York: Charles Scribner's Sons, 1967), p. 14.

[4]Seth A. Fessenden, Roy Ivan Johnson, P. Merville Larson, and Kaye M. Good, *Speech for the Creative Teacher,* 2nd ed. (Dubuque, Iowa: William C. Brown Co., Publishers, 1973), pp. 167-170.

[5]Fessenden et al., *Speech,* pp. 171-172.

[6]Parnes, *Creative Behavior,* p. 3.

[7]George M. Prince, *The Practice of Creativity: A Manual for Dynamic Group Problem Solving* (New York: Harper & Row, Publishers, 1970), pp. 170-171.

[8]Eugene Raudsepp and George P. Hough, Jr., *Creative Growth Games* (New York: Jove Publications, Inc. [a division of Harcourt Brace Jovanovich], 1977), pp. 8-9.

[9]Ibid., pp. 12-13.

[10]Carol Stocker and Martin Cohn, "What Makes Some People Good at Growing Older?" *The Blade* (Toledo), November 12, 1978.

[11]Raudsepp and Hough, *Creative Growth,* p. 13.

[12]Sydney J. Harris, "Often We Try to Solve Our Problems Too Fast," *Detroit Free Press,* August 2, 1976.

[13]Alex F. Osborn, *Applied Imagination: Principles and Procedures of Creative Thinking,* rev. ed. (New York: Charles Scribner's Sons, 1957), p. 157.

[14]Viktor Loewenfeld, "Current Research on Creativity," *NEA Journal,* 47 (November 1958), 538-540. Reproduced in Thomas E. Clayton, *Teaching and Learning: A Psychological Perspective* (Englewood Cliffs, N.J.: Prentice-Hall, Inc., 1965), pp. 166-167. A similar statement, according to Clayton, appears in the Eleventh Yearbook of the American Association of Colleges for Teacher Education, 1958.

[15]See John W. Best, *Research in Education,* 3rd ed. (Englewood Cliffs, Prentice-Hall, Inc., 1977) pp. 8-11; Delbert C. Miller, *Handbook of Research Design and Social Measurement,* 3rd ed. (New York: David McKay Company, Inc., 1977), pp. 44-45; Stephen Isaac and William B. Michael, *Handbook in Research and Evaluation* (San Diego: EdITS Publishers, 1971), pp. 2-11.

[16]Clayton, *Teaching and Learning,* pp. 166-167. Also see Best, *Research in Education,* pp. 9-10.

[17]Carl R. Rogers, "Toward A Theory of Creativity," in *A Source Book for Creative Thinking,* eds. Sidney J. Parnes and Harold F. Harding (New York: Charles Scribner's Sons, 1962), pp. 70-71.

[18]*Ethical Principles in the Conduct of Research with Human Participants,* APA, 1973.

[19]See the special issue of the *American Psychologist,* 22 (May 1967). Also see Guidelines, *American Psychologist,* 30 (June 1975).

[20]In addition to the American Psychological Association, agencies that fund research generally have recommendations about the ethics of research. The Office of the Surgeon General of the United States has issued guidelines for projects funded by the Public Health Service. Agencies such as the National Institute of Mental Health, the National Institute of Education, and the Department of Health, Education and Welfare require an ethical review of funded projects to protect the rights and welfare of subjects. Colleges and universities also have committees or research agencies to review both funded and nonfunded projects to ensure the protection of subjects.

[21]Emanuel J. Mason and William J. Bramble, *Understanding and Conducting Research/ Applications in Education and the Behavioral Sciences* (New York: McGraw-Hill Book Company, 1978), pp. 355-358.

ADDITIONAL SOURCES

Best, John W., *Research in Education,* 3rd ed. Englewood Cliffs, N.J.: Prentice-Hall, Inc., 1977. See especially pp. 108-111.

Koestler, Arthur, *The Act of Creation.* New York: The Macmillan Company, 1964.

Mason, Emanuel J., and William J. Bramble, *Understanding and Conducting Research/Applications in Education and the Behavioral Sciences.* New York: McGraw-Hill Book Company, 1978. See especially pp. 354-358.

Mouly, George J., *Educational Research: The Art and Science of Investigation.* Boston: Allyn & Bacon, Inc., 1978. See especially pp. 50-51.

Osborn, Alex F., *Applied Imagination: Principles and Procedures of Creative Thinking* (rev. ed.) New York: Charles Scribner's Sons, 1957.

Parnes, Sidney J., and Harold F. Harding, eds., *A Source Book for Creative Thinking.* New York: Charles Scribner's Sons, 1962.

Prince, George M., *The Practice of Creativity: A Manual for Dynamic Group Problem Solving* (New York: Harper & Row, Publishers, 1970). See especially Chapter 8, pp. 170-179, "The Uses of Creativity."

Rosner, Stanley, and Lawrence Edwin Abt, eds., *Essays in Creativity*. Croton-On-Hudson, N.Y.: North River Press, Inc., 1974.
Rugg, Harold, *Imagination*. New York: Harper & Row, Publishers, 1963. See especially Chapter 15, "The Creative Imagination: Imperatives for Educational Theory," pp. 288-314.

CHAPTER 12

[1]Claude Shannon and Warren Weaver, *The Mathematical Theory of Communication* (Urbana, Ill.: University of Illinois Press, 1949).
[2]Frank E. X. Dance, "Toward a Theory of Human Communication," in Dance, ed., *Human Communication Theory* (New York: Holt, Rinehart & Winston, 1967), pp. 289-309.
[3]Colin Cherry, *On Human Communication* (Cambridge, Mass.: MIT Press, 1964).
[4]Bernard Berelson and Gary Steiner, *Human Behavior* (New York: Harcourt Brace Jovanovich, Inc., 1964).
[5]Gerald Miller and Mark Steinberg, *Between People* (Chicago: Science Research Associates, 1975), pp. 34.
[6]David K. Berlo, *The Process of Communication* (New York: Holt, Rinehart & Winston, 1960).
[7]Thomas Scheidel, "Commentaries on Process," *Quarterly Journal of Speech*, 58 (1972), 465-469.
[8]Dennis Smith, "Communication Research and the Idea of Process," *Speech Monographs*, 39 (1972), 174-182.
[9]Leonard C. Hawes, "Elements of a Model for Communication Processes," *Quarterly Journal of Speech*, 59 (1973), 11-21.
[10]Teru L. Morton, James F. Alexander, and Irwin Altman, "Communication and Relationship Definition," in Gerald R. Miller, ed., *Explorations in Interpersonal Communication* (Beverly Hills: Sage Publications, Inc., 1976), pp. 105-125.
[11]See for example: P. M. Ericson and L. E. Rogers, "New Procedures for Analyzing Relational Communication," *Family Process*, 12 (1973), 245-267; R. A. Mark, "Coding Communication at the Relationship Level," *Journal of Communication*, 21 (1971), 221-232; L. E. Rogers and R. V. Farace, "Analysis of Relational Communication in Dyads: New Measurement Procedures," *Human Communication Research*, 1 (1975), 222-239; Leonard C. Hawes, "Development and Application of an Interview Coding System," *Central States Speech Journal*, 33 (1972), 92-99.
[12]Paul Watzlawick, Janet Helmick Beavin, and Don D. Jackson, *Pragmatics of Human Communication* (New York: W. W. Norton & Co., Inc., 1967).
[13]George A. Borden and John D. Stone, *Human Communication: The Process of Relating* (Menlo Park, Calif.: Cummings Publishing Company, Inc., 1976).
[14]Kenneth R. Williams, "Reflections on a Human Science of Communication," *Journal of Communication*, 23 (1973), 239-250.
[15]Gerald R. Miller, "Humanistic and Scientific Approaches to Speech-Communication Inquiry: Rivalry, Redundancy or Rapproachment," *Western Speech Communication*, 39 (1975), 230-239.
[16]Various researchers use the term "scientific" in relation to humanistic to mean assumptions of the behavioristic philosophy, not assumptions of the scientific method. A humanistic study can be "scientific" if it follows the scientific method of thinking and organizing.
[17]W. Barnett Pearce, "Metatheoretical Concerns in Communication," *Communication Quarterly*, 25 (1977), 3-6.
[18]Jessie G. Delia, "The Future of Graduate Education in Speech-Communication: A Personal Perspective," *Communication Education*, 28 (1979), 276.
[19]Lloyd F. Bitzer and Edwin Black, eds., *The Prospect of Rhetoric: Report of the National Developmental Project* (Englewood Cliffs, N.J.: Prentice-Hall, Inc., 1971).
[20]Robert J. Kibler and Larry L. Barker eds., *Conceptual Frontiers in Speech Communication* (New York: Speech Communication Association, 1969).
[21]Vincent L. Bloom, "Pragmatism: The Choice of a Critical Perspective for Communication Inquiry," *Western Speech*, 39 (1975), 2-12.
[22]Ibid, 10.

[23]Charles Rossiter, "Models of Paradigmatic Change," *Communication Quarterly,* 25 (1977), 69-73.

[24]Ibid, 72.

[25]Peter R. Monge, "The Systems Perspective as a Theoretical Basis for the Study of Human Communication," *Communication Quarterly,* 25 (1977), 19-29.

[26]Frank E. X. Dance, "Human Communication Theory: A Highly Selective Review and Two Commentaries," in Brent D. Ruben, ed., *Communication Yearbook II* (New Brunswick, N.J.: Transaction Books, 1978), 7-22.

[27]Charles R. Berger, "Interpersonal Communication Theory and Research: An Overview," in Brent D. Ruben, ed., *Communication Yearbook I* (New Brunswick, N.J.: Transaction Books, 1977), 217-228.

[28]See for example: Miller and Steinberg, *Between People*; Charles R. Berger and Richard J. Calabrese, "Some Explorations in Initial Interaction and Beyond: Toward a Developmental Theory of Interpersonal Communication," *Human Communication Research,* 1 (1975), 99-112; M. R. Parks, R. V. Farace, and L. E. Rogers, "A Stochastic Description of Relational Communication Systems," paper presented at Speech Communication Association, Houston, 1975.

[29]Stephen Toulmin, "Concepts and the Explanation of Human Behavior," in T. Mischel ed., *Human Action* (New York: Academic Press, Inc. 1969), 71-104.

[30]Klaus Krippendorf, "Values, Modes and Domains of Inquiry into Communication," *Journal of Communication,* 19 (1969), 105-133.

[31]Jessie G. Delia, "Alternative Perspectives for the Study of Communication: Critique and Response," *Communication Quarterly,* 25 (1977), 46-62.

[32]Delia, "Future of Graduate Education," 272.

[33]Ibid, 272.

[34]Abraham Kaplan, *The Conduct of Inquiry* (San Francisco: Harper & Row Publishers, Inc., 1964).

[35]See Dean E. Hewes, "Interpersonal Communication Theory and Research: A Methodological Overview," in Ruben ed. *Communication Yearbook II,* 155-169, and Bloom, "Pragmatism."

[36]Bloom, "Pragmatism," 5.

[37]Kibler and Barker, *Conceptual Frontiers.*

[38]Leonard C. Hawes, "Alternative Theoretical Bases: Toward a Presuppositional Critique," *Communication Quarterly,* 25 (1977), 63-68.

[39]Delia, "Future of Graduate Education," 276.

[40]Daniel J. O'Keefe, "Logical Empiricism and the Study of Human Communication," *Speech Monographs,* 42 (1975), 169-183.

[41]Charles R. Berger, "The Covering Law Perspective as a Theoretical Basis for the Study of Human Communication," *Communication Quarterly,* 25 (1977), 7-18.

[42]Thomas J. Knutson, "Criticism of Communication Research: An Introduction to Quality Control," *Central States Speech Journal,* 30 (1979), 1-3.

[43]See Gerald R. Miller, "On Rediscovering the Apple: Some Issues in Evaluating the Social Significance of Communication Research," *Central States Speech Journal,* 30 (1979), 14-24; and David R. Seibold, "Criticism of Communication Theory and Research: A Critical Celebration," *Central States Speech Journal,* 30 (1979), 26.

[44]Berger, *Communication Yearbook I.*

[45]Donald P. Cushman, "The Rules Perspective as a Theoretical Basis for the Study of Human Communication," *Communication Quarterly,* 25 (1977), 30-45.

[46]Bloom, "Pragmatism," 5.

[47]Peter R. Monge, "Theory Construction in the Study of Communication: The Systems Paradigm," *Journal of Communication,* 23 (1973), 5-16.

[48]See Berger, *Communication Quarterly,* 1977; Gerald R. Miller and Charles R. Berger, "On Keeping the Faith in Matters Scientific," *Western Journal of Speech Communication,* (1978), 44-57.

[49]William A. Donohue, Donald P. Cushman, and Robert E. Nofsinger, "Creating and Confronting Social Order: A Comparison of Rules Perspectives," *Western Journal of Speech Communication,* 44 (1980), 5-19.

[50]Romano Harré and Paul F. Secord, *The Explanation of Social Behaviour* (Totowa, N.J.: Littlefield, Adama, 1973), 27-43.

[51]Berger, "The Covering Law Perspecive."

[52]W. Barnett Pearce, "Consensual Rules in Interpersonal Communication: A Reply to Cushman and Whiting," *Journal of Communication,* 23 (1973), 160-168.

[53]Donald P. Cushman and W. Barnett Pearce, "Generality and Necessity in Three Types of Theory About Human Communication, With Special Attention to Rules Theory," *Human Communication Research,* 3 (1977), 344-353.

[54]Art Bochner, "On Taking Ourselves Seriously: An Analysis of Some Persistent Problems and Promising Directions in Interpersonal Research," *Human Communication Research,* 4 (1978), 179-191.

[55]Monge, "The Systems Perspective."

[56]Ibid, 53.

[57]Monge, "Theory Construction."

[58]Donald P. Cushman and Robert T. Craig, "Communication Systems: Interpersonal Implications," in Miller, ed., *Explorations in Interpersonal Communication,* 37-58.

[59]Cushman, "The Rules Perspecive."

[60]B. Aubrey Fisher, *Perspectives on Human Communication* (New York: Macmillan, Inc., 1978), 232.

[61]Cushman and Pearce, "Generality and Necessity," 348.

[62]Bochner, "On Taking Ourselves Seriously," 180.

[63]See Cushman and Pearce, "Generality and Necessity." For a reply to Cushman and Pearce, see Vernon E. Cronen and Leslie K. Davis, "Alternative Approaches for the Communication Theorist: Problems in the Laws-Rules-Systems Trichotomy," *Human Communication Research,* 4 (1978), 120-128.

[64]Cushman and Pearce, "Generality and Necessity."

ADDITIONAL SOURCES

Adler, Keith, "On the Falsification of Rules Theories," *Quarterly Journal of Speech,* 64 (1978), 427-438.

Bertalanffy, Ludwig, *General Systems Theory.* New York: George Braziller, 1968.

Bochner, Arthur P., "Whither Communication Theory and Research?" *Quarterly Journal of Speech,* 63 (1977), 325-332.

Bostrom, Robert N., "Epistemological Issues in the Study of Human Communication; Introspection, Objectivity, and Humanistic Psychology." Paper presented at Southern Speech Communication Association, Knoxville, Tenn., 1977.

Buckley, Walter, *Sociology and Modern Systems Theory.* Englewood Cliffs, N.J.: Prentice-Hall, 1967.

Cappella, Joseph N., "The Functional Prerequisites of Intentional Communication Systems," *Philosophy and Rhetoric,* 5 (1972), 231-274.

Cappella, Joseph N., "Research Methodology in Communication Research: Overview and Commentary," in Brent Ruben, ed., *Communication Yearbook I.* New Brunswick, N.J.: Transaction Books, 1977, pp. 37-54.

Cronen, Vernon, W. Barnett Pearce, and Lonna M. Snavely, "A Theory of Rule Structure and Types of Episodes and a Study of Perceived Enmeshment in Undesired Repetitive Patterns (URP's)," in Dan Nimmo, ed., *Communication Yearbook III.* New Brunswick, N.J.: Transaction Books, 1979, pp. 225-240.

Darnell, Donald K., "Toward a Reconceptualization of Communication," *Journal of Communication,* 21 (1971), 5-16.

Fairhurst, Gail Theus, "Using the Functional Prerequisites to Communication Rules as a Structure for Rule-Behavior Research." Paper presented at International Communication Association Convention, Acapulco, 1980.

Fisher, B. Aubrey, and Wayne A. Beach, "Content and Relationship Dimensions of Communicative Behavior: An Exploratory Study," *Western Journal of Speech Communication,* 43 (1979), 201-211.

Ganz, Joan. *Rules: A Systematic Study.* The Hague: Mouton, 1971.

Harris, Linda M., and Vernon E. Cronen, "A Rules-Based Model for the Analysis and Evaluation of Organizational Communication," *Communication Quarterly,* 27 (1979), 12-28.

Krimmerman, Leonard I., ed., *The Nature and Scope of Social Science: A Critical Anthology.* New York: Appleton-Century-Crofts, 1969.

Laszlo, E., *The Systems View of the World.* New York: George Braziller, 1972.

McBath, James H., and Robert C. Jeffrey, "Defining Speech Communication," *Communication Education,* 27 (1978), 181-188.

Meehan, E. J., *Explanation in Social Science: A Systems Paradigm.* Homewood, Ill.: Dorsey Press, 1968.

Monge, Peter R., "Systems Theory and the Structure of Communication Knowledge: An Editorial," *Systemsletter,* 1 (1974), 4-5.

Pearce, W. Barnet,, Vernon E. Cronen, Kenneth Johnson, Greg Jones, and Robert Raymond, "The Structure of Communication Rules and the Form of Conversation: An Experimental Simulation," *The Western Journal of Speech Communication,* 44 (1980), 20-43.

Ruben, Brent D., and John Y. Kim eds., *General Systems Theory and Human Communication.* Rochelle Park, N.J.: Hayden, 1975.

Rychlak, Joseph F., *The Psychology of Rigorous Humanism.* New York: John Wiley & Sons, 1977.

Sanders, Robert E., and Larry W. Martin, "Grammatical Rules and Explanations of Behavior," *Inquiry,* 18 (1975), 65-82.

Scott, Robert L., "Communication as an Intentional Social System," *Human Communication Research,* 3 (1977), 258-268.

Sutherland, John W., *A General Systems Philosophy for the Social and Behavioral Sciences.* New York: George Braziller, 1973.

Suppe, Frederick, *The Structure of Scientific Theories.* Urbana, Ill.: University of Illinois Press, 1974.

Toulmin, Stephen E., "Rules and their Relevance for Understanding Human Behavior," in T. Mischel, ed., *Understanding Other Persons.* Oxford: Blackwell, 1974, pp. 185-215.

Wilder, Carol, "The Palo Alto Group: Difficulties and Directions of the Interactional View for Human Communication Research," *Human Communication Research,* 5 (1979), 158-170.

Author Index

Courtright ✓✓ (Text)

Gerbner, G ✓✓✓

X Habermas, Frederick W. ✓✓✓

Hawes, Leonard ✓✓✓

Aubrey Fisher

Subject Index